D1714940

The Insurgency in Chechnya and the North Caucasus

The Insurgency in Chechnya and the North Caucasus

From Gazavat to Jihad

ROBERT W. SCHAEFER

Praeger Security International

 PRAEGER

AN IMPRINT OF ABC-CLIO, LLC
Santa Barbara, California • Denver, Colorado • Oxford, England

Library of Congress Cataloging-in-Publication Data

Schaefer, Robert W.
    The insurgency in Chechnya and the North Caucasus : from gazavat to jihad /
Robert W. Schaefer.
        p. cm.
    Includes bibliographical references and index.
    ISBN 978-0-313-38634-3 (hard copy : alk. paper) — ISBN 978-0-313-38635-0 (ebook)
1. Chechnia (Russia)—History, Military. 2. Caucasus, Northern (Russia)—History,
Military. 3. Insurgency—Russia (Federation)—Chechnia. 4. Insurgency—Russia
(Federation)—Caucasus, Northern. 5. Chechnia (Russia)—Politics and government.
6. Caucasus, Northern (Russia)—Politics and government. 7. Counterinsurgency—Russia
(Federation)—Chechnia. 8. Counterinsurgency—Russia (Federation)—Caucasus,
Northern. 9. Counterinsurgency—Russia (Federation) 10. Russia (Federation)—
Politics and government—1991- I. Title.
    DK511.C37S29   2011
    947.086—dc22   2010031251

ISBN: 978-0-313-38634-3
EISBN: 978-0-313-38635-0

15   14   13   2   3   4

This book is also available on the World Wide Web as an eBook.
Visit www.abc-clio.com for details.

Praeger
An Imprint of ABC-CLIO, LLC

ABC-CLIO, LLC
130 Cremona Drive, P.O. Box 1911
Santa Barbara, California 93116-1911

This book is printed on acid-free paper (∞)

Manufactured in the United States of America

The contents of this book have been reviewed by the Department of Defense's Office of Security Review (DoD / OSR) and have been cleared for open publication. DoD's clearance and case numbers for the review are 08-S-2567 and 09-S-2106; the DIA case number is 09-272.

The statements of fact, opinion, or analysis expressed in this manuscript are those of the author and do not reflect the official policy or position of the Department of Defense or the U.S. Government. Review of the material does not imply Department of Defense or U.S. Government endorsement of factual accuracy or opinion.

The author wishes to thank the following for granting permissions to use their works in this manuscript: Dr. Bard O'Neil and Potomac Books, Dr. Kalev Sepp, Dr. Moshe Gammer, and Mohammed M. Hafez and Lynne Rienner Publishers.

For my mother, who never let me play with guns.

Contents

Acknowledgments

Although I originally envisioned this project to be a solitary one, reminiscent of my graduate school days of thesis-writing, I quickly learned that writing a book is not a solo project. There were many people involved in the production of this book, and it simply would not have been possible without their help. I would first of all like to thank my wife Olya, who read, edited, translated, transliterated, commented on, and made numerous recommendations to this manuscript and its many versions; she has done much of the yeoman's work for this book and I am extremely grateful to her. I would also like to thank all my colleagues from the Davis Center at Harvard University who helped me with various chapters, in particular the Director, Dr. Timothy Colton, and Professors John Schoberlein and Yoshiko Herrera (now at the University of Minnesota). Dr. Martin Feldstein, the Chief of Economic Advisors for President Reagan and the Chairman of the National Bureau of Economic Research at Harvard, was also instrumental for parts of this manuscript. I am indebted to Dr. Mark Kramer, Director of the Cold War Studies at Harvard. In many ways, this book is a natural progression of the long conversations we had over cups of coffee when the Davis Center was temporarily located in Central Square.

The military historians, analysts, and officers who have assisted me with this project include former Deputy Undersecretary of Defense for Special Operations and Low-Intensity Conflict (and fellow Green Beret) Dr. Kalev Sepp, Colonel Jon Chicky, and Dr. Bard O'Neil from the National War College. Dr. Steven Blank from the National War College was kind enough to give the final version a sanity check, and Charles

Hoing shepherded this manuscript through the myriad Department of Defense gates required to obtain permission for open publication. Sergeant First Class (retired) William J. Dometrich was my early mentor in Special Forces, and when I talk about crusty old Vietnam-era Green Berets who lectured the "candy stripers" about the importance of understanding culture and its impact on counterinsurgency operations, I am talking about him.

I'd like to thank journalist Tom DeWaal for articulating the importance of this work for non-military personnel and encouraging me to write "as much as I could about this topic," Professor Brian Glyn Williams for setting me straight on a few things, and my editor Steve Catalano and Praeger Security International for sticking with me and publishing this book as a stand-alone after the first developmental review concluded that the manuscript didn't fit the planned series.

Amanda Utterback took over the day-to-day compilation of the North Caucasus Incident Database (NCID) when my new assignment precluded finishing the book *and* maintaining the statistics; she also assisted in analysis of the conflict. William C. Schaefer conducted the herculean task of cutting the original manuscript in half, while Rowan and Nicholas Schaefer assisted me with maps, demonstrating that this project was truly a family affair. Thanks to Chadwick Pelletier and Scraper Graphics for the best graphics ever, and Robert Devere Bunn for showing me how it's done—and to both of them for being such great friends. Jennifer Hunt took the manuscript at the last minute and did a wonderful job editing; she ensured that my poor writing didn't get in the way of the concepts and analysis presented herein. Finally, I would like to thank my wife, Olya, again. What was supposed to be a six-month project stretched into years, and her support and willingness to sacrifice so that I could write this book will not be forgotten. I owe you many, many vacations.

Robert Schaefer, Washington, DC

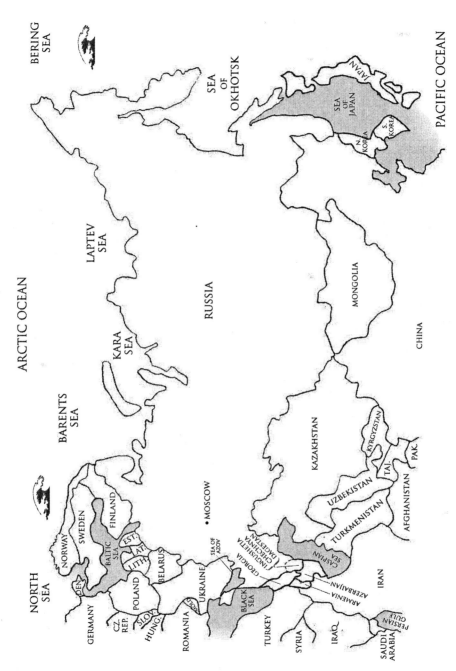

Map of Eurasia

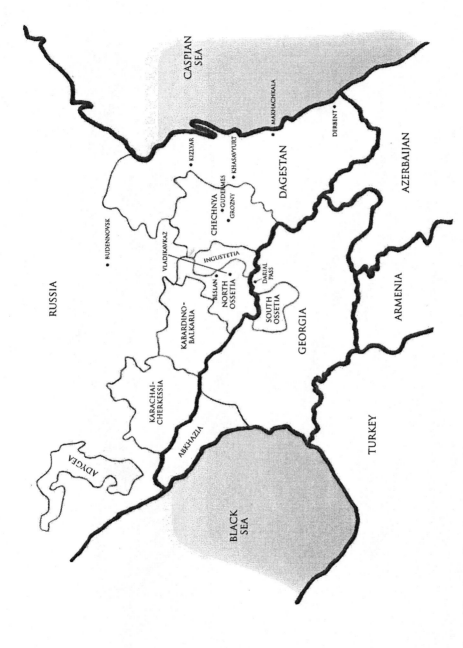

Map of Southern Russia

Introduction

Many fine books have been written about the history of Chechnya, the political events precipitating the wars, the military operations, the terrorist attacks, the human rights abuses, and the trauma suffered by almost everyone involved in the conflict. What has yet to be published is a look at the conflict for what it really is—an *insurgency* and *counterinsurgency* fight, an issue that the United States has also faced since 9/11. Defining the North Caucasus conflict in these terms is imperative if we want to fully understand it—as this class of warfare will become increasingly more prevalent in future conflicts. So as we strive to learn from history in order not to relive it, it is critical to delineate why the Russians claimed the conflict was over when it is becoming increasingly obvious that the upswing of violence in the region is readying it to explode again.

When I began writing this book, the 13-year anniversary of the start of the Chechen insurgency had just passed. At the time, according to the Russian government, it was relatively quiet in Chechnya—an apparent success for former president—now Prime Minister—Vladimir Putin. Now, as this book gets ready to go to print in 2010, the entire "pacified" region is once again embroiled by daily attacks. I was compelled to write this book because I fervently believed in early 2008 that despite what all the pundits, journalists, and analysts said, the Chechen conflict was far from over and I intended to explain why. Unfortunately, the events that have transpired since then suggest that those who claimed the conflict was over must now reevaluate their earlier conclusions based on the extreme level of violence now extant in the Caucasus.

Even as recently as late 2009, most Western reporters and analysts conceded that the Russians defeated the bandits and terrorists in Chechnya. That assessment, however well founded on the "facts," missed one very important point—namely: the North Caucasus conflict is an insurgency, and insurgencies cannot be viewed like other conflicts because they are a fundamentally different type of warfare. Therefore, if one wants to understand why the region continues to see more violence, if one wants to understand why the remedies applied thus far have not worked and will not work in the future, and if one wants to understand the greater context of events in order to explore the merits of a relevant policy option, then it is imperative to view the conflict as an insurgency—and not a counterterrorism operation.

Although much of Prime Minister Vladimir Putin's reputation was built on beating the Chechens, the Kremlin owes much of the current "stability" in Chechnya and the North Caucasus more to the "second front" that the United States opened on the War on Terror than to its own counterinsurgency campaigns. In the United States it is customary to say that the "second front" on the War on Terrorism was opened with the invasion of Iraq. But it was actually the invasion of *Afghanistan* that opened up the "second front" and drew the attention away from Chechnya. Remember, Chechnya was still a full-fledged war in 2001 when the 9/11 attacks occurred and the United States invaded Afghanistan. As a result, many of the foreign fighters left Chechnya. More importantly, the vast majority of jihadi recruits and most of the media attention shifted to the Middle East—providing the Russian government sufficient breathing room to take advantage of the situation. Every month newspaper reports indicate that Afghanistan has been drawing a fresh influx of jihadi fighters from Turkey, Central Asia, the Middle East, and Chechnya.[1]

Moreover, as much as Moscow is fond of saying that the United States is destabilizing the Caucasus by supporting the democratic government in the Republic of Georgia, or even sending in the CIA to destabilize the region, the first major campaign in the War on Terror after 9/11 was a 2002 U.S. Special Forces mission that actually supported the Russians by denying Chechen insurgents their safe haven in the Pankisi Gorge.[2]

Nonetheless, despite the Kremlin's assertions that the Chechen insurgency was over, there were at least 400 attacks in the North Caucasus

---

1. Despite the numerous reports about Chechens fighting in Afghanistan, as of this printing there has not been an officially confirmed Chechen sighting—a name, the mention of a birthplace, an I.D. card, or even an admission from a family in Chechnya that a family member was killed in Iraq or Afghanistan.

2. Although Afghanistan is generally considered to be the first campaign of Operation Enduring Freedom, it was actually the GTEP—or Georgian Train and Equip mission—a 64-million-dollar program which was designed to help Russia in its fight against the Chechens in early 2002. The author was one of the principal planners and executors of that mission. It is ironic that after the Russian-Georgian conflict in August of 2008, the Russians have cited involvement in Georgia as being a destabilizing effort, when, in fact, the GTEP successfully denied both Chechen insurgents and suspected Al Qaeda terrorists a sanctuary in Georgia.

in 2008 and almost 750 in 2009. During one seven-month period in 2008, 173 Russian police and military were killed in the fighting and another 300 were injured. By comparison, during the same period in 2008, U.S. deaths caused by insurgents in Iraq were 148. In 2008, the total number of Russian security forces killed in the North Caucasus was 346, with another 516 reported injured. Compare that with Afghanistan, where the total number of casualties for *all coalition forces* for 2008 was 295.[3] For 2009, there were more than 330 declared deaths (soldiers, police, security forces) in the North Caucasus, but it must be assumed that a portion of the 630+ that were injured died from their wounds. Compare that to the 307 deaths of U.S. soldiers in Iraq during the same period, or even to Afghanistan, which had become the main focus of the jihadis by then, with its total of 520 killed for *all* coalition forces.

Keep in mind that the entire region is five times smaller than Iraq or Afghanistan, it has a fraction of the insurgents, and yet there were more Russian security personnel killed by hostile fire than U.S. forces in Iraq or Afghanistan during 2008 and 2009. Another overlooked statistic is the alarmingly high death rate of FSB agents (successors to the KGB), police chiefs, generals, colonels, judges—far more high-ranking officials than in Iraq and Afghanistan.[4] As of this writing, the statistics for 2010 demonstrate that the trend toward more violence in the Caucasus is continuing.

In addition, the geopolitical environment in the Caucasus changed dramatically after the 2008 Russo-Georgian war. Now that the Russian

---

3. Coalition deaths according to http://www.globalsecurity.org/military/ops/iraq _casualties.htm and http://icasualties.org/oef/. The same figure for the North Caucasus Region are: Mar–11, Apr–26, May–23, June–18, July–31, and Aug–34, for a total of 143. Source: The North Caucasus Incident Database (NCID). The actual number of Russian fatalities is probably far higher as a number of injured soldiers presumably died from wounds—but those figures are rarely reported. As such, the statistics for Ingushetia are very skewed, with only 42 confirmed dead for the period, but a disproportionate 144 wounded. Often the reports list the soldiers as critically wounded, but there are no reports indicating whether or not the critically wounded died from their wounds or recovered.

4. Source: NCID. Using reputable and independent open source reporting, I have compiled a database of every attack (insurgent or terrorist) that has taken place in the North Caucasus since January 2008. Each attack and casualty statistic is annotated with the text of the original reports as well as the URLs where the original citations can be found. NCID statistics cover Chechnya, Dagestan, Ingushetia, Kabardino-Balkaria, and North Ossetia. For each of those regions there is data listing the number of attacks, deaths, and injury statistics for local police, Russian federal troops, and insurgents/terrorists. There are also statistics from open source reporting for civilian casualties and clashes between Russian organizations (i.e., Kadyrovtsy vs. Vostok). Although the data collected may differ slightly from other organizations reporting the same events, that difference is statistically less than 1 percent.

government has so vociferously supported the rights of the South Ossetians and Abkhazians for independence, it will be difficult to claim that the Chechens, the Circassians, and the rest of the North Caucasus peoples should be denied those same rights. Presently, the Kremlin avoids the inconsistency by saying that the Chechen Republic is happy with its status within the Russian Federation, and as long as current President Ramzan Kadyrov continues to speak for the Chechen people, that will remain the case. However, when President Kadyrov begins to lose control of the Chechen majority and they publicly state their desire to be independent again, Russia will be in a difficult spot.

The United States is in a complicated position when it comes to Russia and her handling of the North Caucasus insurgency. On the one hand, as a nation and a government, the United States truly desires to be allies and friends with the Russians and finds every opportunity to work closely with them in counterterrorism and mil-to-mil activities. As a people, Americans also generally desire to be closer to the Russians because they have a profound admiration and respect for Russian culture, history, literature, and scientific accomplishments. As such, the United States aggressively seeks out opportunities to find common ground with the Russians in order to engage with them in cooperative endeavors.

In the same light, it is impossible to forget that Russians have been the victims of the some of the world's worst terrorist attacks—perpetrated against them by Chechens—and that from 2002 to 2004, Russia was virtually the terrorism capital of the world. The recent Moscow subway bombings in March 2010 have once again reminded the West that Russians continue to suffer from terrorist attacks. Some of the terrorists are still in Chechnya, and some of those terrorists had links to extremist Muslim organizations like Al Qaeda. On many levels it makes sense for the United States to support Russia in its campaign in the Caucasus.

Yet, on the other hand, the methods that the Russians employed to crush the Chechens during the wars of the 1990s (most notably the complete devastation of Grozny through indiscriminate carpet bombing) and the continuing "disappearances" of civilians and human rights workers simply cannot be justified by Western standards. Also challenging for the U.S. in dealing with Russia is the fact that Russia is a powerful country that controls critical natural resources and nuclear weapons. Even the most liberal of the Western European nations have had a difficult time criticizing Russia for any reason because Russia provides 25 percent of all natural gas to Europe, and has the ability to negatively impact their lifestyle by cutting off or restricting that flow.

During the August 2008 Russo-Georgian War, the Russians attacked the few gas pipelines that they did not control; this attack strengthened Russia's monopoly over shipping Central Asian oil and gas. A consequence of that action is that some European countries have gone silent on the issue of human rights in Russia. That silence leaves only a few non-governmental organizations, the U.S. State Department, and the European Court of Human Rights willing to raise concerns about the methods currently employed by the Russians in the North Caucasus.[5]

To make matters worse, when Osama bin Laden spoke out against the U.S. position vis-à-vis Chechnya, it became even harder for anyone to speak out against the Russians for fear of somehow colluding or agreeing with Public Enemy #1. In his famous "Crusader" speech, released shortly after the United States began attacking the Taliban in Afghanistan in 2001, bin Laden said:

> Let us look at the second war in Chechnya, which is still underway. The entire Chechen people are being embattled once again by this Russian bear. The humanitarian agencies, even the U.S. ones, demanded that President Clinton should stop supporting Russia. However, Clinton said that stopping support for Russia did not serve U.S. interests. A year ago, Putin demanded that the cross and the Jews should stand by him. He told them: You must support us and thank us because we are waging a war against Muslim fundamentalism.[6]

Although Mr. Putin left the presidency on a high note, by tacitly supporting regimes which support Islamic insurgencies (Iran), and failing to support the West's counterinsurgency efforts overall, he guaranteed a hard road for his successor, current President Dmitry Medvedev, who must now deal with an insurgency that has moved out of the Latent and Incipient Stage, where it was in 2006, and back into the Guerrilla Warfare Stage. Despite the fact that the politicians, pundits, and many analysts stated that the Chechen insurgency was over at the beginning of 2008 due to the relative inactivity over the preceding two years, it was never over—and 300 attacks in the first half of 2008 should have alerted them to the truth. But then it's not surprising that there was a two-year lull in the fighting that convinced everyone that major hostilities were over. That's what insurgencies do—they slide back and forth between stages

---

5. According to Human Rights Watch, in less than five years, the European Court of Human Rights has held Russia responsible for over 119 serious human rights violations in Chechnya alone, including torture, enforced disappearances, and extrajudicial executions. In nearly every ruling, the court called the Russian government to account for failing to properly investigate the crimes. Available at: http://www.hrw.org/en/world-report-2010/russia.

6. Osama bin Laden's November 2, 2001, videotaped statement was broadcast on Al-Jazeera satellite television on Saturday, November 3, 2001. The entire transcript is available at http://news.bbc.co.uk/2/low/world/monitoring/media_reports/1636782.stm; accessed on July 18, 2008.

until they finally win or they are completely defeated—which is precisely why it is impossible to look at the reports coming out of Chechnya and make sense of them unless examined through the lens of insurgency warfare.

Insurgencies are easy. It's *counterinsurgency* that is extremely difficult. Even if a government realizes at the onset that it is dealing with an emerging insurgency and takes immediate and overwhelming action to quash it in its incipient phase, it will still take several years. The Russians themselves admit that they didn't correctly identify what was brewing in the Caucasus in the early 1990s and as a result, they fought two terrible wars in Chechnya in less than ten years—and the losses were appalling for both sides. Entire books have been written about the atrocities and excesses committed by Chechen and Russian alike; even the Russians have prosecuted some of their own officers in recognition of the fact that there were horrific human rights violations.

That's not to say that the Russians aren't working very hard now to contain and defeat the insurgency. The current president of Chechnya, Ramzan Kadyrov, is taking some shrewd counterinsurgency measures to strip away legitimacy from the insurgents. Over 30,000 federal troops, local police, and Russian special police are continually conducting operations to ferret out the remaining 700 or so active insurgents currently operating in the area, and Prime Minister Putin is ensuring that Kadyrov is getting enough money (5.1 *billion* dollars over the next four years) to rebuild Chechnya and build a personal following that will be loyal to him.

Unfortunately, the more important aspects of the Russian counterinsurgency campaigns (good and bad) have largely been overlooked. When writers have thus far attempted to analyze the Russian "counterinsurgency" or "counterterrorism" effort, they have generally focused on the military operations—and in doing so have missed the point. What most military analysts are writing about are the Russian *counter-guerrilla* operations, the tactics, techniques, and procedures (TTPs) that the Russian military has undertaken to retake Grozny, eradicate pockets of guerrilla resistance, establish population control measures, conduct mountain operations, etc. Counter-guerrilla operations are an important part of the military and security activities of a counterinsurgency campaign, but they are merely a *second-echelon subset of activities* that must be conducted as part of a larger counterinsurgency campaign. There is great value in analyzing and discussing the Russian MOUT (military operations on urban terrain) campaign, the impact of secure communications, the lack of armor and mobility for mountain troops, and the efficacy of night-vision optics for helicopter pilots, but those are *tactical* considerations while counterinsurgency is conducted at the operational and *strategic* levels. To look at the counterinsurgency efforts, we must rise above the tactical level and look at operational and strategic plans, which are, not coincidentally, *completely different* from the types of operational and strategic plans that are required for conventional wars.

This is why counterinsurgency (COIN) operations are so difficult; each one has factors that are unique to it; each insurgency must be looked at on its own terms. As Mao Tse Tung said, and David Galula so appropriately quoted in the introduction of his excellent book on counterinsurgency: "The laws of war—this is a problem that anyone directing a war must study and solve. The laws of revolutionary war [insurgency and counterinsurgency]—this is a problem that anyone directing a revolutionary war must study and solve. The laws of China's revolutionary war—this is a problem that anyone directing a revolutionary war in China must study and solve."[7]

This then, is the goal of this book—to get past the politics, the rhetoric, the tactics, the value-judgments, the disinformation, and the condemnations to discover the elements and laws of Chechnya's revolutionary—and Russia's counter-revolutionary—wars.

That is not to say that this book should be read in a vacuum. Close observation of the Chechen insurgency yields important lessons for the insurgencies in Iraq and Afghanistan, Islamic-based insurgencies worldwide, and insurgency movements as a whole. Moreover, this book is useful as a case study for the obverse of the new U.S. counterinsurgency doctrine, the other side of the "COIN," as the Russian COIN campaign is a clear example of an enemy-centric approach in action. Finally, despite the contribution that I hope this book makes to military insurgency literature in general, I also hope that policy makers and Foreign Service professionals will find something valuable in these pages. For, as I will make perfectly clear in the ensuing pages, counterinsurgency efforts throughout the world need experienced and insurgency-savvy diplomats to advise their local counterparts on the government measures necessary to ensure peace and stability throughout the world. There are too few insurgency experts in the military—but even fewer in regular government service.

The bottom line is that the Chechen insurgency is growing and has now spread to Ingushetia and Dagestan, among others. It is more accurately referred to now as the North Caucasus insurgency. It is not a black and white issue, and if one is to discover the reasons why the insurgency is still active, the reasons why it hasn't made further gains, or the reasons why the Russians have not been able to extinguish it com-

---

7. Mao Tse-Tung, *Strategic Problems of China's Revolutionary War* (December, 1936), as quoted in David Galula, *Counterinsurgency War, Theory and Practice* (Westport, London: Praeger, 2006), p. xi (introduction).

pletely, then it is imperative to get below the surface of the vitriol and hyperbole. In order to examine Chechnya through a framework of insurgency and counterinsurgency models, the popular information surrounding it must be stripped of its associated moral "value." To this end, this book endeavors to be an "amoral" examination; judgments about whether an insurgent or counterinsurgent action is "right" or "wrong" will be offered only insofar as that action is consistent with current or historical doctrine and contemporary best-practice approaches to this type of warfare. As such, I expect that everyone will find something objectionable—yet ultimately valuable—in this analysis.

CHAPTER 1

Insurgency

War is not an independent phenomenon, but the continuation of politics by different means.

—*Carl Von Clausewitz*, On War

A group of militants with guns driving VBIEDs (vehicle-borne improvised explosive devices, otherwise known as car bombs) into military checkpoints and shooting mortars into a "safe zone" does not necessarily constitute an insurgency. Depending on the context, those acts could be considered terrorism or lawlessness. Determining whether an explosion in a crowded market is part of a larger insurgency movement and how that particular attack fits into a cohesive insurgency strategy are vital steps in trying to understand what any incident really means. Terrorism and insurgency are not the same, and it's critical to discern the differences between them.

It will prove helpful to start with a primer on insurgency and terrorism to provide a basic background for the analysis. Most people can spot an insurgency if they see one, but don't have the requisite knowledge to fully understand the intricacies of what they're really looking at and the best way to deal with them. All professions have a canon of basic concepts and a lexicon of professional terms that must be understood before it is possible to examine a particular case; the profession of arms is no different.

A GOVERNMENT FIGHT

Make no mistake about it—insurgency is war. As a Special Forces colleague once remarked, "Insurgency is the graduate-level of warfare." Nonetheless, even though the analytical approach used in this book will appear to be military in nature, insurgencies are first and foremost a *political* struggle, and therefore the military should never be the primary agency for conducting a counterinsurgency campaign—unless the military also administers the government.

Why? Well, to start with, from a purely practical standpoint, to defeat an insurgency, regardless of the approach taken, counterinsurgency campaigns require specific actions by the government. The military can't give the government orders; ergo, counterinsurgency campaigns must be *government* campaigns. The second reason is more fundamental: because insurgencies are contests for political power, and because the exercise of political power ultimately depends on the agreement of the people—or their submissiveness—the methods and operations designed to gain the people's agreement must essentially be political in nature—at least if the counterinsurgents are looking for a long-term solution. The other method—enforcing the population's submission, often resulting in genocide—is primarily a military campaign and was the standard counterinsurgency strategy up until World War I. However, even ardent adherents of a pure "enemy-centric" approach still agree that some government engagement is required to avoid military forces being garrisoned permanently and en masse.

Unlike conventional wars where the strategic goal is to destroy the enemy's will to fight through fire and maneuver, the goal in an insurgency is to win the support of the populace through a war of ideas, or *legitimacy*. Whoever controls the "mass base" generally wins. The insurgency does everything it can to destroy the legitimacy of the seated government while simultaneously asserting its own legitimacy based on promises that a new insurgent government will better serve the needs of the people. To counter this threat, the government—not the military—must conduct a counterinsurgency campaign that attempts to point out that the insurgents are criminals and terrorists that are only interested in gaining personal power while simultaneously addressing the population's concerns about security and access to resources.[1]

In a conventional war, each side tries to occupy the "high ground," known as *key terrain*, where it can control the surrounding countryside and avenues of approach. In an insurgency, the key terrain is the *will of the people*. The population will support the government or the insurgency—based upon whoever seems to have the most legitimacy, sometimes perceived as the side most likely to win—and that support will provide the tipping point for one side or the other. Insurgents, terrorists, and even government forces can temporarily control the actions of the populace through fear and

---

1. Enemy-centric counterinsurgency theorists will disagree entirely with this premise, but even they will agree that if a government doesn't do something to convince the local population to stop supporting the insurgents, a constant influx of fresh fighters will keep the conflict smoldering indefinitely. The different approaches to counterinsurgency will be discussed in detail later.

submission—an enemy-centric approach—but that is not the same as having them support one side or the other *because they want to*. Military forces can be a part of this process: they can provide a safe, secure environment so that government reforms can take effect—thereby improving government legitimacy and convincing people that the government way is the best way. However, militaries can also be used to instill fear.

The weapons of an insurgency are different as well. The technological advantage of modern armies is predicated upon *identification* and *stand-off*. Using superior technology, a modern army can find the enemy's tanks, aircraft, and troop formations and use sophisticated weapons to destroy them at distances where the enemy cannot threaten counterattacks.

But if a tank or an F-18 kills an insurgent, it is still unclear whether the threat has been destroyed because the *weapon system* is not a piece of hardware that is easily identifiable. Because insurgencies rely on "human weapon systems," no one knows where the next one will turn up and there is no way to produce a "technologically advanced human." Moreover, it doesn't cost millions of dollars to produce an insurgent like it does a modern weapon; thus, the loss of even a large number of insurgents doesn't destroy the will to fight in the enemy commander's mind—especially if the insurgent leadership has a strong ideological foundation. Insurgents can train just as tirelessly and can obtain much of the same equipment as government forces and, depending on the conflict, the insurgents may even be better trained and equipped than their adversaries.

There is also the concern of collateral damage. Because insurgents are usually dressed like the local population, not only is target identification difficult, but target discrimination can be virtually impossible.

Insurgencies effectively neutralize much of the technological superiority of modern armies and level the playing field, especially when they move the conflict into restrictive terrain—cities, forests, mountains, etc.—because government forces are stripped of their advantages and are forced to fight up close with the insurgents and on equal terms. Insurgents, knowing they don't have the advantage of stand-off (attack helicopters, fighter jets, artillery, missiles, etc.), will stick close to government forces hoping they won't shell, bomb, or strafe their own troops. Ergo, insurgencies, until they become very strong, fight the close battle, which causes significant casualties for government forces. And when sons, daughters, sisters, and brothers are getting killed and wounded at alarming rates, moms and dads will quickly reevaluate the cost of maintaining such an effort on the part of their government.

This is why insurgencies are so difficult and take so long to defeat. Successful counterinsurgency efforts necessitate changing *minds*, and changing minds is a *government* function that is much more difficult than destroying a 50-ton tank or a state-of-the-art missile cruiser. Changing the collective mind of a population requires dedication and committing all the elements of national power—diplomatic, economic, informational, legal, and military—in a synchronized effort so that the total effect is greater than the sum of the individual parts. A military organization can't do this unless that same military organization also controls the government.

Fundamentally, it's a matter of design: militaries are formed to work for their governments and not the other way around. The problem is that insurgencies live and breed in brackish waters by operating on the boundaries of the usual clear-cut federal responsibilities.

But the armed conflict of an insurgency that most people see is only the tip of the iceberg: 85 percent or more of insurgent activity is clandestine and, therefore, goes unseen and unreported. Militaries cannot stop all of those activities, and in some cases are even legally prevented from trying to do so. Moreover, as we will see, an insurgency cannot evolve unless the government is considered to be weak or illegitimate—and the military can't take care of that problem unless it takes over the government itself.

A military organization cannot force a government to deal with the socio-economic factors that make the inhabitants of a particular region susceptible to the insurgents; these factors are often referred to as "root causes." Only governments can address these factors. This is not to say that the military does not play a role here—the security piece is *necessary*; unfortunately, it is not *everything*.

Alas, the study of insurgency and counterinsurgency has been left almost exclusively to the military and a small number of academics— usually those with a military background or those employed by military institutions. A minuscule subset of that group has been given the task of fully understanding insurgencies and being able to plan and execute these complex operations—which has only compounded the problem. As should already be clear, insurgency is a *government* problem and it needs to be studied in-depth by government officials as well.

INSURGENCY 101

Insurgency is one of the oldest known forms of warfare. Certainly since World War II, insurgency has been the predominant type of warfare— and even though they are called "little" wars, they often involve vast resources of major powers and influence stability within an entire region, continent or, since 9/11, the world.

An insurgency is an organized movement aimed at the overthrow of a constituted government through the use of subversion and armed conflict.[2] The term insurgency is often used to cover a wider scope of

---

2. Joint Publication 1-02, "Department Of Defense (DOD) Dictionary of Military and Associated Terms."

low-intensity conflicts and is often linked inextricably to terrorism—as terrorism is a tool that many insurgent groups use to further their agendas. For now, it will be expedient to think of all military action that is not between two nation-states as a type of insurgency.

Insurgencies often begin as a resistance movement, which is an organized effort by some portion of the civil population of a country to resist the legally established government or the occupying power and to disrupt the civil order and stability. Their reasons for doing so are varied, but in its most distillated form, insurgencies are primarily a struggle for power and resources.

WHY DO INSURGENCIES DEVELOP? THE FOUR PREREQUISITES

Historically, certain conditions can transform a dissatisfied portion of a population into an insurgency. People form resistance movements because of a government's (or occupying power's) inability or unwillingness to meet the legitimate needs or desires of the population. Insurgencies develop when those same people believe they have more to gain by resisting the government rather than supporting it and are willing to risk death in violent confrontation to achieve their goals—which may be to overthrow an existing government, expel an occupying power, or change the existing system.

But sometimes, it's not so noble a cause; sometimes it's just about power, money, and status. In many parts of the world, young men do not have many opportunities to succeed in society and a "rifle and a cause" give them a measure of status, power, and money unavailable through respectable vocations. These are the seeds of an insurgency: disaffected and disenfranchised citizens who are given a purpose by a leader who articulates a better vision in a place where they don't have to worry about getting caught. In order for an insurgency to develop in a particular country there are four prerequisites that must be present: *lack of government control*, *available leadership, ideology,* and most importantly, a *vulnerable population*— the future weapon systems of the insurgency.

Lack of Government Control or Illegitimate Government

Governments provide resources and security so their citizens can thrive. When a government doesn't provide enough of either one in a particular region, a vacuum ensues, and the region or country is vulnerable to those forces that would fill the vacuum. Sometimes governments attempt to make up for a shortfall of resources by using repressive security measures to maintain order, but the average citizen realizes that this is illegitimate government, making the message of those rushing in to fill the void—

insurgents—even more believable. Governments who do not "control" their administrative regions by providing proper security and economic resources through effective and representative governance to their populations are vulnerable to insurgents.

It is important to note that the lack of government control can be real or merely perceived, and it is a truism of insurgency that *perception is more important than truth*. This is why the media or the "informational" element of national power is so important—and why so many weak governments spend a lot of time and money on disinformation campaigns aimed at their own people. Insurgency literature and counterinsurgency doctrine spend a lot of time talking about the "fight for legitimacy," and while not completely identical terms, we are essentially talking about the same thing: positive, representative government control = legitimate government.[3] In short, lack of government control gives the insurgency something to point at and say, "That's why *they* are bad and need to be replaced, because *they* don't care about *us*."

Illegitimate governments do not provide state institutions that focus on the social, economic, political, security, or cultural conditions that impact individuals and groups within its society. The basic premise of Ted Gurr's book *Why Men Rebel* is that when people feel deprived of economic, social, or cultural benefits by comparing their position to others in society they often resort to collective mobilization, terrorism, or civil war. When terrorism analysts and sociologists refer to "root causes," they are talking about this type of deprivation or the inherently assumed illegitimacy of occupation forces. Ironically, as much as we tend to hate the seemingly repressive demands of bureaucracy, it is this same bureaucracy that in many ways guarantees our way of life. Weak administrative bureaucratic organizations in remote areas play directly into the hands of insurgents—as insurgencies are "bottom-to-top" movements and governments are "top-to-bottom" organizations. Nature abhors a vacuum, and if there does not appear to be a strong administrative bureaucracy exerting control in a particular region, someone will step in to provide order. Recent literature has begun to refer to regions with insufficient government control as "ungoverned territories," and research shows that these areas are most susceptible to insurgencies.[4]

There is a debate among insurgency and terrorism analysts as to the relative merits of addressing "root causes"; some analysts believe that root

---

3. Except anarchists—who believe all governments are illegitimate, or Islamic traditionalists who see any form of government that is not *shari'a*-based as inherently illegitimate.
4. Angel Rabasa, "Ungoverned Territories," Testimony Before the Subcommittee on National Security and Foreign Affairs, Washington, DC: February 14, 2008.

causes have nothing to do with the real reasons that people become terrorists and insurgents and are merely a smoke screen. Others believe that stopping the violence is as simple as removing the root causes. The point is moot, because both sides are correct: some ideologues—leaders—were never influenced by root causes and will never stop espousing their cause just because a government does or does not do something, but many of the foot soldiers *are* readily influenced by root causes and can often be convinced to change sides if better conditions are presented to them.

Regardless, root causes must be addressed if only to take away the ability of leadership to take actual events and situations and then frame them into an ideology that will influence a vulnerable population. So whether or not root causes affect a given terrorist or insurgent membership is not as important as *how insurgent leadership uses root causes to frame a conflict.* For COIN forces, defeating an ideology is not just coming up with a competing ideology, it's also about being able to "counter-frame" the existing conflict, addressing root causes and providing positive government control. This allows the government to say, "Look, we do care, and here are all the things that we are doing." The obvious danger of government action is that it can actually empower the insurgents by creating conditions where they can say, "See how important and powerful we are, the government does what we tell it to do." But by careful application of the principles of counterinsurgency, a government can marginalize an insurgency's ideology, or at least force it to reveal its true objectives once it has lost its "social and government reform" platform.

Insufficient government control packs a double punch because in addition to creating a breeding ground for root causes, it also creates the conditions for dissatisfied citizens to physically act upon their anger, because in areas with insufficient government control, there is usually insufficient law-enforcement, allowing for low compliance with existing laws. This is why terrorism has become such a popular tool for insurgents: the terrorists' ability to strike at will and disappear showcases the government's inability to protect its citizens. The government's perceived weakness and inadequacy in finding and arresting a small number of criminals is played across the pages of the international press and becomes a daily reminder of the ineffectiveness of the government.

Insurgencies often make excellent use of the media to present the image of an unresponsive or unprepared government, as it is considerably easier and cheaper to erode public confidence through the media than attacking government military forces. Because an insurgent group needs to portray the government as ineffective and unresponsive in order to gather supporters and rally them around a cause, insurgents often initially target minorities or fringe elements of a society—those people who may actually be getting fewer resources and government attention than the primary social group within a country.

Ideology

Insurgencies develop around a common ideology—often intentionally vague and contradictory—which may change as the insurgency gains momentum. This allows the insurgency maximum flexibility to gain support while remaining uncommitted to specific objectives. Usually, in the early stages of an insurgency, the primary effort is made to expose the shortcomings of the existing government followed by sweeping promises of a better system with a more equitable distribution of economic resources to be administered by new insurgent leadership. Insurgency leaders can make grandiose promises at the early stages of an insurgency because they will never have to fulfill them—and they are very attractive to the populace.

The "us against them" construct is probably the single most important element of an ideology. It is one of the most powerful influences on human motivation and the basis for numerous conflicts. An entire academic field, nationalism, has been devoted to the study of why men fight and what motivates them. Two very important ideas have to be addressed here: first—"us versus them" is the reason that the insurgent gets out of bed every morning and says to himself, "I am ready to die for this cause," and secondly—the idea of "us" and "them" is largely constructed—meaning that our ideas about belonging to a specific group, nationality, religion, or other community are largely conceptual, and because they are largely conceptual, they can be manipulated.[5]

The ideology is the message that the insurgents want to disseminate to the people, the central theme around which to rally support. There are different ways of analyzing ideologies, but I believe that Bard O'Neill offers the best framework in his book, *Insurgency and Terrorism*. O'Neill identifies nine basic types of insurgencies (or insurgent ideologies): anarchist, egalitarian, traditionalist, apocalyptic-utopian, pluralist, secessionist, reformist, commercialist, and preservationist—the first five being "revolutionary" movements because they seek a revolutionary transformation of the political system. The broader term of insurgency is therefore used to cover most conflicts directed against a government by a particular sub-national group—as revolutions, secessionist (separatist) movements, and every other type of armed conflict conducted by non-state actors usually fall into the category of insurgency.

Insurgent ideologies cover the complete range of motivation from the *anarchist* ("eliminate all institutionalized political arrangements because they view the superordinate-subordinate authority relationships associated with them as unnecessary and illegitimate") to the *preservationist*

---

5. For the definitive source, see Benedict Anderson's widely acclaimed work *Imagined Communities, Reflection on the Origin and Spread of Nationalism* (London, New York: Verso, revised edition, 1991).

("maintaining the status quo because of the relative political, economic, and social privileges they derive from it").[6] *Secessionists* (one group of Chechen insurgents) reject the political community of which they are a part and seek to withdraw from it and establish their own new and independent government.

Pluralists seek revolution—but not to replace one elite ruling class with another—instead they shun authoritarian governments and seek to establish greater political freedoms and participation through multiparty structures that are "differentiated and autonomous." *Reformists* do not want to change the government or establish their own structures; they simply wish to have greater political, economic, and social benefits for their constituent group, usually ethnic in origin. *Apocalyptic-utopians* believe the world must first be destroyed or ruined so that a savior can emerge and cleanse humanity.

The types we are most familiar with are the *egalitarian* ("impose a new system based on the ultimate value of distributional equality and centrally controlled structures to mobilize the people and radically transform the social structure," i.e., Communism/Marxism in all its forms) and more recently the *traditionalists* who seek to "displace the political system and restore a system that existed in the recent or distant past with values that are primordial and sacred, rooted in ancestral ties and religion." Islamist groups in general—and groups operating in the North Caucasus, in particular—fall into this group.[7] Both egalitarians and traditionalists tend to end up extremely authoritarian, as they are based on the idea that a revolutionary cadre or religious caste knows what is best for the common person. The last group is one that is almost always present as a subordinate group in every insurgency: the *commercialists*—or "profiteers." These groups are often organized on clan or tribal affiliations and, as their name suggests, they tend to be interested in gaining material resources through the control of political power. Groups of profiteers have played an important role in the Chechen conflict.

Available Leadership

As with any organization, leadership is critical. Most importantly for insurgencies, effective leaders at the pinnacle of the organization are

---

6. All of these definitions are from, or based on, *Insurgency and Terrorism, From Revolution to Apocalypse*, Second Edition, Revised (Dulles, VA.: Potomac Books, 2005), pp. 19–29.

7. A much more comprehensive analysis of Islamist ideology is discussed in Chapter 6, where the full extent of that influence on the Chechen insurgency is discussed in detail.

crucial because they frame real or perceived government illegitimacy (root causes) in such a way as to focus the blame on the current administration; then they propagate their own ideology by constructing and articulating a shared vision of a better world under a new insurgent government. Without this vision, it doesn't matter how ineffective the current government is because the population will not see the insurgency as a viable option—or a legitimate alternative. Through this constructivism, the insurgents become the agents of change to improve the lives of the disaffected; they become heroes and martyrs.

Leaders come from all walks of life, but what is really meant by "available leadership" is having leaders that are considered to be legitimate by the population. Often the "available leadership" consists of men with status, prestige, and experience that can be used by an insurgency to legitimize their own actions and draw more of the local population to their side.

Some leaders, however, come from within a community and gain leadership status through their actions or some personal attribute like military experience, personal bravery, intelligence, or natural leadership ability. As these leaders are considered to be "homegrown," they tend to have fanatical followings; government efforts to paint them as "illegitimate" or "criminal" tend to be counterproductive, as the population perceives the attacks against "their" local hero as being directed against them as well—thereby solidifying the "us against them" mentality.

Leadership is critical—it is the first element, or the initiator, of the "acceleration chain" of an insurgency because even the most vulnerable population under the worst conditions will not overthrow their government without someone to lead them; there must be a "head," a leadership element that can light the fire of discontent and then direct the frustrations of the populace along an insurgent strategy.

But insurgencies are less like snakes and more like hydras; there is often more than one head and all of them need to be addressed. Effective junior leaders are just as important to the insurgency and should not be overlooked, as they must be able to quickly and effectively analyze local situations, determine direction for local cells, set a compelling example for the insurgents who are willing to risk their lives, allocate scarce resources, and make appropriate decisions for all manner of day-to-day operational needs. Moreover, if government forces are able to cut off the "main" head, it will be these leaders who will quickly rise to take their place. When it comes to analyzing leadership, it is often more difficult to identify junior leaders, but the effort is worthwhile, as they often harbor different goals than the senior leadership; separating them from the insurgency and co-opting them and their organizations to the government side in a larger

counterinsurgency campaign is one of the most effective means of
ending insurgencies.

Vulnerable Population

The most important prerequisite for an insurgency is a *vulnerable
population*—as it is usually only when the majority of the population is
generally open to change—for economic, social, or political reasons—
that an insurgent leadership is able to mobilize the populace through
ideology and take advantage of the lack of government control.

Insurgent groups attempt to win the support of the population by
promising a better life or coercing them through terror. Although the
vast majority of the population will never take up arms against the
government, *doing nothing* to stop insurgents from operating in their
area still provides enough tacit support and approval for the insurgency to operate successfully.

Counterinsurgency fights are about giving the population a reason to
want to see the insurgency fail. The population must be co-opted into
fighting against the insurgency; they must have something worth losing so they will fight to defend it. People will fight to retain what they
have—even if all they have is their honor, culture, or way of life.

STARTING A CONFLAGRATION

Most books on insurgency don't refer to prerequisites. Rather, when
they refer to different aspects of insurgencies, they will list them as elements, dynamics, aspects, etc. It is efficacious to use those lists to analyze
an insurgency for the purposes of planning a counterinsurgency (COIN)
operation, but I believe that the prerequisite model as explained above
allows for better understanding and ultimately, even better analysis and
targeting. Different actors in the COIN campaign fight at different levels,
so while analyzing likely insurgent weapons and tactics is important
(especially at the tactical level), understanding the interplay of the four
most important factors may present overlooked opportunities to defeat
insurgencies using more efficient and less expensive and exhaustive
measures.

The analogy of a bonfire illustrates the importance of these prerequisites. Every Boy and Girl Scout knows that in order to build a proper fire
there are certain elements that must be placed in the correct order so that
one element will burn hot enough so as to ignite another incendiary element with a higher combustion point. A properly laid fire can be lit with
a single match and each element will "feed" the next until the fire is

self-sufficient and burns hotly on its own. Fires—and insurgencies—
occasionally start spontaneously after an unexpected, catastrophic, or
precipitous event (a lightning strike) that provides such an enormous
initial amount of heat and flame that normal acceleration is significantly
compressed and a conflagration is achieved almost immediately; however, normal fires, either man-made or naturally occurring require an
"acceleration chain" generally expressed as: initiator, tinder, kindling,
fuel (logs).

Insurgencies operate in the same manner; especially when one considers what insurgencies are ultimately attempting to do—destroy an
existing government and raise a new one from the ashes. A vulnerable
population is the fuel of the insurgency, the logs; insurgencies cannot
win unless they can turn the will of the people to their cause. Ideology
is the framing of events in such a way that the population perceives
that there is a problem and that the problem is the government. Ideology is the kindling that lights the log.

But in order to create an ideology (or narrative), there must be events
or facts to interpret. The kindling must be lit by the tinder, and in this
case, the tinder is the lack of government control or an illegitimate government. Moreover, in most cases, it is the lack of government control
that creates the conditions that lead to a vulnerable population in the
first place. And who initiates this acceleration chain? Who constructs
and disseminates the ideology? The leadership. The success of an insurgency or any social movement depends to a large extent on the ability of
the leadership to create and disseminate an ideology that will attract
adherents.

The acceleration chain for a fire is: initiator, tinder, kindling, and
fuel. The acceleration chain for an insurgency is: available leadership,
illegitimate government, ideology, and vulnerable population. And
just as removing a part of the acceleration chain of a fire may prevent
the fire from reaching a conflagration, removing any one of the insurgency prerequisites may cause an insurgency to collapse as well—
which is why these four elements provide the most efficient areas for
targeting.

COMMON CHARACTERISTICS OF INSURGENCIES

Now that it is clear what insurgencies are and the conditions under
which they develop, it is time to examine the different elements that
are commonly found in most insurgencies in varying degrees. No insurgency is ever the same, and it is the combination and strength of
these elements that define the character of a specific insurgency and

often determine its overall effectiveness. Identification of the constituent parts and their relative strengths is the first step in understanding an insurgency and uncovering likely targets for counterinsurgency efforts. These elements are: *organization and goals, environment and geography, external support, strategic approach,* and *phases and timing.*

Organization and Goals

To translate ideology into reality, the insurgency must develop and achieve specific strategic, operational, and tactical goals. The strategic objectives usually address the desired end-state (e.g., an Islamic, *shari'a*-based government); operational objectives address how the insurgency will progress toward its goal (gain the support of foreign governments, capture the support of undecided members of the populace); and tactical objectives address the immediate aims of the insurgency (expand into a new region, conduct an operation against the military, conduct a terrorist attack at the bus terminal). As in any organization, goals must then be turned into plans by senior leaders and executed by workers; mid-level leadership ensures the jobs are completed properly, while others in the organization help to run the infrastructure necessary for the "work" to get done.

Insurgencies are usually organized into three groups of participants that often make finding and destroying a movement difficult. These are *the underground, the guerrilla force,* and *the auxiliary.* The underground is a cellular organization within the insurgency that is responsible for subversion, sabotage, intelligence collection, and other compartmentalized activities. The overall leadership of an insurgency is usually contained within a small cell of the underground.

The guerrilla force is a group of irregular, predominantly indigenous personnel organized along military lines to conduct military and paramilitary operations in government-held, hostile, or denied territory. Generally, this is the group that we see most often as their operations make headlines. Finally, there is the *auxiliary*—a portion of the population that provides active support to the insurgency. This support can take the form of logistics, labor, or intelligence. Members of the auxiliary are part-time members of the insurgency, maintaining their normal positions in society.

The functions of the underground and the auxiliary can be the most difficult to understand. In some ways they are not separate components, but two types of members, making up a single "support" component—complementary rather than duplicative. Historical case studies show a variety of ratios of guerrillas/auxiliary/underground ranging from 1/4/2 to as high as 1/20/10 in urban areas.[8] What's important is that the

---

8. Department of the Army Pamphlet 550–104, Human Factors in Underground Movements, appendix B.

"visible" guerrillas are always the minority—the tip of the iceberg—so even if military forces destroy most of the guerrillas, it doesn't mean the insurgency has been defeated.

Environment and Geography

An insurgency's strategy and tactics will be greatly affected by the geography, environment, and demographics of the region. Insurgencies can be urban-based, rural-based, or a combination of the two. Each type presents its own opportunities and problems for counterinsurgency operations. Although most successful insurgencies have been a combination, the traditional image of the guerrilla is the rural-based "freedom fighter." Historically, strictly urban-based insurgencies failed because of lack of support within cities. However, trends within the last 20 years show an increase in the number of successful urban-based insurgencies as the world's populations move into the cities—but don't find the better life they expected.

These groups usually self-segregate within cities by ethnic groups which create large insular neighborhoods through which the insurgents can move unobstructed; in a sense, these urban environments have become as impenetrable to police as the jungles are to military patrols. More alarmingly, the urbanization of insurgencies has also led to the increased use of terrorism by insurgencies over the last 40 years. This is because urban groups have a difficult time training and organizing for large-scale operations, and security requirements in a city demand higher degrees of compartmentalization within the cells. Although urban areas do have unique advantages in terms of infrastructure, easy access to banking systems, and transportation networks that allow for access to target-rich environments (government organizations, state infrastructure, and large population centers), urban-based insurgencies rarely achieve effects beyond the level of terrorist attacks.[9]

The urbanization of insurgency has also presented numerous obstacles to counterinsurgency efforts. Cities have traditionally administered order through police enforcement, while the military has had the lead in counterinsurgency operations in the rural areas. As insurgencies have moved to the cities, some governments have attempted to use the military in their traditional role, but most modern militaries are wholly unsuited for urban operations or MOUT (Military Operations in Urban Terrain). Huge population densities have obviated traditional government military advantages like tanks, artillery, mortars, and fixed-wing aircraft. So

---

9. Bruce Hoffman and Jennifer Morrison Taw, *The Urbanization of Insurgency* (Santa Monica, CA: Rand, Arroyo Center, 1994), pp. 10–12.

bringing the military into a city (where they are not trained to deal with civilians) is often counterproductive—while police forces are usually outgunned by the insurgents.

External Support

Once an insurgency has started, probably the single most significant factor leading to a successful conclusion is the ability of the organization to attract external support. Most successful insurgencies have received some form of state-sponsored external support, including moral encouragement or political recognition, resources (money, weapons, food, advisors, and training), sanctuary (secure training sites, operational bases across the border, protection from extradition), intelligence, organizational aid, and in some cases, even fighters. Although the impact of external support depends on the stage of an insurgency, third-party state support is often necessary to help insurgents reach a new level of political and military effectiveness.[10] Insurgencies that have a friendly government on their border have a huge advantage over insurgencies that do not because sanctuary, money, advisors, and weapons flowing across a border can sustain an insurgency that would otherwise be eradicated by government forces. And it is the ability to survive for long periods of time that often makes the difference for insurgent movements, because the continued economic and military strain an insurgency puts on an already vulnerable government often brings it to its knees. Regardless of the type—state sponsored, private, or passive—external support is a factor that can be targeted by a government's counterinsurgency campaign through diplomatic or economic pressure and the threat of military force. The flow of money, goods, and services is something that can be tracked if counterinsurgency intelligence agencies are professional and have good relationships with other nations. An oft-heard refrain of COIN professionals is "follow the money"; although in some areas it's as simple as "follow the bread trucks."

Strategic Approach

Finally, each insurgency movement has a plan that it uses to conduct its campaign so that there is a systematic, integrated, and orchestrated use of the various means it has available to achieve its goals. Sometimes insurgents choose to move quickly to take advantage of a particular event, and sometimes they want to move slowly to build their organization.

---

10. Daniel Byman et al., *Trends in Outside Support for Insurgent Movements* (Santa Monica, CA: Rand, National Security Research Division, 2001), pp. 83–100.

Although each insurgency is unique and rarely follows one model exactly, there are four broad strategic approaches that are used as starting points for most insurgency movements: the conspiratorial strategy (Lenin), the strategy of protracted war (Mao), the military-focus strategy (Castro), and the urban warfare strategy (terrorism-based insurgencies like Al Qaeda in Iraq and the PLO).[11] When developing a counterinsurgency campaign, it is important to try to identify the insurgent strategy, because in some cases it can provide an "order of battle" or line and block chart for the organization; at the very least, it gives a good indication of possible targets. Trying to understand an insurgency from the occasional and sporadic encounters with guerrillas or terrorists is like looking at the tip of the iceberg and never seeing what lies beneath the water. Governments have to respond differently to a traditional (Maoist) strategy of protracted warfare than they would to a military-focus strategy, as one moves slowly and depends on winning the majority of the population, whereas the other focuses on decisive military action and demands popular support after the *fait accompli*.[12]

Phases and Timing

All insurgencies pass through various phases and depending on the type of insurgency, the phases may be different. Passing through all phases in the proper order is not a requirement for success, as the phasing and timing of an insurgency is often influenced by external factors; many insurgencies have experienced temporary setbacks, causing them to revert to a previous phase before they could reemerge and become victorious.

Although the time may be appropriate for transition, if the insurgency is not prepared to deal with the new requirements of a new phase—especially if the government has been successful in cutting off external support—then the insurgency may unintentionally overextend itself and allow the government to destroy the majority of the guerrillas in one operation. Other times, insurgencies have surged forward when the government has shown egregious ineptitude in executing its counterinsurgency campaign, thus giving the insurgents opportunities to exploit weaknesses. Insurgencies in Angola, Mozambique, and Rhodesia all succeeded without even reaching the traditional "last" phase. Many observers of Chechnya announced that the insurgency was defeated in 2007 when, in reality, the insurgency moved from a Phase II guerrilla campaign back to a Phase I "rebuilding"

---

11. Galula lists only two types of insurgent patterns, the "orthodox" and the "shortcut" (terrorism).
12. For a much more detailed description of these models, see O'Neill, *Insurgency and Terrorism*, chapter III.

phase, only to reemerge in 2008 with a different ideology and focus. It quickly gained strength, and even those who proclaimed the insurgency "dead" in 2006 do not fail to publicly state that there is an active insurgency conducting guerrilla warfare (Phase II).

Phase I–Latent and Incipient

Phase I is the *latent and incipient stage*, a secretive preparation stage where cadres are recruited and trained, funds are raised, the organization develops an ideology, compartmentalized cellular organization begins in the underground and the auxiliary, attempts are made to infiltrate government organizations, and some civil disobedience may be organized. At this stage it is essential to avoid armed confrontation because the nascent movement is not yet strong enough to withstand the government's police and military forces, and the last thing the insurgents want to do is to tip their hand.

Operating in a hostile environment is common for most insurgencies. As such, travel within the country is often restricted, police and internal intelligence organizations can be omnipresent and heavy-handed, and official state entities unresponsive. In such conditions, recruiting guerrillas is one of the easiest tasks; other requirements such as establishing a logistical system that can cross international borders can take much longer. For these reasons the need for secrecy is vital. Building a legitimate command structure—the cadre—can also take a very long time, and consequently, it's usually near the end of this phase that shadow governments are finally established.

Phase II–Guerrilla Warfare

Phase II is characterized by guerrilla warfare. Trained cadres initiate low-level violence such as sabotage, subversion, and terrorism while constantly attempting to mobilize the masses through propaganda. Now that the insurgency is no longer a secret, the movement aggressively seeks international support and recognition by showing that they can defeat government military forces, thus gaining legitimacy as a "real" organization. Of course it's not a fair fight (or true legitimacy) because the insurgents only choose battles that they know they can win—which is why Phase II consists almost exclusively of ambushes against the military and terrorist attacks against civilians. The idea is to "hit 'em hard and fast" and then run away before reinforcements show up—taking whatever they can.

The guerrilla warfare phase is incredibly frustrating for counterinsurgency efforts; once guerrilla attacks occur, military forces are usually mobilized, but they are forced to deal with a security situation that has already been incubating and festering for many years—so their initial operations are generally unsuccessful. Counterinsurgency efforts must be an all-out fight using overwhelming resources at the very first sign of guerrilla warfare if the government doesn't want to play catch-up for years to come. Unfortunately, most government officials do not understand the full nature of insurgencies and wait too long before committing the kinds of resources required; this is what the insurgents are planning on.

The subject of terrorism will be addressed in the next chapter, but it is important to note that most insurgencies make a conscious decision at this point whether or not to employ terrorism. Unfortunately, the trend lately has been toward greater use of terrorism in order to grab headlines, and the growing number of Islamic insurgencies use passages from the *Qur'an* (Koran) and other sacred texts to justify terrorism against civilians as merely extending the military battle to those who are responsible for supporting the government and their policies.

Regardless of whether or not the insurgents choose to use terrorism, "soft" targets are preferred during the guerilla warfare phase, because they provide the insurgents with additional vital resources—the most important being supplies and "live fire" training. During the incipient stage, insurgents can recruit personnel, but arms and ammunition are often difficult to procure. A basic tactic from the "insurgent playbook" is to initiate attacks in remote areas—requiring the government to send troops outside of the normal radius of their bases or garrisons. Government troops require food, ammunition, and supplies, the bulk of which must be transported by unarmored trucks—the perfect "confidence" target for the insurgents.

In many countries there are only so many high-speed roads that can support trucks and troop movements—meaning the insurgents already have a good idea how government troops will move into their area. During Phase I, the insurgents establish a network of spies and observers around and, most likely, inside military bases. Once the troops begin to move into a remote area being contested by the insurgents, the guerrillas initiate ambushes along the roads and kill many soldiers trapped inside the vehicles; the Chechen ambush that destroyed Russian armored columns as they attempted to take Grozny is one of the best contemporary examples of this. Moreover, when troops initially move to a new area, they expect that *they* will be doing the attacking: they are not expecting to get attacked themselves—making the bulk of young, inexperienced, and mentally unprepared recruits especially vulnerable.

The first ambushes are simple: the insurgents simply set off a few mines, pour bullets into the cloth-covered trucks, killing soldiers who cannot effectively return fire, and then fade away into the woods or dense urban area without a casualty. The ambush is a resounding success, the "green" insurgents gain confidence, and all the media sources report for days on the government and military failure; it usually makes the international news as well. Young men full of idealistic notions and short of cash and opportunities now flock to the insurgency because it has "proven" that it can defeat larger government forces. Money starts to flow into the coffers of the insurgency from outside sources that now see the insurgency as having a chance of winning. Thus, the insurgency is off and running.

Smaller logistical convoys and local patrols are even more vulnerable. They provide the "confidence booster" mentioned above, but are even more important because once the vehicles are stopped and the soldiers killed, the insurgents are able to take all the weapons, ammunition, medical supplies—even vehicles—that they can.

And the government, even a good, effective government, is virtually powerless to stop the attacks. Ambushes are among the easiest attacks to conduct, and a well-executed ambush is able to kill or wound all the troops, take all the equipment, and disappear within minutes; however, the aim is always for some troops to remain alive in order to tell their story to the media and recount the guerrilla force's power.

At this point, the government can't stop sending troops because the guerrilla attacks constantly remind the population of the fact that they are not safe, and the citizens continually scream for protection. The military can't stop doing patrols, although this gives more opportunities for the guerrillas to ambush soldiers. If the military starts using larger convoys, the guerrillas will just plant mines on the road, use shoulder-fired missiles and run away. If the government decides to build a base near the insurgent activity to cut down on vehicular traffic and resupply missions, the guerrillas will start killing all the truck drivers who have to transport the building materials until no one is willing to drive.

Any government effort at this stage is probably already years behind the insurgency, and the insurgents will always manage to stay a few steps ahead—unless the entire government gets involved immediately. Unfortunately, history shows that it will not. Instead, the military will finally begin teaching itself about the military aspects of insurgencies (usually a list of battalion level "tactics") while the government will still conceptualize the conflict as purely military. The local commanders will start using their new basic counterinsurgency tactics—but that will merely play into the hands of the insurgents as well. Once the military begins employing the "new" tactics and the troops begin to have some "apparent" success at defending their convoys and patrols, the insurgents will use those same tactics against the military troops to further destroy local forces and frustrate and demoralize the military establishment and government at large.

Using another tactic from the basic guerrilla "playbook," the guerrillas will attack, observe the military reaction to learn their new tactic, and withdraw without taking casualties. They'll do this a few times to convince the troops that their new tactic is effective, and somewhere around the third or fourth attack, the guerrillas will plan a counterattack designed to exploit the now-established, "successful" military tactic and inflict a crushing defeat on the local forces. And then the cycle begins again. It generally takes about two years for military personnel that are previously untrained in counterinsurgency and counter-guerrilla tactics to gain enough experience to break this cycle—and by then, the insurgency may have grown so strong that the government cannot stop it—especially as the focus will have been almost exclusively on the military aspect of the insurgency.

This is the critical point for the guerrilla warfare stage, because now the guerrilla bands have grown so large that they must physically occupy space, requiring them to operate out of a particular region or town. However, once they are all together in one place (or lots of little places inside of a town), then they can finally be targeted by government forces who will send in helicopter gunships, fighter aircraft, and large troop formations who will establish road blocks, set up curfews, and begin searching every square inch to find the insurgents and their equipment. How well the guerrillas can defend themselves will determine if the guerrilla warfare stage can continue to progress. If government forces are too powerful and the local population is not vulnerable enough, then the guerrillas will simply disappear and the insurgency will temporarily revert back to Phase I (latent and incipient) until it finds a new area from which to start operations. Then it will begin again.

However, if all has gone well, the confident and now well-equipped bands of experienced guerrillas will not only be able to defend themselves, but they will also go on the offensive and conduct larger attacks against government troops and installations in preparation for Phase III—the War of Movement—similar to what we know as conventional warfare.

Phase III–The War of Movement

The war of movement is characterized by the transition into a regular army and large-scale conventional warfare, establishing a national government, and eliminating the former political elites.[13] During the guerrilla warfare stage, the non-guerilla members of the insurgency

---

13. The original Maoist doctrine that this model is based on describes the three phases as the strategic defense, the strategic stalemate, and the strategic offensive. See *Mao Tse-Tung on Guerrilla Warfare*, translated by Samuel B. Griffith (New York, NY: Praeger, 1961), pp. 105–113. Naqshbandi (Sufi Islam) commanders during the Iraq insurgency devised similar doctrine when fighting against U.S. forces, but used the terms "defensive," "balance of power," and "final assault" to describe the phases of their own campaign.

were not idle: they constantly gathered intelligence on the government; fomented unrest with student groups; staged "non-violent" rallies that somehow always turned violent; printed propaganda and fed the media; started a political wing and began lobbying in the legislature; infiltrated police and government organizations at all levels; and planned exactly whom they would assassinate when the time came.

During the war of movement, everyone makes the final "push" and the full extent of the insurgency becomes visible for the first time, even if all the elements are not fully exposed, like the auxiliary. The shadow government emerges and begins operating as a government while the guerrillas—now closely resembling regular army troops, complete with uniforms, heavy weapons, vehicles, and well-disciplined formations—battle government troops. At this point, the conflict has become a civil war, with the insurgency not only controlling, but also administering parts of the country. The insurgency must be sure to provide basic services at a level that was better than the government had provided to demonstrate to the general population—most of whom have not been affected by the fighting yet—that the "insurgent" government has more legitimacy and will do more for the population than the "corrupt" government against which it is fighting.

Transitions between insurgency phases represent significant vulnerable points for government counterinsurgency efforts, as the transitions require changes in tactics to adapt to the increased logistical and communications requirements. Knowing that an insurgency movement is preparing to move from guerrilla warfare to the war of movement tells the government to be on the lookout for shipments of larger weapon systems, the movement of large formations of troops across borders, and preparation for invasion. In 1997, the Kosovo Liberation Army began large-scale recruitment of "regular" soldiers and moved operations and most of its cadre—some of whom had been operating in insurgent and terrorist cells for more than ten years—across the border into Albania and Macedonia. The troops were equipped with uniforms and weapons, trained and organized into conventional combat battalions, and sent back into Kosovo to fight regular Serbian forces. Their successful transition to Phase III resulted in their liberation—or their official recognition as a U.N. protectorate, depending on your point of view—in 1999.[14]

Keep in mind that the example I provided above is merely one example of the myriad permutations that an insurgency can take. If one is to truly understand a particular insurgency, then it is necessary

---

14. Interview with former Brigade Commander of the KLA, August 2001. During this and other interviews, the Brigade Commander, explained how the KLA (UCK) originally started with a cadre of about 30 officers brought together to form a "general staff" and operated in secret for years in order to train a cadre of officers that would be available to lead battalions once the insurgency moved from the guerrilla warfare stage to a war of movement.

to study in detail all the prerequisites and common elements of a particular conflict because the government resources and military tactics necessary for success will be different for an urban terrorism-based insurgency than for a rural-popular-protracted-war insurgency, where terrorism may not play a role and government reforms are paramount.

CHAPTER 2

Terrorism

We argue for the implementation of terror in a whole series of situations.
But for us, terrorist acts can only be part of this struggle . . . interwoven
into a single complete system along with all other methods of partisan
and mass . . . assault on the government.

—Viktor M. Chernov (Russian chief theoretician of pre-WWI
Socialist-Revolutionaries)

If understanding the complexities of insurgency is difficult, then stripping
away the rhetoric to determine which violent acts are considered terrorism and which are considered "legal" under the international law of land
warfare is ten times more problematic. Yet understanding the differences
is central to the question of what is happening in the North Caucasus. To
determine what the insurgency has done and where it is going, then it is
critical to understand what terrorism is and how it relates to insurgencies
in general—and Chechnya in particular. After all, the Chechens have been
responsible for some of the most horrific terrorist attacks in history, most
notably the Beslan School Massacre which left over 180 children dead. But
"terrorism," like "insurgency," is a troubled term—with virtually no consensus on exactly what terrorism means among any two official bodies.
Regardless of the definition that one chooses, it is important to remember
that the central tenet of terrorism is that it uses fear to coerce behavior.
Terrorism cannot change minds, terrorism can only coerce.

According to the Department of Defense, terrorism is defined as "the
unlawful use or threatened use of force or violence against people or
property to coerce or intimidate governments or societies, often to achieve
political, religious, or ideological objectives."[1] The CIA and the State
Department have different definitions. The Department of Homeland

---

1. Joint Publication 1-02, *DOD Dictionary of Military and Associated Terms.*

Security (ostensibly the agency responsible for protecting us from acts of terrorism) doesn't have a definition at all and simply refers one to the U.S. penal code. Everyone seems to know what terrorism is when they see it, but no one can agree on exactly what constitutes an act of terrorism and what doesn't—and that's just within the United States, where we've been conducting the War on Terrorism for over nine years!

The problem becomes increasingly complex as we interact with other countries and their agencies because no two countries can agree on a single definition; ergo, there is no globally accepted definition of terrorism because the word "terrorist" is universally accepted as "bad" and a government that covertly supports an insurgency movement in a neighboring country does not want the insurgency to lose legitimacy on the world stage by allowing it to be labeled as a bunch of terrorists.

TERRORISM, INSURGENCY, OR BOTH?

The preponderance of the confusion about the terms terrorism and insurgency comes from the fact that, although there are groups that conduct terrorism for the sake of terrorism, most terrorism is conducted by insurgent groups who use terrorism as one of the many different kinds of activities conducted as part of an overall insurgency campaign. Unfortunately, because of the success of international terrorism over the past 40 years, terrorism has often become the first choice for insurgent movements rather than something that they attempted to avoid in order to maintain their international credibility—and as such, some "insurgent" groups have adopted terrorism as their primary tactic.

Terrorism is easy. It doesn't require expensive military technology, it doesn't require large numbers of people, it doesn't require a lot of support, and it can be very effective because it gets everyone's attention. The 9/11 attacks were conducted for around $100,000—and caused thousands of deaths and billions of dollars worth of damage. As a result, in addition to the oft-heard "all terrorists are really some sort of freedom fighters" argument, we also have the equally dogmatic obverse: some analysts claim that all insurgencies should actually be referred to as terrorist groups, because if an insurgent group allows any terrorism to be perpetrated in its name, then they are all terrorists.

In an article entitled "Contrasting Secular and Religious Terrorism" in the *Middle East Quarterly*, Jonathan Fine presents a good summary of terrorist activity over the past 60 years. He states:

> Between 1945 and 1979, there were three principle [*sic*] types of terrorist entities: organizations struggling for independence from colonial occupiers such as the Front de Liberation Nationale (FLN) in Algeria or the Mau Mau in Kenya; separatist groups such as the Irish Republican Army (IRA) in

Northern Ireland and the Basque Euzkadi Ta-Askatasuna (ETA) in Spain; and socioeconomic revolutionaries such as the Montoneros in Argentina, the Sandinistas in Nicaragua, the Baader Meinhof Gang in West Germany, and the Red Brigades in Italy. A commonality among all groups, though, would be an attempt to justify their actions in economic or social theory. In most if not all cases, the definition of the opponent by secular agenda guerrillas and terrorist groups was confined to a socioeconomic concept such as "Yankee capitalism" or resisting the imperialism of countries such as Great Britain or France. Even the Palestine Liberation Organization (PLO) infused its national liberation agenda with Marxist rhetoric.[2]

Looking at the three types of groups that Fine describes and thinking back to the insurgent ideologies discussed in Chapter 1, one can accurately attribute secessionist, reformist, and egalitarian insurgent ideologies to them. Indeed, those groups have traditionally been referred to as terrorist groups because they use terror as a tactic. But based on the discussion in the last chapter, it is clear that, for the most part, those groups were insurgent organizations that used terrorism as a tactic—or pure terrorist cells working as proxies for other countries or organizations that were involved in larger insurgent activity.[3]

As Fine pointed out, much of the terrorism of the 1980s and 1990s came from groups like the Red Army Faction in Germany and the Red Brigades in Italy. Those groups, while small and independent of each other, were "state-sponsored" and still worked toward the larger political goal of the group or country that supported them—the Soviet Union in many cases.[4] There are also transnational or international groups like Al Qaeda, whose stated goals include "the removal of American troops from Islamic lands, the overthrow of certain Arab governments, and the creation of Islamic states uncorrupted by the West." However unlikely it is that they will meet those goals, Al Qaeda's demands are clearly political, as they espouse a change of government.

---

2. Jonathan Fine, "Contrasting Secular and Religious Terrorism," *Middle East Quarterly*, Winter Edition, 2008.

3. The situation in Chechnya is complex, but consistent with typical insurgent patterns. There are terrorists operating in Chechnya—indigenous Chechens who have fought as insurgents but also committed acts of terrorism, as well as international terrorists. There are also foreign fighters who are fighting to establish a Caucasian Emirate as part of a larger Caliphate, and there are also bands of Chechen insurgents who have not participated in terrorist activities and who simply want independence from Russia and who meet the international legal standard for "combatants." Not all fighters in Chechnya are terrorists, but neither are they all legally considered combatants.

4. "Scope" is an important concept to keep in mind here, as these smaller "pure" terrorist cells are most efficiently dealt with by law enforcement—and Europe's success in dealing with some of these smaller "pure" terrorist cells has been the basis for their "terrorism policy" in general. Unfortunately, as will become apparent, this approach is insufficient for much of the transnational terrorism that takes place today.

It's no wonder, then, that different journalists or regional experts describe the same incident in completely different terms: some call it terrorism, some call it an attack. Therefore, insofar as many insurgencies use terrorism as a tactic, it is necessary to be able to make the distinctions clear—especially as insurgencies move from one phase to another or even change their strategic approach midstream to attract support. But with insurgents, terrorists, sympathetic farmers, grieving family members, and educated ideologues all part of the same organization, how is it possible to tell the difference between a terrorist organization and an insurgency?

THE NATURE OF THE ACT

Many Western terrorism scholars have begun to surmount the problem by defining terrorism according to the nature of the act and not by the identity of the perpetrator or the nature of their individual cause. This methodology helps to depoliticize the debates and to build consensus among all parties to criminalize a certain mode of political expression or warfare. In other words—if someone commits an act of terrorism (much more easily defined), then he is a terrorist—and the morality or correctness of the "cause" doesn't matter. This approach is an attempt to re-establish the idea that the "end" doesn't justify the "means"; so if a member of the organization kills women and children in a crowded marketplace, they should be legally and internationally branded a terrorist and a murderer.

Terrorism is a crime in the classic sense—just the same as murder, armed robbery, or kidnapping, regardless of the reasons for doing so. And "even if we accepted the assertion by many terrorists that they were waging war and were therefore soldiers—that is, privileged combatants in the strict legal sense—terrorist tactics, in most cases violated the rules that govern armed conflict—for example the deliberate targeting of noncombatants or actions against hostages."[5]

So how is terrorism different from an insurgency? First of all, terrorism is an operational-level tactic; insurgency is a strategic-level campaign. Second, terrorist cells are small—insurgencies are big or aspire to be big. Third, terrorism is a crime that meets the simple universal standard of violence directed at non-combatives,[6] while an insurgency is an act of war: violence directed at the government and its troops. And lastly, there is a

---

5. Ian O. Lesser et al., *Countering the New Terrorism* (Santa Monica, CA: Rand, 1999), p. v.
6. Even this is problematic when dealing with Islamic-based insurgents who state that according to the sacred texts by which they are bound, the world is divided into the land of peace (Muslim countries) and the land of war (everything else). According to them, anyone in the land of war is a combatant.

fundamental difference that can be ascertained simply by looking at their stated goals: terrorism is about fear and the coercing of short-term behavior, while insurgencies are about power and resources; insurgencies may choose to use terrorism as a method, but terrorism and insurgency are fundamentally different things.

When a terrorist cell or group is part of a larger insurgency, it is possible to destroy it by destroying the insurgency—but the methods will be different than if the terrorist cell is acting alone. And because they are fundamentally different in terms of their goals, they require fundamentally different approaches to combat them.

Therefore, terrorism is fought at the tactical level, while insurgencies are fought at the strategic level. The pure terrorist, or a terrorist cell operating in support of a larger insurgency, neither requires nor necessarily seeks popular support, and as we have seen earlier, popular support—winning the hearts and minds of the populace—is often central to an insurgency. Therefore efforts to combat pure terrorism (Timothy McVeigh and the Oklahoma City bombing, the Red Brigades) can more often focus on purely military or law enforcement operations, as there is no great need to deal with economic and political issues through a well-executed information program. This is why counterterrorism campaigns can be led by the military or civilian law enforcement agencies, but counterinsurgency campaigns *must* be led by the government. Governments must *prevent* terrorist attacks, they must *destroy* terrorist cells, but they must *defeat* insurgencies.

Al Qaeda in Iraq's (AQI) use of terrorism perfectly demonstrates this dynamic. AQI conducted hundreds of terrorist attacks in Iraq, but their methods baffled even some of our most prominent terrorism experts because the attacks didn't seem to have a purpose other than creating chaos—AQI didn't appear to be trying to coerce any particular group or behavior. However, *insurgency* experts understood the situation immediately because the reason for AQI's seemingly indiscriminate use of violence was found in the realization that Al Qaeda in Iraq *is not a terrorist organization*, but an *insurgent* organization utilizing David Galula's "bourgeois-nationalist" insurgency pattern—more commonly referred to as the "terrorism" strategy.

This insurgency strategy is designed to seize power quickly from a weak government and not worry about the repercussions until the insurgency has established firm control. Phase I is "blind terrorism" for the purpose of publicity, "conducted in as spectacular a fashion as possible, by concentrated, coordinated, and synchronized waves." Phase II, "selective terrorism," seeks to "destroy all bridges linking the population with the counterinsurgent and his potential allies" by killing local citizens— policemen, councilmen, mayors, teachers, etc.[7] The objective is to terrify

---

7. David Galula, *Counterinsurgency Warfare, Theory and Practice* (Westport: Praeger Security International, 2006, first published in 1964), 39–40.

the population into blind and immediate obedience to the insurgents through abject fear. This approach can be very effective when dealing with moribund counterinsurgency efforts because the population does not feel safe and will support the insurgents because they have more to lose from "trigger-happy" terrorists than they have to gain from supporting an anemic government. This explains why the "surge" was effective in Iraq—people wanted the violence to stop, and once they felt like there was enough security, the population felt confident enough to report on the terrorists. The "shortcut" strategy can be very effective, but its biggest risk is that terrorism may backfire—which it did. AQI was betting that the United States would "cut and run" as soon as casualties started mounting because of the perception that the American people would not support a long conflict. Instead, the United States sent more troops, and AQI "terrorist" cells disappeared as coalition forces and the Iraqi government began to defeat the insurgency.

WHY USE TERRORISM?

If terrorism is not the ultimate vehicle to success, and might even alienate people from supporting an insurgency movement, why do insurgencies use it as a tool? As discussed earlier, terrorism is very cost-effective and garners far more media attention than would an identical attack on soldiers. Moreover, as we've seen from examples above, *as a tactical-level operation,* terrorism works. The March 2004 Madrid train bombings clearly demonstrate the ideal outcome of this tactic—the use of fear to coerce behavior. The attacks occurred a few days before a national election; the sitting conservative government that supported U.S. policy in the Middle East and deployed Spanish forces to Iraq was heavily favored to win. However, in the wake of the attacks, which killed nearly 200 people and injured thousands, a left-leaning government opposed to Spain's presence in Iraq came to power. Consequently, Spain withdrew its troops from Iraq, weakening the Coalition and reducing the Western military presence in the Muslim world.

Another reason to use terrorism is that it shows the government to be illegitimate in two ways, both of which help to fill the ranks of the insurgency. First, insurgent groups that use terrorism initially target large groups of civilians in public places to demonstrate that the government is incapable of protecting its citizens; the message to the population is "join us, the government cannot stop us so we will eventually win." Secondly, a government's response to a terrorist attack is often violent reprisals against suspected organizations. If the government is not careful about managing the informational aspect of the reprisals, they will be seen by the majority of the population—at least the target population of the insurgency—as repressive. This further decreases the perceived legitimacy of the government, which in turn drives members of a vulnerable population into the ranks of the insurgency.

This strategy, while effective, runs the risk of alienating the population and provides opportunities for a well-executed counterinsurgency program to use the terrorist acts against the insurgents. Recent Al Qaeda terrorist attacks against Saudi Arabian citizens have helped to erode much of the tacit support that many of the fundamentalist Muslims in that country had for their native son, Osama bin Laden. Al Qaeda in Iraq's (AQI) attacks on Muslims led to the "tribal awakening counsels" and the alignment of disaffected Sunnis with the Coalition.

A third reason to use terrorism as part of a larger insurgency strategy is to coerce the government into wasting its energy and resources in the wrong area—trying to find small terrorist cells instead of countering the insurgent underground, whose political, informational, and economic attacks quietly but inexorably rot away the foundations of legitimacy. The media hype surrounding a terrorist attack is similar to the misdirection that a magician uses to keep our attention elsewhere while he is executing the real trick, enabling him to take the audience by complete surprise. The battlefield for this confrontation is in the media and, just like the terrorists, the politicians must demonstrate they are taking action in ways that grab headlines. And while the politicians pour money into law enforcement organizations and new technology to prevent attacks, they often fail to allocate resources to items that might not make headlines—like a social program for an unpopular minority group—but that make a difference in the long-term struggle.

Counterterrorism is sexy; counterinsurgency is not. Counterterrorism is an exciting 30-minute operation—fast-roping out of helicopters onto the roof, kicking in doors, and shooting the bad guys; counterinsurgency is months of long, dull visits to the village elder, and drinking innumerable cups of bad tea in order to gain trust and build rapport.

Often, it is the governments themselves who do the work for the insurgents by referring to the insurgents exclusively as "terrorists" for political expediency. This approach accomplishes the short-term goal of attaching the necessary level of political attention to the problem and may make it easier to justify using repressive measures and allocating additional funds and resources toward eliminating the threat. Nonetheless, by referring to all the fighters as terrorists, governments do themselves a disservice by tacitly encouraging a tactical counterterrorism approach when they should be concerned with the "full-court press" approach of strategic counterinsurgency.

The irony is that even apparent government success in the "counterterrorism" fight works to the advantage of the insurgency. When a terrorist is caught or killed, the ensuing media coverage of the event only reinforces the strong tendency of governments—especially Western—to look at the struggle as a tactical battle between the terrorists and law enforcement rather than the larger strategic operation being waged between the insurgents and the government itself. And in Chechnya, where the number of "terrorists" killed annually continues to exceed the government's estimation of the strength of the *entire* insurgency, it only serves to convince the population in the North Caucasus and Russia at large that the government is lying and the insurgency is much stronger than they want to admit.

Yet another reason that insurgencies use terrorism is because of the difficulty linking a terrorist cell directly to the insurgency—unless the insurgency claims responsibility. Terrorists generally work in cells and use "cut-outs" in order to communicate.[8] This ensures operational security and virtually guarantees that the capture of a single terrorist will not lead to the collapse of the larger organization. The loss of a single terrorist cell is minimal; suicide bombers are never the leaders of an organization—they are the "throw-aways," men and women who are not needed for more important work like leading troops or organizing the larger insurgency. This plausible deniability enables the insurgency to claim that although its political wing wants to work for a peaceful resolution to the problem, the angry citizens are taking matters into their own hands because the repressive government is not adequately addressing the legitimate needs of the people. In this way, an insurgency using terrorism can still gain media coverage for its cause as well as maintain the popular support of the citizenry because it can always claim that it wasn't responsible.

Terrorism is also ideal for strategic proxy contests between large countries—and the reason that groups like Abu Nidal and the Red Brigades were used by governments antagonistic to the West during the Cold War. Some governments prefer to fight their enemies through a proxy in a destabilizing terrorist campaign and ensure there is nothing to tie them to the act. In most cases, the "pure" terror groups are recruited, trained, funded, equipped, and managed by governments who wish to do harm to another country for their own purposes. However, proving another country is behind a terrorist attack is extremely difficult; despite expository memoirs from former KGB agents asserting it was the Soviet Union behind all those Red Brigade attacks, no one can really prove it.

---

8. The use of "cut-outs" is basic fieldcraft for any organization requiring secrecy and compartmentalization. A cut-out is any intermediary that eliminates the need to do direct coordination. A terrorist cell is usually small, and communication with "higher" is not done face-to-face, but through a cut-out known as a "dead-drop"—written instructions hidden inside of something and left at a specific time and place. A nondescript, visual signal is left in another place that is regularly visited to indicate that a message is waiting at the drop site. Once the terrorist cell leader has been recruited, he'll be given instructions on how to communicate with "higher" using his cut-out. The person that initially recruits him will not be his "handler," so the terrorist cell leader, if caught, will never actually know who is giving the orders—ensuring complete secrecy of the underground. The terrorist cell leader might be able to identify his recruiter, but since the recruiter will only use one name—and it won't be his real name, and he may be disguised—and since the recruiter is generally moved to a different area and given a new job (or even killed) after he has recruited a few terrorist cell leaders, the chain is effectively broken—especially as some organizations will use multiple cut-outs when appropriate.

It is important to understand that although those pure terrorist organizations were generally engaged at the tactical level by law enforcement agencies, as befits counterterrorist operations, at the international level, there was a much larger strategic campaign called the Cold War that was conducted at the highest levels of government using every element of national power by a coalition of Western nations.

So does that make the Abu Nidal group and the Red Army Faction insurgents? No, they were terrorist cells. However, *as a cellular organization, they worked toward furthering the goals of other entities who had political agendas and who wished to change the governments of the West.* Is Al Qaeda an insurgency? Yes, and it has extremely effective terrorist cells—but that is not the extent of the Al Qaeda organization. Not every terrorist organization is an insurgency—and not all insurgents are terrorists. Just as the military usually works for the elected political officials, so do the terrorists usually work for the larger insurgent organization.

If terrorism can be successful, and if some members of the international community are willing to accept acts of terrorism as an expression of dissatisfaction with "root causes"—such as the presence of foreign troops in disputed lands—and the rest of the international community is later willing to forgive those acts of terrorism in the interests of finding a peaceful solution to the problem, then what do the insurgents have to lose?

This is the critical point in ferreting out the truth behind whether a terrorist attack is somehow connected with a larger insurgency movement. Although the individual terrorist cells can be dealt with by law enforcement agencies, stopping a few terrorist attacks is not sufficient, and law enforcement success does not absolve the affected government from dealing with the legitimate economic and political issues of its citizenry. In cases like this, the affected government must mobilize the police and court systems to combat the terrorism cells in addition to developing and implementing an all-encompassing nationwide strategy that mobilizes all of the government's resources in an effort to keep, or win back, the support of the populace. An already serious problem is magnified exponentially if those in power incorrectly or purposely identify an act as "simple" terrorism—that is, unconnected to a larger insurgency—through ignorance or to downplay the scope of the problem.

THE EUROPEAN VIEW

As those in the international security field know, our Europeans allies generally have a different view on how to tackle international terrorism. They almost exclusively view terrorism as a domestic issue best handled by law enforcement—the idea being that effective policing will discover terrorist cells and plots before they hatch. In the European mindset, going after terrorism outside the borders of one's own country only tends to create more terrorists and makes their particular country a target for more terrorism. And although most European nations rallied behind the U.S. after 9/11 and support the international security mission in Afghanistan, many of those same allies do not see that mission as being a part of a larger counterterrorism campaign in their own countries.

In his book, *Of Paradise and Power, America and Europe in the New World Order*, Robert Kagan speaks at length about the different basic approaches that the Europeans and the Americans take toward security issues.[9] Kagan believes the reason that the United States and Europe disagree on their approaches to geopolitical challenges is that Europe doesn't have the ability to deal with those challenges in any other way except through their policy of engagement. Because they don't have militaries strong enough to force compliance with United Nations mandates or other international agreements, the Europeans *must* focus on their diplomatic, economic, informational, and legal elements of national power to convince recalcitrant nations to do the "right" thing.

Kagan speaks in broad security terms, but if we take his argument and apply it to the specifics of how the Europeans look at insurgency and terrorism, it becomes plain that the reason many Europeans believe the best way to handle terrorism is to use a preponderance of police and courts is because they don't have any other way to deal with it. In many ways Europe has become a continent of laws and lawyers—with the European Union regulating many aspects of everyday life.

However, it is important to remember that the Europeans have been dealing with terrorism a lot longer than the United States; they were the ones who weathered 30 years of proxy-terrorism by the Soviet Union. So some European countries do understand exactly what they're dealing with and have designed their "counterterrorism" strategies to essentially be counter*insurgency* strategies. However, calling everything "terrorism" and not identifying the true nature of the beast causes people—especially politicians who are not trained in counterinsurgency—to scratch their heads whenever the question of terrorism versus insurgency comes up.[10]

---

9. Robert Kagan, *Of Paradise and Power, America and Europe in the New World Order* (New York: Random House, 2004), 31.

10. The French, in particular, are good at counterterrorism/counterinsurgency. Their initial forays into the field began in 1950 when terrorists from the Algerian insurgency began attacking France. Although the French refer to it as "counterterrorism," they are also conducting counterinsurgency as well. The French have a national counterterrorism unit overseen by special magistrates that allows them to bridge the different branches of government to get what they need—in essence making it a full-fledged government campaign. Additionally, the French are authorized to operate outside of France if the suspect or the victim is French. The French do not hesitate to expel those who are espousing radical ideologies. It is no surprise then that France is one of the few European countries that has not had a terrorist attack on its soil since 9/11 and took the number one spot on Foreign Policy's "Worst Places to be a Terrorist 2008." http://www.foreignpolicy.com/story/cms.php?story_id=4316.

And let's not discount the power of "labels" which we addressed earlier. Even those countries with strong militaries don't necessarily want to call something an "insurgency" because to do so might somehow give legitimacy to the insurgents; better to simply call them terrorists, vilify them through the media, but quietly take the steps necessary to defeat the "insurgency." Even many Americans prefer not to use the word "insurgency" because of the inherent implication of greater military and government action—something Americans have been uncomfortable with since Vietnam. This also gives more weight to using the more "sophisticated and progressive" European approach and gives those who desire a smaller response—or no military response—full legitimacy.

So how does one determine whether a "terrorist" incident is really part of a larger insurgency effort? It's simple really; just listen to what the "terrorists" say. The Earth Liberation Front (ELF) is a domestic terrorist group that has claimed responsibility for attacks against U.S. Forest Service stations, a ski resort in Vail ($12 million in damage), universities working on bio-tech research, luxury building sites, bio-engineered seed distributors, and other businesses such as banks and fast-food franchises. The ELF was named the top domestic terrorism threat in the United States in 2001 by the FBI. The now-defunct ELF press office, a legal, above-ground news service dedicated to publicizing the actions of the ELF, stated that the ELF uses economic sabotage and guerrilla warfare to stop the exploitation and destruction of the natural environment. And sympathizers claim that it is an eco-defense group dedicated to taking the profit motive out of environmental destruction by causing economic damage to businesses through the use of direct action.

What does that mean? It is important to listen. None of the ELF literature indicates that its members want to overthrow the government. ELF may be trying to change government policy, but it is not trying to change the government; mostly it is trying to coerce a specific behavior from ordinary citizens through fear. And because the self-proclaimed ideology of ELF is not an insurgent ideology (although one might make the case that they fall under the banner of "reformists"), they aren't insurgents. And despite the fact that they are dangerous, combating the ELF is best left to the FBI and local law enforcement agencies.

RADICAL ISLAMISTS—TERRORISTS, INSURGENTS, OR BOTH?

Islamism, the relationship of Al Qaeda to the North Caucasus insurgency, and its effects on Chechnya will be discussed in great detail in Chapter 6. But to determine the status of Al Qaeda and other Islamist groups, one merely has to examine their stated goals. Al Qaeda has consistently stated in its literature that it wants to end foreign influence in Muslim countries and reestablish a Caliphate. This is very clearly a stated desire to change governments and makes Al Qaeda a reactionary-traditionalist insurgency that uses terrorism. There are those who say that Al Qaeda's rhetoric is only a smokescreen to hide its true intentions, but those same people can't provide a more realistic or believable goal than the ones that Al Qaeda itself states. Michael Scheuer, a 22-year veteran of the CIA and former chief of the bin Laden Unit is probably the foremost expert on Al Qaeda. Scheuer exclusively refers to Al Qaeda as an insurgency and states: "I don't consider Osama bin Laden to be a terrorist. I consider him to be a resistance fighter."[11] One of Scheuer's articles is entitled "Al Qaeda's Insurgency Doctrine: Aiming for a 'Long War.'" In the article, Scheuer states, "The corpus of Al Qaeda's writings on the development and application of its insurgency doctrine is too diverse and voluminous to discuss in a single article." Scheuer's conclusion is stunning for those who espouse a simple "use more police against the Al Qaeda terrorists" and frankly, for anyone who has not studied insurgencies:

> The insurgency doctrine used by Al Qaeda has been evolving for more than a quarter century, and is designed to defeat conventional Western military forces. It calls for the group's fighters to be able to fight in the mountains, in desert regions, in maritime conditions, and to be able to conduct what Muqrin [the late Abu-Hajer Abd-al-Aziz al-Muqrin, an Al Qaeda strategist] refers to as "cover action" in urban areas. These multifaceted military operations must be matched by the mujahedeen "excelling in their organized media action." Tellingly, however, Al Qaeda's insurgency doctrine *pays virtually no attention to what the West would identify as "terrorist" operations.* While such attacks, Muqrin wrote, are an essential contribution to the mujahedeen's war effort—especially "qualitative operations" like those of 9/11—*they are best left to other units of the Al Qaeda organization* (italics mine).[12]

Therefore, Al Qaeda—and its worldwide campaign of terrorism—cannot be stopped simply through law enforcement and legal means. Yes, it may be possible to stop specific Al Qaeda cells within a given country through strictly law enforcement measures, but law enforcement alone cannot stop Al Qaeda. Therefore, our European friends and allies who choose to confront their own Al Qaeda and radical Islamist problems solely through law enforcement and legal means cannot be successful.

This is because, at its core, the "law enforcement-centric" strategy of counterterrorism is based on the idea of a European "Kantian" utopian

---

11. Roundtable discussion on PBS regarding Islam, April 14, 2006, answering a question posed by Ray Suarez.
12. Michael Scheuer, *Al-Qaeda's Insurgency Doctrine: Aiming for a "Long War,"* Terrorism Focus, Vol. 3, Issue 8 (February 28, 2006), The Jamestown Foundation. Found at http://www.jamestown.org/terrorism/news/article.php?articleid=2369915; accessed on May 19, 2008.

paradise. This view is egocentric and socio-centric in the worst sense because it believes that a liberal market economy regulated by international law can compete with the *Qur'an*. Al Qaeda and other Islamist organizations don't care about the bottom line; they don't care if they establish closer economic or cultural ties. What is important to them is that the *only* legitimate form of government, banking system, court system, domestic and foreign policy must be based on their sacred texts—and no one in the West has been able to come up with a competing ideology that can trump that. Most importantly, the European socio-centric approach, *which does not treat ideology as insurmountable*, is mutually exclusive with Islamist ideology, which insists that its ideology is unassailable because it is divinely revealed.[13]

In other words, the Europeans seem to say, "What you believe is important, but it's not the *most* important thing. It's not the most important thing because *we* don't believe it's the most important thing. And it's too bad if you think it's the most important thing, but you can't tell us what to believe. So please don't attack us, and in the meantime we'll sit down and talk about all the things we have in common; and because ideology is not the most important thing, eventually, if we talk long enough, you'll see things our way."

Boiled down, this argument is essentially "you can't force your beliefs on us. Therefore, you leave us alone, and we'll leave you alone." Unfortunately, even this seemingly innocuous statement is logically flawed. The statement, "You can't force your beliefs on me," is, in itself, a statement of belief, and would more honestly be expressed as, *"I believe* that you can't force your beliefs on me and I will force *my* belief on you."[14]

The problem for us is that the logical foundation for this belief collapses as soon as its inconsistency is exposed. But for Islamic insurgent-terrorists, the faulty logic is saved by God; it is literally *deus ex machina*. The argument goes: "If I am an Islamist, it is perfectly acceptable to disregard everything that you say because your laws are built on faulty logic and my belief system comes from God Himself. Moreover, it is perfectly logical for me to tell you what to do because I'm merely passing on the message from God—and we cannot argue with God."

---

13. In Henry Kissinger's book *Diplomacy* (New York, 1994), he quotes the French Prime Minister Leon Blum, who states to a visiting German minister as the Nazis were gaining power in Germany, "I am a Marxist and a Jew, but we cannot achieve anything if we treat ideological barriers as insurmountable," as quoted in Kagan, *Of Paradise and Power*, 15.

14. ". . . and I got together with everyone else who thinks like me and we passed a body of law that guarantees that we can continue to act on our beliefs, and while you're here, you must do as we say."

And so, the European idea that ideology is not insurmountable becomes impotent in the face of divine revelation. No amount of appeasement or engagement will open the Islamists hearts and minds to different ideas. It is true that a small number of hard-core Islamists have renounced terrorism because of their interactions with Westerners who have treated them kindly. But this strategy cannot be effective on a large scale because the vast majority of Islamists are never exposed to "real" Westerners, and those that do travel to the West have already been indoctrinated and are isolated in insular communities that continually reinforce their strident beliefs. By not correctly identifying whether they are dealing with insurgents or terrorists or terrorist-insurgents, some Western countries—and Russia—are designing security strategies that are insufficient to stop the threat.[15]

AL QAEDA EXPLAINS

An enlightening article entitled "Abu Yahya's Six Easy Steps For Defeating Al Qaeda" was published in December 2007, based on Abu Yahya al-Libi's 93-minute video release in September 2007. Abu Yahya is an Al Qaeda superstar. Young, extremely intelligent, and lionized for his escape from Bagram Air Base in July 2005, al-Libi has virtual rock-star status among radical Islamists. Amazingly, during his broadcast, al-Libi gave six steps to the West on how it could better fight Al Qaeda. As expected, trying to figure out why a senior Al Qaeda leader and chief ideologue would voluntarily give advice to the West on how to hurt his own organization overloaded the synapses of more than one counterterrorism analyst. Jarret Brachman, the author of the article and an analyst at West Point's Counter Terrorism Center states:

> Abu Yahya's decision to volunteer strategic advice to the United States was neither out of goodwill nor self-destructive tendencies. Rather, his comments embodied the explosive cocktail of youth, rage, arrogance, and intellect that has made him a force among supporters of the Jihadist Movement. By casually offering his enemy a more sophisticated counter-ideological strategy than the United States has been able to implement or articulate to date, Abu Yahya's point was clear: the United States lags so far behind the global Jihadist Movement in its war of ideas that Al Qaeda has little to fear any time soon.[16]

---

15. The term "Islamist" refers to radical Muslims—not to the majority of people practicing the Muslim faith.
16. Jarret Brachman, "Abu Yahya's Six Easy Steps for Defeating Al Qaeda," *Perspectives On Terrorism* Vol. I, Issue 5. This is a brilliant article that should be read it in its entirety. Available at http://www.terrorismanalysts.com/pt/index.php?option=com_rokzine&view=article&id=18&Itemid=54; accessed July 16, 2008.

Personally, I believe al-Libi's motives are more sinister and insidious than what Brachman asserts, but what is more important for our purpose here is the fact that he did give us advice—and it is brilliant.[17] Al-Libi offers the West the following six pieces of advice: (1) weaken the ideological appeal of Al Qaeda's message by highlighting the views of jihadists who have renounced violence, (2) discredit the actions of the Jihadist movement (i.e., show them to be illegitimate) by publicizing stories about jihadist atrocities against Muslims, (3) enlist mainstream Muslim clerics to issue *fatwas* (religious rulings) against Al Qaeda and use derogatory language whenever they refer to AQ (again, show as illegitimate), (4) offer a competing ideology in order to unleash a "torrential flood of ideas and methodologies which find backing, empowerment, and publicity from numerous parties" against them, (5) shut down the key luminaries of the movement (the leaders who are articulating the ideology), and (6) sow dissention among the ranks (aka "split the insurgency"). This is a very condensed version of Abu Yahya's recommendations—in his video he goes into detail about exactly how to accomplish each of those tasks and his recommendations are good ones. In many ways, they are the same kinds of tactics that Al Qaeda routinely uses against its enemies.

However, there is an additional strategy that Brachman divines from al-Libi; Brachman states: "Yahya's most important contribution is identifying

---

17. Al-Libi wants to fight a decisive battle with the West, but he believes that most of the West hasn't figured out the real field of battle—ideology—the fight for hearts and minds. The West has not sufficiently attacked Al Qaeda's ideology (as it is afraid of getting it wrong and offending the greater Muslim community), and the more moderate Muslims have been slow to offer competing ideologies. Al-Libi is giving us advice because he unquestionably believes that the Islamist ideology is unassailable and he wants the West to hurry up with a counter-ideology so he can deliver a crushing blow. An audio release by bin Laden in May 2008 hints at this strategy. In his statements, bin Laden attacks Arab governments, he attacks other Islamist groups like the Muslim Brotherhood, and he attacks moderate Muslim clerics who have begun to attack him (and Al Qaeda's ideology). Although largely not understood by the West, bin Laden's attacks are devastating to those who understand the Muslim faith—which is Al Qaeda's target audience. By invoking the actions of *Salah al Deen* (Saladin) and comparing his actions with those of present-day leaders, clerics, and Islamist organizations, he delivers withering attacks against their legitimacy *in the minds of Muslims* by accusing them of deviating from the real principles of Islam. This then is the reason that al-Libi is giving advice to the West. Al-Libi understands warfare and he wants an ideological fixed battle with the West and its allies because he believes that Al Qaeda's ideology will crush all competing ideologies. If the Islamists can do that, they will take the moral high ground and gain legitimacy with billions of Muslims around the world. In Al Qaeda's mind, this is what's needed to get the greater *jihad* moving. Al-Libi is on the battlefield with weapons locked and loaded, tapping his foot impatiently and looking at his watch waiting for the enemy to show up. His "advice" to the West is the same thing as calling over the radio saying, "Hey blockheads, the battlefield is over here, hurry up and get here so I can destroy you!"

that the best way to defeat Al Qaeda is by tying it up in knots: Al Qaeda must be continuously forced into a series of compromising positions from a variety of angles so that it hangs itself over the long term."[18] In military terms, what Brachman really means is to go on the offensive against Al Qaeda, as going on the offensive allows us to get inside of Al Qaeda's decision cycle (or "OODA loop"), and forces them to react to us instead of us reacting to them.[19] Brachman is right on the money—as this is the one true thing that the West can do that cannot be turned against it, for generally the best defense is a good offense—and that goes for terrorism as well.

Al-Libi's video is also important because it clearly indicates that Al Qaeda thinks of itself as an insurgency, fights as an insurgency, and must be defeated through counterinsurgency means. However, the most important part of al-Libi's statement is what he *doesn't* say. Note that Abu Yahya doesn't say that it would be a good idea for the West to negotiate with AQ. He doesn't recommend starting a dialogue or opening trade talks. In fact, he doesn't advocate engagement of any kind except ideological and informational warfare, and he doesn't recommend that we take any defensive actions—increase police presence, install better sensors in the airports, etc. Al Qaeda and other radical Islamists do not want to talk, and they don't want to negotiate—they've stated numerous times what they want—we're just not listening.

Al Qaeda's message is loud and clear: "Non-Muslim influence must be eradicated from traditional Muslim countries. Those who call themselves Muslim rulers must revert to the true teachings of Islam, or they will be killed. If the billions of Muslims in the rest of the world want to be 'good' Muslims, they must conduct *jihad* and establish *shari'a* wherever they are living—and if anyone tries to defy those efforts, they must be killed."

---

18. Brachman, "Abu Yahya's Six Easy Steps for Defeating Al Qaeda."
19. The "Boyd Cycle" or "OODA" loop is a technical term used by military planners, but is increasingly finding its way into business circles as well. Conceived by Air Force Colonel John Boyd, it is a cycle of four interconnected processes that are used by all opponents (even in sports) to conduct their own actions. Boyd's contention is that by properly analyzing the individual processes of both your own and your opponent's "loops," it is possible to find opportunities to "get inside" the opponent's decision-making cycle and disrupt his plans and actions—allowing for the possibility of decisive outcomes. The processes are: Observe, Orient, Decide, and Act. This short footnote is too small to give the concept the credit it is due, but suffice to say that it is all about speed—the ability to think faster than your opponent and thereby obscure your own intentions while simultaneously divining more of his. In so doing, one is able to constantly stay one step ahead of the enemy because he is constantly reacting to your moves instead of making his own. Terrorists and insurgents are generally far better at this than larger conventional militaries, as virtually nothing is known about the terrorists or insurgents (and they work very hard to keep it that way), while government policy and basic military strategy and capabilities are an open book.

INSURGENCY, TERRORISM, RADICAL ISLAMISM, AND THE NORTH CAUCASUS

Defining terrorism and discussing counterterrorism approaches, European soft power, and Islamist ideology are important in reaching a comprehensive understanding of the situation in the North Caucasus because the role of radical Islamic fundamentalism—and how the Russian government counters it—is crucial in understanding how the battles are fought and why the insurgency is surviving. The Russian government will not publicly refer to the attacks happening in the North Caucasus (Chechnya, Dagestan, Ingushetia, North Ossetia, Kabardino-Balkaria) as an insurgency. Instead, for reasons that have already been discussed, they refer to all the groups currently conducting attacks in the region as terrorists. In addition to labeling all the fighters as terrorists, the Russians also claim that all of the fighters are Muslim extremists (Wahhabists in the Russian vernacular), and the media and official statements from the Kremlin paint the entire group as members of a transnational Islamic extremist organization affiliated with Al Qaeda. Because the Russians classify the fighters as transnational terrorists, their campaign to defeat the "terrorists" is more tactical and less strategic than it should be.

Regardless of their reasons for doing so, the Kremlin is wrong in labeling the fighters in Chechnya and the North Caucasus as simply terrorists, and their aversion to addressing the situation for what it really is—and to rely so heavily on police and special units—has been to its detriment. Terrorism in Russia is a very real threat; the situation is bad, and it is getting worse. And while it is undisputed that some Chechens have committed heinous acts of terrorism and others have perpetrated other egregious crimes, 95 percent of the attacks in 2008 and 2009 were directed at government targets (usually federal forces like Ministry of Internal Affairs troops, federal soldiers, border guards, and local police).[20] The insurgents universally call for a change in government and independence from Russia, the actual fighters (guerrillas) number in the several hundreds (by the Russians' own accounts), and a good portion of the population supports them (again, by the Russians' own accounts). This is not terrorism; this is insurgency—an insurgency that also uses terrorism as one of its tactics.

If we look back to how terrorism differs from insurgency, we can see that the activity in the North Caucasus region of Russia is undoubtedly an insurgency in that it is a strategic level campaign coordinated across the North Caucasus region with at least some international support. But even if the Russians were correct and the entire insurgency was affiliated with Al Qaeda (which it isn't), the Russians would still be using the wrong tactics because Al Qaeda is an insurgency and not

---

20. 94.8 percent, North Caucasus Incident Database.

simply a terrorist organization. Regardless of whether or not Al Qaeda is involved, there is a large group of radical Islamists who want to establish a regional Emirate—again, a very clear indication that it is an insurgency and not a terrorist group operating in Chechnya, Ingushetia, Dagestan, and the rest of the republics in southern Russia. The insurgency is already large, and by some estimates the total number of fighters presently operating in the region is only marginally less than when the Chechens actually won de facto independence from Russia in 1996. The majority of the attacks do not meet the standard for terrorism (violence directed at non-combatives), and the fighters operating in the North Caucasus are focused on obtaining political power instead of trying to coerce the general population to adopt a change in behavior. Yet the Russians are still choosing to deal with the problem using primarily law enforcement or special operations assets. They have not integrated the security effort with a broader approach that includes economic development (Chechnya being the only exception—and that largely only for rebuilding so that Grozny doesn't look so terrible when journalists visit) and government reform.

Contrary to what the Russians might say to their own citizens and the rest of the world, the Chechen insurgency is alive and well—and in better shape than it has been for much of the last 300 years.

CHAPTER 3

Histories, Narratives, and Legends

With a better understanding of insurgency and terrorism, it is now possible to examine how the history, narratives, and legends of Chechnya and the North Caucasus still resonate within their respective psyches and help to drive ideologies on both sides of the conflict. As in many conflicts extant in the world today, especially those with an ethnic aspect, the sources of enmity and conflict in the current quarrel are still shaped in many ways by how the participating groups view the history of the last few centuries.

Since the Russians first had contact with the Vainakh (Chechens and Ingush) in the mid-1500s, the history of Chechnya, Ingushetia, and Dagestan was primarily the history of insurgent warfare against Russia. The tides of North Caucasus independence have been inextricably tied to Russian (later Soviet, and again Russian) history. One need only to look at the campaigns of Shamil to get a flavor for the bitter and relentless crusades that were waged once Ivan the Terrible conquered the Astrakhan Khanate and pushed the edge of Muscovy into the North Caucasus for the first time.

GEOGRAPHIC, GEOPOLITICAL, AND ECONOMIC FOOTPRINT

Because of the unique geopolitical position that the North Caucasus occupies, it has been impossible for the Chechens, the Ingush, the Dagestanis, the Circassians, the Georgians, the Azeris, and the other ethnic groups that live in and around the mountains to avoid conflict. The Caucasus Mountains are an incredibly high wall that extends west to east from the Black Sea to the Caspian Sea with very few ways to easily traverse them. Those passes and corridors have literally been the gateways between Europe and the Middle East for thousands of years. To the east, there is but a single long, narrow corridor along the Caspian Sea to allow north-south movement. And to further restrict passage, the ancient Persian rulers of Derbent (in present-day Dagestan) built a 60-foot-high stone wall that extended a mile-and-a half from the eastward edge of the mountains to the Caspian Sea; this barrier allowed the ruler of Derbent to control movement between Europe and the Middle East. The only other easy way through the mountains—the Darial Pass (in present day North Ossetia)—is a legendary gorge running through the mountains that has been fortified and defended since 150 BCE.

South of the mountains was the Silk Road, and north of the mountains were rich pasturelands fed by the Don and Volga Rivers which, at their closest points (300 miles north of Chechnya), are only 65 miles apart. The area between the two rivers was called the Volga-Don Portage, or the Khazarian Way. To protect this vital area which allowed trade to go by ship from the Caspian Sea out through the Black Sea and to the rest of the world, a fortress called Sarkel (White Tower) was established as early as 833 near the present-day city of Volgograd, where the Don-Volga canal was eventually excavated in 1952.

What completed the strategic importance of the region was the triumvirate of "superpowers" that constantly warred with one another and needed to cross the mountains. Whether it was the Mongols, the Huns, or the Russians, there was always a power seeking to extend its influence to the south and control trade. Whether it was the Romans, the Byzantines, the Ottomans, or NATO, there was always a power seeking to exert its influence to the east and to the north. And whether it was the Persians, the Muslim Caliphate, the Safavid Dynasty, or present-day Iraq or Iran, there was always a power seeking to expand west and north. For at least 2,000 years, great powers have been vying with each other for control of the passes and the mountains.

The earliest "superpower" struggle for the Caucasus started after Pompey and the Roman legions came into the area around 66 BCE and began fighting with the Sassanid (Persian) Dynasty for control of the area. The Roman-Persian War was a series of conflicts that would last almost 600 years and eventually morph into the Sassanid-Byzantine wars (same players, different names). Mark Antony led a huge Roman army into Azerbaijan with his Armenian allies in 36 BCE, but had to withdraw when his siege trains were isolated and wiped out. Nonetheless, the Roman Empire established dominance over the region for about 200 years until the door swung the other way and the Sassanids became the dominant force in the Caucasus. Even the Huns swept down from the north for a while late in the 4th century—occupying the Dagestani and Chechen lowlands and driving the Chechens and Ingush up into the mountains.

The constant fighting depleted their strength—making them all susceptible to the armies of Mohammed. Around 650, the earliest Muslim
Caliphates began expanding into the Caucasus. In so doing they brought
the region into the middle of yet another set of conflicts—the Byzantine-
Arab Wars (same players, but now the Persians had converted to Islam)—
which lasted about 600 years, from 634 until the Mongol invasions, and
included the western Crusades. The Kazars (including the Chechens,
Ingush, Alans, and Dagestanis) fought the Muslims, but slowly Islam
began to spread throughout the region. As the Caliphate took advantage
of the Caspian Corridor (the Derbent Pass) and began expanding north-
ward into Dagestan, they also began moving eastward into what is now
known as Chechnya, Ingushetia, North Ossetia (Alania), and the rest of
the northern slopes of the Caucasus.

Around 1200, the Mongols began their inexorable advance along all
points of the compass, and established the largest empire the world has
ever known. But once the Mongol hordes began to fight amongst themselves, even the hordes adopted the age-old superpower patterns
described above. The Golden Horde became the "north-of-the-Caucasus
power," the Il-Khanate adopted the role of the "southwest-of-the-Caucasus
power," with yet another horde playing the role of "southeast-of-the-
Caucasus power." Luckily for Medieval Europe, an unnamed battle on the
banks of the Terek River in present day Dagestan between elements of the
Golden Horde and the Il-Khanate would become the "linchpin of history"
and save both Europe and the Middle East from further subjugation by
the Mongols.

Later, the Russians and the Ottoman Empire would fight for nearly
400 years—with both of them fighting the Persians to the east on and
off during the entire period. Much of this fighting either centered on,
or was facilitated by, movement through the Caucasus.

There is an abundance of early history written about the Azeris and certain areas of Dagestan. And there is also quite a bit known about the
Alans (North Ossetia)—who were the people that controlled the Darial
Pass to the west of Chechnya. However, virtually nothing was written
about the people in between. One map of the area during the Mongol period gives us a clue why there was not much written about the Vainakh—
as the area of Chechnya-Ingushetia on that map is simply marked as
"ungovernable."

This is not surprising, as the majority of armies moving north or south
would be interested in passing through the mountains and getting to
their ultimate destinations as quickly as possible—leaving the peoples
between the two passes relatively unmolested. Besides, the mountains
are high and the roads are narrow—not good places to take armies. So it
would have been important to control or ally with the people that
owned the passes, but not the inhabitants of the mountainous areas in

between. Additionally, there hadn't been much reason for the Vainakh to come down into the lowlands during the early periods because the mountainous area where they lived had been self-sustaining and fertile until the end of the Middle Ages when a phase known as the "little ice age" resulted in cooler temperatures and shortened growing seasons at higher elevations, thereby requiring the mountain people to move down into the valleys.[1] If one wants to know why it is so hard to get information on the early Chechens, I submit it is for these two reasons—they were in the middle and out of the way. It just wasn't worth the time and effort to go chasing after people who generally stayed out of *your* way, didn't have anything you wanted, and who weren't on the army's direct line of march: no battles + little trade = few records. This would also explain why we have written histories starting in the 1500s—they stopped being in the middle.[2]

In the 1550s, Ivan the Terrible defeated both the Kazan and Astrakhan Khanates (Mongol remnants), a huge territory that essentially doubled Muscovy's size and gave Ivan control of the longest and one of the most important rivers in Europe—the Volga. Although it would not be accomplished in Ivan's lifetime, a series of canals would be built linking the existing waterways to the Volga and make it possible for ships to travel from the Atlantic Ocean all the way to the Caspian Sea. Ivan built St. Basil's Cathedral in Moscow to celebrate his victory over the Muslim Mongols (they had converted to Islam in the 1300s), built a fortress at Astrakhan (on the Western Shore of the Caspian), and established Russia in the Caucasus as far south as the Terek River, in present day Chechnya and Dagestan.

Ivan also established a fort along the Sunzha River—which runs through Grozny—the capital of Chechnya—and stationed (cajoled) the Greben and Terek Cossacks in northern Dagestan to serve as a kind of frontier force. The Muscovite state was dependent on the Cossacks because as the Cossacks continued to add regions of fertile land to their own possessions, so too did Muscovy grow. The Cossacks were the people that lived on the edges of the nascent Russian empire, and they constantly pushed it farther and farther from Moscow. When the Vainakh came down from the mountains to escape the little ice age in search of fertile lands, they ran into the Cossacks. Tolstoy wrote that the Cossacks felt a certain kinship with the Chechens because of their

---

1. John B. Dunlop, *Russia Confronts Chechnya: Roots of a Separatist Conflict* (Cambridge, Oxford: Cambridge University Press, 1998), 3; and V. A. Tishkov, O. L. Belyaeva, and G. V. Marchenko, *Chechnskii krizis* (Moscow: Tsentr kompleksnykh sotsial'nykh issledovanii I marketinga, 1995), 6.
2. It also doesn't help that Stalin's purges of the Chechens entailed destroying the few books written about Chechen history in an attempt to erase them completely from history. The 1994–1996 war also saw the destruction of the national archives in Grozny.

similar ways of life. If so (and there is no reason to doubt Tolstoy, as he served as an army officer in the region and his accounts are often more accurate than the "official" reports of the day), then it was the kind of kinship that leads to bitter family feuds, as the Chechens regard the Cossacks as culpable in much of what transpired since those early days.

About this same time, the Ottomans (Sunni Muslim) began their 400-year war with Russia. By the time Peter the Great assumed the throne in 1689, Russia had experienced military success and expansion in every direction but the Caucasus—having extended Russian lands all the way to the Pacific Ocean. Although the eastward expansion encountered only sporadic tribes engaged in hunting and raising cattle, any southward expansion met with resistance from the Persians, the Ottoman Empire, or the few remaining Mongol hordes scattered about in the southeast. Having overreached to the east, Russia had never been able to put enough forces and resources into effectively controlling the Caucasus; it had just been easier to let the Cossacks roam in the area to keep the Persians and the Ottomans from getting any closer. It would be Peter the Great that would make the first real push into the Caucasus in an attempt to finally and firmly establish the southern border of the empire.

The Russo-Persian War of 1722–1723 was a Russian success and, for the first time, Russia took control of the Caspian corridor—taking Derbent, Baku, and all the provinces along the southern bank of the Caspian Sea (now Iran). Peter got his victory easily as the Persians were forced to come to terms with him quickly because the Ottomans took the opportunity to take up the fight against their old enemies, and attacked into southern Persia as soon as Peter did.

Notable in Chechen and Ingush history, the Russo-Persian War of 1722–1723 was the first time that Imperial Russia had a formal military encounter with the Vainakh.[3] As the Russians took control of the Caspian corridor and moved into Dagestan, Peter's forces ran into mountain tribes. Peter sent a cavalry force to subdue them, and the Chechens routed them. As most invading armies had done, the Russians simply pushed on toward their larger objective and bypassed the people in the middle.

In 1732, having once again lost effective control of the region to the Vainakh and having pulled the Russian line back to the Terek River, Imperial Russian troops clashed with the Chechens in a village called Chechen-aul along the Argun River. The Russians were defeated again and withdrew, but this battle is responsible for the apocryphal story

---

3. In 1721, after he finally made peace with Sweden, Peter was acclaimed "Emperor of all Russia" in addition to his traditional title of Czar. Thus the Russian Empire was born, although many European rulers did not acknowledge the title.

about how the Nokhckii came to be known as "Chechens"—the people ostensibly named for the place where the battle had taken place. Although this is the most popular story about how the Chechens got their name, the term "Chechen" was actually used as early as 1692. Official Russian maps from 1719 depict an area in the North Caucasus called "Chechnya."[4]

In 1735, Empress Anna went back to war with the Ottomans and the Crimean Tatars, in part because of the Crimean Khan's military campaign in the Caucasus which threatened the already tenuous hold that Russia had in the area. This time, instead of fighting the Tatars near the Caucasus where the mountainous tribes could assist them, the Russians went for the heart of the Tatars, sending troops into the Crimea itself. The Russians destroyed the fortress of Perekop, which stood at the head of the isthmus leading to the Crimea, thus opening the door for Imperial Russian troops. Another Russian flotilla retook Azov (which had fallen to the Tatars), and Russian generals took additional cities along the coast of the Black Sea. An outbreak of plague and the inability of Russia's ally, Austria, to make any headway against the Ottomans forced an end to the conflict in 1739.

Another Russian victory over the Ottomans in 1774 finally saw the end of Ottoman influence in the North Caucasus, as the Ottomans ceded Kabardia and Ossetia to the Russians.[5] As the Ossetians controlled the Darial Pass, Russia finally gained control of one of the routes through the mountains. Catherine the Great then began to build a series of forts and Cossack settlements in the Caucasus in order to establish a firm border. It was in this war that Grigory Potemkin distinguished himself. In 1774, Catherine ennobled him as a count and gave him the areas of Azov and Astrakhan as a reward. It was Potemkin that encouraged Catherine to move forward with the "Greek Project"—which aimed to break up the Ottoman Empire completely, sweep aside the Muslims, and place a Christian ruler (Catherine's grandson Constantine) once again on the throne in Constantinople. Potemkin encouraged Catherine to consolidate

---

4. Amjad M. Jaimoukha, *The Chechens: A Handbook* (New York: Routledge Curzon, 2005), p. 12.
5. It also resulted in the independence of the Crimean Tatars, who were actually *not* seeking independence. The Ottomans would not cede the Crimea to the Russians, but the Russians were tired of the Crimean Tatars raiding Russian settlements—especially as any form of retribution meant yet another war with the Ottomans. So, more specifically, the Ottomans renounced their political right to defend the Crimean, giving the Crimeans de facto independence and making them an easy target for the Russians next time something happened. They didn't have to wait very long, as Russia annexed the Crimea in 1783 and began colonizing it with Slavs—forcing a mass exodus of Tatars to Turkey. Over the next 100 years, an estimated one million Tatars abandoned their homeland.

Russia's holdings in the Caucasus so as to be able to move against the Ottomans from both land and sea.

It wasn't just Potemkin who was encouraging Catherine to continue to move south. The Georgians (Orthodox Christians), who were sandwiched between the Ottomans in the west and the Persians (a different dynasty but still Shi'a) in the east had formally requested that Russia extend itself through the Darial Pass and, for the first time, expand the Empire across the Caucasus. In 1783, Catherine signed the Treaty of Georgievsk and the Russian Empire accepted the eastern part of Georgia (the kingdoms of Kartli-Kakheti) under its suzerainty. In exchange for becoming a part of Russia, the Georgians were given a guarantee that Georgia would maintain its internal sovereignty and territorial integrity—and, most importantly, Russia would regard the enemies of Georgia as her own. Religion definitely played a part in this exchange as the bond of Ortho-doxy was acknowledged in the treaty and the primate of the Georgian Church became a member of the Russian Holy Synod and a permanent Archbishop.

Catherine took her new responsibility seriously, especially as she real-ized that, in time, "protectorate" would turn into "part of," and Georgia would simply become another territory she could add to the ever-expanding Empire. As a result, she began construction of the "Georgian Military Road" which transformed the Darial Pass into what we refer to in military parlance as a "high-speed line of communication (LOC)." To guard this new road, she began constructing an enormous fortress called the "Ruler of the Caucasus," or Vladikavkaz. And then, the real trouble began.

THE FIRST CAUCASUS JIHAD

It is quite in vogue these days to talk about how the radical Islamists associated with Osama bin Laden hijacked the populist Chechen inde-pendence movement of 1991–1996 and turned it into a religious war in 1999. Although there is some truth to this assertion it is disingenuous because the Vainakh have been fighting religious wars against the Rus-sians from the 1780s onward. Despite the rhetoric, it was the demo-cratic, secular movement of the 1990s that was the exception to the rule—and not the other way around. By the 1780s, large parts of the Caucasus had been Muslim and part of both the Ottoman and Persian empires. That Islam had been established as a major religion in the region is beyond question—different historians may argue that the level of religiosity was higher in Derbent than in Vladikavkaz in 1780, and they would be right. Some would argue that the Chechens weren't Muslims at all until the late 1700s, and I'm sure that there were some mountain clans that remained pagan for a while.

What everyone does agree on, however, is that something new started after Vladikavkaz was built. From this point forward *every* Chechen insurgency movement (rebellion/insurrection) would be fueled, at least in part, by the ideology of conservative and fundamentalist Islam, and was accompanied by a call for a more stringent interpretation of Islamic Sacred Texts and law. Moreover, just as the actions of Catherine the Great and later, General Aleksei Yermolov, helped to bring about the rise of Islamic fundamentalism in the region, we'll see that the "fundamentalism" of the current conflict is simply part of a pattern that was started in 1780.

Sheikh Mansur

The first *Gazavat*,[6] or holy war, directed at the Russians by the people of the Caucasus was declared by a Chechen named Ushurma, who was from a small village on the Sunzha River (near present-day Grozny) called Aldy-aul. Chechnya was not a particularly devout area during the 1700s; so when Ushurma went for religious training, he went to neighboring Dagestan, which, as discussed in a later chapter, was a well-respected center for Islamic learning at the time. He returned as *Al-Imam al-Mansur al-Mutawakil 'ala Allah*, more commonly referred to as Sheikh or Imam Mansur. Sheikh Mansur was a Naqshbandi imam, and Naqshbandi Sufism is a "strictly orthodox"[7] order that believes that the misfortunes that have fallen upon the Muslim world are a result of straying from the righteous path, and that only by returning to strict observance of Muslim religious law will the Muslims return to their former glory: "Only once the s*hari'a* had been re-established and Muslims had returned to the right path would they become virtuous and strong again and able to wage *jihad*—holy war—in order to liberate themselves from foreign threat or occupation."[8] Thus Mansur ordered the Chechens to stop practicing many of their old traditions. This was difficult for the Chechens, as their Islamic traditions had not been as strong as those in Dagestan. However, as the Chechens saw the encroaching Cossacks (yet another Cossack host had been added to the "Caucasian Cordon Line" and the Cossacks had formally become members of the Empire) and the construction of the new fort in Vladikavkaz, Mansur's message of "strict observance before *jihad* to eject the invaders" began to attract supporters.

---

6. *Gazavat* is old term meaning *jihad;* it is more associated with folk Islam.
7. Hamid Algar, "The Naqshbandi Order: A Preliminary Survey of its History and Significance," *Studia Islamica*, 44 (1970), 124.
8. Moshe Gammer, *The Lone Wolf and the Bear, Three Centuries of Chechen Defiance of Russian Rule* (Pittsburgh: University of Pittsburgh Press, 2006), 19. This book is required reading for a thorough history of the Chechen conflicts from 1780.

As Mansur's message continued to resonate with the populace, the Russians became wary. They first tried to discredit him—and later arrested him. In 1785, the Russians sent a regiment under Colonel Pieri (some sources say up to 5,000 soldiers and Cossacks) to Mansur's home in Aldy-aul. The Chechens, following a tactic that they had developed against earlier Russian patrols and still use to this day, withdrew and let the Russians come all the way into the village without engaging. Finding the *aul* (village) deserted, the Russians plundered and set fire to everything and started back through the forest. Mansur, now having seen what the Russians had intended, declared *gazavat*—holy war—on the Russians and then ambushed the retreating regiment and destroyed it at the Battle of the Sunzha River. Historical documents show that Colonel Pieri, his deputy, and many of his senior officers were killed along with hundreds of men. Casualty estimates are from 300–600 dead, hundreds more wounded, and hundreds more taken prisoner. The rest of the force disintegrated without senior leadership to guide their efforts, and the Chechens hunted them as they ran through the forests.

Thus began the first war between the Russians and the Chechens. That war established a pattern that has continued for over 200 years: the Russians send in large forces and raze the places where the Chechens live; the Chechens retreat to the dense forests and high mountains where the "war leader" announces a holy war to expel the Russians from Chechen lands; all the Chechens rally around the "war leader," and under his leadership they ambush and kill startling numbers of Russian soldiers in well-executed guerrilla attacks.

Although Mansur had significant support from the people, he could never match the numbers of troops or the firepower that the Russians possessed, and after a failed attempt to escalate the conflict into open battle (Phase III insurgency—war of movement), Mansur did what all insurgencies do at this point and reverted back to guerrilla warfare (Phase II). The Chechens used their natural advantages and conducted concentrated hit-and-run guerrilla raids along the Caucasian line of Russian forts, convening large groups of guerrillas from far off areas, striking suddenly without warning, and then disappearing. Mansur hoped to export the insurgency throughout the entire Caucasus so that he might raise enough troops to take on the mighty Russian Army; he hoped to convince men from other regions to fight by demonstrating that the Russians could be beaten through guerrilla attacks.

These attacks began the cycle of North Caucasus insurgencies that continues to this very day. The Russians responded by sending in even more troops, destroyed more villages and towns, and ground down the Chechens until they couldn't fight anymore. A period of relative peace ensued during which the Chechen birthrate spiked to more than four times the national average, and then the Chechens rebelled again.

Although Mansur was not successful militarily, his most enduring legacy was his influence in spreading a more fundamentalist and strict interpretation of Islam throughout the entire Caucasus region. This Islamization process would lay the foundation for those who followed—especially Shamil, who would be born a few years after Mansur's death.

Mansur's death in 1794 did not mean an end to the fighting in the Caucasus. The Russian forts still stood in the Chechen lowlands, and the Chechens still wanted them out. Inasmuch as "raiding" on horseback was part of the usual maturation process for Chechen boys, there were numerous small raids and ambushes on Russian forces throughout the area. After Mansur's death, the Russians conducted two large excursions deeper into Chechen-controlled territory, but both were promptly driven out by combined Chechen and Dagestani fighters. One took place under a commander named Bulgakov, who foolishly attacked into a ravine, which resulted in casualties similar to the Pieri episode. The Russians had bigger problems to deal with at the time (Napoleon, the Persians, the Swedes, and the Ottomans), and couldn't afford casualties on such a scale, so no more expeditions were sent to attempt a decisive battle with the Chechens. Nonetheless, the Caucasus Line of forts stood and continued to expand. The Russians could not best the Chechens in the forests—where the Chechens could fight man-to-man. But Russian cannons provided the technological advantage that prevented the Chechens from driving the Russians out of their fortresses.

After defeating Napoleon and establishing a successful alliance to ensure peace, Czar Alexander believed he could direct his attention to the south again. He needed to establish a secure border and establish a base of operations in order to reunite all the Georgians and expand their borders against the Ottomans and the Persians. To do that, he first needed to subdue all the disparate groups to the north of the Caucasus Mountains and establish control. In 1816, after having wrapped up his Napoleon problem, Alexander sent one of his most trusted confidants, one of his best generals, and one of the heroes of the Napoleonic wars to solve his Caucasus problem: Yermolov.

General Yermolov

"I desire that the terror of my name should guard our frontiers more potently than chains or fortresses, that my word should be for the natives a law more inevitable than death. Condescension in the eyes of Asiatics is a sign of weakness and out of pure humanity I am inexorably severe."[9]

---

9. John F. Baddeley, *The Russian Conquest of the Caucasus* (London: Longmans, Green & Co, 1908), 97.

With those words, General Aleksei Yermolov, the new Governor and chief administrator of Georgia and the Caucasus, Commander-in-Chief of the Georgian Army Corps of the Russian Empire, and Ambassador Plenipotentiary to the Court of the Shah, made clear his Caucasus policy from the very beginning. Yermolov (who took to calling himself the Proconsul of the Caucasus, probably because it was shorter), was a brilliant officer who achieved rank, decorations, and fame at a young age and was well loved by his men and Russian society. With the death of General Kutuzov, Yermolov had become the most accomplished and respected officer in the Russian Empire.

He was also, according to multiple sources, a butcher. Every source, including the generally favorable Russian ones, indicates that Yermolov considered the non-Russian peoples of the empire to be of a lower order; and in the Caucasus, he treated them accordingly. As far as Yermolov was concerned, the Russian border was now on the other side of the mountains and extended into what is now Georgia and Azerbaijan, which had been won from the Persians in 1813 in the Treaty of Gulistan. Yermolov intuitively understood that, from a military and administrative point of view, you simply cannot have groups of people running around in the interior of the country raiding and causing trouble. And (in Yermolov's view) if those groups of people wouldn't willingly submit to the authorities—him—then the simple answer was to get rid of them.

Yermolov decided to start with the Vainakh because it was the tactically sound decision. The fortress at Vladikavkaz was the strongest in the region and allowed him to move troops back and forth between Chechnya and his headquarters in Georgia as he needed them via the Georgian Military Road, thus ensuring his supply lines stayed short and behind friendly lines. He planned to start from his secure strongpoint and move eastward until he reached the Caspian Sea—meaning that the Vainakh were first in his sights. With a line of smaller forts already along the Terek, he used Vladikavkaz as his anchor and built a new line of forts further south along the Sunzha River—moving Chechens and Ingush out and resettling Cossacks in between the two lines of forts. Resettling the Vainakh ensured a secure rear area, and also allowed him to levy food and grain from the newcomers as part of the deal for their new land. He needed to establish a steady food supply before he could continue eastward into Dagestan, which was rocky and barren and would not support large standing garrisons of troops.

More importantly, resettlement would deprive the Vainakh of their traditional agricultural and grazing lands and drive them up into the mountains where their herds could not survive the winter. He believed that depriving the Vainakh of their lands would force them to submit—and he was prepared to allow those who cooperated with him to move back into the valley and retain their lands. If the Vainakh agreed, they would be left alone in peace; but if they didn't, then obviously they were no more than brigands and criminals, and he would treat them as such.

And so, in 1818, to realize this plan, Yermolov began building. From a purely military standpoint, his plan for establishing forts was quite good—if not the obvious choice. He began construction of a major fortress almost halfway between Vladikavkaz and Kizlyar (on the Caspian Sea), along the Terek River and in a position to control the last major valley between his new line and the Caucasus Mountains proper. This large fortress supported two additional smaller fortresses, one to the west and one to the east of the central one. From this new southern line of forts, his soldiers would be able to ride out and destroy all the crops each autumn in order to starve the Chechens into submission. He called the central fortress *Grozny* ("Menacing"), and that's exactly what he meant for it to be. In addition to forts along the Sunzha, Yermolov also built a smaller fort across the valley from Grozny at the edge of the mountains at Urus Martan, to allow him to more effectively control that valley. And in 1821, he built one called *Burnaya* ("Stormy") at the easternmost edge of the Caucasus near Makhachkala (the present-day capitol of Dagestan). Although nowhere near the line of forts along the Sunzha River, Burnaya was nonetheless strategically significant as it was the northernmost point of the Caspian Corridor (Derbent being the southern "gate"), and allowed the Russians to more effectively control all north-south traffic through both passes.

Yermolov's construction frenzy started an escalating firestorm of violence. The Chechens attacked the new forts and slaughtered the soldiers; Yermolov responded by wiping out entire villages and taking the remaining Muslim women as slaves. The emperor eventually heard of the brutalities being committed in his name and called on Yermolov to restrain his troops, but Yermolov justified his actions by telling him that the Chechens were evil criminals that did not want to be civilized and thus had to be destroyed.

In June 1821, as the construction of Burnaya was near completion, the Chechens held an all-Chechen gathering in a mosque to bring the clans together and fight the encroaching Russians. Thus began another long religious war (guerrilla campaign) that ended with Yermolov marching through Chechnya, burning everything in his way, and driving the Chechens into their mountain strongholds.

Much has been written about Yermolov's legacy: that he permanently set the savage tone for all future Russian-Chechen conflicts; that by forcing the Chechens back up into the mountains he retarded the very "civilization" process that he sought to bring to the region by forcing the Chechens to revert to their clan-based society, instead of progressing to a more feudal system that may have allowed more opportunities for societal integration; that by coercing behavior through fear for so long and with such vigor, he made the Chechens immune to the fear of death; that by forcing the Chechens to band together and search for an ideology that would facilitate the integration of disparate clans, Yermolov was the one that was responsible for the rise of fundamentalist Islam and its subsequent dominance in the region. Regardless of what the academics say, ask any Chechen about Yermolov—they still revile him today.

Looking at Yermolov's campaign from a counterinsurgency standpoint, and aided by the clarity of hindsight and the emergence of insurgency literature with which to conduct analysis, there is another legacy that should be added to his list: Yermolov established in the Chechens' collective minds that the Russian Imperial government could not be trusted and could therefore not be legitimate, essentially guaranteeing that revolts would follow. Yermolov was the confidant of the emperor—the embodiment of Russian generalship who had helped defeat Europe's mightiest army and greatest general—Napoleon. Yermolov was also a Russian ambassador, and as an official representative of Imperial Russia his actions in the Caucasus impacted the Chechen's perception of Russia in general. He forcibly took Muslim women to use as "field wives," destroyed entire villages of innocent civilians, and invited the Chechen elders to come "talk," then attempted to coerce them into turning on their neighbors. Because Yermolov was only concerned with coercing behavior, he lost the battle for the Chechen hearts and minds, and poisoned entire generations. And because the Russian government never had a chance to be perceived as trustworthy or legitimate, once fundamentalist Islam was firmly established in the region with its complete package of government and moral and legal codes, *there would be no chance for the Russians to construct a competing ideology.*

Ideology is the key to insurgency, and not only did Yermolov inadvertently encourage the growth of Islamic fundamentalism, not only did he cement the clan-based social structure (which is almost perfect in its cell-like structure for decentralized guerrilla or terrorist attacks) which prevented the growth of feudalism, he also made it impossible for future Russian campaigns to have any kind of success because, until the Bolsheviks overthrew the existing Russian government, there could not be a competing ideology. This is why the Communists initially succeeded with the Chechens where the emperor could not—the Chechens saw the possibility of a new government that sounded as though it could be trusted.[10] However, because of their short-term success, Yermolov's tactics were much studied, and this "enemy-centric" approach was considered to be standard military doctrine for over 100 years.

---

10. The Chechens were instrumental in helping the Communists (Reds) defeat the Czarist forces (Whites) during the Russian civil war. Tragically, the Communists then subjected the Chechens to even greater traumas than those perpetrated by Yermolov.

THE THIRTY YEARS WAR AND THE AGE OF SHAMIL

The Great Gazavat (1829–1859) was preceded by a few years of relative peace between the Chechens and the Russians. Flush with recent victories over both the Persians and the Ottomans, the new emperor, Nicholas I, wished to consolidate power in the Caucasus once and for all and "ordered his Commander-in-Chief in the Caucasus to add to that 'glorious' deed, another . . . in my eyes as glorious and . . . by far more important,' that is 'to tame forever the mountain people, or *exterminate the insubordinate'* [emphasis added]. This had to be done in one mighty blow, 'as decisive as it should be unexpected.'"[11] General Vel'yaminov, the former chief of staff for Yermolov and the originator of the extremely effective deforestation strategy which denied the Chechens the advantage of surprise and cover, began a new operation in which he destroyed over 30 Chechen villages and demanded that the Muslims abandon the *shari'a.* This once again inspired the Chechens to find a war leader to organize a resistance and drive the Russians out.

This time, however, it would be the Dagestanis who would take the lead. After seeing Vel'yaminov's campaign through Chechnya, the Dagestanis knew that it would only be a matter of time before the Russians came after them as well. It was apparent a religious leader was required to transcend the numerous clan affiliations across the entire region, and as Dagestan was still the more "religious" area, in 1829 the Dagestanis held a council and elected *Ghazi Mohammed ibn Ismail* as imam (he is also referred to as Kazi Mullah or Gazi Mullah in some sources), who promptly declared *gazavat* on the Russians yet again. Once again, the new war leader's immediate emphasis was to return the people to a more fundamentalist approach to Islam.

After 40 years of almost constant guerrilla warfare, the insurgents had learned a few lessons about fighting the Russians. They had learned to avoid big pitched battles like Sheik Mansur had tried and focus on protracted guerrilla warfare in order to wear the Russians down. Moreover, the Chechens, Ingush, and Dagestanis had learned the need for unity of command, and as the first true North Caucasus insurgency leader, Ghazi Mohammed organized the population and moved the entire population to a war footing. He prepared them for a long struggle by exhorting them to move out of large villages and into the forests so that they wouldn't present targets for the Russian reprisals that he was sure would come. He had the population start growing maize instead of wheat, which allowed for greater yields, is more water-efficient, does

---

11. V. G. Dadahiev and Kh. Kh. Ramazanov, eds. *Dvizhenie gortsevv severo-vostochnogo Kavkaza v 20–50 gg. XIX v Sbornik dokumentov* (Makhachkala; Dagestanskoe Knznoe Isdatel'stvo, 1959), 58–59, document no. 32. Letter from Nicholas I to Paskevich, September 25 [October 7], 1829. Quotations from p. 58, as quoted in Gammer, 46.

not require the same plowing requirements to sow, produces about twice the food nutrients of wheat (the ears), but—and perhaps most importantly for a culture moving to a war footing—the stalks make excellent fodder for horses, being more digestible than the normal fodder of hay and clover.[12] This allowed the mountaineers to use the same crop to feed both people and horses. Maize, or corn, cannot be grown everywhere, but the Chechen lowlands have good conditions for maize, and Ghazi was clever enough to exploit this new crop.

In addition to directing the logistics of food production for his fighters, he also encouraged the nascent arms-manufacturing industry that was developing in Dagestan. Because Dagestan had so little arable land, they had always depended on skilled metalwork for income, and as they could not contribute to the fight with food, a cottage industry developed in which manufacture of different rifle parts were fabricated by different villages. Under Ghazi's leadership, Dagestan soon became an important area for rifle manufacture during the mid-19th century. At the peak of this industry, it is estimated that Dagestan was producing up to 20,000 rifles per year and the majority were "grooved-barrel rifles of remarkable quality and shooting precision."[13] These were the weapons that made guerrilla ambushes so effective. Unlike the muskets of the Imperial Russian Army, in the hands of an experienced marksman—and all the mountaineers were skilled hunters—one shot meant one kill, and the grooved barrels meant the mountaineers had the advantage of "stand-off." Being able to obtain these weapons locally and at relatively low cost was a huge advantage to the insurgents.

Ghazi began by attacking the fort at Kizylar (killing 150 civilians in the process), and then captured forts at Nazran and Tarki (Makhachkala), as well as others; he threatened Vladikavkaz, Vnesapnaya, Derbent, and more. He ambushed a Cossack unit of more than 500 and killed nearly one-third of them. At the same time, Ghazi was attempting to negotiate with the Russians, trying to convince them that the Caucasus peoples would always be too much of a problem—better to let them live in peace and just go away. Packs of wolves cannot be tamed, so if you don't encroach on their territory and give them a wide berth, then you won't have to worry about getting attacked.[14] The Russians, however,

---

12. Thomas Forsyth Hunt, *The Cereals in America* (London: Orange Hall, 1904), 202, 221, 264.

13. L. I. Astvatsaturyan, *Oruzhie narodov Kavkaza* (Nalchik: El-Fa, 1994) as quoted in Georgi M. Derlugian, *A World History of Noxchi* (work in progress), http://www.yale.edu/agrarianstudies/papers/11noxchi.pdf, p. 7.

14. The lone wolf is the Chechen national symbol. The Chechens themselves say "the wolf is the only creature that dares to take on someone stronger than himself. The wolf's insufficient strength is compensated by limitless audacity, courage and adroitness. If, however, he has lost the battle he dies silently, expressing neither fear nor pain. And he always dies facing his enemy." Lema Usmanov, *Nepokorennaia Chechnia* (Moscow: Isdatel'skii dom Parus, 1997), 42.

weren't interested.[15] They followed up with another massive march
through the Caucasus under General Rosen that resulted in the usual
swath of destruction and the death of Ghazi.

The Russians hoped that Ghazi's death would mean the end of the insurgency, but Yermolov's earlier campaign and Rosen's recent repetition
had convinced the mountaineers that living under Imperial Russian rule
could never be an option. Moreover, as the population had become
increasingly more conservative, the people became more committed to
the *gazavat*. *Gazavat* was the *jihad* of its day. *Gazavat* meant putting yourself on the right path (what Muslims refer to as the lesser *jihad*) as well
as expelling the invader (what is referred to as greater *jihad*). Being a
conservative Muslim means living under *shari'a*, and any government
that is not based on the *shari'a* is illegitimate by its very nature. Naqsh-
bandii Sufism, the predominate form of Islam practiced in the region at
the time, is a fundamentalist sect of Islam and it therefore required all
"good" Muslims to conduct *jihad* (*gazavat*) in order to expel the invaders
with their illegitimate (non-Muslim) government. According to this ideology, it was Allah himself who demanded the Russians be expelled so
the Chechens, Ingush, and the Dagestanis could live under *shari'a*.

Ghazi was succeeded for a short time by another imam, and then two
years later Shamil assumed the leadership of the insurgency. For the
next 25 years, he conducted a brilliant guerrilla war against Russia. More
significantly, during this period, Shamil proved to the world that if a
small group of guerrillas fought hard enough and believed hard enough,
they could take on the great Russian Empire. It is this unwritten narrative, passed from generation to generation, that inspired countless North
Caucasian boys to dream of one day taking up Shamil's cause and
finally freeing the Caucasus from the Russians. Shamil's legend started
when the Russians invaded Ghazi's stronghold in his native village
of Gimry (Dagestan) at the end of Rosen's campaign. There, Ghazi
Mohammed and 50 of his men were cornered in a ravine and chose to
make their last stand. Shamil, also born in Gimry, participated in the battle and was one of the two survivors; he is reported to have rushed out
of the house that he had been defending, leapt over the first rank of soldiers, cut his way through the second with *kinzhal* (the traditional mountaineer fighting knife) and bayonet, and disappeared into the night. In
Gimry, there is still a sign that marks the spot where Shamil supposedly
landed when he vaulted over the soldiers.[16] There is a mausoleum

15. Do not overlook the significance of Ghazi's message to the Russians. This is the same
message that radical Islamist groups use today: "Go away. Leave Muslim lands or we
will attack your soldiers, we will kill your civilians, we will never stop, and we will
wear you out until you tire of this constant battle and give up."
16. Sebastian Smith, *Allah's Mountains, the Battle for Chechnya* (London, New York: I. B.
Taurus and Co., Ltd., 2006), 44.

marking the spot where Ghazi fell, and the entire area is a place of pilgrimage.[17]

Shamil initially sought reconciliation with the Russians, but they would not accept Shamil's conditions—the sticking point being the right to practice *shari'a*. In exchange for this, Shamil was prepared to accept Russian sovereignty and to prohibit the mountaineers from raiding the lowlands, which were now occupied by the Russians and their allies. But the Russians did not trust Shamil and instead gave him the option of unconditional surrender—either voluntarily or by force. Shamil refused, and another destructive Russian march commenced. Despite the devastation inflicted upon the people, it was this march—as well as the poor governance of the Russian administration in the lowlands—which convinced the general population to support Shamil and sustain the insurgency for almost 30 years. Despite their promises of fair treatment, the Russian-installed local governments in the lowlands continually took advantage of the indigenous residents and heaped humiliations upon them; virtually the entire populations of Chechnya, Ingushetia, and Dagestan eventually joined the insurgency.

Shamil began his military campaign, as had his predecessors, by demanding stricter adherence to conservative Islam. The people had come to Shamil asking to be delivered from the Russians because of his growing reputation as a sagacious and fair leader, but they were also coming to him and asking him how to *live*. Although the previous imams had preached a return to fundamentalist values, orthodoxy had not taken hold in all the areas. Shamil now used the universal support that he had been promised by the local leaders to once and for all firmly establish the conservative Naqshbandiyya sect in all parts of Chechnya and Dagestan. As before, Shamil preached that the people had to purify themselves before Allah and this would allow them to expel the invader; this time they listened—and if they didn't, he made them.

Shamil next reinstituted more of the practices of Ghazi Mohammed and Sheik Mansur, but improved on them. He started by organizing a professional full-time force of religious warriors (*murtazeks*), who were the local administrators. The *murtazeks* were considered to be an elite group, both extremely devout and fearless, who, along with the *naibs* (who also fought and were extremely loyal) and local judges who adjudicated according to the *shari'a*, helped to finally add some hierarchy and structure to the previously fractured mountaineer society. Shamil resumed the practice of having one man in ten from every village take

---

17. If there is any question about how history affects current conflicts, one need look no further than Gimry, where present-day residents still revere the memory of their two imams, and the Russians still routinely lock down the village for up to six months at a time—convinced the residents are aiding the insurgents.

part in the standing military force, while the other nine houses were required to take care of the fighter's family. Not only did Shamil regulate military and religious life, he also set up an able administration, which is what the *shari'a* is supposed to be—a complete system of life to include government that dealt with taxes, fines, road building, and sorting out blood feuds. Ironically, in reacting to the Russian attempt to subdue and "civilize" the mountaineers, Shamil was successful in uniting several hundred smaller political units that had previously been unable to agree on much, thus creating the first truly united government in the region. With the people finally united, Shamil fought the Russians continuously for another 19 years.

Despite Shamil's success, his bid for independence was doomed from the start—as were all the Chechen insurrections except in 1994. Keep in mind when reading about the mountaineers' victories that no matter how successful they have been in guerrilla warfare, they have only once been able to move into Phase III (the war of movement): every other time a group in the Caucasus became large enough to conduct major operations against the Russians, they also became large enough for the Russians to effectively target them and destroy their bases. Things were dramatically different in 1994, and because the Chechens were able to get the heavy weapons, vehicles, sanctuary, and time to actually conduct large-scale operations against the Russians, they were finally successful. Even though Shamil ran roughshod over the Russians for many years, in the end he was not able to convert his mounted warriors into anything more than ambushers and skirmishers. To win against an army as enormous and sophisticated as the Russians, Shamil needed outside support and sanctuaries—neither of which he ever got.

In fact, Shamil had sought such assistance from the Ottoman Empire. At this point, the Ottoman Empire had been fighting with the Russians for over 250 years for hegemony in the Black Sea region and the Caucasus. Shamil, a devout Muslim imam who had successfully converted the region to a strict form of Islam, should have gotten assistance from the Ottoman Sultan and Caliph—the titular leader of Muslims worldwide. Not only would the Ottomans have been helping their fellow Muslims, this could have created conditions for the Ottomans to take back some of the lands they had been consistently losing to the Russians. It was this hope—that the almighty Caliph would someday cross the mountains and assist them—that kept the insurgents fighting for so long when all their possessions were constantly taken and their villages, farms, orchards, and homes burned to the ground. But the Crimean War would end all their hopes.

The Crimean War is important to this study for many reasons; however, insofar as Shamil's insurgency is concerned, what is most notable about the Crimean War is the greater context it provided for the mountaineers' struggle. First of all, it is important to recognize that Shamil's insurgency occurred during the first "Cold War." The Cold War that was fought between the Soviet Union and the West in the late 1900s was in reality "Cold War II." The first Cold War (also referred to as the "Great Game") was between the Russian and British Empires over Russian influence in Central Asia from 1813 to 1907, and specifically during this period—Afghanistan. Coupled with spreading Russian influence in Persia, the czar's push toward Afghanistan threatened the "jewel of the crown" of the British Empire—India. Britain allied with France and the Ottoman Empire as part of her campaign to block Russian expansionism.

The second and most immediate cause of the Crimean War was religion—specifically the Ottoman's concession to Napoleon III to recognize France as the sovereign authority in the Holy Land. Russia objected, drawing the Sultan's attention to two earlier treaties that he had signed with Russia giving the Orthodox Church sole authority over Christian holy places and the keys to the Church of the Nativity. Napoleon insisted, making a military show of force, and convinced the Sultan to sign a new treaty and to entrust the Catholic Church with the keys. The Russians attempted to convince the Sultan to sign yet another new treaty, but the British, who had considerable influence in Constantinople, were also working behind the scenes against the Russians, and convinced the Sultan to reject the new treaty. Hostilities soon broke out, and the Crimean War began. Although Russia was not the clear winner in a war that was often characterized by tactical and logistical incompetence on all sides, Alexander II was able to conclude a peace treaty through the Congress of Paris in which both Russia and the Ottomans agreed not to establish any military posts in the Black Sea region and all the European powers agreed to respect Ottoman territory. These were not great terms for the Russians, as it meant giving up its naval base at Sevastopol, but it enabled the Empire to survive a two-year ordeal—including a devastating blockade of all its ports—against three major powers.

For Shamil's fighters, the effect was devastating. The psychological impact of the realization that the great Ottoman Sultan—even with the help of the mighty English and French—could not beat the Russians dealt an almost immediate deathblow to Shamil and his insurgency, validating Napoleon's maxim that, in war, the moral is to the physical as three to one. After having fought for decades against the Russians, constantly having to rebuild their villages and go hungry, waiting for the Sultan to send aid to his people bravely fighting for the right to live under *shari'a*, the mountaineers had placed their hopes on the major powers to weaken Russia to the point where their attacks might finally convince Russia that the Caucasus was not worth the effort. Seeing Russia emerge virtually unscathed after such a war and against such global power made the mountaineers lose their will to resist.

Following the Congress of Paris, delegations from virtually all the clans went to Shamil to ask him to seek terms from the Russians. Shamil agreed, asking only for a two-month delay in order to work out the best terms he could manage. It looked as though the Russians would finally have peace in the Caucasus.

Shamil went to the Russians to ask for terms: the Russians offered Shamil resettlement. Shamil was, no doubt, stunned. I'm sure that he was hoping to get *something* in return for giving up the fight; after all, Shamil had been besting the Russians for the better part of 20 years. Instead of concessions, he was told that in exchange for peace all the mountaineers would have to leave their ancestral homeland (an impossibility for Sufi Muslims who consider pilgrimages to the graves of their saints and ancestors a sacred duty) and their beloved mountains to move over 200 miles north to Manych—halfway between the Caspian and Azov Seas.[18] Not surprisingly, Shamil refused. Once the rest of the clan representatives heard about the Russian plan, they rediscovered their earlier passion to defend their homeland and set the stage for another few years of conflict. However, the Russians now had the advantage of an extra 200,000 men (freed up from the recently concluded Crimean War) and they used their overwhelming numbers to finally crush the insurgency and then move west to take care of the Circassians.

With all organized resistance gone, the Russians were able to commence their forced resettlement program, and hundreds of thousands of

---

18. Do not underestimate the power of religion and tradition; this is not ancient history. Although the Russians were not culturally aware in this case, they were very adept at using this very same emotional driver and religious obligation to their advantage during the 1999 Chechen War. In fact, the issue of paying homage to saints and relatives was manipulated into a compelling narrative and presented as *the* turning point for the Russians during the war. Akhmad Kadyrov was the Chief Mufti of the Ichkerian Republic (Chechnya) during and after the First Chechen War. At the outbreak of the second war, he switched sides, breaking his allegiance with then Chechen/Ichkerian President Maskhadov—in large part (according to the narrative) over the issue of the tomb of Sufi Saint Kunta-haji's mother, Kheda, which is considered sacred. Chechen President Aslan Maskhadov had been pressured by the radical Wahhabis/Salafists to destroy the tomb, as they consider reverence of the tomb to be heretical. Although the tomb was saved, this issue became emblematic of the differences between the Sufis and the Wahhabis—and the threat presented by "newcomers" to the traditional form of Sufism that had always been practiced in the region. The Russians deftly exploited this rift among the insurgents and promptly appointed Akhmad Kadyrov as the president of the Russian Republic of Chechnya. Many Sufis followed Kadyrov, which fundamentally changed the conflict to what it is today—insurgents fighting former insurgents (with help from the federal government). Although Kadyrov was assassinated by a bomb in 2004, Vladimir Putin appointed Kadyrov's son Ramzan as president in February 2007 after he turned 30—which is the minimum age for the post. To this day, Ramzan Kadyrov makes regular pilgrimages to the holy places in Chechnya associated with Kunta-haji.

mountaineers and a half-million Circassians were invited to leave the Caucasus for the Ottoman Empire. Many died during the exodus, and many more expired upon arrival; the Ottoman Empire was in no condition to receive almost a million people from Russia. Sources estimate more than 100,000 Chechens left and a third died. Those who remained were resettled to the lowlands, and many mountain villages were destroyed. Missing their homeland and not able to make a new life for themselves in the Ottoman Empire, many of the mountaineers attempted to return to their villages, but were turned back by the Russians. A few managed to find their way home after the next Russo-Turkish War in 1878, although sizeable North Caucasus diasporas remain in Turkey, Jordan, and Syria to this day—some of which have become quite powerful in their new countries and routinely send support to the current insurgents.

Nonetheless, even though the Russians rid themselves of a sizeable portion of the mountaineers and repopulated the area with Russians, Ukrainians, Cossacks, Georgians, and Armenians (all Orthodox), a number of the remaining fighters took to the mountains and continued to attack the Russians in uprisings and guerrilla assaults for the next ten years—similar to the situation in the North Caucasus at the moment.

THE QADIRII

> War—it is savagery. Remove yourself from anything that hints of war if the enemy hasn't come to take away your faith and honor. Your strength is wisdom, patience, fairness. The enemy will not withstand this strength and sooner or later will admit his defeat. No one will have the strength to defeat you and your truth, if you don't turn away from the path of your faith—the tariqat.
>
> —from the teachings of Kunta-haji[19]

After 20 years of almost continuous warfare, the majority of the mountaineers were tired of fighting; they wanted peace and an opportunity to make a life for themselves and their families. And so, whether they liked it or not, they either moved to the Ottoman Empire or accepted Russian rule. However, Shamil's insurrection hadn't been "over" for a year before small groups of insurgents once again began fighting the Russians. From 1860 to 1877, they occasionally instigated localized insurrections and exhorted the people to fight. The Russians responded to each local uprising with the

---

19. Julietta Meskhize and Mikhail Roshchin, *Islam in Chechnya*, Krotov Library, 2004, available at http://www.krotov.info/history/20/tarabuk/chechn.html#777; accessed July 25, 2008.

tactics that they felt had worked for them before—large scale punitive expeditions that would essentially erase entire settlements and villages from the map. This was usually followed by a large-scale deforestation campaign in the area, and finally, in addition to the large scale "invitation" to leave Russia, the military would also forcibly resettle recalcitrant villagers into areas within the lines of their fortifications in the lowlands to more easily control them.

Whereas current counterinsurgency doctrine emphasizes the need to "clear, hold, and build," the Russian tactic was closer to "clear, destroy, and remove." The Russians also utilized a "divide and conquer" policy during the period as well—impressing or enlisting the Chechens into military units that would then deploy elsewhere—allowing the Russians to remove a large part of the militant population from the Caucasus (with all their horses and weapons) while using their formidable martial skills against other rebels—like the Polish.

This new situation, coupled with the thought that they would never be able to defeat the Russians, demoralized the mountaineers. In much the same way as the Muslims of the Abbasid Dynasty felt defeated and searched for a new way to define themselves and their situation following the fall of Baghdad in 1258, now the Naqshbandiyya Sufis of Chechnya did the same. And just as many of the Sunnis of Baghdad turned to a more mystical and personal relationship with God after the fall of their empire—resulting in an increase in the Shi'a—so now did the Naqshbandiyya Sufis search for a way to do likewise.

Qadiriyya (Qadiri, Qadiriyah, Qadiriya) Sufism was brought to the Caucasus in the 1850s by Kunta-haji (al-Sheik al-Hajj Kunta al-Michiki al-Ilishkhani), who had shown great piety and aptitude at an early age and had been given the opportunity to study with the most revered scholars. Some sources say that Shamil encouraged the youthful Kunta to continue in his pious ways and therefore allowed him to make the Hajj at a young age. During his travels, Kunta-haji traveled to Baghdad and soon became an adherent of Qadiriyya Sufism. The Qadiriyya place great importance on the purification of the self and, according to their philosophy, "purification of the mirror of the heart from the rust of carnal, animal, and satanic qualities is an essential part of one's spiritual journey." Once the rust is removed, the mirror of the heart will reflect the beauty of God clearly.

When Kunta-haji first returned to Chechnya in 1850, he was initially brought to Shamil and had long debates with him, but within a few years he was "invited" to make the Hajj again. Shamil forced Kunta-haji to leave the Caucasus because, not only did he preach that it was not against the Qur'an to submit rather than resist the superior Russian power, but moreover because "he demanded a halt to the resistance, which he deemed not only futile but also a sin against God. He even predicted the downfall of Shamil's imamate."[20] Thus Kunta-haji was a direct threat to Shamil's leadership when he preached that it was possible to live under Russian rule and still be a good Muslim.[21] Moreover, Kunta-haji had attracted a large number of followers who found relief from their despair in his message; finally, they could stop fighting and be even *better* Muslims than they were before. The Russians should have been ecstatic because here was the answer to their prayers—a revered Muslim scholar who was offering a counter-ideology to what was being preached by Shamil. And indeed, it was the Russians who brought Kunta-haji back to Chechnya after Shamil's surrender in the early 1860s and tried to use him and his teachings to finally put an end to the fighting.

However, after a few years, even the pacifist Qadiriyya began to worry the new Russian administration, who saw the large number of Kunta-haji's *murids* (or followers[22]) as a threat. Despite the fact that Kunta-haji repeatedly refused to accept the title of imam, by drawing 5,000 mountaineers to the ideology of non-violence, Kunta-haji had, ironically, become dangerous. The Russians claimed that the Qadiriyya were assembling in much the same way as the Naqshbandiyya had previously, and that Kunta-haji was really just waiting for the proper time to whip his followers into a frenzy and start another rebellion. The Russians took Kunta-haji into custody, and when 3,000 of his followers gathered to protest and began the ritualistic whirling *zikr* dance, the Russians perceived it to be an attack (the followers were all wearing their ceremonial daggers) and opened fire on them in what is now known as the Battle of Daggers. Most of Kunta-haji's followers were killed, and their lands were expropriated and redistributed to the Cossacks or the Orthodox Church. After the Battle of Daggers, Chechen lands were reduced to one-quarter of what they were prior to the start of Shamil's Great Gazavat. Not unexpectedly, the population once again turned against the Russians.

---

20. Gammer, *The Lone Wolf and the Bear*, 75.
21. Refer to the earlier note about Akhmad Kadyrov (a Qadiriyya) about breaking away from the rest of the Chechens in 2000 and siding with the Russians. His son, the current President Ramzan Kadyrov, makes regular pilgrimages to Kunta-haji's holy sites in Chechnya and has used essentially the same argument to convince Chechens to leave the insurgency and live as members of the Russian Federation.
22. Murid is a Sufi term meaning "committed one," as well as "willpower." A Murid is a follower or initiate of Sufism. Although not mentioned previously, the term "Muridism" was used commonly to refer to Muslim resistance in Russia during the 1800s. In Tolstoy's illuminating book *Hadji Murad*, he uses the term almost exclusively as was the custom of the day ("Hadji Murad had only brought two of his murids, Khanéfi and Eldár, with him").

A PARADIGM ESTABLISHED

There is considerable value in examining the early North Caucasus campaigns, because the patterns established in those early conflicts repeat themselves in every generation and still have relevance to both the conflict today and counterinsurgency practice in general. No doubt veteran Chechnya observers have already been making these connections—especially in light of the insurgency and terrorism framework presented in the first two chapters. Nonetheless, before listing the numerous uprisings since the Battle of Daggers, it will be beneficial to illuminate these patterns so that all subsequent action can be put into proper context.

The first and most obvious pattern is the presence of Islam as the unifying ideology used to fight the "invader." Frankly, when I first started researching this topic in depth I was stunned to discover the effect that religion has *always* had on the Chechen conflict. Like everyone else studying the Chechen Wars of the 1990s, I assumed that the "religion factor" had entered the picture sometime around 1995. Although the religious aspect of the war in 1994 seemed to be diminished to the point that it was rarely reported on, reporter Sebastian Smith who was in Chechnya for much of that war has written that, during the fighting in the mid 1990s, bands of Chechen soldiers often got together and danced the *zikr*—sometimes while the Russians were dropping bombs nearby. While the politicians may have done their best to keep the undercurrent of the Muslim faith in the background, Islam has been the most often used ideology to move the common man to fight.

The importance of religion is prominently emphasized in current counterinsurgency doctrine, so much so that many experts now add a "C" (Culture—to include religion) to the old standby term that has been used by security professionals for years—DIME (diplomatic, informational, military, and economic)—to discuss the elements of national power that must be used to defeat insurgencies. Look again at the words Kunta-haji used to describe what constitutes a people's honor and freedom—"language, culture, and customs." And although religion might not be the strongest motivating factor for every individual involved (especially those today that want to keep the conflict "secular"), it is simply counterproductive to argue that religion doesn't matter—or that this ideological influence is not the most repeated throughout the history of conflict in the North Caucasus.

In addition to religion, "splitting" the insurgency emerges as a significant theme, which results from coupling both Islam and the local culture. Research on the *wirds* and *teips* (clans and families) of the Chechens is difficult to collect and the findings generally frustrate the Western desire for order and clarity. But what this research has demonstrated by its inability to draw straight lines is that *there aren't straight lines* and the Chechen and

Dagestani (or Ingush, Kabard, and Balkarian among others) cultures are not vertical structures, or "power verticals" to use the current Russian vernacular. The Muslim faith is a relatively flat hierarchy to begin with, but by looking at the mountaineer culture and its imposition of yet another layer of clan hierarchy on top of the religious one, it is easy to understand why the Caucasians have so much success at insurgent warfare.[23] North Caucasus social structures are perfect for conducing guerrilla and terrorist activity because their societies are already a culture of "cells," and as we've seen, cellular organizations with a high degree of loyalty are paramount to insurgencies. Because familial loyalty sometimes trumps religious authority, and because those same clans are often competing among themselves for status and hegemony, those societal "fractures" were—and still are—exploited by the Russians.

Moreover, Kunta-haji's influence on the region cannot be underestimated; the additional rift in mountaineer society that occurred after the introduction of a competing counter-ideology to the more fundamentalist Naqshbandiyya had an effect that can still be seen 150 years later.

This particular characteristic of Caucasus culture is what gives it strength as an insurgency and yet ultimately keeps it weak when it comes time to make the final move toward independence.[24] Although the Chechen tradition is to be like a herd of horses and stay dispersed until such time as a crisis causes the herd to come together and move as one, not even the elected "war leader" is always accepted by everyone. The longer the conflict drags on, the more likely these splits are to occur. Current counterinsurgency doctrine places great emphasis on analyzing the links between political, religious, tribal, familial, social, and other networks, and how those groups interact with each other—specifically for the purposes of determining where counterinsurgency forces can exploit weak links. As emphasized in Chapter 1—insurgencies at some point always become about power and resources. The success of the "Awakening Councils" in Iraq is a perfect example of this dynamic at work. Although the Russians have historically referred to this concept by a different name, "divide and

---

23. To be examined in detail in Chapter 6.
24. Although Chechnya has been the primary focus of this book thus far, the Dagestanis have been as much a part of this conflict as anyone else. As of this writing, there are more attacks taking place in Dagestan than in Chechnya. The internal dynamics of Dagestan are even more fractured than Chechnya. Aside from the religious and family aspects, Dagestan is made up of more than 13 different ethnic groups—of which the Avars, Dargins, and Lezgins still comprise less than 60 percent of the population. In addition, there are Laks, Tabasarans, Rutuls, Aguls, Tsakhurs, Kumyks, Nogais, Azeris, Chechens, and Russians, and another 40 or so tiny groups numbering only about 200 total—and they all speak their own language—making Chechnya and its Vainakh cousin Ingushetia look downright homogenous.

conquer," this policy is the crucial part of the strategy that the Russian government currently employs in Chechnya.

The most successful example of the Russian divide and conquer policy during the 1800s was in North Ossetia and Kabardia. During Shamil's rebellion, the Circassians (the North Caucasus nation that lived along the Black Sea to the west) were also fighting the Russians. Although Shamil sent emissaries to the Circassians in an attempt to coordinate their actions, his expeditionary forces were denied transit to the Circassians by the Kabards, and Shamil's dream of having the entire Caucasus region join together against the Russians was unfulfilled. The Kabards and North Ossetians had long received preferential treatment from the Russians because of their location astride the Darial Pass.

During this period, the Russians were even more demonstrative of their appreciation. However, the Kabards would later pay heavily for their decision not to join Shamil, as they would eventually suffer much the same fate as the Chechens and the Circassians—and their priceless herds were eventually decimated to the point that their famous horses were almost brought to extinction. Having two separate insurgency movements cut off in the middle and then sending in overwhelming force to deal with one and then the other is the most literal of "divide and conquer" or "splitting the insurgency" policies.[25]

Additional fault lines in Caucasus society are found between the lowland dwellers and the mountaineers—despite the fact that the two groups depend on each other for survival. The lowlands produce the food and the mountains provide a kind of internal sanctuary that prevented all but the largest of Russian expeditions to pry them out. Nonetheless, it was often the lowlanders who were most eager to stop the fighting under any terms because they had the most to lose. The Russians have always used those divisions to their advantage.

Shamil established yet another enduring pattern of the insurgency when he moved his headquarters from his home in Dagestan deep into the mountains of Chechnya early in his campaign. Although "terrain" always favors the defender, when terrain such as the Caucasus Mountains is involved, it increases the difficulty and complexity of counterinsurgency operations exponentially. Terrain dictates tactics—the mountaineers did not have the manpower to defeat the Russians in open battle, but they did

---

25. The Ossetians, on the other hand, have always fared well with the Russians, and the Russian attack into Georgia on August 8th, 2008, was specifically to protect the Ossetians—many of whom had been given Russian citizenship. Ironically, Prime Minister Putin described Georgia's attempt to subdue its own breakaway province as "complete genocide," and that Georgia had "effectively lost its right to rule the breakaway province." AP, August 10, 2008, David Nowak, http://www.miamiherald.com/news/top-AP-stories/story/636123.html; accessed August 10, 2008.

have superior rifles, outstanding shooting skills, plenty of rocks and trees for cover and surprise—and lots of fast horses with which to evade. As a result, the Imperial Russian Army simply could not compete with the insurgents man-to-man once they retreated to their mountains or forests.

It was exactly the constancy of the Chechen belief in the power of their mountains, their forests, their martial culture, and their faith that produced the greatest paradox of the entire history of Chechen rebellion and insurgency. The factors that made it impossible to completely subjugate them using an "enemy-centric" approach to COIN *are the very same factors that have prevented the mountaineers from winning their independence* from Russia.

The basic theme of Chechen resistance has always been, "We are Muslims and this is the land of our ancestors and saints, and we cannot leave. We are magnificent fighters, we have the mountains from which the Russians cannot pry us out of, and we are willing to die for our beliefs. If we just keep to the path, the Russians will eventually tire of this 'death by a thousand stings' and leave." The paradox is that it is exactly this combination of factors: terrain, ideology, and small unit guerrilla tactics conducted by extremely loyal and committed decentralized clan groups that have allowed the Chechens to win many battles but lose the war. They have a hard time winning the war because eventually there has to be some sort of Phase III insurgency operation where there is a "real" plan for large Chechen units to seize key terrain and then successfully defend against determined Russian attacks supported by heavy direct and indirect fire.[26] You can feel good about yourself if you are confident that as a man you can take on ten enemy soldiers and win. You can feel good about your nation if you know that every one of your clansmen can do the same; but when the enemy has the resources and the national will (which was singularly lodged in the person of the czar) to send 11 soldiers for every one of your clansmen, eventually you'll have to run away or die fighting.

The Chechen strategy has always been to conduct Phase II guerrilla warfare as long as possible and hope that the Russians will give up and go away. As anyone who has ever worked as a battalion-level staff officer will tell you, *hope is not a method*. The Chechen success on the

---

26. Although Russian military officers will contend that they did not "lose" the First Chechen War in the same way that the U.S. military argued that it did not lose the Vietnam War, the signing of the Khasavyurt Agreement in August 1996 gave de facto independence to Chechnya until the start of the "Second" Chechen War in December 1999. However, the fact that the Chechens won at least one "war" does not negate the premise. In fact, as will be discussed in a later chapter, it was precisely *because* the Chechens were able to transition to the War of Movement in 1995 that allowed them to achieve their independence.

battlefield and their natural advantages are the very same factors that have led them to believe that the Russians will simply give up and go away if they just keep at it long enough.

Historically, this is not a bad strategy—but it usually only succeeds when the "occupier" is deployed far from home and is not a "great" power. In this case, Chechnya was (and still is) attempting to secede from what Russia considers its southern border. And as far as Russia is concerned, a far better and more easily defendable border is the great wall of the Caucasus Mountains. As long as the Russian national will supports keeping Chechnya within the Russian Federation (the Nord-Ost, Beslan, and Moscow subway bombings are just a few of the terrorist attacks directed at the Russian population specifically to diminish the national will), and as long as Chechnya continues to be denied substantial external support (and seriously, what country is willing to start a war with Russia), then the Chechens will not progress beyond guerrilla warfare—meaning they will continue to win numerous battles and inflict terrible casualties on the common Russian soldier, but still lose the war.

The Chechens continued to be successful in guerrilla warfare because there was never a lack of volunteers to fill the ranks, regardless of the casualties they suffered. True, the number of forces available to the early insurgencies waxed and waned depending on the successes of the mountaineers and the level of commitment that the Russians were showing at the time. But recruits continued to flow to the insurgencies because the common man felt that the traditional, clan-based, (semi) Muslim society was not only inherently legitimate, but it was also superior to the culture against which they were fighting. If they only held on long enough, surely some of their Muslim brethren to the south would give them assistance.

This brings up another theme that is repeated over and over again— the lack of external support for the Chechens. The Russians were attempting to force the mountaineers to live under a different set of beliefs, but the groups with which they were culturally and spiritually linked were not helping them. Every single insurgency leader has called for international help—and received nominal support at best. After giving up his ambitions for southern Russia in the 1500s, the Ottoman Sultan provided only sporadic and nominal aid, despite his titular responsibilities as the leader of the world's Muslims. As for other countries, the Estonians gave all their Russian rubles to Chechnya when they underwent currency exchange in the early 1990s, the Nordic countries grant liberal asylum to Chechens and speak out on human rights issues, and there has been substantial private funding and fighters from the Islamic community—but no country has been willing to send the kind of support that really matters because they can't afford to start a war with Russia.[27] The only country that has ever given any kind of official external support to the Chechens was the Taliban-led country of Afghanistan, which granted Chechnya full diplomatic recognition and sent money and fighters to help in the 1990s. Keep in mind that Al Qaeda was very much behind the scenes in Afghanistan at the time; so ironically, the AQ fighters that went to Chechnya could actually be considered "official" support from a foreign government. Tragically, during WWII, the Germans sent some agents to the Caucasus to help foment revolution in the region and facilitate the German advance, but the handful of soldiers were virtually worthless. Stalin nonetheless used it as an excuse to resettle the entire Chechen community after the war.

This brings up the issue of resettlement which, as discussed earlier, is an emotionally charged subject as the peoples of any resettlement campaign have suffered great losses of life and further deprivation upon arrival at their new location. Resettlement of the Vainakh is a pattern that began during this period. It was also used on a smaller scale prior to Shamil's defeat, prompting some prominent historians to refer to the deportations of the 1860s as the "third deportation." It would be used again by the Russians and later, on a grand scale, by the Soviets. Less than 20 years ago, the Russian Minister of Defense, Pavel Grachov, circulated a secret memo stating, "It has been decided to take advantage of the anticipated mass, but disorganized, resistance by implementing mass deportation of the local population under the guise of orderly evacuation from the theatre of military operations to other regions of the Russian Federation," as the way to settle the Chechen problem.[28] Even in 2010, the Kremlin is discussing resettling some of the Ingush population to reduce tensions over the Prigorodnyi Raion.

Because terrain always gives an advantage to the defender, removing insurgents from their "home turf" has resulted in pacification, and it has been a favorite tactic of those who advocate "the end justifies the

---

27. All the Baltic countries had significant reasons to support the Chechens. In addition to the fact that Latvia, Lithuania, and Estonia share a common history of Soviet occupation, Dzhokar Dudayev, the first democratically elected president of Chechnya, had been a general in the Soviet Air Force and commander of the Soviet Air Force in Tartu, Estonia, one of the most important strategic air bases of the USSR. When the Soviet government ordered him to crush the Baltic independence movements in the late 1980s, Dudayev refused, and even allowed Estonian demonstrators to enter the base—effectively ending any possibility for the Soviets to regain control of the Baltics. As such, the Estonians actually came very close to giving official, diplomatic recognition to the Chechen Republic of Ichkeria (ChRI) in 1996, and for many years one could see the Ichkerian flag hanging opposite the parliament building in Estonia's capitol or visit the Embassy of the Chechen Republic of Ichkeria in the heart of Tallinn.

28. Official statement from the chairman of the government of the Chechen Republic of Ichkeria, Akhmed Zakayev, February 23, 2010, at http://www.chechenpress.co.uk/content/2010/02/23/main01.shtml; accessed on February 22, 2010.

means." In the case of the Chechens, removing them from their mountains and dense forests resulted in long periods of relative peace. However, because Chechnya and Dagestan contain the sites of many sacred
religious sites, the Vainakh have always found a way to get back home,
and eventually the fighting starts again.

On a smaller scale, the "scorched earth" policy that the Russians
employed liberally during this period was perhaps another kind of resettlement. The Russian practice of destroying all the homes, gardens, crops,
fruit-bearing trees, wells, etc., in an attempt to erase villages from the map
would be repeated throughout all the conflicts. Although the reduction of
the city of Grozny during the Russian carpet-bombing campaigns in the
1990s might seem to be the culmination of that trend, it was probably the
Stalin-era resettlements that were more emblematic—as the Soviets *literally* erased Chechnya from the map as if it had never existed.

For the majority of Americans, the wars in Iraq and Afghanistan under-
scored just how many troops are needed for effective counterinsurgency
operations, but the early Chechen conflicts also make it clear why the
Russians needed an enormous amount of manpower to achieve results. In
1897, 30 years after the end of the Great Gazavat, the Imperial Russian census reported the total Chechen population as 226,171. Assume that the casualty rate during the earlier wars was high (a reputable source puts the
number at over 50,000 for the years 1830–1860),[29] but was somewhat offset
by the traditionally high mountaineer birthrate (at least four times the
national average in every census ever taken). In addition, assume that half
of the 100,000 Chechens who left for the Ottoman Empire came back—
although most historians would say that 50,000 returnees is far too high a
number—and that the Dagestani population was as high as the Chechen
one (again, a bit unreasonable considering that most of Dagestan is rocky
and mountainous and cannot produce food like Chechnya can). Add all
that up, and the number for the total population of the mountaineers still
comes to less than half a million—of which, the highest number of "active"
fighters ever reported never exceeded 18,000. Historically, successful counterinsurgency campaigns have had to operate at a level of 20 law enforcement and military to 1,000 civilians.[30] To subdue Shamil's insurgency,
it required about an 11:1 ratio of soldiers to guerrillas and 40 soldiers
for each 1,000 civilians (assuming the highest possible population of
500,000)—at least double the usual number required for the job.[31] In

---

29. Mairbek Vatchagaev, *Chechnya in the 19th Century Caucasian Wars* (Moscow, 1995), 35.
30. Kalev I. Sepp, "Best Practices in Counterinsurgency," *Military Review*, May-June 2005,
    8; and Bruce Hoffman, "Insurgency and Counterinsurgency in Iraq," (Washington,
    DC: Rand Corporation, 2004), 14.
31. These are very generous figures, as they assume forces at their highest peak of
    strength when, in fact, at the end of the conflict when all 200,000 Russian soldiers
    were thrown in the fray, Shamil's forces probably never exceeded 8,000—putting the
    combat calculus for active fighters at about 25:1.

every successful Russian counterinsurgency campaign, the Russians (Soviets) had to send in overwhelming forces approximating those same odds.

OTHER LESSONS FOR COUNTER-GUERRILLA OPERATIONS

The Russians couldn't reduce the mountains, but they could remove the forests. And although it was an ecological disaster, the Russian deforestation campaigns established during Yermolov's time were nonetheless an effective means of securing the Russian lines of communication (LOCs)—enabling soldiers and supplies to move rapidly and securely without fear of ambush. As even the casual reader of the current Afghanistan campaigns knows, most Coalition casualties come from traveling on the roads, making convoy security one of the most dangerous jobs in the theater. Armies need supplies, and supplies move in big, slow carts—or trucks—over roads to outposts, and remote roads are excellent places for ambushes. The Russian solution was to remove the ambush sites by removing the trees for close to a thousand yards on either side of a road—outside of the range of the rifles used by the insurgents. This ensured that the Russians could not be surprised by ambushes or killed by snipers. Securing LOCs is extremely difficult under any situation, and operating in areas where one never knows where the next guerrilla will pop up makes the job almost impossible. Nonetheless, despite the fact that securing LOCs is not mentioned as a "principle" or "best practice" in any of the counterinsurgency literature as of late, the modern day equivalent of what the Russians did—secure road building—is an effective tool for counterinsurgency campaigns.[32]

Closely connected with road-building and securing LOCs were the series of fortifications that were built throughout the region. The Russians quickly realized that they could not control the region operating out of a few large, well-defended forts, but instead needed to build entire lines of smaller, interconnected forts. As the fighting got worse, they increased not just the number of troops, but also the number of forts. The forts were situated in such a way that they were mutually supportable, making it much easier for the Russians to exert positive control over the entire region—especially when it came to the smaller resettlement campaigns. The idea was to establish a line, clear out anyone behind the line that wasn't a "friendly," backfill the areas with "friendlies," then start moving forward again in order to establish a line even farther out where the process would be repeated. The additional two lines of forts put in after Shamil took over, combined with the deforestation campaign made it possible for the Russians to move the Chechens out, bring the Russians and Cossacks in

---

32. I am not advocating deforestation; for an example of what I do mean, see David Kilcullen, "Road-Building in Afghanistan," *Small Wars Journal*, April 24, 2008, available at http://www.smallwarsjournal.com.

and little by little control larger and larger areas. This "clear, hold, move" tactic is similar to "clear, hold, build" except that there was little focus on maintaining the good will of the "friendlies" once the army moved on. Corrupt and untrustworthy local administrators took advantage of the situation for their own gain, and soon there was unrest in previously "cleared" areas—highlighting the need for legitimate government.

There are also a multitude of lessons learned from those early conflicts that can be applied to any counterinsurgency campaign: the importance of artillery; the importance of intelligence to identify networks and links; the difficulty of determining the enemy when everyone is wearing civilian clothes and carries a weapon; the need to stay ahead of an "adaptive" enemy, etc. However, the most significant "best-practice" counterinsurgency tactic that the Russians used was "presence and persistence" or, to use the doctrinally correct term, "long-term commitment." As the national will was embodied by the will of the czar and the national objective seemed to mirror U.S. "manifest destiny," albeit to the south and east instead of the west, the Russians maintained a presence and a large force in the Caucasus for 60 years—something that most countries might not have the stomach for. However, if a country is willing to put an overwhelming number of soldiers in an area for an unlimited amount of time and isn't particularly fussy about high numbers of casualties, then to some extent, success will follow even if the conduct of their operations do not follow "best practices" for a "population-centric" approach to counterinsurgency.

CHAPTER 4

Revolutions, Total Wars, and Final Solutions

THE RUSSO-TURKISH WAR

In 1877, Russia went to war with the Ottoman Empire in order to reestablish itself on the Black Sea, gain more territory from the Ottomans in the Caucasus (near Armenia), and to help Serbia, Montenegro, Bulgaria, and Romania gain independence from the Ottomans—as those Orthodox populations had been subjected to increasingly more severe repressions, culminating in particularly violent measures in 1875. In many ways, the Ottomans and the Russians had the same problem—each had territories that constantly rebelled (with populations belonging to the "other's" religion)—and both countries dealt with their problems in a similar manner. In a war that was described by Prussian Emperor Frederick II as a "war between the one-eyed and the blind," Shamil's heir was promoted to general by the Ottomans and given a division of ex-patriot mountaineers to go and fight in the Caucasus with a 20,000-man Ottoman Army. Yet another Chechen uprising started as Ali Bek-haji roused the population to hope for independence, and they began to make gains due to the reduced Russian troops in the area.

The Russians eventually won the war on all fronts, but lost a staggering number of soldiers. They accepted a truce from the Ottomans, but continued to march toward Constantinople—sensing that the Ottomans were too weak to resist. The British and the French were alarmed at what it might mean for them if the Russians took Constantinople, and sent the British Fleet to stop the Russians from entering the city. The Russian advance was stopped at San Stephano, where a treaty was signed. The Ottomans recognized the independence of Romania, Serbia, Montenegro, and the autonomy of Bulgaria, and gave Russia a significant amount of territory in the Caucasus—including the strategic port of Batum (Batumi).

Under increasing pressure from European countries, the Ottomans agreed to establish some basic human rights for the Christians in the rest of the Ottoman-controlled Balkans and declared the empire to be a constitutional monarchy—but subsequently suspended the constitution.

Nerses II, the Armenian Orthodox Patriarch in Constantinople, reached out to the Russians for protection and convinced them to insert a clause into the treaty stipulating that Russian forces in the Ottoman-held Armenian provinces would withdraw only with full implementation of Ottoman reforms.[1] British and French influence on the part of the Ottomans served to have this clause removed in the subsequent "Congress of Berlin," as the British were more concerned about the "Great Game" with Russia. For her part, Russia never forgave Britain for interfering in what could have been a return of Orthodoxy to Constantinople.

Ali Bek-haji's revolt (some sources state he was a Qadiriyya) was joined by Qadiriyya and Naqshbandiyya alike and he successfully conducted guerrilla attacks and struck the Russians seemingly everywhere at once. Initially, the Russians responded slowly, but as the months went on and more and more communities joined Ali-Bek, the Russians resorted to standard operating procedure and sent in 15 soldiers for every inhabitant of Chechnya. The Russian General Svistunov decided that "merciless punishment of the guilty was the only way to re-establish peace in the *oblast*. The destruction of *auls* [villages], fields, cattle, and everything at hand should strike the mutineers as just retribution and by denying them means for survival should force them to come out of the forests and submit."[2] This action only spread the revolt further. In the end, a massive Russian effort to surround Ali Bek-haji and his men did not result in his capture, but at least had the effect of dispersing his forces—many of whom went to Dagestan and continued fighting under Muhammed-haji—who soon had the support of

---

1. According to the *Qur'an*, non-Muslims may continue to live in Muslim lands without converting to Islam as a *dhimmi* (conquered person) and gain the protection of the state if they pay the *jizyah* (poll-tax). Over the ages, according to scholarly Islamic legal consensus, in addition to the *jizyah*, *dhimmi* had to wear a wide cloth belt to distinguish them from the Muslims and keep to the side of the streets. They were also prohibited from building as high or higher than the Muslim buildings, displaying crosses or ringing church bells, reciting their own holy books aloud, making public displays of their funerals and feast days, building new churches or synagogues and, by the mid-1800s in the Ottoman Empire, they were not allowed to ride horses, or be accepted as a witness in any trial (meaning a Muslim could steal from a Christian and the Christian could not appear in court to present his case). The Armenian Patriarch additionally complained of atrocities such as forced conversion, arson, extortion, rape, and murder at the hands of the Ottomans—similar to the charges leveled against the Russians by their own Muslim populations.
2. N. Semenov, "Khronika chechenskogo vosstaniia 1877 goda" [Chronicle of the Chechen insurrection of 1877], Appendix to the *Terskii Sbornik*, Vypusk I (Vladikavkaz, 1891), 26, as quoted by Gammer, 92.

almost all of Dagestan—including areas that had not supported Shamil during the 1850s.

The Russians moved operations to Dagestan and were eventually able to regain order. They promised Ali Bek-haji and his men that no harm would come to them or their families if they surrendered. They complied and were immediately imprisoned, tried by courts-martial, and 23 of them were executed. More than 5,000 mountaineers (entire villages) were resettled to Siberia and their lands given to the Cossacks. A period of relative peace ensued for the next seven years as many of the mountaineers were resettled outside of Chechnya and Dagestan. However, they slowly began to filter back to their native homeland, especially as they watched others flock to the region seeking to deprive them of yet another of their natural resources—the recently discovered oil fields.

By the mid 1800s oil had been discovered in the Caucasus, and by 1887, French, English, and Dutch firms had already established refineries and were producing 1,600 tons annually. Three years later the number had skyrocketed to 263,000 barrels per year.[3] Because Chechen oil is of very high quality, needing little refining and often bubbling up in pools on the surface, Grozny would later become the center of refining for specialized aviation petroleum products during the Soviet period. But even in the early 1900s the Russians sent thousands of oil workers to Grozny—reaching 12,000 by 1906, and 22,000 by 1912—and a new mountaineer legend, the "abrek," was born.

The combination of new money from the oil-boom, an influx of foreigners to the region, and the relative deprivation of the mountaineers (combined with their cultural tradition of "raiding") spawned a generation of "highwaymen," turning the region into a kind of "Wild, Wild East." Some historians have expressed surprise that the mountaineers didn't rob each other (making the highlands relatively safe), but this is easily explained by what Islamic law refers to as hiraba (gangsterism), which is only prohibited against other Muslims and was the "preferred form of jihad when fighting a superior force and represents the first organized form of jihad in early Islamic warfare."[4] These abreks attacked travelers, trains, farms, factories, and state institutions as well as carried out the occasional attack on the Russian military and police. Some of the abreks banded together and would conduct larger assaults, but they were protected by the locals and even lionized for their resistance to the Russians and the boldness of their actions—in one case sending a note to the commander at Kizylar announcing they would rob the bank on a particular day. They then dressed up as Cossacks, rode straight past the troops sent to guard the town, robbed the

3. Gammer, 105.
4. Stephen C. Coughlin, "To Our Great Detriment, Ignoring What Extremists Say About Jihad," National Defense Intelligence College, July 2007, 291.

bank in broad daylight, and later sent another note to the commander asking where he had been.[5]

THE RUSSO-JAPANESE WAR AND THE WAKE OF REVOLUTION

In the meantime, Russia had gone to war with Japan in 1904 over Russia's expansion in the Far East and ambitions in Manchuria. The Russians had leased Port Arthur from the Chinese in 1898 and finally had a warm water port in the Pacific. In 1899, they sent troops to China to help quell the Boxer Rebellion and safeguard their interests. But when the Russians failed to meet the agreed-upon timetable for withdrawing—and actually increased their holdings in Manchuria, the Japanese conducted a surprise attack on the unsuspecting Russian fleet before the czar had a chance to complete the Trans-Siberian Railroad—cutting off the Russian troops in the east. The czar's forces, vulnerable and without hope of resupply or reinforcement, lost a series of battles which culminated in the naval Battle of Tsushima; another Russian fleet was virtually annihilated, and Russia sued for peace. Having lost both the Pacific and Baltic fleets in the war, Russia's reputation with the major European powers declined rapidly and Russia was thrown into tumult—causing the first failed revolution.

The 1905 Russian Revolution began with "Bloody Sunday" in December 1904. A peaceful demonstration in front of the Winter Palace in St. Petersburg, characterized by families holding crosses and praying, ended with participants being shot and ridden down. Estimates of the casualties range from 96 dead and 333 injured (official report) to 4,000 dead. Among other things, the people had petitioned the czar to abandon the war with Japan because of the huge number of casualties. Immediately following Bloody Sunday, the population mounted a mass demonstration and, after three days of riots, Czar Nicholas II, knowing he didn't have enough troops to restore order unless he massacred the population, finally capitulated and signed the October Manifesto. This established a new organization, the Duma, as the primary legislative body in Russia, and also granted basic human rights to the population. Although the majority of Russians rejoiced, there was a backlash against the original organizers. The Bolsheviks made their first appearance at this time, staging a two-day strike which devolved into a week-long street fight where 1,000 workers were killed before the Bolsheviks surrendered.

In 1907, Russia took control of Azerbaijan from the Iranians, and in 1911, Russian troops entered northwestern Iran, hoping to take advantage of the country's instability and take more territory. In the Caucasus,

---

5. Chechen oral tradition, as relayed by Said X.

the *abreks* continued their constant raiding, causing general instability, but their attacks against the Russians were largely symbolic as neither side had the strength to engage in major campaigns. Once again, world events and the machinations of the major powers would soon bring war back to the North Caucasus.

WORLD WAR I AND THE CASE OF THE MISSING *JIHAD*

World War I began in June 1914. It was started by a Serb (Bosnian) who assassinated Archduke Ferdinand, the heir to the Austro-Hungarian Empire. Austria-Hungary retaliated against Serbia (Russia's ally) and Germany declared war on Russia in August. Germany and Austria-Hungary convinced the Ottomans to join the Central Powers and the Ottomans agreed, but waited to officially declare war in order to make secret preparations. Russia began fighting Germany on the Eastern Front (where trench warfare did not develop) and declared war against the Ottoman Empire on November 2, attacking in the Caucasus along the Armenia-Ottoman border. This preemptive strike was designed to quickly crush the Ottoman troops that had massed on the border and prevent a threat to the Port at Batumi—Russia's main oil exporting hub—which received regular shipments from Baku and Grozny via the now-completed trans-Caucasian railroad.

The Russians' larger goal, however, was to finally fulfill the dream of every czar since Peter the Great (as well as to complete the last march of the War of 1878) by conquering Constantinople, taking control of the Black Sea, re-consecrating the Hagia Sophia, and reestablishing Orthodoxy in its rightful home.[6] Specifically, Russia told England and France (the countries that prevented Russia from taking Constantinople in 1878) that if they wanted a lasting settlement after the war, then Russia wanted full possession of Constantinople, the Bosphorus and Dardanelles straits, and the Sea of Marmara—giving Russia complete control of access to the Black Sea. Moreover, Russia demanded no international resistance when they implemented their standard method of expansion and *resettled the Turkish population out of Anatolia* and replaced them with Cossacks.[7] The Russians' first move—attacking the Ottomans in what is known as the Bergmann Offensive—did not go well and the Russians lost 40 percent of their troops. This apparent Russian weakness emboldened the Ottoman Minister of War and Commander-in-Chief Enver Pasha (one of the three

6. The traditional seat of the Patriarch of Constantinople and the religious focal point of the Eastern Orthodox Church for nearly 1,000 years.
7. As voiced by the Russian foreign minister to the British and French ambassadors in March 1915, the documentation made available by the Russian newspaper *Izvestia* in February 1917 to gain Armenian support. R. G. Hovannisian, *Armenia on the Road to Independence, 1918* (Berkeley: University of California Press, 1971), 72.

leaders of the "Young Turk" movement) to implement his own grandiose plan to take back the Caucasus and reunite all the Turkic peoples throughout the region.

The Ottoman Empire had long endeavored to regain its lost territories from previous Russo-Turkish wars, and ultimately, to regain all of the Caucasus as far as the Caspian Sea. Unlike earlier wars, this time the Ottomans had powerful allies—including a massive German contingent on Russia's western front. To further help coordinate the total war effort, Ottoman Sultan (and Muslim Caliph) Mehmed V issued the first of his two significant acts—formally declaring global *jihad* against the Allied powers following the Russian attack—followed up by a call to all Muslims worldwide to kill their Christian oppressors.

Although some historians claim that the call to *jihad* had no noticeable effect on the war because the Arabs eventually turned on the Ottomans in 1916 (with the help of Lawrence of Arabia and the British), it did have the effect of inciting the Ottomans to rid themselves of Christians within their empire, and as the Ottomans were now fighting against the Russians in Armenia, it would be the large Armenian population that would suffer the most.

The initial call for *jihad* was followed by another in 1915 with the publication and distribution of *A Universal Proclamation to All the People of Islam*—more commonly referred to as the 1915 *Fatwa*. This *fatwa* (religious ruling) was far more explicit in its instructions and included the line: "No one is exempted from it, not even the Muslims who dwell in the interior of the land of Russia."[8]

Enver Pasha disregarded German advice to not attack the Russians during the winter. He took personal command of the Ottoman 3rd Army and attacked the Russians at Sarikamis, where they were, literally, decimated (only 10 percent made it back). Enver Pasha publicly blamed the disaster on the Armenians for siding with the Russians and acting as a fifth column. A month later, Enver ordered that all Armenians serving in Ottoman military units be disarmed and sent to labor battalions. In April, the Ottoman propaganda drive against the Armenians went into full swing, and the Ottomans arrested 250 Armenian intellectuals and civic leaders on the same day that the Allies landed at Gallipoli. After that, what is commonly referred to as the Armenian Genocide proceeded in earnest. Characterized by massive deportations, massacres, and forced marches, the number of Armenian deaths is generally accepted to

8. National Society of Defense—The Seat of the Caliphate, *A Universal Proclamation to All the People of Islam*, The Seat of the Caliphate: The Ottoman Empire: Muta'at al Hairayet, 1313/1915, trans. American Agency and Consulate, Cairo, in U.S. State Department document 867.4016/57, March 10, 1915, page 23, as quoted in Coughlin, 173. Cited hereafter as 1915 *Fatwa*. The State Department kept this document classified until 1961 due to its inflammatory speech.

be about a million people (in addition to up to 700,000 Assyrians and 300,000 Greeks).[9]

THE 1915 *FATWA* AND THE MISSING TURKISH "FIFTH COLUMN"

The violence directed against the Armenians could not be justified by either of the Sultan's *fatwas*, which called on Muslims worldwide to rise up against their oppressors—and the Armenians living in the Ottoman Empire were hardly oppressing Ottoman Muslims. However, the *fatwas should have* resulted in a "Muslim" fifth column in the Caucasus, to create the same kind of chaos in the Russian rear areas as the Christians were allegedly causing the Ottomans. The second *fatwa* was considerably longer than the first and described in great detail exactly what the Sultan expected Muslims to do, explaining the different levels of war and the types of *jihad* he expected of the Muslims. In a section entitled "The Kinds of Holy War," the Sultan, relying on legally consistent and appropriate Islamic scholarly consensus,[10] explains the three types: the "Heart War," the "War of Speech," and "True War" (*jihad*). The "Heart War" is defined in the *fatwa* as "the lowest form of the war. And it is that the Muslim should believe in his heart that the infidels are enemies to him and to his religion, and that he should desire their disappearance and the destruction of their power . . . Verily *all the people of the Faith are under obligation to this amount without any question whatever*" [italics mine].[11] In other words, the Caliph specifically states that all Muslims must believe that non-Muslims are their enemies regardless of their circumstances.

When describing the third type, "True War," the Caliph lays out the three types of *jihad* that Muslims are to undertake given their current ability: individual *jihad*, *jihad* by bands, and *jihad* by campaign, which, if one reads the descriptions closely, sounds very much like the three phases of insurgency.[12] However, what is most interesting about the 1915 *Fatwa* is that the Caliph *specifically exempted the Caucasus from*

---

9. Sources range from 300,000 (Turkish Government), 600,000 (Arnold Toynbee—a British foreign officer stationed there at the time who did extensive research and whose figures were used by *Encyclopedia Britannica*) to 1.5 million (Armenian government).

10. "Scholarly Consensus" is an important term that denotes that scholars from all four of the classical Sunni schools of jurisprudence agree on a particular statement or interpretation based on their knowledge of the *Qur'an* and *Sunna*. Scholarly Consensus carries at least the same legal weight as a Supreme Court ruling does in the United States.

11. 1915 *Fatwa*, page 22, as quoted in Coughlin, 285.

12. Discussed further in Chapter 6. However, veteran Chechnya observers should note the name of the second form of *jihad*—by *bands*—and compare that with the term the Russians formerly used to describe the insurgents—"бандформирования"—(*band formirovania'*). This usage may actually legitimize the insurgents in the eyes of Muslims by using a term that essentially recognizes the insurgents as fulfilling a religious duty.

conducting jihad. Instead, the Caliph explained the War of Speech (the second type of war) and simultaneously exempted the mountaineers from *jihad* (the third type of war) when he wrote:

> The war of speech, and that may be with the tongue and the pen, and that in the condition of some of the Islamic kingdoms before this date. This applies in times like those of the Muslims of Caucasia which in a condition which did not admit of their being under obligation to do more than the war of speech, because their condition did not aid them to do more than this. And if there does not exist an excuse which permits contentment with the heart-war, the war of speech is strictly enjoined upon all Muslims, and it is the duty of the masters of the pen to dissipate the darkness of the infidels and of infidelity with their pens, and the people of eloquence with their tongues; and the war of speech today is a duty decreed on the Islamic world in its entirety. No one is excepted from it, *not even the Muslims who dwell in the interior of the land of Russia. But this kind of war is strictly enjoined upon all of them.*[13] (italics mine)

Why were the mountaineers only required to participate in the *war of speech* against Russia; why were they not required to fight as well? After all, the 1914 *Fatwa* (the initial call for global *jihad*, often referred to as the Berlin *Fatwa*) was issued because the German Kaiser asked the Sultan to declare *jihad* to generate Muslim uprisings within *British and French colonies.* Why not inside of Russia as well? Why decree jihad *only* to benefit your allies? The 1915 *Fatwa* was issued from the seat of the Caliphate and carried "the presumption that it is a legally sufficient document that accurately states the legal requirements of *jihad* that carried the force of law."[14] Why not level it against the Ottoman's main enemy in the war, its nemesis for 400 years *and the country from which it hoped to regain its former territories?* Why not use it to create a "fifth column" in the Caucasus?

From a purely strategic viewpoint, the mountaineers were in *exactly* the right place in which to conduct guerrilla operations that would strategically influence the main campaign a few hundred miles away. The Russians were fighting a tough campaign against the Germans and the Austrians on the Eastern Front, especially as the Germans made the Eastern Front their main effort in 1915, and could only commit 60,000 troops to the Caucasus campaign. Any sustained attacks in the immediate rear of current combat operations and *especially in the area around the main supply route (MSR—the Georgian Military Highway and Vladikavkaz)* would have drawn off a significant number of Russian troops from the main campaign in Anatolia. *If the Ottomans were so worried about the effect of an alleged Armenian fifth column that they designed a campaign to eliminate them, why would they not foment the*

---

13. 1915 *Fatwa*, page 23, as quoted in Coughlin, 286.
14. Coughlin, 171.

very same kind of unrest in Russia—especially when the Sultan was already writing a *fatwa* designed to weaken the English and the French?

I think the Sultan gives us the answer in the *fatwa* itself: at that point it was understood that the mountaineers simply didn't have the strength to incite insurrection within Russia. The Russian resettlement of a million Muslims to the Ottoman Empire or to Siberia had so weakened the Chechens, Dagestanis, Ingush, Circassians, and Tatars that they simply did not have the manpower or the strength to rebel—and even the Ottoman Sultan, in the midst of his own war, realized it. Did the idea that the Russians had a "fifth column" advantage (the Armenians) inside of the Ottoman Empire motivate the Ottomans to get rid of them? Ottoman records indicate that their reason for the forced marches and relocation program directed against the Armenians was specifically for this reason.[15] Some historians say that the Ottomans simply wanted to eradicate the Armenians out of hatred and that the military threat was merely pretext. If so, why did the Ottomans choose, as they called it in their own documentation, "relocation and settlement" of their Christian populations to get rid of the "threat?" Was it because they had seen firsthand the success that the Russians had using this same technique, a technique so successful that when the Sultan wrote the 1915 *Fatwa* against the English and the French that he couldn't use it against his own foe—the Russians? Although interesting in its own right as a previously unknown historical mystery, the real significance is, despite its immorality, the efficacy of resettlement as a means of quelling insurgencies.

THE BOLSHEVIK REVOLUTION AND THE CAUCASUS MOUNTAIN REPUBLIC

In 1916, the Allied forces retreated from Gallipoli, and the Ottomans were reinvigorated. For his actions at Gallipoli, Mustafa Kemal (Ataturk) began his meteoric rise, while Winston Churchill was demoted from First Lord of the Admiralty. Russia was in trouble, as Germany and Austria blockaded her via land, and the German Baltic fleet from the sea. Russia had desperately needed the Allies to win Gallipoli in order to open the straits and allow supplies to flow in from the West. On the Eastern Front the Germans were advancing, and each successful Russian attack was thwarted by an even more successful German counterattack. Only in the

---

15. Tetik, Dr. Alb. Ahmet, *Arsiv Belgeleriyle Ermeni Faaliyetieri 1914–1918*, Volume I, (Ankara, Turkey, Genelkurmay ve ATASE ve Genel Kurmay Denetleme Baskanligi Yayinlari.), available at http://www.tsk.mil.tr/8_TARIHTEN_Kesitler/8_1_Ermeni_-Sorunu/konular/ermeni_faalitetleri_pdr/Arsiv.

Caucasus, against the Ottomans, were the Russians successful, gaining additional troops from the Armenians who now flocked to their side.

By 1917, the Russian economy was close to collapse. Food shortages caused by the blockades and the alarming number of casualties led to civil unrest throughout Russia, culminating in what some sources call a "spontaneous" revolution in March (The Russians use a different calendar which accounts for the "February" Revolution). Czar Nicholas II was forced to abdicate and the Romanov Dynasty and Imperial Russia came to an end. A provisional government was formed between liberals and socialists and it created an elected executive branch and assembly. The new government tried to end the war immediately, but German demands were insuperable and it wasn't until February 1918 (the Treaty of Brest-Litovsk) that fighting on the Eastern Front finally ceased.

The collapse of the government created a power vacuum in Russia which impacted the mountaineers directly when the imperial viceroy was removed and the position replaced by smaller administrative bodies belonging to the provisional government. In the Caucasus, the news of the czar's abdication, the disorganization of the imperial army, and the resulting *lack of government control* were seized upon as a chance for the mountaineers to regain their independence. There were many who still remembered Shamil personally or had grown up listening to his legends; without an organized force to stop them, independence could finally be achieved. Despite the fact that the Sultan had thought them too weak to support his own efforts, the mountaineers found renewed energy for yet another revolution.

Immediately following the czar's abdication and collapse of the government, groups sprang up to fill the void. A Chechen congress elected a committee of sheiks and, in May, the first North Caucasus Congress met in Vladikavkaz to establish a central committee to act over an independent North Caucasus. In August, the Islamic religious leaders demonstrated their power to the secularists, who were espousing a democratically elected government, by bringing 20,000 supporters for the second North Caucasus Congress. Sheik Najmuddin Hotso (also referred to as Najm al-Din or Najjmutdin Gosinsky) called for establishing the *shari'a* and expelling the Russians. Another sheik, Uzun Haji, who would himself become the imam of the Caucasus Emirate in 1919, went to the conference to support Nahm al-Din and called for him to be proclaimed imam. The sheiks were not successful in convincing everyone to declare *shari'a*, but the congress did ratify a provisional government for the state.

The impotent new Russian government could not withstand the Bolshevik machinations against it. On November 7, 1917 (October in the Russian calendar), the Bolsheviks seized power and issued the "Declaration of the Rights of the Peoples of Russia." The declaration allowed for the right of secession, the right of self-determination, and freedom of religion—which the mountaineers interpreted as a clear guarantee to live under *shari'a*. Any possibility of forming a government with the Cossacks quickly died as the mountaineers, especially the Chechens and Ingush, swept out of the mountains to retake their ancestral lands from them. The Cossacks retaliated with a series of raids that culminated in the deaths of the most influential Naqshbandiyya sheik in the region and his closest followers.

In 1918, civil war between the "Reds" (Soviets) and the "Whites" (imperial supporters) engulfed Russia; but the conflict was actually far more complex, as the empire was essentially shattered into hundreds of small groups that would sometimes band together against a common foe and later split apart to fight with each other. The Soviet government could not defend against the Whites and the Germans at the same time and finally signed a peace treaty with the Central Powers, but relinquished huge amounts of land to secure the agreement.[16] The Ottomans regained all the territories lost during the war with Russia in 1878. Moreover, Transcaucasia (modern-day Georgia, Armenia, and Azerbaijan) were declared autonomous—meaning that the Russian Soviet Federative Socialist Republic (the Russian SFSR—as Russia was then called) did not have the right to defend those populations. In May 1918, the three countries declared themselves to be independent democratic republics, but were now ripe to be picked off one by one.

Enver Pasha had been forced by his allies to suspend operations against the Russians while the Central Powers were negotiating a treaty; now he had a free hand to finally realize his dream and immediately started to retake Transcaucasia. He formed a new army composed entirely of Turkic-speaking Muslims called the Army of Islam and kept marching until he reached the Caspian Sea and retook Baku.[17] As the Ottoman Army of Islam began moving into the region on the other side of the mountains, the Vainakh realized that their time had finally come. When Georgia, Azerbaijan, and Armenia declared themselves independent, the All-Mountaineer Alliance of the North Caucasus followed suit and on May 11, 1918, declared itself to be the Independent Democratic Republic of the Mountaineers of the Northern Caucasus (or

---

16. This was the reason the Germans gave permission to Vladimir Lenin to traverse Germany in a sealed diplomatic train car; they had rightfully guessed that Lenin's return would politically disrupt Imperial Russia and facilitate ending the war on their eastern front.
17. The Germans were upset by Enver Pasha's advance, believing that they had done most of the heavy fighting against the Russians and so deserved Transcaucasia as their reward. They sent troops to defend Georgia, which the Ottomans bypassed.

the Mountain Republic), which roughly encompassed the majority of present-day Stavropol, Abkhazia, Adygeia, Kabardino-Balkaria, North Ossetia, Chechnya, Ingushetia, and Dagestan. The new republic was recognized by Germany, Austria-Hungary, and of course, the Ottoman Empire. The mountaineers immediately reached out to the Ottomans and signed a treaty of "peace and friendship," and a small Ottoman force moved north into Dagestan and eventually into Chechnya.

Despite their seemingly divine deliverance, the Mountain Republic was not a cohesive, unified group, and the new mountaineer government's control over their region was spotty—for just as Russia was divided because of the Bolshevik message, so was the Caucasus. The Chechens were split between pro-Soviet members who believed that they could remain part of a larger federation, and a more conservative pro-independence faction. Additionally, other groups that had moved into the Caucasus during the past few hundred years created their own organizations, and many of them were aligned with the Bolsheviks. Ironically, it was the Cossacks who helped foster a Soviet-Mountaineer relationship. As the Bolsheviks gained more power, the Cossacks, being landowners and loyal retainers of the czar, realized that they had the most to lose if the Soviets came to power. The Cossacks began attacking the "Reds," who then called upon the Vainakh (who fell neatly into the category of dispossessed proletariat) to save Soviet power—and their newly won independence. What had previously been a cultural and religious clash had now become a class war. The Chechens and Ingush were anxious to regain their lost properties from the Cossacks, and the Soviets were eager to use them for their own ends, so for once, the Cossacks became the target of Russian power and the mountaineers the instrument of a government they despised.

Unfortunately for the mountaineers, the Ottoman victory was short-lived. Germany and the Austro-Hungarian Empire had also suffered great economic losses during the war, and when German attacks designed to end the war before the Americans could land in force failed (they did get close enough to Paris to use artillery and force the civilians to evacuate), the Central Powers knew that the end was near. As such, the Central Powers began suing for peace, beginning with Bulgaria. The Ottomans capitulated to the Allies in October and were forced to retreat to their pre-war boundaries, leaving the Caucasus forever—and the mountaineers without their ally and patron.

But things were to get even worse for the Ottomans in the next few years. As part of the Armistice of Mudros, the Ottomans were forced to accept Allied occupation of the forts that controlled the Dardanelles and Bosphorus straits. The Ottoman army was demobilized while its railways, ports, and other strategic points were taken over by the British and French, who used them to begin the partition of the

Ottoman Empire.[18] Ironically, the same forces who had stopped the Russians from taking Constantinople 30 years earlier and who had promised it to the Russian Empire at the start of the war, would now accomplish that feat themselves. French General Franchet d'Esperey began the occupation of Constantinople by riding into the city on a white horse— exactly as Mehmed the Conqueror had done in 1453 to mark the end of the Byzantine Empire. This humiliating defeat and occupation mobilized the Turkish national movement and would bring about the Turkish War of Independence in 1920, the downfall of the Ottoman Sultanate, and the modern Turkish state led by Ataturk (formerly Lieutenant Colonel Mustafa Kemal, the hero of Gallipoli). The 400-year struggle between the Ottoman and Russian Empires was finally over, and both had lost. The Sultan, Mehmed V, did not live to see his empire dismantled; he died on July 3, 1918, four months before the end of the war. Czar Nicholas II and his family were executed by the Bolsheviks two weeks later.

General Denikin and the Volunteer Army (White) had started moving into southern Russia in early 1918. The farther they moved into Cossack territory, the more recruits Denikin got, until his forces—now called the Armed Forces of South Russia—numbered about 40,000 and were organized into the Caucasus and Volunteer armies. In late 1918, Denikin defeated the Soviet 11th Army and moved into the North Caucasus. He wanted to use the relative safety of the region—the mountains at his back, the Caspian and Black Seas on his flanks, and major rivers like the Don

---

18. This partitioning is cause for much of the current unrest in the Middle East. To defeat the Ottomans, the British successfully fomented an Arab revolt, and the sons of Hussein (Sherif of Mecca and former commander of the Arab forces) were rewarded by establishing the Hashemite Dynasty in Jordan, and modern-day Iraq. Iraq's present-day borders, including a Shi'a majority in the south, and Sunni and Kurdish minorities in the center and north, are by design. By specifically denying the Kurds a separate state, the British tried to balance out the Shi'a in the south with the Kurds in the north to keep control over the oil fields. One of the principal architects of this plan, Gertrude Bell CBE (Commander of the British Empire) wrote to her father about her reasoning for this plan stating: "You can never have 3 completely autonomous provinces. Sunni Mosul must be retained as a part of the Mesopotamian state in order to adjust the balance . . . I don't for a moment doubt that the final authority must be in the hands of the Sunnis, in spite of their numerical inferiority; otherwise you will have a mujtahid-run, theocratic state, which is the very devil" (available at http://www.gerty.ncl.ac.uk/letters/l1380.htm; accessed on August 13, 2008). The French were responsible for Syria and Lebanon. Palestine was originally designed to have an international administration, but when the Balfour Declaration of 1917 (originally a classified British government policy statement) was made public by the Soviet government, it significantly changed the original plan. It stated, "His Majesty's Government views with favor the establishment in Palestine of a national home for the Jewish people, and will use their best endeavors to facilitate the achievement of this object, it being clearly understood that nothing shall be done which may prejudice the civil and religious rights of existing non-Jewish communities in Palestine."

and Volga to protect his front—to mount his attack on Moscow and the Bolsheviks. Initially, he left the mountaineers alone, setting up his own administration north of the mountains and controlling the lowlands, but not interfering. However, after he focused his main effort on attacking north toward Moscow with other White armies as support, he encountered heavy resistance and casualties and sent an order to his administrators in the south to draft all available men. The Mountain Republic refused to support the draft and Denikin, whose slogan was "one undivided Russia," decided that he first had to subjugate the mountaineers before turning his full attention on Moscow.[19]

Denikin has been vilified for allowing Communist rule to take hold in Russia because he split his forces trying to subdue the Caucasus and, in so doing, lost the war against the Reds. It is hard to defend Denikin's decision from a strategic standpoint, especially as Denikin was using his best forces to conduct major operations against the mountaineers at the "decisive moment of the civil war when the fate of Moscow itself hung in the balance."[20]

Denikin started by taking over Kabardia and Ossetia—areas traditionally loyal to the empire. Then in May he subdued Dagestan, the seat of the Mountain Republic's Government, thereby putting an end to the new state. At this point, the Sufi population was split. Sheik Nahm al-Din (a Dagestani Avar) believed that the Communists were the bigger threat while his former supporter, Sheik Uzun-haji (a Chechen), and his followers now believed that Denikin and the Whites posed the greatest risk to Mountaineer independence. Even though Uzun-haji had previously called for Nahm al-Din to be named imam, the majority of the population considered the Communists to be the lesser of two evils and rallied to his call to fight the Whites. The Bolsheviks flocked to the area to forge alliances with Uzun-haji, and once again promised the mountaineers that they would keep their earlier promise about freedom of religion and recognize their right to live under *shari'a*.

With those reassurances—and Denikin burning villages throughout Chechnya and Ingushetia—Uzun-haji (a Naqshbandiyya) broke with Nahm al-Din and declared himself to be the emir and imam of the new Emirate of the North Caucasus in September 1919, in Vedeno, Chechnya (Shamil's old capital). Uzun-haji was, as had been Shamil and Mansur before him, extremely well-respected for his personal reputation and

19. General Denikin was highly respected and led the last successful Russian campaign of WWI. He would later go into exile, first to France and later to New York, where he wrote books and lectured on military matters. He was buried with military honors in Detroit, and in 2005, Russian President Putin had his remains transferred to the Donskoy Monastery in Moscow.
20. Richard Pipes, *The Formation of the Soviet Union: Communism and Nationalism, 1917–1923* (Cambridge, MA: Harvard University Press, 1957), 215.

scholarly credentials. Thousands flocked to his call to expel the invader, including the secularists who had originally formed the Mountain Republic. The secular "professionals" formed the backbone of a highly sophisticated and organized government, with a strategic fiscal system that collected taxes, printed its own money, and had an advanced judicial system.[21] Soon, Uzun-haji had 10,000 mountaineers under his command to send against Denikin; by the end of September, the Whites had been defeated and driven out of the Emirate and the Soviet Union was saved. The Chechens, Dagestanis, and Ingush were once again independent; it lasted about six months.

THE SOVIET PERIOD

If the past 200 years of history with the Russians had been brutal, it was nothing compared to what would happen under the Soviets who, arguably, owed their very existence to the peoples of the North Caucasus. In 1920, the Soviet 11th Army had begun to counterattack Denikin's White Army after they had been driven out of the Emirate and only Grozny remained to be retaken. The Red Army was originally welcomed in the city as allies and liberators; but once the Red Army arrived, it never left. Uzun-haji died in March at age 90, and after moving on to retake Georgia, Armenia, and Azerbaijan, the Red Army—mostly comprised of ethnic Russians and commanded by former imperial officers—moved back into the Dagestani lowlands. There, it began to treat the mountaineers as poorly as the imperial forces had in the past. Shamil's grandson, Said-Bek, joined forces with Nahm al-Din and took the 10,000 men who had fought against Denikin and turned them against the 35,000-man Red Army— whom they had always considered to be the real threat. Using tactics learned from the imperial age, the Red Army moved methodically through the valley and surpassed its predecessor in savagery, killing or deporting everyone in its path.

In January 1921, Joseph Stalin went to Vladikavkaz to meet with representatives of the mountaineers. It would still be a few months before the Communists would finally defeat the White Army, and Stalin needed to quiet the Caucasus Front in order to free up the 9th and 11th Red Armies; he would not repeat Denikin's mistake. He offered amnesty to all those who were fighting, and told them that if the mountaineers recognized the Bolshevik government, then the Soviets would create an autonomous Soviet Mountain Republic. The mountaineers responded by saying that the Soviets would have to agree that the *shari'a* would be recognized as constitutional law, the lands taken from them by the Cossacks would be

---

21. Mairbek Vatchagaev, "Uzun Haji's and Dokka Umarov's Emirates: a Retrospective," *Chechnya Weekly* IX:10, March 13, 2008. Available at http://www.jamestown.org/chechnya_weekly.

returned to them, Arabic would be an official language, and the Soviets would not interfere with the internal affairs of the Mountain Republic. Stalin gave his word, and the majority of the mountaineers accepted his offer.

However, Nahm al-Din and Said-Bek didn't trust Stalin and continued to fight the Communists. In May, the Red Army overtook the last mountaineer stronghold at Gidatl (Dagestan) in an epic battle where "no more than 300 rebels with four machine guns were pitted against six infantry regiments and four cavalry squadrons. The Rebels fought to the end and there were virtually no survivors."[22] Nahm al-Din and Said-Bek escaped and continued to conduct guerrilla warfare against the Soviets until convinced to surrender and executed in 1925. The White Army was finally defeated in September 1921, and the Red Army moved back into the Caucasus and slowly but surely began to renege on all of its promises.

In early 1922, the Soviets appeared to be keeping their word and moved several Cossack settlements out of the Mountain Republic—giving the land back to the Vainakh. Additionally, they supplied seed and grain to the population during a famine to keep the locals quiet until they had consolidated their power. They made preparatory moves by severing Chechnya from the rest of the Mountain Republics (Dagestan was already separate) and establishing a Chechen Autonomous Oblast—which left Grozny and the surrounding oil fields under Soviet control. They would later use this divide-and-rule tactic to pacify each Chechen region in turn. The Soviets also moved in large numbers of troops and began to disarm the population. The insurgents conducted relatively large attacks and inflicted heavy losses on the Red Army. The Soviet commander at the time wrote: "The fear of repression and confiscation of property forces the rebels to defend their villages fiercely and defiantly, fighting over every bit of soil in every *aul*. In some villages even women and children are fighting against the Red Army. Such fighting takes time and inflicts on us colossal losses."[23] Some 10,000 Chechens were moved from the mountains into the lowlands during the period.

The Soviets continued to move carefully in 1923–24, convincing Sufi sheiks to join "revolutionary committees" in order to make it seem as though the Chechens were part of the government. However, the Soviets began the process of Sovietization by introducing the Latin alphabet (as the intermediate step to Cyrillic) and began cracking down on some Islamic practices—including the use of Arabic. The most influential sheik and the

22. Sebastian Smith, *Allah's Mountains, The Battle for Chechnya* (London: Taurus Parke, 2006), 56.
23. Russian State Military Archive (Rossiiskii Gosudarstvennyi Voennyi Archiv–RGVA), fond 39247, opis 1, delo 101. Telegram from the commander of the Terek-Dagestan Group with copies to Ordzhonikidze and Krov, Petrovsk, February 1, 1921, as quoted by Gammer, 138.

main Chechen advocate for *shari'a* were invited to visit Lenin in Moscow but were instead taken to Rostov-on-Don and strangled to death. For their part, the Chechen guerrillas continued to attack the Red Army, sometimes individually and sometimes in small bands.

In 1925, Soviet troops massed along the borders of Chechnya under the guise of participating in training maneuvers. They attacked Chechnya from all sides and began a concentrated campaign to disarm the citizens and destroy the last of the guerrillas. They surrounded the remaining leaders and forced them to surrender by dropping bombs on the civilians until they turned themselves in to prevent further casualties. Other influential leaders that had earlier supported the Soviets, but had now outlived their usefulness, were rounded up; some were deported and others were executed.

The Soviets cracked down on religion and began closing mosques and religious schools. "Popular Courts" were designated as the arbiter of law, and *shari'a* courts were abolished. This campaign was designed to transfer authority and legitimacy from the local religious leaders— most of whom had supported the Bolsheviks in the early days because of Soviet propaganda aimed at the poor—to the Soviet authorities.

In 1929, the Soviet apparatchiki swept into Chechnya and introduced collectivization by confiscating lands and allocating them to collective farms. Combined with the campaign against culture and religion, this new step to take away their lands spurred the Chechens into action, and revolts sprang up across the country. The uprisings gained momentum, and before too long the Chechens had seized Soviet power structures, institutions, and even refineries. The Chechens formed a provisional government and demanded that the Soviets keep their bargain with them— return their land and allow the practice of their traditions without Soviet interference. The Soviets sent in a special delegation from Moscow who listened to the Chechens' grievances, put on a show of conducting an investigation, and then told the Chechens that the local authorities had overstepped their bounds and had definitely not met the terms of the 1921 agreement. The delegation went on to say that the local authorities would be removed and dealt with accordingly and, in the future, the Chechens would settle their own internal matters. They advised the Chechens to go back home and relax, and sent a special unit of the GPU[24] to round up the

---

24. The State Political Directorate or Gosudarstvennoye Politicheskoye Upravlenie of the NKVD was the dreaded secret police of the early Soviet Republic. They were ruthless and brilliant—their most spectacular success being the "Trust" operation of 1924–1925 where they contacted Russian émigrés in Europe, convinced them they were setting up an organization to get rid of the Soviets, coerced large sums of money from them (and foreign governments), discovered the identities and addresses of all the major figures, lured them back into Russia, and executed them. They were responsible for the Gulag system, and the systematic persecution of the Orthodox Church and all other religious organizations in the Soviet Union.

"inept" Soviet authorities who had caused the problem. However, when they were done, the GPU went after the Chechen leaders as well. The leader of the Chechen uprising, Shita Istamulov, fought back like every other Chechen had before him and managed to hold off over 100 GPU members until Chechen reinforcements arrived. The Chechens destroyed the GPU unit, and Istamulov once again called the mountaineers to *gazavat* to expel the infidels from the Caucasus. Once again the Caucasus exploded.

In 1930, unable to stop the insurgency through subversive means, the Soviets literally sent everything they had into the region to "liquidate the anti-Soviet demonstrations." The Soviets threw airpower and artillery at the mountaineers, but by now the insurgency had spread to Dagestan, North Ossetia, Kabardia, Balkaria, and Karachai. The Soviets suffered staggering losses—sometimes an entire division at once.[25] The Central Committee of the RSFSR (Russian Soviet Federative Socialist Republic—as Russia was then known) decided that the Caucasus wasn't ready for collectivization. They called back the Red Army, condemned those who had attempted collectivization, granted amnesty to all the mountaineers, and flooded the area with large quantities of industrial goods at very low prices. The mountaineers took the bait and went back to their villages—convinced that they had shown the Soviets that it was just "too hard" to take the Caucasus.

But when the chief of the regional GPU met with Shita Istamulov, he handed over the official amnesty document with one hand, then shot him with the other. Istamulov managed to kill the GPU chief before he died, but that didn't prevent the GPU from beginning a very quiet campaign of rounding up troublemakers in the countryside and making them disappear—most of them were executed.[26] The Soviets managed this by taking family members as hostages until a suspect turned himself in (having received promises that he wouldn't be killed), then executing the suspect and sending the family to a Gulag in Siberia. The Vainakh responded by conducting disorganized guerrilla attacks and raids against the Soviets—especially the GPU and NKVD (The People's Commissariat for Internal Affairs, predecessor to the KGB and its current incarnation, the FSB) in retaliation for attacks against the locals.[27]

In 1934, the Soviets combined the Chechen Autonomous Oblast with the Ingush Autonomous Oblast and redrew the borders in order to

25. A. Avtorkhanov, "The Chechens and the Ingush during the Soviet Period and its Antecedents," in M. Bennigsen-Broxup (ed.), *The North Caucasus Barrier: The Russian Advance towards the Muslim World* (London: Hurst, 1992), 159. Also quoted in Gammer, 150, and Dunlop, 51.
26. Ibid., 161.
27. This is very similar to the situation in the region today. Most of the guerrilla attacks are directed against law enforcement personnel, with favorite targets being members of special police and FSB units that have been responsible for "disappearing" the locals.

dilute the Chechen and Ingush majorities. The Soviets also reintroduced collectivization of farms, and little by little began resettling the population onto them. However, the Communists kept at least one of their promises and the proportion of indigenous people serving in the regional and local bureaucracies reached 70 percent by 1937.[28]

THE GREAT PURGE

The Great Purge of 1937 (also referred to as the Soviet holocaust and the Great Terror) affected the entire population of the Soviet Union—and targeted Communist Party leaders everywhere. The official Communist figures put the number of deaths at 681,692; unofficial estimates put the number in the millions. Lenin had died; Stalin was in charge and was tired of hearing about Lenin, so he basically got rid of everyone who made him angry, who had been loyal to Lenin, or whom he couldn't trust. Stalin seemed to have been especially angry with the Chechens, and he and the NKVD exacted their revenge on the Chechen-Ingush Republic with the "General Operation for the Removal of Anti-Soviet Elements," which began the night of August 31, 1937. Over the course of the next few days, the NKVD arrested almost 14,000 men in Chechnya alone and every night there were mass executions; this represented 3 percent of the total population in one blow.[29] And it didn't stop; within a few months virtually every civil servant, every Communist Party member, and all leadership—even those outside of the republic—were rounded up, sentenced by a special NKVD tribunal, and either executed or sent to Siberia. Over the next two years, 35,000 people would be arrested, tried, and convicted by a special GPU tribunal called the "Extraordinary Commission of Three." The official census in 1937 shows the number Chechens living in the USSR to be 435,922; two years later the number was 400,344.

As for long-term counterinsurgency planning, this was not in the best overall interests of the state, as the purges destroyed the nascent Chechen and Ingush intelligentsia which were slowly being integrated into the Soviet system. They may have one day been able to lead the mountaineers away from parochialism toward the very civil society that the Soviets were advocating. Instead, the Chechen population once again took to the hills and filled the guerrilla units with thousands of new recruits who were anxious to attack the Soviets—their favorite targets being the NKVD and the Red Army.

---

28. Valery Tishkov, *Chechnya: Life in a War-Torn Society* (Berkeley: University of California Press, 2004), 23.
29. Avtorkhanov, 175.

WORLD WAR II AND STALIN'S REVENGE

In 1939, there was a cautious alliance between Stalin and Hitler, and with Stalin's blessing, Germany invaded Poland and started World War II. Three months later Stalin attacked Finland and, although the Red Army initially outnumbered the Finns 200 to 1 in tanks, 30 to 1 in aircraft, and 4 to 1 in men (the percentages would go up dramatically as the war went on), the Finns mounted one of the most heroic resistance efforts in history and inflicted huge losses on the Red Army.[30] The Great Purge had eliminated close to 50 percent of the Army officers and 80 percent of the senior leadership. Thus, the new "senior" leadership had either been junior officers only two years before—or mid-level officers who were spared because of their loyalty to the party and not because of their military prowess.

The Finnish resistance, and the weaknesses it exposed in the Red Army, inspired another full-fledged revolt in the Caucasus that started in Balkaria and Karachai and soon spread to Chechnya-Ingushetia. The movement was led by former Communist Party member, poet, and playwright, Hassan Izrailov, who had earlier been imprisoned by the Communists for writing about government abuses in Chechnya. Released in 1934, he was thrown in jail a second time in 1937 for warning the Communists that if they didn't change their policies, there would be a general uprising. Released again in 1939, he proved himself prescient and started the uprising himself. Within a few months, Izrailov's forces controlled large parts of Chechnya and despite Finland's eventual loss to the USSR, the resistance continued to grow. Izrailov's insurrection was significant because it is *the first time* in the long history of the North Caucasus insurgency that the call to arms was not made by a religious authority, and it is the first time that the war leader did not call the people to *gazavat* or *jihad*—the first time that the ideology was not based on Islam.[31] The Sufi sheiks were still an important part of Izrailov's organization and commanded large numbers of insurgents, but they were now *part* of the organization instead of leading the insurgency.

In 1940, Izrailov convened a national congress which proclaimed the establishment of the "Provisional Popular Revolutionary Government of Chechnya-Ingushetia" with Israilov as their leader. Finland finally lost the Winter War—as well as 9 percent of its territory and 20 percent

---

30. Finland held out until March 1940. The Finns showed the rest of the world how to fight in the winter and how to take advantage of the Soviets. Corporal Simo Häyhä was credited with 542 confirmed sniper kills in four months. Because the temperature averaged 40 degrees below zero for a good portion of the conflict, the heavily outgunned Finns developed the tactic of destroying Soviet field kitchens instead of attempting large scale attacks on Soviet troops—which had devastating effects.

31. Note, however, that all the prerequisites for insurgency were present: Lack of Government Control (the Red Army is weak), vulnerable population (the purges), available leadership (educated Muscovite Israilov), but now for the first time the ideology became secessionist and traditionalist.

of its industrial capacity to the USSR. Despite its victory in the Winter War, the Red Army's weaknesses had been exposed; convinced that the Wehrmacht could beat the Communists, Hitler began planning the invasion of Russia a few months after Finland's capitulation.

Almost a year later, in June 1941, Hitler double-crossed Stalin and launched Operation Barbarossa. The plan was to seize everything from Archangelsk in the north to Astrakhan on the Caspian Sea. Once they reached the "A-A line," the Nazis would control the Black Sea and the Crimea, all of the USSR's industrial centers, major food production centers, and all of its oil industry—centered around Baku and Grozny. The Nazis advanced rapidly, and Stalin was forced to evacuate all heavy industry deep into the interior of the USSR. He relocated 226 factories to the Caucasus and built railroads between Moscow and Transcaucasia—creating a new industrial center in the region. Despite this economic gift to the region, Stalin hadn't forgotten his hatred of the mountaineers, and when there weren't German Army targets close at hand, the Communists routinely carpet bombed Chechnya-Ingushetia to try and destroy the remaining insurgents.

In February 1942, another Chechen insurgent group led by Mairbek Sheripov took control of the southwest mountains of Chechnya-Ingushetia and linked up with Izrailov's forces, giving the insurgency control of almost the entire mountainous southern region. To the west, the Germans had captured Ukraine, and in anticipation of further German advances, Izrailov and Sheripov issued a joint "Appeal to the Chechen-Ingush People," stating that the Germans would only be welcome if they recognized Caucasian independence.[32] The NKVD reported at the time that almost 25,000 men were ready to rise up at Izrailov's orders, cells were active in Grozny, Gudermes, and Malgobek (Ingushetia), and high-ranking government officials were communicating with the Germans.[33]

Anxious for quicker results, Hitler divided Army Group South into Army Groups A and B. Army Group B continued east to Stalingrad where it would become embroiled in that epic battle, while Army Group A turned south and conducted "Operation Edelweiss" to seize the Caucasus. Because the objective was the oil fields, the Germans also took 15,000 oil industry workers with them to immediately restart production. The Germans strongly believed in the idea of a Caucasian fifth column, and to prepare the way for the German Army, the *Abwehr* (German intelligence unit similar to the U.S. OSS or British SOE) planned a special operation designated as "North Caucasus Special Commando [operation] 'Shamil'" (Nordkaukasische Sonderkommando Schamil). The plan was to parachute special forces behind the lines at several points in Chechnya, link up with partisans,

---

32. Avtorkhanov, 183.
33. Gammer, 161. However, it was also possible that the NKVD fabricated documents for later purges.

seize the Grozny petroleum refinery, and defend it from destruction by a retreating Red Army until the German First Panzer Army arrived.[34]

Rostov-on-Don (The Gates of the Caucasus) fell to the Germans on July 23, and within 11 days, the Germans had moved another 200 miles south and captured Stavropol. From there the Germans spread out along the northern slope of the Caucasus Mountains, and within a month captured (from east to west) Novorossiysk, Maikop, Pyatigorsk, and Mozdok (one of the original forts established by Yermolov). The retreating Red Army blew up the oil wells in Maikop, confirming German suspicions that the Red Army would destroy any important petroleum infrastructure they could not control—and highlighting the need to secure the all-important refinery in Grozny *before* the Red Army retreated. Operation "Shamil" commenced on August 25, 1942, with four squads of commandos (less than 50 total) landing in different *auls* throughout Chechnya. They succeeded in seizing the oil refinery in Grozny, but were forced to retreat when the German Panzer Army was stopped just nine miles away from the Chechen-Ingush border (55 miles from Grozny).

Although the Chechen insurgents had drawn significant manpower away from the Soviet defense, even the addition of two Dagestani insurrections (Novolakskaya and Dylym) could not prevent the Red Army from halting the German offensive. And even though the German commandos linked up with Izrailov's forces, the inability of the German Army to break the Soviet line and liberate the mountaineers took much of the fight out of them. The line stabilized at Mozdok for two months—a disaster for the insurgents. The Germans could not mount offensive operations because the fight at Stalingrad had siphoned off too much of their strength, so the Red Army took advantage of the situation and mercilessly pounded both the German lines and suspected insurgent positions with artillery and aerial bombing. With the front line mired directly in Chechnya-Ingushetia, and with the Germans unable to do anything but hold their own positions, the Soviet North Caucasus Front was free to use its massive size and airpower to regain control of the region. When the Red Army went on the offensive against the Germans in early 1943, the insurgency had been defeated and many Vainakh had crossed the lines to join the Germans. Others fled to the mountains to hide and conduct guerrilla attacks—some for decades.[35]

Not all the Chechens and Ingush supported the Germans. Many of them enlisted in the Red Army and fought against both the insurgents and the Germans. Stalin didn't see it that way.

---

34. Franz Kurowski, *The Brandenburger Commandos, Germany's Elite Warrior Spies in World War II* (Mechanicsburg, PA: Stackpole Books, 2005), 207–209.
35. Izrailov was hunted continuously by the NKVD. He was finally killed by two of his own bodyguards (for money from the NKVD) in December 1944.

Operation "Lentil" (Chechevitsa)

On February 23 (Soviet Army Day), 1944, more than 120,000 special troops (NKVD, N'KGB, and SMERSH)[36] began the resettlement of the entire Chechen and Ingush populations. They had come to the region a month before dressed in normal Red Army uniforms and billeted themselves among the people in each village saying that they were going to repave roads and bridges. The newspapers continued the disinformation campaign as well. On the evening of February 22nd, the troops celebrated Soviet Army Day with the people; later that night they surrounded the villages to prevent escape. At dawn the villagers were brought into the village center, read the order of deportation, and given 30 minutes to pack no more than 45 pounds per family. They were stuffed into cargo trucks, taken to the train stations, and packed into cattle cars so tightly that there wasn't room to sit down. They traveled almost a month with little food or water; typhus broke out, and many died along the way.

The majority of the Vainakh were sent to Kazakhstan; the remainder to Kyrgyzstan. Once they arrived they did not have adequate housing or supplies, their food rations were often appropriated by the local Communist administrators, they were forced to do hard physical labor, and were prohibited from traveling more than three kilometers from their settlements. They were the lucky ones. Those Vainakh that had been too weak to travel or lived in villages that were too remote were simply killed, the villages burnt down, and the area put off limits. Official NKVD statistics show that 145,000 died just during the deportation years, although most historians place the figure much higher. No official figures are available for the dead during their exile, but some sources speculate that 60–65 percent of those that had been resettled died in the first few years.[37]

Stalin's desire to rid himself of the Chechens and Ingush culminated in literally erasing them from existence, history, and the map. Most of the towns and districts were renamed with Russian names, immigrants from other parts of the Soviet Union were brought in to repopulate the area, and a new state (oblast) was created and called "Grozny," which was considerably smaller than Chechnya-Ingushetia had once been. The surrounding territories of Dagestan, Georgia (Stalin's homeland), and North Ossetia were given large parts of what had been Chechnya and

---

36. SMERSH (Smert' Shpionam or "Death to Spies") was a real Red Army counter-intelligence unit responsible for securing the rear lines from partisans, saboteurs, and spies, and arresting conspirators, mutineers, "traitors, deserters, spies, and criminal elements" at the combat front. For a while it was under Stalin's direct control. Ian Fleming based his nemesis for James Bond on SMERSH.

37. There are many excellent books that specifically discuss the deportations and give accounts of the victims and their deprivations. There is not sufficient space in this book to give this episode the attention it deserves.

Ingushetia, and the two nations literally ceased to exist. During the period of forced exile, there were no reports of major Vainakh guerrilla attacks, demonstrating why resettlement has been used throughout history as a counterinsurgency technique.

In 1953, Stalin died and Communist Party leaders feared that the new First Secretary, Lavrenty Beria (another Georgian), would have them all killed to secure his own power. Beria had been the head of the NKVD and chiefly responsible for the Great Purges—Vyacheslav Molotov's memoirs state that Beria also admitted to poisoning Stalin. What had made Beria so indispensible to Stalin was now used against him, and he was arrested and later executed. Nikita Khrushchev eventually rose to power, and the Soviet Union began to relax a little—especially after Khrushchev began to dismantle Stalin's cult of personality. During this period, some of the Vainakh began infiltrating back to Chechnya. By 1955, large numbers of them were returning to the Grozny Oblast and demanding the return of their homes from those that had occupied them for the past 11 years. When they were unable to take their homes back, the Vainakh "would make dugouts next to them and settle in, and in an immensely symbolic move, they also brought back the remains of relatives who had died in Central Asia, so that they could find rest in the land of their ancestors."[38]

Khrushchev, doing everything he could to be as anti-Stalin as possible but saddled with his legacy nonetheless, was faced with the problem of the Vainakh, who would not accept anything less than a return to their ancestral lands and the removal of the settlers that Stalin had brought in years before. All attempts to placate the Vainakh failed; they were offered incentives to stay in Central Asia but they kept returning to Chechnya and Ingushetia in droves, creating a difficult and volatile situation, as most of them did not have a place to live or any kind of employment.

After Khrushchev's (now) famous "secret speech" to the Communist Party Congress, the Central Committee moved in 1956 to resurrect the national autonomy of the populations that had been deported—the Chechen and Ingush included. The Soviets tried to get concessions from the Chechens and Ingush so that they would not attempt to reclaim their old homes and properties, but many of the Vainakh refused to sign. The government planned a phased approach to bring the Vainakh back, but many of them returned as quickly as they could arrange transportation. Settlements and working cooperatives were created in the lowlands and around Grozny to encourage the Vainahk to integrate into the new reality that had overcome their old homeland and prevent them from moving back into the mountains and their traditional

---

38. Dunlop, 76.

strongholds where bands of insurgents still roamed and occasionally attacked the authorities. Additionally, the Soviet government now had to go back and redraw the administrative boundaries to include the new Chechen-Ingush Autonomous Soviet Socialist Republic (ASSR), but in such a way as to ensure that the returning Vainakh were still a minority of the population, thus leaving control of the region to the Russian and Cossack populations. Not surprisingly, large-scale clashes broke out between those who had moved into Chechnya in 1944 at the invitation of the government and the returning mountaineers, but the insurgency appeared to have died—as guerrilla attacks were few and far between.

For the next 30 years, Chechnya was quiet. The Soviets appeared to have finally completed the subjugation of the Caucasus. However, in hindsight, it is possible to see that the Chechens hadn't really given up—they might not have been actively fighting, but they had reverted to a condition known as "passive resistance." In insurgency terms, we are talking about Phase I—the latent and incipient stage where an "underground" movement is formed, along with parallel legal and social institutions. In the Muslim faith, this is referred to as the "war of thought." This is not to say that an active insurgency movement was being directed along a particular path. In the vacuum of alternatives in which the Vainakh found themselves, many adopted the attitude that the Soviets would never take care of them, and they would therefore have to find a way to take care of themselves.

The Soviets had used a "coerce behavior" strategy prior to the 1956 "rehabilitation," and had they now attempted the "change minds" strategy during the peaceful period that ensued, they might have ended the insurgency once and for all. However, this was not the Communist way, and they continued the "coerce behavior" strategy, designed to keep the population weak, which merely gave the insurgency time to rebuild and gain strength. This is the primary drawback with military-based "coercion" campaigns: they produce short-term results, but they do nothing to take care of the problem. The only way to stop the Chechens from fighting for their independence would have been to *give them a reason to stop wanting independence* or to kill them all. Although Stalin might not have balked at the latter, Khrushchev was a different sort of man. Yet despite the potential advantages of the Soviet system, the Communists never made it worthwhile for the Vainakh to even consider thinking about being anything other than Chechens and Muslims—meaning that it was merely a matter of time before the conflict would erupt again.

In practical terms, the Soviets continued to encourage the Vainakh to think in terms of "us against them"; so much so that the Vainakh went about creating underground communities and organizations. Instead of growing a blue-collar middle class that was fully invested in the economy with resources and wealth that would be lost in the event of insurrection, the Soviets continued to bring more ethnic Russians to the area, gave them the most prestigious and best-paying jobs in the oil industry, and kept the Vainakh a minority by restricting their representation in local governments.[39] It wasn't until Gorbachev's Perestroika in the late 1980s that local administrations weren't run by Russians or until a Chechen was finally named the leader of the Chechen-Ingush ASSR.

The Chechens responded to this lack of power in their traditional way. They produced three times as many children as the outsiders, relied exclusively on their clans for mutual support, and developed underground (criminal and black market) organizations that eventually infiltrated governments and businesses, creating a loose command structure that became especially powerful during the Brezhnev years of corruption.

Another part of the Sovietization program from the 1930s to the 1980s was to eradicate religion. But attempts to convince the mountaineers that Islam and Sufism were bad fell on deaf ears. Lectures and decrees claiming Communism had saved the population from a life of backwardness (bereft of the benefits of modernity), only convinced the Vainakh that the Soviets were immoral and their system illegitimate. In trying to pretend that the earlier Soviet repressions had never happened, by never offering an apology, and never publicly acknowledging the events of the early Soviet period, the Vainakh were never given a chance to come to grips with those events themselves and "move on" as a society.

As such, the only legitimate authority for the Vainakh continued to be Sufism, and the more Soviets tried to get rid of the Sufis, the more the Sufi brotherhoods extended their control. During this period there were "large parts of the Chechen-Ingush ASSR [where] the Sufi sheikhs and elders regulated life according to *shari'a* and the *'adat*, not the Soviet legal system."[40] These were not isolated communities. Chechens responded to Soviet attempts to eradicate their religion with the strongest adherence to religion of all the Muslim populations within the USSR; and this did not change over time. In 1970, according to Soviet statistics, 90 percent of all Chechens were still getting married in the Muslim faith, 99 percent were

---

39. What I refer to as the "blue-collar effect." I believe that one of the most important counterinsurgency factors is the strength of the middle class. As the leaders of insurgency movements are often from the educated, intellectual elites (the "haves"), and the fighters are usually from the underprivileged segments of society (the "have-nots"), what can keep a population from tipping to insurgency is the strength and percentage of the middle class (the "have-somethings"), which is actively engaged in making a living and caring for their families. People who have something to lose do not advocate for radical change, and when a family member attracts bad attention, it imposes legal and financial penalties as well as societal opprobrium; thus a society is more apt to "police itself."

40. Gammer, 196.

given religious funerals, and religious holidays were still celebrated by the majority of the population.[41] Twenty years later in 1993—just prior to the 1994 Russo-Chechen War, 98 percent of the Chechen population considered themselves to be religious and 74 percent said they both believed in and practiced their religion. Even today, most Chechens still observe Ramadan and the current president, Ramzan Kadyrov, released a statement in 2008 exhorting all the Chechens to more closely observe the fast during Ramadan.[42]

The Soviets also conducted campaigns in the Chechen highlands until the mid-1960s to keep the mountain villages free of people. The Chechens responded by slowly taking back the Cossack villages in the north—and then repopulated the mountain villages once the Soviets stopped their campaigns. As for the Ingush, they have never been able to regain their beloved Prigorodnyi Raion directly to the east of Vladikavkaz, which was given to North Ossetia following Stalin's dissolution of Ingushetia in 1944. The Ingush returning from Central Asia were denied access to their homes in Prigoridnyi, but they have never given up hope. In the 1970s they protested heavily for its return, and in 1992 fought a short but bloody battle with the North Ossetians; the Soviets supported the Ossetians.

It is generally believed that it was Prigorodnyi that finally split the Vainakh cousins and prompted Ingushetia to separate itself from Chechnya prior to the 1994 war of independence. The Ingush believed that by not supporting the Chechens, they would finally gain Russia's support for regaining their lost territory from North Ossetia. This historic split between the two cousins went unrewarded by the Russians, and Prigoridnyi is still a source of contention in the region.[43]

For 50 years after the resettlement, the Caucasus was quiet—one of the longest periods of peace the region had seen since the 1700s. It appeared that the Vainakh were changing and adapting to Soviet life, but that was wishful thinking. The peoples of the North Caucasus were merely responding to the external pressures placed upon them. As they had done ever since the Russians had appeared in the Caucasus, they waited. They turned inward toward their families, their clans, and Sufism, growing stronger in number, organization, and belief in the idea that the Soviet (and later Russian) government did not present a future for them.

---

41. Yaacov Ro'I, *Islam in the Soviet Union: From World War II to Gorbachev* (London: Hurst, 2000), 81–82, quoted in Gammer, 192.
42. Interfax, September 3, 2008, http://www.interfax-religion.com.
43. Not only did the Russians not help the Ingush regain their territory, they also reneged on their promise to develop a new capital city—Magas. To add insult to injury, after the Russian-Georgian war in 2008, Russia put South Ossetian refugees into Prigorodnyi Raion. Ingushetia is now one of the centers of the insurgency.

CHAPTER 5

The Chechen Republic of Ichkeria

By the 1980s, the Soviet Union was beginning to show visible cracks as Mikhail Gorbachev (general secretary of the Communist Party of the Soviet Union) began a series of domestic reforms designed to stimulate the economy, known as *glasnost* (openness) and *perestroika* (restructuring). In early 1990, under Gorbachev's direction, the Central Committee of the Communist Party agreed to give up its monopoly of power and, soon after, the 15 republics of the USSR began conducting their first ever democratic (or at least truly competitive) elections. Gorbachev continued to move forward with what he thought was best for the Soviet Union, and his reward for allowing greater freedom of speech was to become the target of constant public criticism.

A similar dynamic was operating in the Chechen-Ingush Republic, and after the republic's Communist Party raised the issue of officially recognizing the deportation and genocide of 1944, the *Russian*-born first party secretary of the republic was fired. Surprisingly, he was not replaced by an even more strident Communist, and for the first time a Chechen—Doku Zavgayev—was selected to lead the Chechen-Ingush Republic. Through skillful maneuvering, Zavgayev managed to become a member of the Communist Party's Central Committee, and by early 1990 he had become the most powerful Chechen since the Communists had taken over.

During that same time, a group of reformers within Chechnya-Ingushetia began to speak out about creating a sovereign Vainakh republic. In May 1990, Zelimkhan Yanderbiyev (poet, scholar, children's book author, president of Chechnya after Dudayev, strident Islamist, and accused terrorist) formed the Vainakh Democratic Party—the first party devoted to creating an independent state. They were emboldened by Gorbachev's *glasnost* and freedom of speech, as well as the Baltic Republics, which by

1988 had already established independence movements and on the 50th anniversary of the Molotov-Ribbentrop Pact (August 1989), formed a 600-kilometer human chain that stretched from Tallinn, Estonia, to Vilnius, Lithuania, and represented the united wish of the Baltics for independence.

The real backstory to all of this maneuvering, however, was the contest being waged between Gorbachev and Boris Yeltsin, the "leader" of Russia—technically chairman of the Presidium of the Supreme Soviet of the RSFSR (Russian Soviet Federative Socialist Republic), by far the biggest and most influential of all the Soviet republics. The Soviet Union was a slightly deceiving construct; the Bolsheviks took over the Russian Empire in 1917 and then recaptured areas that declared independence, and granted them "statehood" within the USSR to give the entire endeavor validity and legitimacy. For all intents and purposes, the Soviet Union was a new name for the territory that had been known as the Russian Empire. For its 70-year reign, the Soviet Union, in all practicality, had been Russia and Russia had been the Soviet Union. Now however, Yeltsin was using his position to challenge that old paradigm. There was bad blood between Yeltsin and Gorbachev, and had Yeltsin not been selected as the president of "Russia" a few years earlier, it would not have been a cause for concern. In the past, the "Russian president's" post had traditionally been little more than ceremonial, as "Russia" didn't really have any autonomy under the Soviet Union. It was just a large "state" responsible for its own internal administration.

Unfortunately for Gorbachev, during *perestroika* and *glasnost*, Yeltsin had become a popular figure. And, because the Supreme Soviet was split between hard-line Communists and reformers, Gorbachev became more and more impotent because he wasn't perceived as a dedicated reformer, while Yeltsin gained more and more support. Yeltsin's "Russia" declared sovereignty from the Soviet Union, and Yeltsin resigned from the Communist Party so as not to be bound by party connections and to prove he was a "real" reformer to the general population. A contest now ensued where each man tried to weaken the other through a series of laws and counter-laws. Yeltsin sought to seize power by eliminating Gorbachev's position, and Gorbachev fought back by attempting to do the same thing to him.

On April 26, 1990, Gorbachev signed USSR Law No.1457-I, which made the rights of autonomous republics within the Soviet Union (Chechnya-Ingushetia among others) equal to those of Soviet republics, like Russia, Ukraine, or Lithuania. Hoping to gain their support against Yeltsin, Gorbachev had now increased the number of entities within the USSR that owed allegiance to him personally because the law took regions like Chechnya away from Russia and made them federal subjects—giving the Chechen-Ingush Republic *equal status* with Russia. This law was the legal basis for Chechen independence once the Soviet Union dissolved. It gave the Chechen-Ingush Republic a legal right to claim independence in the same way that the Baltics, the "Stans," and the Trans-caucasus countries could. Conversely, when Moscow later invaded Chechnya to regain "its" territory, the act was illegal according to international law.

Following the passage of Law No.1457-I, some autonomous republics began to assert their newly won sovereignty—Tatarstan being the most active and, as far as Russia was concerned, the most dangerous. After all, if Russia, Georgia, and the Baltic republics could declare autonomy based on ethnic and nationalistic claims, why couldn't republics *within* Russia (that had now been given equal status) claim the same rights? This fight between Gorbachev and Yeltsin created a constitutional crisis that would cause the break-up of the Soviet Union and threaten to break apart Russia in much the same manner—as Russia itself was only slightly more homogenous than the Soviet Union. Yeltsin had to somehow figure out how to knock out the superstructure of the Soviet Union without causing the foundation of Russia to collapse in the process.

Yeltsin attempted to co-opt the republics, and in August 1990 famously called upon them to "take as much sovereignty as you can swallow." Yeltsin hoped to quell the budding independence movements in his breakaway Russian provinces by giving regional governors another option besides secession; it worked in many republics because it allowed them to take advantage of the Russian superstructure, while still being essentially independent and keeping 100 percent of local revenues.

In November, Gorbachev tried to "one-up" Yeltsin and drafted a new [Soviet] "Union Treaty" which would confer rights to "republics that are part of other republics" and allow them to participate in the Union Treaty with the same status as a Soviet republic. This treaty draft was disseminated to the citizens of the Soviet Union before the nationwide referendum to vote on whether or not to remain a part of the Soviet Union. Just as Yeltsin was trying to eliminate Gorbachev's position, Gorbachev now tried to do the same and make Yeltsin superfluous. His new Union Treaty would maintain the Soviet superstructure, but break up Russia into 85 little pieces—meaning Gorbachev was offering Chechnya the opportunity to have the same power as Ukraine or Kazakhstan or Russia.[1] He hoped that by offering Tatarstan and Chechnya and all the other republics in Russia a framework through which they could be autonomous—but remain in the same economic and security framework of the *Soviet Union*—they would choose the Soviet Union over Russia.

This battle between Gorbachev and Yeltsin resonated throughout all of the Soviet Union, but in the Chechen-Ingush Republic the looming constitutional crisis was seen primarily as a sign that the current government

---

1. The Soviet Union had 15 Soviet republics which became independent countries when the Soviet Union dissolved: Russia, Ukraine, Moldova, Belarus, Estonia, Latvia, Lithuania, Georgia, Armenia, Azerbaijan, Kazakhstan, Uzbekistan, Kyrgyzstan, Turkmenistan, and Tajikistan.

was weak. The Vainakh were not thinking in terms of which side to choose; for many Chechens, as soon as they heard the words "take all the autonomy you can swallow," the only option was complete independence. It is significant to note that this view was not purely emotional or nationalistic; ignoring for a moment the bitter memories ingrained in the Chechen psyche, the Chechens, *as a nation*, also ardently believed that Chechnya would be better off economically as an independent state and had no need for any kind of shared economic sphere. They believed that Chechnya-Ingushetia could become a "Caucasian Kuwait" because of its high-quality oil reserves and its petroleum-processing infrastructure.[2] And so, while the rest of the Soviet Union was debating the new Union Treaty, in accordance with Law No.1457-I, the autonomous republic of Chechnya-Ingushetia convoked a national congress and invited recently promoted Air Force Major General Dzhokhar Dudayev to come to Chechnya-Ingushetia and lead the nascent nationalist movement.

Ironically, it had been Zavgayev who had convinced the Soviets to promote Dudayev to general a few years earlier. Now that he had created a national hero for the Chechens, Zavgayev was now competing for power with his own creation. A few days after the congress, the Chechen-Ingush ASSR's Supreme Soviet published the "Declaration of State Sovereignty of the Chechen-Ingush Republic," and a few days later (on December 1), General Dudayev, although still the garrison commander of the Soviet Air Base in Tartu, Estonia (as well as the division commander of the associated Soviet Air Wing of Strategic Bombers), accepted the position as chairman of the executive committee of the Chechen National Congress.

The conditions and prerequisites for insurgency were all in place: a central government that had lost control, available alternative leadership, a vulnerable population, and multiple ideologies—any one of which was sufficient to move the people toward secession. Throughout the first half of 1991, a continuous power struggle raged throughout the entire Soviet Union—at both the national and local levels. Zavgayev (Yeltsin's man) and Dudayev vied for power in Chechnya, while Gorbachev fought with Yeltsin. Gorbachev was more worried about Zavgayev, while Yeltsin was more worried about Dudayev—but, at this point, everyone was more worried about Tatarstan, or a civil war between the Ingush and the North Ossetians (over the Prigorodnyi Region), or the Georgians and the Abkhaz, and especially the Armenians and the Azeris (over Nagorno-Karabakh) than they were about the Chechens.

After all, by this time, virtually all the Soviet and Russian republics were clamoring to swallow more of the promised autonomy, and the Chechens

---

2. Robert W. Schaefer, "The Imagined Chechen Economy," available online at http://jsis. washington.edu/ellison/reecasnwconf2008.shtml, presented at the 2008 NW REECAS conference. The economic factor played a critical role in the movement towards independence. Although not a "framed" argument, it was nonetheless fatally flawed and therefore used erroneously by the Chechens to further their cause for independence.

were simply one of many. By March, Dudayev had resigned his commission and moved to Grozny to take over the day-to-day operations of the Chechen National Congress (which had no official power, but plenty of support), and when Yeltsin made his next move against Gorbachev in April by getting the Russian Supreme Soviet to pass a law on the "Rehabilitation of Repressed Peoples," he, like many other Chechens, saw it as an opportunity to more aggressively seek independence.

In May 1991, Dudayev declared Zavgayev and the Supreme Soviet of the republic to be illegitimate, and stated that "his" Chechen National Congress would assume power until a general election could be organized. Despite Dudayev's announcement, both the Chechen-Ingush Supreme Soviet and Zavgayev continued business as usual and, as a response to Dudayev, banned all opposition activity and arrested some opposition leaders.

In June 1991, Yeltsin won 57 percent of the popular vote in the democratic elections for president of the Russian Republic—defeating Gorbachev's candidate, Nikolai Ryzhkov, who had managed only 16 percent. This election was important for many reasons: first, it was the death knell for Communism inasmuch as it was a referendum against Gorbachev and his desire to keep the Soviet Union together. Moreover, in Chechnya-Ingushetia, it was seen by Dudayev and the radicals as a signal to push ahead with their agenda; after all, Yeltsin had promised "as much sovereignty as they could swallow," and Yeltsin had won.

In his memoirs, Zelimkhan Yanderbiyev states that two weeks after the election, Yeltsin sent an unofficial representative to meet with him (Yanderbiyev was deputy chairman of the National Congress at the time). Now that Yeltsin had won the election, Yanderbiyev and the nationalists were told to back off, and Yeltsin's representative gave clear indications that Russia would not support Chechen self-determination: "He openly threatened the use of any and all force and measures in order to cut off the attempts of Chechnya to separate, 'up to a return to the situation of the middle of the previous century [i.e., the Caucasus War],' as he put it."[3] However, Dudayev (the nationalist), Yanderbiyev

---

3. Zelimkhan Yanderbiyev, *V preddverii nezavisimosti* (Groznyi: author publication, 1994), 37, and Dunlop, 99. Unlike most of the Chechens, Yanderbiyev did not fight during most of the 1994 war, seeing his role as more of the spiritual and intellectual architect of the movement. As such, he spent the years of the war writing about the events of the independence movement and exhorting Muslims worldwide to support the Chechens. He was a strong proponent of an Islamic state and was later instrumental in securing Taliban Afghanistan's recognition of Chechnya's independence. He had ties to radical Islamists and was eventually put on the UN Security Council's Blacklist of Al Qaeda-related terrorism suspects. He later served as vice president under Dudayev and interim president once Dudayev was killed. However, his vision of an Islamic Chechnya was defeated when he came in a distant third in elections—behind Maskhadov and Shamil Basayev. He was assassinated in Qatar in 2004 by Russian agents (acknowledged).

(the Islamist), and the rest of the secessionists continued to push for independence.

At the same time, Gorbachev was struggling to keep the Soviet Union together and he was scheduled to sign the new Union Treaty into law in August (a few weeks away). This treaty would convert the Soviet Union into a federation of independent republics that would still share a single economic and defense space with a common president and foreign policy. On August 19, 1991, the Soviet vice president, prime minister, minister of defense, and chief of the KGB organized a coup to stop the Union Treaty from being signed. Gorbachev had gone to his dacha in the Crimea, and the conspirators arrested him and issued an emergency decree suspending political activity and banning independent media. They ordered tanks and troops into Moscow and surrounded the Russian White House (the Russian Parliament building). Because the majority of the population had just voted to retain the Soviet Union, the conspirators expected the public to support their move—but it did not turn out that way. Instead, the acting chairman of the Supreme Soviet of the Russian Federation, Ruslan Khasbulatov (a Chechen), and Boris Yeltsin went to the White House and began denouncing the coup.

By the afternoon, both Gorbachev and Yeltsin supporters began filling the streets of Moscow and erecting barriers around the White House to protect it from being taken over by the military. Why the plotters hadn't also detained Yeltsin is unclear, but the oversight would be their undoing, for late in the afternoon Yeltsin climbed on top of a tank to address the crowd and forcefully called on the coup conspirators to stop their illegal actions. Some of the tank units guarding the White House stated that they would support Yeltsin and Russia. Supporters flooded in from everywhere to defend the White House against an attempt to seize it by force. The next day Muscovites blocked bridges and tunnels with trolleybuses and street-cleaning machines and some attempted to set fire to the infantry fighting vehicles trying to push their way through. On the third day, the half-hearted efforts of the military were repulsed, the attack on the White House was called off, and the conspirators went to the Crimea to negotiate with Gorbachev. Gorbachev refused to meet with them. The KGB eventually restored telephonic communications to his vacation home, and Gorbachev immediately nullified all the actions of the conspirators and removed them from their posts.

Chechnya had also been cut off from communications, and with Zavgayev and other party members in Moscow to sign the new Union Treaty, the remaining government officials in Grozny were frozen with indecision. Although Zavgayev and the rest of the Chechen-Ingush ASSR leadership were in a difficult spot—all of them being members of the Communist Party and concerned about their own survival—Zavgayev in particular made a critical error by not taking a stand and coming out strongly against the coup.

In so doing, he convinced the Chechens and the Ingush that he was nothing more than an apparatchik and, more importantly, this showed Yeltsin that Zavgayev was not reliable.[4] Shortly thereafter, according to Khasbulatov, Yeltsin made the decision to replace Zavgayev with someone he could trust,[5] mistakenly believing that the problem in Chechnya rested solely in the person of Zavgayev, and that the independence movement in Chechnya could be stopped with some reforms and promises. Yeltsin didn't know Chechen history, and Khasbulatov either didn't explain it to him or was unfamiliar with it himself.

On August 22nd, the day after the coup in Moscow ended, demonstrators in Grozny seized the local television station and Dudayev went on the air to broadcast a Chechen revolution. Zavgayev flew back to Grozny to try and restore order, but he was restrained by Yeltsin and Khasbulatov because "at this stage, both men were evidently obsessed with consolidating their power and getting rid of the remaining pro-Gorbachev elements in the administration. They evidently saw Dudayev and the Chechen Congress as allies in this struggle, and . . . gave a strong warning to Zavgayev not to use force to crush the protests."[6] This was the final blow to Zavgayev, who might have been able to stop the events that now transpired, as an overwhelming majority of the Ingush (14 percent of the total population of the Republic), none of the ethnic Russian population (26 percent), and 40 percent of the Chechens themselves did not support the revolution.[7]

By September, the demonstrators had seized government buildings and Yeltsin tried to get Zavgayev to resign. Instead Zavgayev imposed martial law and called for elections later in the month. The Chechen National Congress felt that the time was right to make its move against the Communist leaders who were still in power, especially as Yeltsin's and Khasbulatov's messages to Zavgayev could not have gone unnoticed by the secessionists. On September 6th, having already declared the Supreme Soviet to be dissolved, supporters of Dudayev's National Congress stormed the parliament building in Grozny. Zavgayev resigned, tried to un-resign the next day, made further attempts to regain his power, and finally fled Grozny on the 15th of September—the same day the Chechen-Ingush Supreme Soviet (personally chaired by Khasbulatov, who had flown in from Moscow the day before) voted to dissolve itself.

---

4. Sometimes discretion is the better part of valor. Unlike many of the main players during the period, Zavgayev is still alive and in 2009 was appointed as the Russian ambassador to Slovenia.
5. Dunlop, 104.
6. Anatol Lieven, *Chechnya, Tombstone of Russian Power* (New Haven, CT, and London: Yale University Press, 1998), 60.
7. Emil Pain and Arkadii Popov, "Rossiiskaya politika v Chechne," *Izesvtiya*, February 7, 1995, 1, 4, as quoted in Dunlop, 103.

Also on the 15th, Ingush radicals declared Ingushetia separated from Chechnya—and still a part of Russia—a decision that would be ratified soon after. On October 27th, presidential and parliamentary elections were held and Dudayev won by a landslide (90 percent of the 72 percent that voted). On November 2nd (two months before the dissolution of the Soviet Union), the new parliament of the Chechen Republic of Ichkeria (ChRI) held its first session, declared complete independence from Russia and the Soviet Union, and swore in Dudayev as the first president of the *Islamic* Republic—on the *Qur'an.*

The consequences of Yeltsin and Gorbachev's power struggle had finally caught up to them—and Yeltsin was left with few options. Although he was seeking to deconstruct the Soviet Union, Yeltsin couldn't let the same thing happen to Russia, and he had to respond to the Chechen provocation, otherwise it had the very real possibility of destabilizing the entire region. Yeltsin had promised sovereignty—the ability to control one's own resources; Yeltsin didn't mean independence. And although Soviet Law No.1457-I was in effect, Yeltsin didn't recognize it. On November 7th, Yeltsin declared a state of emergency in Chechnya, but by then, it was too late because all the organs of national power had already been seized by the Chechens. The Soviet army would not fight Dudayev's 60,000-plus National Guard troops without an order from Gorbachev, and even then, considering how the political winds were blowing, the generals were hesitant to conduct any operations that might cause bloodshed. The lack of government control provided the critical opening that the Chechens needed to mobilize.

However, Yeltsin's Ministry of Internal Affairs Troops belonged to him, so he deployed 300–600 (depending on the source) lightly armed paratroopers to the Grozny Airport on November 9th. The Chechens immediately blockaded them and wouldn't allow them off the airfield. The troops remained at the airport in limbo while Gorbachev criticized Yeltsin's state of emergency decree, and even Yeltsin's own Supreme Soviet annulled his order. Two days later, the paratroopers handed over their weapons to the Chechens and were shipped out on buses.

November 9th was also the day that Shamil Basayev conducted his first terrorist attack. He and two other Chechens hijacked a plane and forced it to fly to Turkey, where they planned to hold a press conference to tell the world about the Russian "invasion" of Chechnya. The Turks let the plane land, but refused to hold a press conference so as not to anger the Soviets. The plane was released and Basayev and his compatriots eventually made their way back to Chechnya where they were hailed as heroes.

The events of November demonstrated that Russia was not capable of doing anything to stop the Chechens, but it's also important to remember that at the time, Chechnya was not the most important item on the agenda. During this same period the Soviet Union was engineering an overthrow of the Georgian president, Zviad Gamsakhurdia, who had declared independence from the Soviet Union earlier in the year and was denouncing the Soviet involvement in South Ossetia since 1989 as an attempt to destabilize Georgia.

Gamsakhurdia and Dudayev shared a common goal—to be free of Russia and the Soviets. Gamsakhurdia, an ardent nationalist, was overthrown by a Russian-assisted coup in December and replaced by the former Soviet Foreign Minister Eduard Shevarnadze. Shevarnadze just happened to be available to accept the Presidency because his old job had just been eliminated. On December 8, 1991, Ukraine, Russia, and Belarus met and signed an accord which declared the Soviet Union dissolved. By the 21st, the rest of the republics (minus Georgia) had joined in, and on December 25, 1991, the Soviet Union ceased to exist. Later that night the Soviet flag with its emblematic hammer and sickle was lowered for the last time from the Kremlin; Gorbachev resigned and ceded his remaining powers to the president of Russia, Boris Yeltsin.

Regardless of the recklessness of the Chechen decision to unilaterally declare independence in November, the dissolution of the Soviet Union made the decision moot, as, having been given equal status with all other republics within the Soviet Union, the dissolution of the Soviet Union meant that legally Chechnya, Tatarstan, Abkhazia, and all the other autonomous republics were now independent. Naturally Russia (and Georgia) didn't see it that way.

RUSSIA ARMS THE INSURGENCY

As discussed in Chapter 1, one of the most crucial elements to the survival of an insurgent movement is external support. In one of the more ironic episodes of insurgent warfare, for once Chechnya was provided sufficient external support—and by the very country it was seceding from. Usually insurgencies aren't able to capture enough arms and ammunition from the enemy to be effective—they must be provided from an outside source. However, in just a few months, the Chechens were able to seize enough Soviet equipment so that, for the first time in 200 years, a Chechen insurgency would have the means to progress from guerrilla warfare to a Phase III war of movement.

A few weeks before Gorbachev ceded his power to Yeltsin, the USSR deputy minister of defense, Pavel Grachev, traveled to Chechnya and worked out a deal with President Dudayev to arrange for an orderly withdrawal of Soviet troops—contingent upon leaving a large portion of arms for the Chechens; Dudayev wanted 50 percent. Further talks didn't happen because the Soviet Union ceased to exist, but the Chechens, wanting to equip their new republic, began raiding Soviet depots within

Chechnya. There were no casualties from these raids because no one tried to stop the Chechens; the "Soviet" troops stationed in Chechnya (which could have been from any ethnic group or nationality, including members of former Soviet states that were now independent) were more interested in getting home alive and making money than they were in defending arsenals for a country that had ceased to exist. No one knew when, how, or if "Soviet" soldiers were going to get paid any more. However, they couldn't go home yet because, as military personnel, their quarters were in Chechnya, and until such time as their units were officially moved, they literally had nowhere to go. Their choice was to give the Chechens what they wanted or face the threats that were leveled against them and their families by the Chechens.

The Russian military's situation in Chechnya was not helped out by Yeltsin's crude attempts to remove Dudayev from power, as had been done with Gamsakhurdia a few months before. Yet despite Yeltsin's machinations, the Russian government recognized the independence and sovereignty of Chechnya on three different occasions in 1992—March 14th, May 28th, and September 25th—each one preceding or following an attempt by Moscow to remove Dudayev by force.[8] Dudayev still had quite a few critics at the time, but each attempt to remove Dudayev had the effect of rallying all the Chechens around him. More importantly, the constant negotiation and recognition, followed by more attempts to overthrow the democratically-elected Dudayev did nothing to convince the Chechens that the current Russian government would act legitimately— meaning if they hoped to discourage the Russians from future armed incursions, the Chechens needed to arm themselves with all the weapons and ammunition still physically located in Chechnya.

On March 31st, following the first failed Russian-backed coup d'état attempt, the Chechen Parliament passed a resolution that all cantonment areas, military equipment, and supplies were the property of the ChRI. The Chechens began taking possession of the bases, but had trouble collecting the equipment because the ex-Soviet (now mostly Russian) troops were still there and controlled the weapons and vehicles. Russia went back to the negotiating table with the Chechens and at the end of May signed an agreement confirming an earlier settlement (which had recognized independence and sovereignty). A few days later Dudayev demanded that all Russian forces leave Chechnya within 24 hours and leave all arms and ammunition behind. As the representative of the USSR, Pavel Grachev (now the *Russian* minister of defense) had flatly denied Dudayev's request for a 50/50 split back in December; now he pressed for Russia to get "its half." When that failed, the order was given to rig the arsenals for

---

8. Dunlop, 170–173.

demolition; but in the end, Grachev cancelled the destruction order and the Chechens got everything except for a large number of light weapons.

It is apparent that the Russians didn't feel particularly alarmed by the amount of weaponry left to the Chechens (many still claim the bulk of it was unusable), because in September 1992 they attempted to seize Chechnya by trying to send two battalions of interior ministry special troops (with only 70 armored vehicles) into Chechnya through Dagestan. This raid, a precursor to the 1994 war, was indicative that Russia still did not view Chechnya as anything more than a local nuisance. The attempt failed because local residents blocked the movement of the troops (and took some officers hostage) before the column could even reach Chechnya. The Russians retreated, the officers were released, and the Russians went back to the negotiating table to stall for time in order to deal with Georgia again.

Given the current geopolitical situation and the 2008 war between Russian and Georgia—as well as an appreciation of the fact that there are still many unresolved ethnic conflicts in the Caucasus—it should come as no surprise that, in 1992, Russia, Georgia, Chechnya, and Ingushetia were involved in two short wars in Abkhazia and Ossetia.

Abkhazia

The Abkhaz problem started with the Soviets in the early 1920s, when, after re-conquering Georgia, the Soviet Union created the autonomous Abkhaz Republic *inside of* the Georgian Soviet Republic—similar to the way the Chechen-Ingush Autonomous Republic had been created inside of the Russian Soviet Republic. While the Soviet Union was in charge, the strong central authority it exerted over the entire Soviet Union kept everyone in check. However, once the Soviet Union started to break up, ideas like national identity and independence came to the forefront again. There were demonstrations in 1989 when Georgia tried to make the university in Sukhumi, Abkhazia, part of the broader Georgian university system and Soviet troops were dispatched to Tbilisi.

Deposed President Gamsakhurdia still ran a government in exile, and had the support of many democratic European nations; he was also a friend of Dudayev's. Clashes between Gamsakhurdia's and Shevardnadze's forces continued throughout 1992 and 1993, and Gamsakhurdia supporters often took the new government's personnel as captives. The Abkhaz government was supportive of Gamsakhurdia because Gamsakhurdia had always been in favor of autonomy for Abkhazia, which only intensified the friction between Georgia and Abkhazia. In August 1992, after the Georgian government accused Abkhazia of harboring Gamsakhurdia supporters, Georgia sent 3,000 troops into Abkhazia to restore order. At which point, regular *Russian* forces joined up with the Confederation of

Mountain Peoples of the Caucasus (including the Chechens) to defend Abkhazia. It was here that Shamil Basayev and many future insurgent commanders received training from Russian Military Intelligence (GRU).[9] Initial Georgian successes were quickly reversed, and the Abkhaz and their allies retook a significant amount of land.

This conflict was the progenitor of the civil war in Georgia, and with the help of the Confederation of Mountain Peoples and the Abkhaz, Gamsakhurdia was able to seize large portions of Georgia—including major ports. It was at this point that Russia was successful in getting Georgia, Azerbaijan, and Armenia to join the Confederation of Independent States (CIS)—Russia's new version of the Soviet Union, only now with Russia in charge. Armenia and Azerbaijan were dependent on Georgian ports and now—with the rebels in charge—the danger was too great. They agreed to Russia's terms, and Russia now "officially" entered the conflict by sending 2,000 troops into Georgia to crush the rebellion and set up the "frozen conflict" that would result in de facto independence for Abkhazia.

Prigorodnyi Raion

There was also a short war between Ingushetia and North Ossetia in the summer and fall of 1992 over the Prigorodnyi region: this war would be used as a pretext by Russia to try and reestablish control over Chechnya. Russian experts say that the two main reasons the Ingush split from the Chechens in 1991 was because the Ingush feared their culture was being sublimated by the larger Chechen one, and that by staying within the Russian Federation, they had a much better chance of having the Prigorodnyi region returned to them. Just as the Chechens had seen the bulk of their best land go to the Cossacks, the Ingush had watched as their lands were given to the North Ossetians—the most significant being the Ingush village of Zaur—later known as Vladikavkaz. In 1934, when the Bolsheviks merged Chechnya and Ingushetia, they gave Vladikavkaz—the most important fort and city in the Caucasus—to their long-time supporters, the Ossetians. "Prigorodnyi" means "suburb" in Russian—and that's exactly what the region was—the suburbs of Vladikavkaz—with rich agricultural lands. Even though the Bolsheviks secured the town and fort of Vladikavkaz by giving

---

9. On November 4, 1990, 16 nations of the Caucasus including many pro-Kremlin groups such as the Cossacks, Ossetians, and Russian paramilitaries formed a loose, unofficial confederation designed to give a greater voice to the Caucasus in the ongoing struggle between Russia and the Soviet Union. Comprised primarily of militants, its original purpose was not well defined, but the Georgian assault clarified their purpose and, with Russian financial aid and support, they created detachments of volunteers to go to Abkhazia and fight against the Georgians. About half of the total 1,500 volunteers were Chechens.

it to the Ossetians, even the Bolsheviks didn't dare to take away this prime real estate from the Ingush. However, in 1944, when Stalin resettled the Vainakh to Central Asia and made Chechnya and Ingushetia disappear, he immediately gave the Prigorodnyi to the Ossetians. When Khrushchev allowed them to return in 1957, every attempt was made to prevent the Ingush from coming back to Prigorodnyi, but many still managed to return to their homes.

Once the Soviet Union began to splinter, ethnic tensions between the Ingush and the Ossetians came to the surface. When Gorbachev passed laws on territorial rehabilitation in an effort to reduce Yeltsin's influence, the Ingush were able to use it to lay claim to the Prigorodnyi and things quickly deteriorated. During the summer, the Ingush continued to become more militant in their stance and the Ossetians responded through harassment, kidnappings, and rapes. According to an official report by the Helsinki Human Rights Watch, in late 1992, the North Ossetians began an ethnic cleansing campaign against the Ingush living in the Prigorodnyi—which resulted in more than 600 Ingush deaths and 60,000 Ingush being displaced from their homes.[10] In an attempt to stop the Ossetians, the Ingush and Chechens flooded into the Prigorodnyi, which then prompted the Russians to send in troops to restore order. As Ingushetia had chosen to remain a part of the Russian Federation, the Russian troops went all the way through Ingushetia and into Chechnya—the border between the two now-separated entities not having been clearly defined.[11]

The Chechens responded by sending their own tank regiment to stop the Russians from continuing further into Chechnya, and Dudayev issued an ultimatum: if the Russians did not leave Chechen territory, there would be war. Thankfully for Dudayev, the Confederation of the Peoples of the Caucasus, feeling empowered by their success in Abkhazia, threatened to send half a million volunteers to fight the Russians if they didn't withdraw. Russia was in no shape to fight a major Caucasian war in 1992, and they eventually backed out of Chechnya—at least most of the way.

By then, Dudayev had dissolved the parliament and introduced direct presidential rule in order to deal with the state of emergency and the poor economic situation. Yeltsin, experiencing similar problems, announced in 1993 that he would assume special powers and rule by decree in order to

10. *Russia: The Ingush-Ossetian Conflict in the Prigorodnyi Region* (Paperback), by Human Rights Watch Helsinki Human Rights Watch (April 1996).
11. If this situation reminds you of the recent Russian-Georgian war in August 2008, it should. There is still sharp debate among analysts, journalists, and observers as to whether or not Russia and South Ossetia engineered the conflict to provoke a Georgian response. Ironically (or not), the South Ossetian refugees from that conflict were moved into the Prigorodnyi region.

implement his program of reforms. In September 1993, he disbanded the Russian parliament (led by former friend and Chechen Ruslan Khasbulatov), which then turned around and declared his actions unconstitutional and removed him from office—which resulted in a constitutional crisis. In a complete about-face, Yeltsin now got the army to attack the very same Russian White House (parliament building) that he had once defended—but this time there were hundreds killed and thousands wounded. Afterwards, Yeltsin threw the leaders of the "coup" in prison and dissolved the old parliament for good. The first elections for the current parliamentary system—the Duma—were held in December, and a new constitution that greatly expanded Yeltsin's powers was passed. This election also packed the Duma with "hard-liners" that were ready to support Yeltsin's position vis-à-vis regaining Chechnya. That same month in Grozny, the Russian-backed opposition staged another unsuccessful coup attempt and then organized a provisional council (mostly former power elites of the former Communist era and supporters of Zavgayev) to serve as a shadow government—and publicly called on Moscow to assist them to reestablish order in Chechnya.

What is important to keep in mind about the constant attempts to remove Dudayev is that the Russians didn't invade earlier because *they didn't think they needed to.* They knew the political situation in Chechnya was precarious and Dudayev had so little support that if they just waited long enough and sowed enough discord, eventually Dudayev would fall; hence, they would be able to install their own people or justify sending in a peacekeeping force as they had done in Georgia. But Chechnya was not Georgia.

Many sources refer to this period as Russia's attempt to "stamp out a three-year-old secessionist movement," but by 1994 it would be more accurate to say that Russia was now conducting an *insurgency* campaign against the Chechen Republic of Ichkeria through the FSB, who have a lot of experience and are very adept. Russia was not "defending" its local Chechen government against Dudayev and a group of outsiders seeking to take power—that was already a fait accompli; by 1994, Chechnya was defending itself against Russian attempts to take Chechnya back. Russia was attempting to subvert the Chechen government, and the Chechens should have been conducting COIN against the Russian proxies. The conditions were ripe in terms of vulnerable population and lack of government control, but what the Russians didn't have was available leadership or a competing ideology. As such, the Russians continued to support anyone who might be able to represent an "opposition" that would be supported by the general population. They even pardoned Ruslan Khasbulatov for his part in the coup against Yeltsin and sent him to Chechnya to see if he could garner enough popular support to serve as the leader of the opposition.

Umar Avturkhanov was one of the first Dudayev supporters to break from him and call for a return to Russia. In August 1994, the Russian government chose to back Avturkhanov and recognized the Chechen Provisional Council as the only legitimate government in Chechnya. Russia then began a blockade of Chechnya, suspending civilian flights to Grozny while border troops cut off the roads. In the fall of 1994, unmarked aircraft began bombing Grozny, while attack helicopters and tanks fired on villages. Avturkhanov's opposition forces launched a ground attack but were repulsed by Dudayev's troops. Avturkhanov admitted that he had a large number of Soviet-built attack helicopters, and Russian newspapers confirmed that Russian soldiers were taking part in the hostilities (the Chechens had captured some). There was a second attack in late November, and it was during that month that Dudayev referred to the "beginning of the second Russian-Caucasian war."[12]

President Yeltsin, despite having been publicly embarrassed that Russian troops had already been involved, tried to appear as an arbitrator and announced that the warring factions in Chechnya should cease fighting and disarm. When Dudayev refused, Yeltsin ordered an attack to restore "constitutional order." By December 1st, Russian forces were engaged in the heavy bombing of Grozny and military targets. The Russian government was immediately besieged by Western leaders, who decried Yeltsin's use of violence and began to question whether he was a true democrat and reformer. On December 6th, Dudayev and Pavel Grachev met and once again agreed to avoid the further use of violence, but five days later Russian forces entered Chechnya in a three-pronged attack to "establish constitutional order in Chechnya and preserve the territorial integrity of Russia."[13] The Russians believed that they would be able to topple the Chechen government within a "couple of hours with a single airborne regiment." Instead they were handed a humiliating defeat.

ANALYSIS OF THE INSURGENCY PRIOR TO DECEMBER 1994

To understand why the Russians thought that a "bloodless coup" in December 1994 would be over in less than ten days, it is imperative to examine both the actual situation and the Russians' perception. To say that there had been a *lack of government control* in Chechnya prior to the declaration of independence would be a gross understatement. In Chechnya there was *no* Soviet or Russian government control—and the little that might have been exerted was wasted by Yeltsin and Gorbachev fighting each other. The lackluster leadership demonstrated by Zavgayev and his attempts to play

---

12. Radio Free Europe—Radio Liberty, *Daily Report*, November 21, 1994, 1.
13. Aleksandr Goltz, "Shtoby pravil'no ispol'zovat' voennuyu silu, eyu kak minimum nado raspologat,'" *Krasnaya zvezda*, September 7, 1996, p. 2.

it safe did not engender him to either the Soviet or Russian authorities, so when he needed help from the central government to deal with the nascent insurgency in Chechnya, he did not have the support he needed. This created the necessary vacuum for Dudayev and the secessionists to fill.

However, Dudayev's regime was not much (if any) better in this regard, giving the Russians an opportunity to foment insurrection against him. Initial Russian efforts were poorly planned, but subsequent attempts met with more success, especially as the Russians tried to portray Avturkhanov's provisional council as being more legitimate than Dudayev's. Using Kremlin-supplied cash, Avturkhanov began paying pensions and salaries to ordinary Chechens and creating strife among Dudayev's government by supporting his opposition groups with resources—thereby forcing Dudayev to suspend the parliament.

Dudayev may have been president, but he had never been given the necessary mechanism with which to administer a state—namely, a monopoly on violence. He didn't have a police department to speak of, and if he had, he didn't have a way to pay them. The National Guard worked for their commanders, who often argued with Dudayev and competed with him for power. Without a functioning economy, Dudayev did not have "purse strings" to control, and there were many funding sources that kept the militias functioning independently from Dudayev. There were no jobs to speak of, so lawlessness, black market deals, and other extra-legal activities became the way that most people survived. Dudayev's government did not have money to pay pensions and salaries. And so, paradoxically, as in many insurgencies, it was precisely at the point where the insurgency appeared to have finally achieved success that it became vulnerable. Russian attempts to take back Chechnya during this unstable transition period represented good counterinsurgency doctrine and strategy; failing to commit sufficient forces to accomplish the task did not.

As discussed previously, Chechen attempts to win their independence have always been successful at the tactical level, but strategically they've been hamstrung by their inability to stay united unless they are actually fighting a war. And ironically, in one of the very few times that the Chechen independence movement was *not* primarily driven by an Islamic ideology, it achieved its goal—only to suffer from the lack of a government and social system that it could turn to once it took the reins of power. This would have been more than amply provided for had the primary ideology been Islamic (*shari'a*-based) as in the past—because fundamentalist-based ideological strategies share that strength with the Mao protracted-war strategy—there is a plan for running the government and society once the battle is won. It was therefore no coincidence that during this period the traditionalists (Islamists, led by Yanderbiyev) began to exert their influence against the secessionists (Dudayev).

Dudayev had been admired early on, but the longer he remained in power, the less popular he became—especially to the Russians. To a very large extent, the problem lay in the personal enmity between Yeltsin and Dudayev. Dudayev's original position had been in support of Gorbachev's new Union Treaty, so he did not necessarily want full independence from some sort of mutual union, he just wanted Chechnya to be on par with every other republic—especially Russia. The original conflict had always been against Russia, so Dudayev and many of the secessionists were prepared to stay a part of a "New Soviet Union" as long as they were no longer part of Russia; more specifically, they wanted "independence" and a functioning economic sphere where the Chechens and the Russians shared the ruble. Chechnya would guard the southern border, but Chechnya would have its own laws and Dudayev would be on an equal footing with Yeltsin. One can only imagine what Yeltsin thought about this. This personality conflict was further played out in the choice of advisors that each chose to represent their respective sides during negotiations, and ultimately resulted in little more than constant bickering. But the longer it went on, the more the balance of power shifted to Russia.

During the same period, Russia had its own problems. Yeltsin had sent tanks against the parliament, and the question of whether or not the Russian Federation would survive the constitutional crisis was very much in the forefront of everyone's mind. In addition to the terrible economic conditions in Chechnya and Dudayev's inability to do anything about it, there was the equally bad economic situation gripping the rest of Russia. So if the average Chechen was asked to pick which side he would fare better under and which side could claim the mantle of legitimacy, it would still have to be Dudayev, as he had been popularly elected by a wide margin and carried the popular will of the population.

Leadership

That the Chechen insurgency had available leadership in 1991 is obvious given the large numbers who came out to vote for Dudayev. Russia could have (and should have) moved decisively in 1990 and 1991 to provide alternative leadership to Dudayev. Moscow miscalculated and believed Dudayev, as a member of the Soviet system (with a general's pension), would want to remain within that system. Yeltsin believed that in the short term, Dudayev would be instrumental in removing some of the old Communists that threatened Yeltsin's liberal reforms. Therefore, one can forgive Moscow for not moving decisively when available leadership in the form of Dudayev showed up in Chechnya in the early 1990s. However, from a strategic viewpoint, one can't excuse the Kremlin or the

FSB for not providing strong *legitimate* leadership to Dudayev's opposition once Yeltsin made the decision to take Chechnya back.[14]

Their combat calculus was wrong: the Russians assumed that negative marks for Dudayev would automatically mean positive marks for anyone who opposed him. But in an insurgency, the leadership must *frame the conflict* and provide a reason for the population to follow them. In this case, the majority of the negative framing came from Moscow (generally official statements about how bad the situation was in Chechnya or how Dudayev had no principles), which was necessary to get the population to consider someone besides Dudayev, but not sufficient to move them to support the Russian-backed opposition.

Ideology

There were competing and sometimes overlapping ideologies during the period from 1990 to 1994. Even within the ranks of the secessionists there were multiple ideologies that complemented each other at first and then served to create splits in the overall movement once their objective was attained. It's important to state again that not all ethnic Chechens wanted to separate from Russia—especially in the north and lowlands. But those who did want independence were secessionists who favored a democratically elected constitutional government, and traditionalists who favored a return to an Islamic-based government. As for the secessionists, the idea of democracy was not as strong as the basic nationalist ideas of independence, but nationalism combined with (one's own interpretation of) Islam proved to be the most effective form of social mobilization, and this hybrid became part of the official style of the politicians during the period. Sebastian Smith writes that "religion played a crucial supporting role to the resistance. . . . their beliefs and the tradition of Sufi brotherhoods was one of the most important elements in maintaining morale and a sense of ethnic identity."[15] Moshe Gammer writes: "Being Chechen has always *ipso facto* meant being (Sunni) Muslim. Even the most secularized and Westernized [Chechen] nationalists have always regarded Islam as one of the principal components of Chechen identity, tradition and culture. . . Islam thus became the antithesis of everything Marxist and Soviet. The Islamic alternatives to the Soviet state and code of law, so deeply engraved in national history and

---

14. Following the coup attempt against him Gorbachev disbanded the KGB and split up its many directorates so that it wouldn't be so powerful. As a result, many sources during this period refer to the FSK—which was the successor to the KGB and the precursor of the FSB. In the interests of keeping it simple, any references to the FSK are listed here as the FSB.

15. Smith, 154.

tradition, are the *imama* and the *shari'a* respectively. Therefore it was natural that Dudayev took his oath as president on the *Qur'an* and that the republic was termed 'Islamic.' . . . Furthermore, Islam proved the strongest rallying call inside Chechnya and was more effective than secular ideologies in calling for unity and mobilizing support among other North Caucasus nationalities."[16] Despite the fact that Dudayev said, "I would like the Chechen Republic to be an institutional secular state," he himself was sworn in on the *Qur'an*. And it was exactly this combination of nationalist secessionism and Islam that provided the real ideology in the early years of the 1990s—creating a hybrid "third" ideology—not uncommon for insurgencies.

There was yet another ideology operating in Chechnya at the time: profiteering. The Profiteers thrived in this unstable environment where the lack of a strong legal or religious authority made it easy for them to make large sums of money in illegal activities. Very recent insurgency literature has finally officially recognized these groups, and Steven Metz has referred to them as "commercial insurgents." The Chechen profiteers were (are) primarily interested in their own opportunities and not overly concerned about the fate of the Chechen nation or a Chechen state. During the Soviet years, even privileged ethnic groups who had access to official goods and services participated in a thriving black-market economy to make extra money and to obtain necessities. The Chechen family and village-based clans, being largely shut out of any opportunities by the Communists, were able to survive by working together and operating almost exclusively in the underground economy. This fourth ideology would become prevalent among many clans and family groups—the *teips*—in Chechnya after the end of hostilities in 1996.

As for the provisional council and all others who supported returning to Moscow, their ideology was "preservationist," as they wanted the old system back—the system that would continue to provide them the political, economic, and social privileges that came from being part of Russia. However, this ideology was not compelling for the majority of the general population—whose support was necessary for the oppositionists to succeed. The pro-Russian factions never gave the average citizen a reason to want to go back to the days of Soviet or Russian suzerainty.

There definitely was a *vulnerable population* for the available leadership to direct along any one of those insurgent ideologies because the Chechen population has *always* been vulnerable. Although there was a section of Chechen society that wanted to maintain its ties to Russia, the majority of Chechens voted for Dudayev—and independence—in 1991. There were no riots in the streets in Grozny protesting his actions; in fact, quite the opposite happened and a large portion of the population rejoiced.

16. Gammer, 214.

In 1994, the population was perhaps even more vulnerable than it had been in 1991. When the Kremlin was analyzing the possible outcomes of any planned military action, they asked, "How many people are currently unhappy with the situation in Chechnya?" And indeed, many people were unhappy—indicating a vulnerable population. The problem for the Russians was that without a sufficient *counter*-ideology, the population was not vulnerable *for them*. Better questions would have been, "How many people are willing to rise up against Dudayev?" and "What percentage of the population is willing to sit on the sidelines and wait to see what happens if there is an invasion?" The ultimate question should have been, "If forced to make a decision, which side will *each group* choose and why?" If they could have answered the "why," they would have been more successful.

External Support

The issue of arms has already been discussed and regardless of the type, quality, and total quantity, by mid-1992, Chechnya had a national guard with enough arms and ammunition to make Russia think more about negotiations than outright military action—and much of that "external support" had been supplied courtesy of the Soviet Union and Russia. As for the other types of external support critical to maintaining an insurgency (or maintaining a nascent state that had emerged from a successful insurgency), it was a different story entirely.

What happened between 1991 and 1994 could be referred to as a "missed opportunity" by the Chechens, but that wouldn't be fair. In the first place, Chechnya was in no condition to be economically independent, it didn't have a professional cadre of bureaucrats necessary to run an administration, and it hadn't been politically recognized by anyone (with the exception of Gamsakhurdia's Georgia for a few months and later Taliban Afghanistan). Moreover, it wasn't getting the external support necessary to establish itself in the world community because Russia prevented other countries from establishing economic and trade ties with Chechnya. But most importantly, there was no rule of law.

The economic factor is critically important for understanding subsequent events, but for now, it is important to note that Dudayev now fell prey to the same predicament that all successful insurgencies go through once they have reached their goal—dividing power and resources. Moreover, the time of "promises" was now past; the secessionists had rallied the population under the banner of "Chechnya for Chechens," and now were required to make good on their promises. Because Chechnya did not have a functioning economy, and because it did not receive sufficient external support at this critical early stage of inchoate statehood, the successful independence movement was doomed to eventually wither on the vine.

THE "FIRST" CHECHEN WAR

In many ways the Chechen War of 1994–1996 resembled the earlier conflicts between the Russians and the Chechens. It started off with multiple columns of Russians thrusting into Chechnya, the Chechens countering with fierce resistance, the Russians reacting by grinding down the Chechens while the Chechens conducted devastating ambushes—especially on supply routes. The war would eventually move to the traditional defensive areas of the mountains and forests, but the new addition of built-up cities provided a new kind of "forest" where the traditional form of Chechen guerrilla warfare could be carried out as well.

Russian tactics were similar to earlier campaigns: send a lot of troops; attempt to coerce behavior; and reduce population centers where the Chechens could hide. Although the Russians did not literally deforest insurgent strongholds as they had in the past, they did conduct the modern-day version—reduce the cities and buildings where the Chechens were able to successfully conduct urban warfare. As in the past, the Chechens had the home team advantage of terrain, a highly motivated and well-trained force, the ability to appear and disappear almost at will, a short logistical tail, and the ability to blend in with the surrounding population; the Russians, as usual, had overwhelming firepower and troops.

This war was characterized by brutality on both sides. However, it should be said that there were a great many Russian officers and soldiers who refused to participate (some sources say up to 800), and at least 83 were later convicted by courts-martial. Some refused because they believed the invasion to be morally wrong, while others objected to the fact that it was so poorly planned. The morale of troops was very bad; many of the conscripts deserted, allowed themselves to be stopped by civilians blocking their path, surrendered, or even sabotaged their own equipment so it would be incapable of moving. The Russians began with an aerial campaign to take out Dudayev's small air force and establish air superiority and, once it became apparent that the initial advance of ground columns would not immediately take Grozny without a fight, began an aerial and rocket bombardment of Grozny that was described as the heaviest Europe had seen since the firebombing of Dresden in WWII. Many of the bombing casualties were ethnic Russians because, unlike the Chechens who could escape and stay with relatives in the countryside, the Russians had nowhere to go and no way to get out. Following the almost two-week-long bombardment of the city, a

Russian armored assault began with the objective to occupy Grozny. But a well-prepared and well-executed ambush decimated the armored columns and resulted in *thousands* of Russian casualties. It is important to note that the Chechens fought in much the same way they always had—in small decentralized cells—in family or clan groups with a high degree of trust between fighters. Each group controlled their "own" sector of the city, acting independently but with full knowledge of the "commander's intent." They also denied the Russians' use of their superior firepower by keeping the fighting up-close where they had an advantage. The battle for Grozny would continue until the beginning of March, with estimates of the civilian deaths as high as 35,000.

In the meantime, the Russians began using cluster bombs against villages, and the lists of atrocities committed by both sides grew. Human rights groups have documented instances where Russian troops targeted civilians and committed other human rights violations whenever they experienced strong resistance from the Chechens. There are numerous sources that document those events, and serious students of the conflict should examine those sources to fully understand how those events became "root causes" and still affect the overall insurgency today.

That is not to say that the Chechens could claim the moral high ground either. There are many techniques that insurgents use to gain popular support, but two that the Chechens used during the first war were terrorism and provocation of government repression; the second isn't far removed from the first. Bard O'Neill describes the second as "attacks to provoke arbitrary and indiscriminate government reprisals against the population, calculating that this will increase resentment and win the insurrectionary forces more support."[17] That is exactly what happened: some Chechens devolved into barbarians and there are still videos available showing Chechens beheading Russian soldiers. Harsh Russian reprisals resulted, and many of the uncommitted civilians who had not supported Dudayev earlier now flocked to his forces. Thousands more created their own poorly equipped self-defense forces to defend their homes, families, villages, and culture once the Russian troops began using indiscriminate violence.

It was not hard to provoke a strong Russian response, as the Russian strategy was still a "coercive" strategy designed to force compliance through fear. It would be incorrect to label the Russian strategy as "enemy-centric," because even advocates of the "enemy-centric" approach state that it requires some steps toward engaging the population. There are reasons why the Russians chose the coercive strategy; adopting a "population-centric" approach requires an extremely professional, well-trained, and exquisitely disciplined force that will not give in to provocations and

---

17. O'Neill, *Insurgency and Terrorism*, 104.

"create more terrorists." Because even if the force is exceptionally professional and disciplined, the enemy will fabricate lies and frame half-truths
to paint the government as butchers—no matter what the actual truth is.
Eventually, the people will stop believing the disinformation if they continue to see a professional force that does not use indiscriminate violence
and they feel protected. Counterinsurgency is contingent upon the four
"P's"—presence, patience, persistence, and professionalism—and if
practiced religiously, this will eventually pay long-term dividends.

However, this strategy is costly in terms of time, resources, troops,
training, and national will. The Russians, having just come through a
revolutionary period, had a military establishment in disarray and their
soldiers were barely trained conscripts. Therefore, they chose the short-
term, easier solution in an attempt to coerce behavior which, unfortunately, resulted in numerous human rights abuses.

Although protecting human rights is important for its own sake, from
a long-term counterinsurgency success point of view, it is important to
understand that doing the humane thing results in strategic and operational success and is necessary to defeat the insurgents. Bombing apartment buildings, hospitals, and orphanages[18] only motivates more people
to fight, gives the opponent plenty of facts with which to frame the conflict,[19] and destroys the national will required to maintain a campaign of
such length.

As the Russians continued to pour in soldiers and the greater numbers
of Russian troops and superior firepower began to take its toll, the Chechens abandoned large-scale Phase III war of movement tactics—as trying
to take on the Russians in open battle is generally suicidal—and reverted
to what the Chechens have always done best—guerrilla warfare—hit-and-
run tactics, ambushes, mining supply routes, booby-trapping equipment
with improvised explosive devices, etc. As in campaigns past, the Chechens were eventually driven back to mountain strongholds where smaller
numbers of Chechens held off significantly larger Russian forces.

During this period, the Russian media—having been restrained for so
many years by Communist control—reveled in the opportunity to conduct real journalism. And for a while, the accurate story of what was
happening in Chechnya played out in newspapers and televisions all
across Russia. As the Russians (and all the other nationalities whose sons
had been drafted to fight a war they didn't want to fight) saw their children being killed and injured, and as they saw their fellow Russian civilians being killed by their own troops, the national will for fighting such a

---

18. Smith, 150–151.
19. "They call us terrorists, but you would become a terrorist too if you lost your mother,
    your sisters, your nieces and nephews, your whole family to those animals who bomb
    everyone." Interview with former Chechen fighter, February 2009 (S.A.).

war began to turn and President Yeltsin, who had been promised a quick victory that would help him politically, was now faced with a morass.

The Chief Mufti of Chechnya, Ahkmed Kadyrov (later Kremlin-approved president of Chechnya) called for *jihad* to evict the "occupiers." Many fighters from the Confederation of Mountain Peoples came to their assistance—including many Dagestanis, Georgians, Abkhazians, Ingush, and Azeris. Volunteers also came from ex-Soviet republics (the Baltics and Ukraine) who were eager to see yet another Russian vassal become independent.[20] Moreover, many Russian Federation autonomous republics passed laws prohibiting their native sons from being used by the Russian government to participate in Chechnya or other similar conflicts. However, the Cossacks, who had historically fought against the Chechens, began to organize themselves to assist the Russian government once again. Although the Cossacks have always *fought* for the Russians, they had *sympathized* with the Vainakh during the early 1990s, until the terrorist attacks began to turn public opinion against the Chechens.

TERRORISM

There are numerous documented cases of Chechen terrorism and other violations of the law of war during the conflict. Most concerned the use of civilians as shields, kidnapping and killing civilian collaborators, killing prisoners of war, and even beheadings. However, at some point, Shamil Basayev, who had successfully hijacked a plane in 1991, led the Chechen battalion in Abkhazia in 1992 and 1993, and commanded the central sector in Vedeno during the 1994 war, began to conduct large acts of terrorism in an attempt to erode the national will and coerce the Russians to end the conflict. After the Russians finally took Grozny in March 1995, they spread south across the plains that led to the foothills of the Caucasus. The open fields gave the Russian mechanized forces a marked advantage because they could now use the "standoff" potential of their weapons. In an attempt to reduce their own casualties, the Russians only advanced after they had conducted a full artillery preparation—meaning they leveled the area with rockets and artillery—turning each village and town into a mini-Grozny. By mid-1995, it appeared as though the Russians were in a position to defeat the faltering Chechen forces. As in campaigns past, the Russians drove the Chechens into their mountain strongholds, but this time the Russians had air superiority and clear skies. As the Chechens continued to lose battles, and as morale in the last stronghold of Vedeno continued to drop, Shamil Basayev and 150 volunteers decided to take the fight into Russian territory. Basayev would later say: "We won't sit here

20. However, the foreign fighters who got the most attention came from Turkey, Iran, and other Arab nations—the most influential being a Saudi called Ibn al-Khattab.

in Chechnya and be exterminated. I warned that we would fight in Russia and there are a lot more targets . . . That's what we did and we'll do it again."[21]

On June 14, 1995, Russian troops entered the mountain fortress in Vedeno without a fight, thinking that they had won a great victory. What they found instead was that Basayev had evacuated his command and infiltrated Russian lines with his best soldiers. They traveled 70 miles north of the Chechen border into the next "state" (Stavropol Krai) to the town of Budennovsk, where the main Russian air base for the Chechen campaign was located. Basayev's men simply drove from Vedeno, bribed their way through Russian checkpoints, stopped in the center of Budennovsk, dismounted their vehicles, attacked police and government buildings, and started killing policemen and soldiers. After shooting a few civilians on the streets, they began rounding up the citizens and taking them to the hospital, where, by the end of the day, they had managed to gather more than 1,500 prisoners in one of the largest hostage-taking terrorist attacks in history. The Chechens emplaced mines and booby traps at all the entrances and prepared the building for an anticipated Russian assault. They threatened to kill the hostages unless the Russians immediately stopped combat operations and bombings in Chechnya and began negotiations with the Chechen leadership to find a peaceful resolution.

On June 15th, Basayev demanded that journalists be allowed into the hospital because he felt the Russians were dragging their feet and preparing to assault instead of complying with his demands. The Russians did not respond to his request, and Basayev killed six hostages—three military helicopter pilots and three policemen; after which the Russians granted Basayev's request for journalists to be allowed to enter the building. On the fourth day the Russian Special Forces assaulted while Russian news crews filmed the entire event. The Chechens anticipated the Russian assault and placed hostages in front of all the windows and points of entry. Instead of using snipers to try and kill the terrorists without inflicting civilian casualties, the Russians assaulted the building as if there were no civilians, using tanks and APCs to provide direct covering fire. The Alpha group commandos did not use non-lethal "flash-bangs" after the initial breaches, but instead used shrapnel grenades to try and gain a foothold in the building. The Chechens forced their civilian hostages to remain at the windows and wave white flags while roving Chechen groups defended breach points. The Russians were driven off, but many civilians died in the attempt. A second and third attempt to take the building by force was also repelled.

---

21. As quoted in Smith, 200.

It was the Russian press that stopped Budennovsk, because the Russian people witnessed the actual events without the old filter of Communist disinformation. The stark reality of the situation simply could not be missed and, as Basayev had hoped, in the eyes of the average Russian, the hospital siege became a microcosm for everything happening in Chechnya. Indeed, the lesson was not missed by the Russian government or military, and they haven't made the same mistake since. One can easily trace the precipitous decline of the independent Russian media to the Budennovsk incident, where the Russians had made no attempt to control the media. As a result, the Russian national will was manipulated and turned against the government. President Yeltsin was conspicuously absent during the hostage situation (at a G7 meeting with other world leaders in Nova Scotia), evidently sure of the eventual success of the Russian commandos to retake the hospital. However, after the third attempt failed and civilian casualties began to mount, Prime Minister Victor Chernomyrdin stepped in to personally negotiate. The prime minister did much to restore the public's faith in their government when they watched the televised phone conversation between him and Basayev and witnessed (in Chernomyrdin's own words) "the first time in Russian history that saving lives has been put above the interests of the state."[22]

In exchange for the release of the hostages, Chernomyrdin agreed to immediately cease all air and ground combat operations in Chechnya and promised that the Russian government would release "all the children, women, elderly, sick and wounded, who have been taken hostage." Admitting to holding hostages was a bold statement on behalf of the Russian government, as it clearly implicated them in violating the Geneva Convention and the laws of land warfare. The Russian government also agreed to appoint a delegation authorized to "negotiate the terms of the peaceful settlement of conflict in Chechnya," as well as give Basayev and the rest of the Chechens safe passage back to Chechnya.[23] On the 19th, Basayev released most of the hostages and took over 100 volunteers (including nine Duma deputies and 16 journalists) to ensure their safe trip back to Chechnya. Once in Chechnya, the rest of the hostages were released, although some of the journalists chose to stay with Basayev.

Despite the Duma's vote of no-confidence for Chernomyrdin's government and Yeltsin's rage at the peace deal (he fired his interior minister and the head of the FSB, Sergei Stepashin, who would later become prime minister), the Russians kept their bargain, and signed a cease-fire on June 21st. Shamil Basayev had saved the Chechen state through terrorism, but in so doing, initiated a tragic cycle that would eventually take thousands of innocent lives. Basayev, flush with victory, never doubted that terrorism

---

22. As quoted in Gammer, 202.
23. Ibid.

could succeed and never stopped trying to engineer a terrorist attack "big enough" to stop the Russians. For their part, the Russians would never again give in to terrorism, even if it meant sacrificing the lives of their own citizens. As the scope of Basayev's terrorist attacks grew, so would the number of civilian deaths. Total casualty figures for Budennovsk start at 140 dead and 200 wounded and go up from there. According to the hostages' own accounts, most of the casualties were from the Russian artillery and direct fire attacks; only 11 terrorists were killed.

With a cease-fire in place, the Russians and the Chechens sat at the table to hammer out an agreement in Grozny while hordes of journalists, bodyguards, and worried mothers congregated outside. They talked of Chechen disarmament and Russian troop withdrawals, but both sides were merely catching their breath and reorganizing. The Russians believed that they had perfected the technique necessary to finish the war once it re-started, and the longer they negotiated, the harder it would be on the Chechens—who would have to fight in the mountains during winter without shelter. The Chechens had been given new hope by Budennovsk and were now busy re-arming and re-fitting, infiltrating back into areas that had been previously lost and working out their plans to retake Grozny. The Russians offered Dudayev huge incentives to step down; Dudayev offered to step down as soon as the Russians acknowledged Chechen independence. For months the negotiations went on despite increasing attempts by unknown parties to derail them. It was in the best interests of the separatists and the average Russian soldier to continue negotiations, but a lasting peace deal would have been a personal disaster for the provisional council (the Chechens that Moscow had now put in power to administer Grozny), or Yeltsin; a peace deal would probably not have suited the FSB or senior army leadership either. Regardless of who did it, an assassination attempt against the chief Russian military negotiator General Romanov threw the two sides back into war.

Once hostilities began anew, the Russians immediately began implementing an updated COIN strategy, an "enemy-centric approach" with population measures resembling "clear, hold, build." They began by going back into all the villages that the Chechens had infiltrated back into during the cease-fire, and established some government control by bringing in pro-Kremlin Chechens who established a local administration within a zone of "peace and accord." The army provided security, the bombings stopped, and the new administrations began providing basic services, rebuilding homes, and paying wages and pensions. In exchange, the villagers had to agree to prevent the guerrillas from coming back and to give information to the troops if someone did show back up. Presumably, the authorities would also ensure that any soldiers in the area would not harm the civilians. The Russians assumed (rightly) that if they could convince the people that the pro-Russian Chechen government would take care of them and provide security, then the civilian population would stop providing support to the fighters and the fighters would run out of supplies—especially as they would be in the mountains during the winter.

The Russian plan might have worked but for a few significant errors in their COIN analysis and planning. The first problem was the decision to bring Zavgayev back to lead the pro-Russian Chechen Administration; there was nothing wrong with Zavgayev per se, but he was not far enough removed from the Russians, and he was not a strong enough figure to draw the Chechens away from Dudayev. Secondly, the unprofessionalism of the troops undercut the promise of security. The soldiers and the police—although not firing on the villagers anymore—still took liberties with them, treated them poorly, and did not fulfill the contract that the Russians had made to keep the people safe. And because the troops did not provide security, their presence and actions simply reinforced the idea that the Russians (and by association any Chechens who sided with the Russians) were illegitimate and could not be trusted. However, the final blow to this strategy was a failed Chechen military raid-gone-bad against the helicopter base at Kizylar (the site of the first Russian fort and many historical battles) that turned into a terrorist act and destroyed any ideas that the Chechens had about the Russians safeguarding them.

In January 1996, after Zavgayev had returned to Chechnya to start the new Russian "clear, hold, build" campaign and hold elections, a force similar to the one that Shamil Basayev used at Budennovsk infiltrated Dagestan and attacked the Russian helicopter base south of Kizylar—about a mile-and-a-half from the Chechen border. This raid had a legitimate military target: destroy aircraft, flight and navigation equipment necessary to run air operations, and kill as many military personnel as possible (especially pilots) to prevent future air operations against Chechnya. The operation was led by Salman Raduyev, Dudayev's nephew, and according to Raduyev, the original plan (the military raid) was approved by Dudayev. Although Dudayev would later deny giving permission for the attack, it bears remembering that, as a military mission, a raid on an enemy airfield less than two miles from your own border and across relatively flat, easily traversable terrain is a high-value military target. Thus, despite the fact that the Russians frame the Pervomayskoye affair as the "terrorist act in Kizylar," the initial raid met the internationally accepted standard for legal war, and Dudayev, an air force general, would have known the best way to attack such an installation and would have seen the value in such a raid—especially as it was Russian airpower that was most effective against his forces and most devastating to the Chechen civilians.

The military raid was unsuccessful because the Russian Quick Reaction Force (QRF) responded to the attack promptly (evidently having gotten serious about airfield security following the Budennovsk raid), and there were very few helicopters on the base to attack. The 200 Chechens[24] withdrew from the air base after having destroyed only three helicopters and killing 33 base personnel. However, the retreat back into Chechnya was poorly planned and, pursued by the Russian QRF, they copied Basayev's actions at Budennovsk, retreated back into the city, seized the hospital in Kizylar, and took at least 2,000 civilians hostage.

President Yeltsin was livid. In just a few months he would be running for re-election and at the beginning of 1996, his approval ratings were close to zero. He was facing possible defeat by a strong Communist Party, and the Chechen conflict was supposed to have given him a boost (á la "wag the dog"), but it just kept getting worse. In an attempt to prevent the situation from becoming another public relations disaster, the authorities quickly agreed to safe passage back to Chechnya for the terrorists and some volunteer hostages, and the next day the guerrillas-turned-terrorists released almost all of the prisoners. The terrorists and 150 hostages boarded buses and departed for Chechnya with a police escort. It is a relatively short drive, only about five miles from the hospital to the Chechen border. However, as the 13-vehicle convoy approached the border (and the point where Raduyev would release most of the remaining hostages), a helicopter gunship fired at the head of the convoy to force it to stop; the Dagestani interior minister (who originally orchestrated the deal) also claims that the Russians destroyed the bridge in front of the convoy to ensure the Chechens did not escape this time.[25] The Chechens immediately turned around and entered the small village of Pervomayskoye (really just a small settlement on the outskirts of Kizylar) and set up defensive positions to await the Russian attack.

This was a sound tactical decision on the part of the Russians: get the majority of the hostages released to prevent massive casualties, give the terrorists a false sense of security by providing them safe passage, choose the time and place of battle instead of letting your enemy dictate the venue, and most importantly, put the battle in a place where it was possible to control access, and effectively encircle the area and cut off any possible escape routes. Budennovsk had been a disaster for the Russians and by getting the Chechens away from the built-up area of the major city, the Russians gained the advantage of being able to control information and collateral damage; Pervomayskoye was not very accessible, and the Russians controlled all the roads. Journalists, cameras, and

---

24. Accurate numbers are difficult to get, as President Yeltsin would later claim that Russian forces had killed 153 terrorists and wounded another 30, but the number of Chechen survivors make that claim improbable.

25. Tony Barber, "Fog of battle clouds Pervomayskoye's ugly truth," *The Independent* (London), January 20, 1996, available at http://findarticles.com/p/articles/mi_qn4158/is_19960120/ai_n9638659.

witnesses were prevented from getting any closer than 4 km (2.5 miles) away from the village, and all camera film was confiscated.[26]

Both sides negotiated for five days, but both were really just using the time to prepare for the upcoming battle. President Yeltsin could not afford to have another defeat at the hands of terrorists—especially with an election so close, so the Russians used the time to move assault teams, tanks, APCs, and Grad rocket launchers into position; the chief of the FSB flew down to Dagestan to personally take charge of the operation. For their part, the Chechens prepared a diversion on their side of the border to give the terrorists a chance to break out of their encirclement. After five days, the Russians were ready, and according to their press reports, had deployed 2,000 soldiers in a triple-ring security zone around the area, with "38 snipers" tracking every move of the terrorists that would kill them all surgically without harming the civilians.[27] To give pretext for an immediate need to assault the village, the Russians claimed that the terrorists had lynched six Russian policemen and killed village elders—all of which was later proven to be untrue (one journalist for *Izvestia* managed to sneak through the Russian cordon and observe events firsthand).[28]

With the conditions set, the Russians started their assault—not with snipers as President Yeltsin had promised, but with tanks. The Chechens had dug in, and despite multiple rocket salvos, helicopter gunship and direct fire tank attacks, the Chechens held off the Russians for three days. On the third day, according to journalist Sebastian Smith, the FSB spokesman told reporters: "I want everybody to understand that now we have a situation which is not about liberating hostages. If you're following military rules, the task here is to capture a military fortress held by a battalion strength unit in urban conditions. This is about liberating a city." When Smith asked about the lives of the hostages, the FSB spokesman replied that, according to their information, "There are very few left alive."[29] The FSB chief who had flown in from Moscow to take charge of the operation also gave a press conference and falsely claimed the Chechens had "executed all of the hostages."[30] The Russian commanders were given the order

26. Smith, 212. Smith was one of the journalists reporting from the scene, and his account of the events is startling and elucidating. He interviewed Raduyev immediately afterwards as well.
27. "Reinventing Tsar Boris," *The Moscow Times*, April 12, 1997, available at http://www.moscowtimes.ru/article/850/49/308772.htm.
28. Alessandra Stanley, "Yeltsin Criticized for Handling of Chechen Hostage Crisis," *The New York Times*, January 20, 1996, available at http://query.nytimes.com/gst/fullpage.html?res=9507E3DC1E39F933A15752C0A960958260.
29. Smith, 213.
30. Eileen O'Conner and Steve Harrigan, "Scores dead at end of hostage siege" CNN, January 18, 1996, available at http://www.cnn.com/WORLD/9601/chechen_rebels/01-18/chechnya_update/index.html.

to flatten the city. Following that, the Russians fired salvo after salvo of 120 mm missiles into the village and strafed it continuously for hours with helicopter gunships. Smith, watching the scene from the edge of the Russian cordon, wrote that he prayed that the hostages would be lucky enough to die quickly.

But the Chechens managed to break out in groups of 50 and, according to accounts of the hostages themselves, it was the *Chechens* who saved them from annihilation by the Russians. After a Chechen volunteer force attacked the Russian encirclement from the rear to provide a diversion, Raduyev and his men led the hostages to safety. In an interview with the hostages only hours after their escape into Chechnya, Smith wrote, "The hostages say they heard on the radio that they were all presumed dead in Pervomayskoye and that executions had begun. They realized this meant carte blanche for an assault to wipe out the village . . . during the breakout fighters went first, followed by the hostages carrying ammunition and the wounded on stretchers. No one was left behind. The group crossed a minefield, and hostages say . . . boyeviks [Chechens], not hostages, cleared the way." Smith quotes one former hostage (a Russian) as saying: "At about 6:00 A.M. they came [helicopters], three of them, firing machine guns at us . . . Do you know what a lamb feels when the wolf is near? That's how we all felt, and here the wolf was all Russia."[31]

When it was over, the Russians claimed success and did much to cover up what really happened at Pervomayskoye. They claimed they killed over 150 terrorists, but a truer number of total casualties is 96 Chechens, 26 hostages, and 200 Russian military killed and wounded.[32] More importantly, however, this crisis demonstrated to the Chechens that if the Russians would not guarantee the safety of their own citizens, they could not be counted upon to protect the Chechen people. Moreover, despite Russian attempts to control the media around the event, the press still reported what they could see—which was rockets fired into the village. They heard the tanks firing, and later, they listened to the hostages vent their anger at their own government and *thank the terrorists for saving them*. This then was a monumental failure on the part of the Russians, and demonstrates why an counterinsurgency must be a government-led initiative using a *synchronized* effort of all the elements of national power—military, diplomatic, economic, informational, and *legal*. After all, this was undeniably a *terrorist* attack and yet the Russians came out looking like the butchers.

Despite the Russian attempt to control the "informational" aspect, it demonstrates perfectly why a fifth element of national power must be considered in any COIN plan. The *rule of law* (or legal element),

---

31. Smith, 216–217.
32. Carlotta Gall and Thomas de Waal, *Chechnya: Calamity in the Caucasus* (London and New York: New York University Press, 1998), 303.

expressed in military operations as the ROE or "rules of engagement," is specifically designed to reduce civilian casualties. While the primary role of the ROE is to prevent unnecessary casualties, the ancillary effect of a professionally trained and disciplined army with a proper ROE is that not only does proper "security" ensue, but the "atrocities" necessary for framing conflicts and blaming government forces are denied to the insurgency's propaganda spinmeisters. The failure of the Russians to learn this lesson meant that Pervomayskoye would be used against them with devastating effects.

Considering that the Chechens never had a chance to win the war against the Russians militarily, their best chance was always to make the Russians believe that it would simply be too costly to care about such a small place like Chechnya. In military terms this is referred to as trying to defeat the national will—or, raising the cost of winning a war that does not have vital national interests at stake to unacceptable levels. To be fair, the Russians initially started the war with a pretty restrictive ROE, but later they took the gloves off and used more tanks because, as the Russian minister of defense stated, "There was no other way."

But here, not only were the the Russians not attempting to minimize Chechen casualties, they also proved they were willing to kill Russian civilians as well, and their attempts to deny their actions publicly only backfired as the media exposed the lies to the Russian public. The Chechens, for their part, had always used the media effectively, knowing that any victory they might gain was not based on defeating the Russian army, but rather on convincing the Russian people to stop the war. After Pervomayskoye, even Russian politicians were condemning the Yeltsin government and applying political pressure to stop the war—not exactly what Yeltsin needed before an election. There was, however, another very important "lesson learned" for the Russians, something that had been slowly dawning on them since the beginning: the West was not going to do anything significant to try and stop them, regardless of what they did. Knowing that the West wouldn't (and later couldn't) do much to interfere made the Russians more confident in their actions and even less concerned about any international censure.

By the spring of 1996, the Chechens had regained their momentum and even though Russian bases were dotted all throughout Chechnya, the Chechens owned the night and were able to move freely and strike throughout the country. They had given up on the idea of fixed bases and according to Basayev, they were now "fighting clever," which meant simply reverting back to guerrilla warfare. In March, they launched a three-day "raid" on Grozny, driving out Russian troops, capturing soldiers, and seizing weapons depots. In the run-up to the election, President Yeltsin claimed impending victory and refused to deal with Dudayev directly. This became a moot point on April 21st when Dudayev was killed in a missile attack while talking on his cell phone.

Some have alleged U.S. collusion in the attack based on President Clinton's desire to help President Yeltsin defeat his Communist rivals. President Clinton was also up for re-election and he did not want to be accused of being the man who lost Russia to the Communists, especially given his previous efforts to help President Yeltsin. He had also publicly promised to help President Yeltsin with the Chechnya problem earlier in the year, but hadn't specified exactly what that meant. Finally, there was the odd circumstance that the U.S. State Department was one of the first sources to issue an official confirmation of Dudayev's death. Assistance of this nature would explain why Russia seems anxious to maintain a close relationship with the United States in counterterrorism cooperation while regularly finding fault with the United States in every other major area, and why days after the 2008 Russo-Georgian war, President Medvedev made a speech indicating the same.

Nonetheless, whether the Russians had help or whether Dudayev stayed on the phone too long,[33] after numerous attempts by the Russians to assassinate him, they finally succeeded. Vice President Zemilkhan Yanderbiyev, the poet and Islamist, became the head of state and remained in that office until elections were held again in 1997.

With Dudayev out of the picture and elections around the corner, President Yeltsin seemed more eager to negotiate. On May 28, 1996, Yeltsin signed a cease-fire agreement with Yanderbiyev and declared victory. As one of Yeltsin's campaign promises was to end the war in Chechnya, this may have helped him to win re-election on June 16th. Although the Russians and the Chechens were still talking during the cease-fire, once the elections were over, the Russians immediately began advancing to the south toward the Chechen mountain strongholds. General Shamanov, the commander of the Ministry of Defense troops in Chechnya, indicated that the Russians were working more seriously on their COIN strategy when he stated in July, "We have to wage a cruel campaign against those bastards in every field—military, political, economic, and in the media."[34]

The Chechens, once again seeing the possibility of being overwhelmed by the Russians, made another bold move—one they had been planning for months. A few days before Yeltsin's second inauguration, in a stunning surprise attack, 800-plus Chechens emerged from pre-planned hiding places in Grozny to take on the 12,000-plus well-entrenched Russian troops stationed there and overran the key districts within hours, isolating the

---

33. Dudayev evidently loved to talk on his cell phone. The director of the Davis Center at Harvard, Prof. Timothy Colton, relates that during one of his seminars, someone asked a question regarding the ongoing war. In the middle of class, Colton called Dudayev and despite the danger, Dudayev took the call and answered the question.
34. General Vladimir Shamanov as quoted by Smith, 239.

Russian outposts from support, allowing the Chechens to methodically attack and reduce them one-by-one, while ambushing and obliterating any relief columns. Simultaneously, they took the second and third largest cities in Chechnya—Gudermes and Argun—with barely a shot fired.

The credit for this attack generally goes to former Soviet Colonel Aslan Maskhadov (later president) as the overall architect, but Chechen fighters I've talked to say that in reality it was a group effort by all the main commanders. The previous "raid" on Grozny a few months earlier, discounted by the Russians as a mere demonstration or a *"nabeg* by *abreks"*[35] was now revealed as a critical part in the overall strategic plan—a full-up rehearsal on the actual terrain. And what had the three-day "rehearsal" accomplished? It validated infiltration routes and approaches for getting past the Russian outposts and into the city, and although the Chechen intelligence had already accurately determined the exact positions of all the Russian strongpoints within the city, the March attack allowed the Chechens to gauge Russian reaction times and the routes the relief columns would take—making it easy to pre-plan ambushes and counterattacks. Moreover, it allowed the Chechens to arm themselves for the August assault by seizing Russian weapons depots, which they then cached *within the city*. Three days before the attack, the main force began infiltrating the city and a good portion of their weapons and ammunition were already waiting for them; the rest was taken from the Russians after the initial attack succeeded, as were vehicles, weapons, ammo, and even defensive positions.

The Chechens moved quickly and initiated the attack with simultaneous raids on command and control elements at airfields, and FSB and GRU headquarters. They also conducted supporting attacks and established blocking positions along the three main avenues of approach into Grozny. Individual Russian positions were bypassed but "overwatched" by a machine gun or sniper to ensure that the Russian soldiers did not attempt to break out and provide mutual support to each other. The main Chechen forces then occupied their ambush points and roadblocks and determinedly defended their positions. In a single day the Chechens had turned the tables: they were back in Grozny and were defending—much easier than attacking. Moreover, the bulk of the Russian troops were in the city, pinned down and isolated, without food or water, with poor (or no) communications, and in terrible fear. The poor coordination between the army and the interior troops delayed the initial attempts to relieve the isolated soldiers, and when relief troops did come, they were cut to shreds; the Russians admitted to losing six helicopters and almost

---

35. The *nabeg* was the traditional Chechen-style raid where the Chechens would ride into an area on horseback, shoot their guns in the air, and make off with as much as possible. "Abrek," has now come to mean "robber."

30 tanks and APCs within two days. The Russian soldiers trapped in the city were petrified, not only because of the possibility that they might be overrun any moment by the Chechens, but because the Russian helicopters overhead were now shooting at everything that moved; tragically they often hit those they were attempting to rescue. But more than anything, the troops in Grozny feared that at any moment their government might decide to simply level the city to destroy the Chechens, regardless of whether they were still alive.

Initially, the Russians were not prepared to engage in saturation bombing as they had in the past—not with thousands of their own soldiers in the city. There was also the matter of the almost 250,000 civilians that had been convinced to move back to Grozny in order to demonstrate that the pro-Moscow government was in control. If the Russians wanted to take back Grozny, they would have to do so with infantry, room by room, house by house, street by street, block by block—a scenario that Russian conscripts with less than two years of total experience were unprepared to execute—a scenario that Russia could not win. They tried for five days, but more than 200 soldiers were killed, more than 800 were wounded, and an undetermined number went missing in action. On August 19th, the Russian commander gave an ultimatum for the Chechen fighters to leave the city or he would level it in a massive aerial bombardment. Panic ensued, and chaotic civilians fled the city in droves. The frightened and frustrated Russian soldiers panicked and "refugee columns were shot up, the 4th City Hospital was rocketed by a plane, roads were bombed and strafed miles away from any sign of *boyeviks*, and civilians were taken hostage by stranded [Russian] units."[36]

The ultimatum was rescinded by President Yeltsin's national security advisor, General (retired) Alexander Lebed (who had recently come in a respectable fourth in the Russian presidential elections), who immediately began talks with the Chechens. His negotiations ultimately concluded with the signing of the Khasavyurt Accord, where both sides agreed to remove their military forces from the city and to create numerous joint headquarters called *komendatura* to ensure safety and preclude looting. The most important part for the Chechens was the agreement by Russia to remove all its forces from Chechnya by December 31, 1996, and by that same date in 2001, a treaty "regulating the basis for mutual relations between the Russian Federation and the Chechen Republic" would be reached.

The war was over, and the Chechen Republic of Ichkeria had seemingly done the impossible, winning independence from a great power and then winning a war to maintain it with very little external support.

---

36. Smith, 248.

However, as in all previous fights with the Russians, the overall casualty figures were enormous for such a short war: documented casualties are above 50,000 (the Chechens say 100,000; human rights groups say that 80,000 is probably accurate) and another 300,000-plus became refugees. The Russians have not released reliable casualty figures for the war, but reputable sources put the numbers at 25,000-plus killed, wounded, or missing in action. The country and the cities were ruined from the saturation bombing, much of the land was still strewn with mines, the already small economy had fled with the refugees, and there were no jobs or homes to return home to. Nevertheless, Russia had promised to help rebuild, and following the Khasavyurt agreement, Maskhadov traveled twice to Moscow to meet with President Yeltsin and sign further agreements. On May 12, 1997, after having been elected the president of Chechnya, Maskhadov signed a peace treaty with Yeltsin stating that both sides were "desiring to end their centuries-long antagonism and striving to establish firm, equal and mutually beneficial relations, hereby agree . . . to reject forever the use of force or threat of force in resolving all matters of dispute."

CHAPTER 6

From Gazavat to Jihad: The Role of Islamic Fundamentalism in the Chechen Insurgency

The leap from high-risk activism to self-sacrificing violence is not a gigantic one.

—*Mohammed Hafez*, Suicide Bombers in Iraq

Analysts who discuss the conflict in Chechnya after the Khasavyurt Accord in 1996 generally fall into one of two diametrically opposed camps—those who believe that Russia is almost entirely to blame for the "second" (1999) war (and cast doubt on the veracity of any supposed Al Qaeda connection), and those who believe that the rise of Islamic fundamentalism turned the conflict into another front of Al Qaeda's campaign directed at the West. Members of these two groups are often so polarized in their views that arguments between well-respected academics and professionals turn into ad hominem attacks.

So what is the truth surrounding the post-Khasavyurt Accord Chechen conflict? If academics and analysts argue about this topic, how do others begin to navigate through the mass of reporting and conjecture to determine what actually triggered the events and, more importantly, how they were used to either further the cause of the Chechen independence movement or shut it down. Was Chechnya an Al Qaeda operation from the start, or were all the claims of a plot to establish a Caliphate merely a pretext used by the Russian government to crack down on the region?

The answer lies not in understanding the Russians or the Chechens or the history of the region—but in understanding insurgencies. As is typical with insurgencies, the answer is not clear-cut. Insurgencies evolve: the membership changes, and ideologies often shift back and forth between groups. Fundamentalist Islam has always played a role in Vainakh independence movements, so it should not be surprising that it would play a role in the 1999 war as well; nevertheless, *something* changed, and that something had to do with the introduction of a different kind of fundamentalist Islam. Examining which changes occurred and *how* they occured is not only critical for understanding the current conflict in the North Caucasus, but is also important for insurgency research overall, as the *modus operandi* used in the North Caucasus will continue to be used by other insurgent groups to infiltrate and influence nationalist movements in the future.

Therefore this chapter closely examines the relationship between Islam and the insurgency in Chechnya to show what was—and what is—the relationship of conservative (and later radical) Islam throughout the history of the Chechen conflict. As should be clear by now from previous chapters—Islam has always been a part of every phase of the 300-year-old insurgency, but it has evolved and it is currently changing.

DIVISIONS WITHIN THE MUSLIM FAITH

The role of religion and culture in insurgencies is often overlooked by observers, but understanding the role of Sufism in Chechnya, and realizing the Shi'a-Sunni split is only the tip of the iceberg when it comes to divisions within the Muslim faith, is a critical step in understanding the North Caucasus insurgency since 1996. Inasmuch as the conflict has lately been portrayed as a battle between the Sufis and the Wahhabis (not high-frequency terms in the general Western lexicon), an explanation of terms will be useful. Most people are familiar with the two best-known branches of Islam, Sunni and Shi'a, and most have also probably heard of Sufism, or Sufis, but are generally unsure of what Sufism is or how it fits into the Islamic faith. Much like the Christian faith is broken down into different branches (Catholics, Protestants, Lutherans, Adventists, etc.), so are the Shi'a and Sunni communities divided into smaller sub-sects, schools, and cults—which are then divided still further. Wahhabism, for example, is a sect of the Hanbali school of Sunni Islam.

After the Sunni and Shi'a, the two best-known Islamic sects are the Sufis and the Ismailis (the "Assassins" were a subset of the Ismailis). Sufism is a mystical branch of Islam that emphasizes prayer and transcendent rituals such as ecstatic dance (the *zikr*—sometimes referred to as "whirling dervishes"). Because Sufis believe that God reveals himself to individuals on a personal level, and because of their reliance on teachers, Sufism is considered to be heretical by more fundamentalist sects of the Sunnis such as the Wahhabis (the official sect of Saudi Arabia) that demand a literal interpretation of the *Qur'an*.

Sufism is a movement of organized brotherhoods, or *tariqas,* who are grouped around a spiritual leader, and is characterized by the veneration of local saints and by brotherhoods that practice their own rituals. There are many Sufi *tariqas,* but the four predominant ones are the Naqshbandiyya, the Qadiriyya, the Chishtiyya, and the Mujaddiyya—of these, the first three are the most prominent and the first two are the main *tariqas* in Chechnya, Dagestan, and Ingushetia. Even the *tariqas* are further divided, with the *Khalidiyaa* branch being the form of Naqshbandiyaa practiced most in the region.

Sufi followers understand Islam in a mystical, personal way. Sufi Islam doesn't differ from Islam theologically, but the Sufi interpretation is simply a different way to look at Islam. Ardor is the medium required to get in touch with God, and therefore Sufi followers use a variety of techniques to move toward God like singing, circular dances, etc. Sufism follows the basic tenets of Islam but not all *tariqas* follow all of the orthodox practices of Sunni or Shi'a Islam. Sufism has come to mean those who are interested in finding a way or practice toward inner awakening and enlightenment.

In the early days, Sufis tended to be lone ascetics who wore rough wool garments known as *suf.* Later, they began to gather around learned spiritual leaders called *sheikhs* or *pirs* and developed into religious orders, known as dervishes. Others forsook the orders and became mendicants, traveling around the countryside and living off the charity of others. Not all Sufis were accepted by the more conservative elements of Islam due to their unorthodox habits and beliefs, yet Sufi influence has grown over the centuries and today there are literally hundreds of mystic orders with millions of adherents. The Sufi tradition is rich in scholarship and philosophy.

The Qadiriyya (Qadiria, Qadiriya) Order was founded in Baghdad by Abd al-Qadir al-Jilani (1078–1166) and is the most predominant order in the world—as well as in Chechnya today. The second most prominent order is the Naqshbandiyya (Naqshbandiya, Naqshbandia) which was brought to Iraq from India by Sheik Khalid Naqshbandi in the early 13th century and later moved into Chechnya.

There is a distinction between official and "folk" Islam. Official Islam stresses religious texts, the *shari'a* (Islamic law), the literal interpretation of religious teachings, and worship at mosques. Folk or popular Islam, reflecting Arabic and Turkic nomadic heritages prevalent on the Russian steppes, emphasizes sacred forces, the symbolic interpretation of texts, and worship at shrines. Popular Islam in the form of Sufism continues to flourish in rural areas and has been especially popular in Central Asia for the past thousand years. Sufi orders, like all folk religions, focus on the allegorical interpretation of texts and have historically been organized around a pious founder or saint.

Although the majority of Caucasus Muslims are Sunnis belonging to the Hanafi school, it was "popular Islam" in the form of Sufism that largely survived in the North Caucasus during the Soviet period because its focus on the individual relationship with God allowed adherents to practice their faith secretly and not alarm the Communists. Perhaps because of Sufism's ability to adapt and survive almost anywhere, Sufism and popular Islam have been discriminated against by other Islamic sects for centuries, as they have been accused of incorporating "un-Islamic" beliefs into their practices such as celebrating the birthday of Mohammed, visiting the shrines of "Islamic saints" (like Kunta-haji), dancing during prayer (the *zikr*), etc. This tension between sects played an important role in the interactions between actors after the Khasavyurt agreement.

Historically, Sufism has always been an integral part of conservative Islam, and some of the most vitriolic and incendiary language and legal rulings have come from Sufi religious authorities throughout the ages— some of whom have been universally heralded by all Muslims as great scholars and authorities. Abu Hamid Muhammad ibn Muhammad al-Ghazali (1058–1111) is often referred to as "the greatest Muslim after Mohammed" for his pioneering works that effectively discovered philosophical skepticism well before Descartes and Hume. Many of his writings had profound influence on Western scholars and theologians—including Thomas Aquinas.

Nonetheless, when it came to Islam, Al-Ghazali wrote "one must go on jihad at least once a year . . . one may use a catapult against them [non-Muslims] when they are in a fortress, even if among them are women and children. One may set fire to them and/or drown them . . . if a person of the Ahl al-Kitab [People of the Book—primarily Jews and Christians] is enslaved, his [or her] marriage is revoked . . . One may cut down their trees . . . One must destroy their useless books. Jihadists may take as booty whatever they decide . . . they may steal as much food as they need. . . ."[1] This particular ruling by Al-Ghazali is still used as justification for contemporary jihadists to use weapons of mass destruction (WMD) against the West—as catapults were the WMDs of Al-Ghazali's day.[2]

1. Al-Ghazali (d. 1111), *Kitab al-Wagiz fi fiqh madhab al-imam al-Safi'i*, Beirut, 1979, 186, 190–91; 199–200; 202–203 [English translation by Dr. Michael Schub] as quoted by Andrew G. Bostom, "Sufi Jihad," *American Thinker*, May 15, 2005. Available at http://www.americanthinker.com/2005/05/sufi_jihad.html; accessed on August 21, 2008. This article lists a great many quotes from respected Sufi scholars, and shows that their statements regarding *jihad* and treatment of non-Muslims is at least as bellicose as the prominent Hanbali jurists Ibn Qudama and Ibn Taymiyya.
2. Don't overlook the hypocrisy of the Salafists who dismiss Sufism as heretical while simultaneously using the legal justifications of one of its foremost scholars.

SUFI WARLORDS IN THE CAUCASUS

The very first *gazavat* in the North Caucasus was started in the 1780s by Sheik Mansur (a Khalidiyya Naqshbandi sheik) who promoted orthodox Islam over the prevailing "folk" Islam so as to unite all the people of the North Caucasus as well as obtain help from the Ottoman Sultan. The second *gazavat* (1825–1859) was also started by the Naqshbandiyaa, and the eventual leader of this holy war would be the legendary Shamil. Nonetheless, even when the "peaceful" Qadiriyya arrived in Chechnya following the fall of Shamil in the late 1850s, they soon rebelled after the Russians first supported—but later arrested—their leader, Kunta-haji. After the Bolsheviks seized power and Russia was thrown into civil war, General Denikin's White Army conquered the lowlands in Ingushetia, Chechnya, and Dagestan all the way to Derbent, where his powerful army was defeated by the Naqshbandi Sheikh Uzun-haji, who established the first Islamic Caucasus Emirate in the area. It wasn't until WWII that the war leader of a Chechen insurgency wasn't a religious figure who didn't first call the people to orthodox Islam and enforce a strict interpretation of the *shari'a* and the practice of daily obligations. Keep in mind, however, that the most successful units during that conflict were the sheiks and their followers who did call for *gazavat*.

Every time the Chechens have declared war on the Russians, Islamic fundamentalism has provided at least part of the ideology which the leaders have used in an attempt to obtain support from other Islamic countries as well as unite the local population. When Wahhabis moved into the North Caucasus in the mid-1990s, their message of orthodoxy *was not* the introduction of a new and foreign concept to the Chechens, *it was merely a different version of the orthodox ideology that the Chechens had used every time they went to war with the Russians.*

WAHHABISM

Wahhabism is a sect of the Hanbali school of Sunni Islam. It is essentially a reform movement that began 200 years ago to rid Islamic societies of cultural practices and interpretations that had been acquired over the centuries. It derives its name from its founder, Muhammed ibn Abd al-Wahhab (1703–1792). Wahhabism is a fundamentalist sect in that it calls for the purification of Islam by declaring ideas and philosophies developed after the death of Mohammed to be untrue and impure because they did not come from the Prophet or his teachings (the *Qur'an* or the *Hadith*—a collection of the sayings, practices, and deeds of the Prophet and his followers). It prohibits the veneration of saints, mysticism, innovations, dancing, and music.

Democratic forms of government are heretical to Wahhabism because Wahhabis (often referred to as Wahhabists in Russian texts and newspapers) believe that the only law can be the one that God decreed through his Prophet Mohammed. Allowing "the people" to elect leaders (who craft laws and societal norms) is essentially placing man before God. Wahhabism was a small sect until it came under the protection of Muhammad ibn Saud, who used this particular form of Islam as a means of "cleansing" the other tribes and establishing the House of Saud as the ruling house in Saudi Arabia.

Wahhabism does not advocate violence, but because of its fundamentalist teachings, it is sometimes used as part of an ideology that encourages violence. Because Wahhabism teaches that all good Muslims must constantly strive toward establishing a government based on *shari'a*, Wahhabis can never accept a secular government as a legitimate government and must always strive to change the system. Extreme forms of violence have become part of some Wahhabi strategies—especially in cases where its adherents believe there is no other way to remove a non-Islamic government.

Wahhabism is a strict fundamentalist form of Islam and as such, it is often criticized harshly by many other Muslims throughout the world (in much the same way as many Christians criticize fundamentalist Christian sects). However, in order to properly understand the significance of Muhammad ibn Abd al-Wahhab's ideas, they must be considered in the historical context of Islamic practice. In al-Wahhab's time, there was a clear difference between the rituals defined in religious texts and popular Islam as it was practiced at the time. Muhammad ibn Abd al-Wahhab was concerned about the way the people of his town of Najd engaged in practices he considered polytheistic—praying to saints; making pilgrimages to tombs; venerating trees, caves, and stones; and making sacrificial offerings. He was also concerned by what he viewed as laxity in adhering to Islamic law and in performing religious devotions, such as indifference to the plight of widows and orphans, adultery, lack of attention to obligatory prayers, and failure to allocate shares of inheritance fairly to women.

SALAFISM

Wahabbism is sometimes incorrectly referred to as a branch of *Salafism*, which has been described as a "militant group of extremist Sunnis who believe themselves the only correct interpreters of the *Qur'an* and consider moderate Muslims to be infidels; seek to convert all Muslims and to insure that its own fundamentalist version of Islam will dominate the world."[3] Although Wahhabism and Salafism share many similarities, and although the philosophical and religious differences between the two sects are best explained by a religious scholar, what can be said definitively is that Salafism and Wahhabism cannot automatically be considered

3. Princeton University Online Dictionary.

synonymous. What is important for understanding the conflict in the North Caucasus is that the terms Wahhabi and Salafi are often used interchangeably by the Russians, the Western press, and even analysts discussing conservative Muslim thought.

WAHHABIS, SALAFIS, QUTBISTS, OR AZZAMISTS?

Despite the fact that the Russians (and even some Chechens) always refer to the insurgents as "Wahhabists" in an attempt to paint the insurgency as an Islamic extremist/terrorist movement, it must be said that the radical Islamists in Chechnya have never called themselves Wahhabis and have refuted the term numerous times in the press and elsewhere. The government of Saudi Arabia (officially Wahhabi) disavows any relationship with the Islamists in Chechnya, or Osama bin Laden, or Al Qaeda or any other radical organization. It is therefore problematic to label the radical Islamists in Chechnya as Wahhabis, because, although Wahhabism is a very fundamental sect of Sunni Islam, it does not call for violence to overthrow existing non-Islamic regimes.

Simply stated, the fallacious Russian argument is: many of the outsiders who went to Chechnya were (are) Wahhabis, those Wahhabis turned the local Chechens into religious extremists, the extremists began committing terrorist attacks, therefore all those fighting in the Caucasus are Wahhabis and each one of them is a terrorist. This is why the Russians rarely refer to any of the fighters in the North Caucasus as "insurgents"; they are usually referred to as Wahhabis or terrorists.

Defining terms and understanding the difference between sects is important; it is one thing to believe that an Islamic government based on *shari'a* is the only legitimate form of government and all Muslims must work to establish it. It is a big jump to adopt extreme acts of violence as a tactic to achieve it. "Wahhabi" does not equal "terrorist," and in this, the Russians are wrong. Therefore, if we want to identify the specific ideology of the radical jihadists in Chechnya (and elsewhere), it would be more accurate to ascribe it to the teachings of writer and activist Sayyid Qutb, and scholar Abdullah Azzam.

Sayyid Qutb is considered by many in the West to be the "godfather" of all contemporary radical Islamic thought; he is acknowledged by everyone to be one of most influential Muslim intellectuals in modern times. Born in Egypt in 1906, Qutb is reported to have memorized the *Qur'an* at age 12. He began his career as a teacher, but quickly became famous as a literary author and critic. He became a civil servant for the Egyptian Ministry of Education in the late 1940s and went to the United States to study the American educational system.

Qutb's writings are inflammatory to say the least, and Qutb's impact on ultra-conservative Islamic thought is profound. A quick check of the scholarly articles and investigative journalist reports available on the Internet shows that the influence of Qutb on bin Laden and other extremists is well-documented. Youssef Choueiri describes Qutbism as comprising those who believe that "the world is thus divided into two diametrically opposed camps; the believers and the unbelievers (or infidels)," and that his central task was to "topple idolatrous governments and wrest power from their representatives."[4]

Abdullah Azzam was a Palestinian who earned his PhD at Egypt's most prestigious Islamic university and, after seeing the success of the international cadre of mujahadeen against the Soviets in Afghanistan, took Qutb's earlier idealistic writings and gave them practical application by advocating for the creation of transnational Islamic brigades to travel the world in defense of Muslim communities.[5] It would be exactly this kind of "international Islamic Brigade" that al-Khattab formed in the North Caucasus during the first war—and what he would continue to create in the region for the rest of his life.

But, as the Wahhabis are quick to point out, Sayyid Qutb was Egyptian and Azzam studied there. Qutb belonged to the Muslim brotherhood in Egypt, and his brand of ultra-conservative Islam has never been accepted in the countries where the Wahhabis are the majority.

So were the men that brought radical Islam to Chechnya Wahhabis? Yes. Although they would not refer to themselves as such, their cultural and religious heritage would be Wahhabism—and they would continually strive toward establishing Islamic governments based on the *shari'a*. But was it Wahhabism that was responsible for the terrorist incidents in Russia? Was it Wahhabism that drove the Chechens to seize 1,200 hostages at School Number One in Beslan or take over the Dubrovka Theater in Moscow (referred to as the Nord-Ost incident)? No. That particular radical influence comes from Qutbism, and although we will not see the term "Qutbists" or "Azzamists" used to describe or label the Muslim extremists in Chechnya (or Afghanistan or Iraq or anywhere else Al Qaeda is operating) *it's actually Qutbist/Azzamist-inspired Salafists who are committing terrorist acts*, even though they are labeled "Wahhabists."

The North Caucasus is, and always has been, a region of Sufis. Outside groups of Muslim fundamentalists, traditionalists, and extremists—lumped

---

4. Youssef Choueiri, "The Political Discourse of Contemporary Islamist Movements," *Islamic Fundamentalism*, edited by Abdel Salam Sidahmed and Anoushiravan Ehteshami (Westview Press, 1996), 19–28.
5. Brian Glyn Williams, "Allah's Foot Soldiers, An Assessment of the role of foreign fighters and Al-Qaida in the Chechen Insurgency," 160, available online at www.briangynwilliams.com.

together and referred to almost exclusively as Wahhabis—entered the area much later and played (and continue to play) an important role in the conflict. In their role as "purifiers of the Islamic faith" they oppose all practices not sanctioned by the *Qur'an*, and perceive the Chechen form of Sufi Islam as a deviation from the original Islamic rules.

These ultra-conservatives deny the role of the teacher, which for Sufis is very important. They also condemn the widespread Sufi practices of venerating saints and making pilgrimages to shrines. The inner link with God, typical for Sufi followers, is rejected by the newcomers.

The clash between these two polarized forms of Islam had a major impact on the course of the interwar period (1996–1999) and is the basis for a part of the internal conflict within Chechen society today. During the 1994–1996 war, the pro-Kremlin Provisional government did not have a competing ideology that was both necessary and sufficient to convince the majority of Chechens to support it. The Russians quickly learned from their mistake, and the 1999 war was characterized by the Russians as a clash between Islamic ideologies—the "traditional Sufi Islam that had always been practiced in the North Caucasus" and the "Wahhabists bent on establishing a world-wide Caliphate." And in 1999, it would be the *Russians* who would be seen as the guarantors and protectors of traditional Chechen culture and religion. The Russians very adeptly "stole" the religious-based ideology from the insurgents and turned it against them.

ISLAM AS A MOBILIZING FRAMEWORK

Islamic insurgencies are very successful because the organizational structure inherently built into Islamic society is what is generally required for successful insurgent organizations: cellular, loosely organized, sanctuary, external support, leadership, ideology, legitimacy. And because the problem with most insurgencies is that there isn't a solid plan on how to run society after the insurgency is successful, and because any religion can provide the moral justification required to overcome an inner revulsion to killing and other types of dangerous behavior, the inherent strengths of the Muslim religion make Islamic-based insurgencies extremely difficult to defeat by non-Muslims.

Let's be very clear, practicing Islam does not cause Muslims to become insurgents. However, to deny the fact that the Prophet Mohammed was a great warrior, general, and statesman is to deny the Muslims a proud part of their history and heritage. Islam is a great religion because it is a "complete" religion that covers all aspects of life. For the Muslims of the Prophet Mohammed's time, war was a way of life; ergo, the instructions that Allah would give to his people through his Prophet Mohammed would of course include instructions on how to wage war. Perhaps this explains why the armies of Mohammed created one of the largest empires in history.

The Structure of Islamic Organizations

As discussed earlier, insurgency movements develop around a vague common ideology which may very well change as necessary to maintain support. This flexibility also allows insurgencies to remain uncommitted to specific objectives. Ideology is essentially a frame or set of frames constructed from subjectively drawn facts, histories, legends, and literature that provides an organized system of beliefs, values, and ideas which shapes the way an individual thinks and understands the world. It supports the foundation of a program and suggests modes of behavior.

A frame is an "interpretive schemata that simplifies and condenses the 'world out there' by selectively punctuating and encoding objects, situations, events, experiences, and sequences of actions within one's present or past environment."[6] Ideology is problematic as the underlying characteristics are often based on nationalism or nationalistic ideas that are not readily identifiable in the "frame." But as we've seen already, at some level, ideology is an attempt to define a conflict as "us against them."

A basic tenet of Islam is that there is the *Dar al-Islam* (the world of peace where all members are Muslims) and the *Dar al-Harb* (the world of war where non-Islamic people live). It doesn't get much more "us versus them" than that. Radical Islamic organizations by their very nature are "traditionalists" because they seek to displace the existing political system and restore a system based on *shari'a* with values that are primordial and sacred, rooted in ancestral ties and religion. In Islamic communities, the religious authority is also the political authority, so to disregard one is to be in violation of the other—the minimum penalty being censure from friends, neighbors, and family.

The strength of a particular ideology also lies in its ability to resist hostile attempts to construct counter-ideologies or show that the insurgent ideology is flawed. Any counterinsurgency strategy that tries to develop a competing ideology against Islam will have a very difficult time as it will be directly contravening the divinely revealed word of *Allah* to his people. As we can plainly see in the fight against Al Qaeda and the insurgencies in Iraq and Afghanistan, Islam itself is unassailable. This has been one of the most significant challenges in battling Al Qaeda; there are more established and respected scholars to be found, it's just that, from a conservative point of view, Al Qaeda's interpretations of the sacred texts is doctrinally correct and often carries scholarly consensus; therefore, there are few respected scholars who can speak out against Al Qaeda because there aren't grounds to do so.

---

6. David A. Snow and Robert D. Benford, "Master Frames and Cycles of Protest," *Frontiers in Social Movement Theory* (New Haven, CT: Yale University Press, 1992), 137.

Unlike Western jurisprudence, there is very little interpretation in contemporary Sunni legal discourse because "the gates of *Ijtihad*" (independent or personal interpretation of legal sources) were closed for the Sunnis in the 10th century. Western society has a problem with this, as we believe that things have changed and rulings made 1,000 years ago, however brilliant, have to be integrated with the realities of contemporary life. Sunnis, however, don't have a problem with this idea at all—in fact they consider us to be floundering because we have lost our moral anchor, and our relativism destroys our previously strong bond with God. Their belief is quite uncomplicated: Allah spoke through his Prophet; Allah doesn't need to say something more than once; if Allah wanted to give further instructions he would do so; thus, because Allah has not sent a new prophet or given further instructions, what Allah said before is still in effect.

Thus, in a traditional society, where political and religious authority is amalgamated by design, one gains secular power and authority by becoming a religious scholar first. The more one knows about the ancient, fundamental writings, and the more one can use that knowledge to make rulings *without personal interpretation*, the more conservative one becomes; and consequently the more rank and power one earns. Thus, the most respected and revered Islamic scholars are, by design, the most conservative. Moreover, when that scholar acts as the war leader as well, when he goes into battle, he does so with the greatest ideology that he could possibly have: he has God Almighty sanctioning his efforts.

As discussed earlier, legitimate leadership is crucial because an insurgency doesn't start spontaneously; someone has to light the match, and that person has to be sufficiently intelligent and well respected that people will follow him into dangerous situations. Moreover, leaders are the critical link in the process of taking grievances and constructing the frame that both links the "root causes" to the government and also provides a better alternative. Most Islamic movements are led by religious leaders who already have the advantage of legitimacy because of their education and status. They are already leaders in their communities, but in a time of conflict, Islamic religious leaders also have the ability to issue *fatwas* in order to condone or justify violent behavior, making their decisions a religious duty before God.

Religious leaders also have the advantage of having their houses of worship considered to be inviolable. And because there is no concept of "separation of church and state," it is expected that religious leaders will speak freely about government injustices in the mosques—five times a day—when the faithful are called to pray. And unlike other insurgencies with charismatic leaders at the helm, Islamic insurgencies tend to be less prone to having the insurgency crumble if a leader is killed, as slain leaders become *shahid* (martyrs), who are celebrated, honored, and remembered.

Usually an insurgency movement attempts to attack the government by showing it is not legitimate (it commits atrocities against the people, etc.) while proclaiming that the insurgency is a more legitimate guarantor of the people's welfare. While most non-religious movements find it difficult to achieve legitimacy without the use of highly framed arguments, religious groups in general have immediate and unimpeachable legitimacy. What could be more legitimate than a government that was designed by God himself? For this purpose, there has never been a more perfect system than Islam—in that both parts of the legitimacy question (I am legitimate, you are not) are addressed in the sacred books themselves—namely, because *shari'a* was divinely revealed by Allah through the Prophet, it is the only legitimate form of government. Ergo, any government that is not based on the *shari'a* is inherently illegitimate, and all Muslims must strive to work toward the establishment of *shari'a*.

In the West, there is currently much debate as to whether Islam is a religion of peace or a religion of war. Some analysts argue that Islam is being misinterpreted when terrorists invoke the *Qur'an*, while some claim that Islam itself drives its adherents to violent behavior in the service of religion. The argument is irrelevant; what is important is that, correctly or incorrectly, some groups use Islam as an ideological framework for both insurgency and terrorism. The statement of the 9/11 terrorists is perhaps the most illustrative example of this framing, for, even if the majority of Muslims do not believe that Islam condones violence, those who espouse terrorism do.

> Therefore killing you and fighting you, destroying you and terrorizing you, responding back to your attacks, are all considered to be great legitimate duty in our religion. These actions are our offerings to God.[7]

To translate ideology into reality, a movement must develop and achieve specific strategic, operational, and tactical goals. The strategic objectives usually address the desired end-state (e.g., an Islamic, *shari'a*-based government), operational objectives address how the movement will progress toward its goal (gain the support of foreign governments, capture the support of undecided members of the populace), and tactical objectives address the immediate aims of the movement (recruit more members, conduct a protest, etc.). Again, by its very nature, radical Islamic movements have their goals built into their operating structure,

---

7. *The Islamic Response to the Government's Nine Accusations*, Official statement of the 9/11 Shura Council, Khalid Sheikh Mohammed, Ramzi bin As-Shibh, Walid bin 'Attash, Mustafa Ahmed Al-Hawsawi, 'Ali 'abd Al-'Aziz 'Ali, Sunday, 3/1/1429, Guantanamo Bay, Cuba (March 1, 2009). Available at http://www.defense.gov/news/orderpercent 20regardingpercent20properpercent20sepercent20filingpercent20topercent20islamicpercent 20resppercent20topercent20govpercent209percent20accusations.pdf.

and more importantly, these goals are the same for every radical commu- nity large or small. No communication is necessary between "headquar- ters" or "adjacent units."

One of the most important factors in a movement is its ability to attract outside or external support, especially sanctuary, political support, and resources. Radical Islamic organizations have external support simply by virtue of their shared values with other Islamic organizations throughout the world. Moreover, the inviolability of the local mosque gives the Muslim insurgent an additional advantage—a local sanctuary. In most pla- ces where insurgent groups are operating, governments can find methods for controlling public gatherings or assemblies. Muslims, however, are required by their faith to pray at least five times per day, and no one can really prevent them from going to the mosque to fulfill their religious duty. No government can risk closing mosques and still be considered legitimate in the eyes of the world at large—and such a closure would immediately support the insurgents' claims that the government is illegitimate. Islam puts the government in a Catch-22 situation where it can't do anything even if it knows the local mosque is fomenting insurrection. But perhaps the biggest advantage that Muslim insurgencies have is their worldwide support from billions of other Muslims around the world who routinely support Muslim causes with money or even go to fight for the insurgency.

As for organization, by its very nature, Islam establishes parallel com- munities with non-governmental power and political structures when- ever it operates outside of an Islamic government. Because of the requirement for an Islamic education (which requires reading the *Qur'an* in Arabic), Islamic communities run their own education systems that distribute religious literature, *Qur'ans*, and written sermons that some- times question government decisions that are not within the religious teachings of Islam. Islamic communities often have their own media out- lets, usually with their own newspapers and sometimes broadcasting over their own radio stations. Because these communities are often dia- sporas that welcome relatives or refugees that do not speak the local lan- guage, the communities can become insular, turning away from the government and turning toward the Muslim structures and authorities who regulate daily life through the *shari'a*. This is not a phenomenon found only in developing countries; there are currently *shari'a* courts legally operating in London, Birmingham, Bradford, and Manchester, England, with more being planned in Glasgow and Edinburgh, Scot- land.[8]

The cumulative effect of this internal organization is that alternative government structures are already in place in many Muslim areas. If

---

8. Abul Taher, "Revealed: UK's first official sharia courts," *The Sunday Times*, September 14, 2008, available at http://www.timesonline.co.uk/tol/comment/faith/article4749183.ece.

those communities are called upon to defend themselves or their culture (religion, values, members, whatever), then it is easy for leadership to mobilize the membership to action. But by itself, that organization is not sufficient to move human beings to violent behavior.

Mobilizing Youth

Within the highly structured Muslim communities, radical Islamic groups have been very successful in reaching out and mobilizing large groups of educated professionals and uneducated youth. Carrie Rosefsky Wickham addresses the mechanisms used by radical organizations to attract new members by combining the two primary strands of literature on the subject—the "rational actor" model of human behavior (self-interests) and the normative rational of "motivational framing" (ideas). In her article, "Interests, Ideas, and Islamist Outreach in Egypt," she looks closely at the efforts of Islamist groups in Egypt in the 1980s and 1990s and addresses the "micro-mechanisms of mobilization," which are the methods that movement leaders use to forge and sustain relationships with potential recruits that become stronger over time and are difficult to sever.[9]

She argues that radical organizations attract young Muslims (vulnerable population) by offering incentives that they cannot get anywhere else, like social venues that both men and women are allowed to attend, and networks that expand their potential to meet prospective marriage partners. They are then encouraged to participate in low-risk, political activities to introduce them to the idea of activism on behalf of their religion. From there, they are exposed to an ideological framework that is tailored specifically to them, delivered by people they respect, and reinforced by other members of the community with whom they have formed bonds.[10]

WHY MUSLIMS REBEL

In his book, *Why Muslims Rebel*, Mohammed M. Hafez describes in detail the interplay between the four prerequisites for insurgency, and argues that terrorists and insurgents are able to coerce violent behavior from otherwise non-violent Muslims through "anti-system ideological frames that develop under conditions of repression" within Islamist groups because the anti-system frames "facilitate . . . 'moral disengagement,' which deactivates self-sanctioning norms against brutality and makes anti-civilian

---

9. Carrie Rosefsky Wickham, "Interests, Ideas, and Islamist Outreach in Egypt," *Islamic Activism, A Social Movement Theory Approach*, edited by Quintan Witorowicz (Bloomington and Indianapolis: Indiana University Press, 2004), 231–247.
10. Ibid., 232.

violence a permissible, indeed legitimate, mode of contention." He states that anti-system frames permit (1) ethical justification of violence, (2) advantageous comparison among episodes of violence, and (3) displacement of responsibility for violence, and finally that "anti-system ideologies deny the possibility of personal or group neutrality; every individual is responsible for maintaining or overthrowing the system under which he or she lives."[11]

Examples of how ethical justification is achieved include "framing" violent action as the only way to draw attention to an issue or to stop real or perceived social or economic inequalities. It is also used as a way to stop a "foreign" enemy or "foreign" ideas from controlling the faithful, their way of life, or their political environment. Advantageous comparison is used by many groups to legitimize their violence by framing their attacks as minor compared to the damage that has been inflicted by the government or other enemy. Displacement of responsibility is most often heard in the rhetoric of Islamist groups as being "forced to react" to the actions of the government, or that their attacks were in "self-defense." The idea is to shift the blame. When a group states that "Because civilians elected the 'bad' government, they therefore support its policies, and are therefore not innocent and can be attacked," it is an attempt to displace the responsibility from themselves to another group in order to justify their violent actions. "Those who brought about or maintain such a system are the culprits, not the rebels who are seeking to rectify the injustice."[12]

> Anti-system ideological frames portray the institutional political system and the state elite as fundamentally corrupt and deny (them) legitimacy. . . . They depict social ills and individual grievances as manifestations of problems deeply rooted in the system, as opposed to products of misguided policies or ineffective leadership. . . . Second, anti-system frames are polarizing. They represent the relationship between the movement and its opponents as a conflict between two antithetical opposites—us versus them, just versus unjust, faithful versus impious. The sharp dividing lines drawn by such frames depict the opponent as a monolithic entity that is incapable of adjustment due to intrinsic characteristics that preclude reform; the opponent must be displaced.[13]

In other words, the *leadership* develops an *ideology* addressed to a *vulnerable population* that describes how *illegitimate government* is either not taking care of the needs of the *vulnerable population* through *lack of government control* or is actively hurting the *vulnerable population* through the

---

11. Mohammed M. Hafez, *Why Muslims Rebel, Repression and Resistance in the Islamic World* (Boulder, CO: Lynne Rienner Publishers, 2003), 156–159.
12. Ibid.
13. Ibid., 157.

use of government repression (both *illegitimate* and indicative of a *lack of control*). Since the government does not have the ability to *control* itself or take care of the population, leadership argues that it is obviously *illegitimate* and must be replaced. And when it refuses to step aside, leadership has already framed the situation as *us against them* and the only morally responsible thing to do is to replace the government. If violent action is required, it is unfortunate, but the government has brought it upon itself, and the insurgents are not to blame.

Although Hafez writes about Islamist organizations in particular, this system of radicalization is not unique to them. Whenever we hear how a government's actions or a military campaign is "creating" new insurgents or terrorists, these are the mechanisms that are at work. And this is why the "population-centric" approach to COIN has become the only acceptable method for Western governments. Nonetheless, this approach is dependent upon establishing a secure environment so that moderate voices within society can step forward to find solutions to the conflict.

In a "coerce behavior" approach, moderate voices are never given a chance to be heard because the radicals accuse anyone who seeks to work with an already-deemed illegitimate government of being immoral. As more moderate voices are silenced, the radical voices become more influential and more violence ensues. Tragically, the radicals will appear to have been justified because their spectacular acts of violence will bring in ever increasing numbers of fighters and external support. Government repressions destroy whatever legitimacy the government had left, and in so doing, destroy the legitimacy of *any* moderate voices that support reconciliation. This is the current situation in the North Caucasus today—the few moderate voices calling for peaceful solutions have been marginalized and no longer even live in Chechnya.

By framing non-Muslims as non-believers, infidels, and crusaders, as well as the characterization of Muslims that do not support the insurgent cause as apostates and sinners, Islamist organizations make committing violence against those groups (both governmental and civilian) a religious imperative and a holy deed: "Ethical justification for violence, in other words, becomes bound to God's word as if God has ordered it himself."[14] This is why Sufi imams supportive of the current pro-Kremlin regimes throughout the North Caucasus are routinely targeted and attacked by the insurgents and terrorists.

Observers of Caucasus conflicts know that Chechnya has been nothing if not a crucible, and as seen above, crucibles + framing ideologies = radicals. The war in Chechnya has seen atrocities on both sides and perhaps no place has witnessed such reactive and indiscriminate repression as Chechnya did in the mid-1990s. Hafez asserts that the bombings of

---

14. Ibid., 188.

civilian cities and villages, brutal interrogation at filtration centers, and recurring human rights violations by undisciplined soldiers directly contributed to rebellion in Chechnya between 1994 and 1996.[15]

Unsurprisingly, vows of vengeance abound in Chechnya, and despite local and federal efforts to reduce the number of young men joining the insurgency, the insurgency does not appear to lack recruits; in fact Dokku Umarov, the current leader of the insurgency, has even publicly called for young men to stop seeking them out because they already have enough to fill the ranks.[16]

Under such circumstances, killing President Maskhadov—who constantly called for Russia to engage in peace talks, and often declared unilateral cease-fires to demonstrate his willingness to find a solution that didn't involve weapons—has made it harder than ever to draw moderates into the peace process. In fact, the last of the moderates seem to have been pushed away now that Dokku Umarov has declared a North Caucasus Emirate and "fired" the European-based secular government. Moreover, to this day, Chechnya remains an economic wasteland from which over 100,000 Chechen refugees have fled to live in squalor elsewhere—meaning that many of those who might have called for more cooperation have simply quit the area instead of working for a safer environment.[17]

THE HISTORY OF ISLAM IN THE CAUCASUS—ISLAM AS IDENTITY, IDEOLOGY, AND STRUCTURE

With an understanding of the different Muslim sects involved in the conflict, as well as the underlying structures of Muslim communities that make them successful social movements, and the ways that radical leaders use ideological frames to move members of exclusive communities toward violent behavior, it's time to overlay that framework upon the history of the North Caucasus insurgency in order to properly understand the role of religion—and especially Islamic fundamentalism—in the North Caucasus insurgency.

---

15. Ibid., 96, 97.
16. In June 2010 the U.S. State Department designated Dokku Umarov as a terrorist because he claimed responsibility for the 2009 Nevsky Express train attack and the March 2010 Moscow subway bombings. There are many who claim the designation was a political move designed to soften the relationship between the United States and Russia; they are wrong. The State Department didn't designate the entire insurgency as a terrorist organization because it understands the difference between terrorism and insurgency; Umarov claimed he ordered the terrorist attacks so the United States designated him as a terrorist.
17. Rajan Menon and Peter Reddaway, "Putin Should Defuse the Chechnya Time-bomb," *The Financial Times* (UK), May 12, 2005.

The people of the North Caucasus are Muslims and have been so for hundreds of years. Numerous sources state that Islam first arrived in the Caucasus area around 1,200 years ago. Look at any map that shows the extent of the original Muslim Caliphates, and you'll see that the line of demarcation in the north was the Caucasus Mountains—and we've already discussed the importance of Derbent and the Darial Pass as being the only "easy" ways to get past the mountains. Originally appearing in Dagestan, Sufism spread quickly and deeply, and Dagestan soon became a major center of Islamic culture and scholarship.

By the time that the Russians started to make serious attempts to take control of the Caucasus region in the early 1700s, the vast majority of the population in Dagestan was Muslim and the Dagestanis "produced the largest number of Islamic scholars (*ulema*) who were recognized in the Islamic world . . . The 'youngest' Muslims of the region were the Chechens and the Ingushes [*sic*]. Their Islamicization began only in the eighteenth century."[18] It was Catherine the Great's full-scale campaign to subjugate the Caucasus in 1780 that helped to firmly establish Islam in Chechnya, as the "Russian invasion of the North Caucasus in the eighteenth and nineteenth centuries stimulated political and military functions of *tariqatism* which were not characteristic of mainstream Sufism. The Naqshbandi *tariqa* provided a mobilizing framework [ideology] for resistance to Russian expansion in the region. . . . In the case of the Chechens and the Ingushes [*sic*], the Caucasian war was also a strong catalyst in the process of their Islamicization."[19]

The harsh campaign, led by Russian General Yermolov—who is reputed to have vowed to rid the area of anyone who was not Russian—forced the Chechens up into the mountains and into an economically and socially deprived situation that essentially provided a "crucible" which forged the Chechens through the medium of Islam into a fierce, dedicated, insurgent force. In an attempt to prove to the Chechens that they could not win, the Russian army destroyed villages and conducted increasingly harsh punitive actions that drove many more Chechens into the arms of Shamil.[20]

Despite the fact that the Russians eventually subjugated the area and the bulk of the Naqshbandiis were either deported, or rounded up and killed by the secret police, Sufism still remained strong in the area. The remaining Naqshbandiis went into the mountains in Chechnya or

---

18. Galina M. Yemelianova, *Russia and Islam, A Historical Survey* (London, UK: Palgrave 2002), 47.
19. Galina M. Yemelianova, "Sufism and Politics In The North Caucasus," *The Nationalities Papers* Vol. 29, No. 4, 2001, 663.
20. Matthew Evangelista, *The Chechen Wars; Will Russia Go the Way of the Soviet Union?* (Washington, DC: Brookings Institution Press, 2002), 13.

became Qadiriyya in order to evade further repression. In many cases during the early period, the Qadiriyya did not fight against the Russians and were rewarded by receiving government and clerical posts from the Russians.

SUFISM UNDER THE COMMUNISTS

In general, Communist rule in the Soviet Union was not good for religion, and Galina Yemelianova states that the Bolsheviks targeted Sufism in particular.[21] Stalin's crackdown on religions resulted in a severe decline of Sufism, resulting in mass deportations, executions of clerics, and the eradication of Sufi books and culture. The Communists saw Islam as a "harmful rudiment of the past," and the Soviet state took over the business of religion by taking control of clergy and reducing or eliminating religious activities.[22]

Yet despite their attempts to eradicate religion, Soviet policies actually strengthened Sufism among the Vainakh—especially during the Central Asian resettlement. Religion is culture—and once the Vainakh were deported from their ancestral lands, the graves of their saints, and everything else that was a part of their heritage, they clung even more tenaciously to the one thing that the Soviets could not physically take from them: their religion, which was their identity and their culture. The deportations unraveled (in some cases destroyed) the existing social network that had been predominate before the move—the clans and village structures—which meant that by default, *Sufism now became the single most important unifying element among the people.* Not only did Sufism serve as the repository of Vainakh culture, it became a symbol of their nationhood in exile, a mechanism with which to organize themselves, a conduit through which to communicate between communities, and a source of solace for the exiles in Central Asia.

Later, it would provide the Vainakh with the motivation to return to their homeland, and give them the shared communal bond that allowed them to endure the subsequent years of economic hardship they experienced after they returned to Chechnya in the late 1950s. As such, the Sufi brotherhoods not only survived in Central Asia, they became strong enough that they actually expanded into areas of Muslim Central Asia, particularly Kazakhstan and Uzbekistan.[23]

21. Yemelianova, "Sufism and Politics In The North Caucasus," 665.
22. Valery Tishkov, *Chechnya; Life in a War-Torn Society* (Berkeley: University of California Press, 2004), 164.
23. Alexandre Bennigsen and S. Enders Wimbush, *Mystics and Commissars* (Berkeley: University of California Press, 1985), 30.

THE END OF COMMUNISM AND THE ARRIVAL OF WAHHABISM

Wahhabism first entered the North Caucasus through Dagestan around 1986, although it would take another ten years before it would reach Chechnya. As Gorbachev's Perestroika was taking hold, religious leaders in Chechnya began to reestablish their religion on a more visible level—openly preaching Islam, celebrating religious festivals, publishing religious materials, exercising their new right to make the pilgrimage to Mecca, and increasing contact with Islamic communities outside of the Soviet Union. This trend was further accelerated by the decree on "Freedom of Religious Persuasions" passed by the Russian Parliament in 1990, which facilitated a marked increase in the level of religious schools, the rebuilding of mosques and cultural centers, and an increased role in internal politics for religious leaders.

However, despite the fact that Chechens, Ingush, and Dagestanis had once again begun to see themselves as Islamic, *it was not* this resurgence of religious independence that gave rise to the parallel move toward political independence from Russia in the early 1990s. Although there were some calls for *shari'a* and independence from the council of elders (the *Mekh-Khel*), Dzhokhar Dudayev, the Chechen leader that declared independence from Russia in 1991, drafted a constitution and a declaration of sovereignty that were purely secular.[24]

So how central was radical Islam to the conflict up to this point? Not much. Despite Kremlin efforts to paint the entire conflict (starting in the early 1990s) as one of Al Qaeda's campaigns against the West, there isn't any reliable information to support that claim. Sufi Islam has served as the identity for the Chechen people for at least a few hundred years. A more conservative form of Sufism—*muridism*—which emerged during the first Caucasian war with Russia (1800s) has also served as an ideological frame to rally the population to fight against the Russians—and those same Naqshbandiyya established a short-lived independent *Emirate* in the early 1900s as well.

Despite the fact that the Sufi religious leaders were involved in the overall effort, there is no evidence to suggest that any form of Salafism or Wahhabism played a role (much less the central one) in the decision to declare independence from Russia in 1991. And all available literature shows that the first serious foray of radical Islam into Chechnya occurred after the war had started—making radical Islam a consequence rather than a cause of the first Chechen War. The brother of al-Khattab, Chechnya's most famous foreign Salafist, states that it was the news reports about the fighting in Chechnya that convinced his brother to go there. Although some Islamists were already in Chechnya at the time of

---

24. Tishkov, 168; although it was an Islamic Republic and Dudayev swore on the *Qur'an*.

the first war, the foreign "Wahhabis" (as the Russians refer to them), came as a result of the first war, they were not the cause.

THE RISE OF RADICAL ISLAM

Predictably, it was once again war itself that brought in a more radical form of Islam to Chechnya. It was predictable because, if one examines all the conflicts that the Chechens have fought with the Russians since the mid-1700s, it is clear that once the Chechens have felt the need to rise up against the Russians, they have turned to the rallying call of Islam and, more specifically, turned to a more orthodox practice of their religion. However, orthodoxy is not necessarily radicalism, and what moved into Chechnya after the first war was a radicalism that was based on Qutbism, a new form of orthodoxy hereto unknown in the Caucasus.

Almost all observers agree that a more radical form of Islam, commonly referred to as Wahhabism, did not enter Chechnya until the mid 1990s—once the first Chechen War had been underway for at least a year. Although Vice President Yanderbiyev was a fundamentalist and a proponent of *shari'a* from the beginning, neither he nor his followers were Salafis. Although there were undoubtedly a few radicals running around in the early 1990s, the major infusion came in the form of Omar ibn al-Khattab, a veteran of the Afghan war against the Soviets who came to Chechnya looking to continue fighting the international *jihad* and who brought with him a group of Arab guerrillas financed by Salafi/Wahhabi NGOs, such as *al-Haramayn* operating out of Baku.

Earlier attempts by members of the Islamic Party of Renaissance to encourage Chechens to reject Sufism and follow a fundamentalist interpretation of Islam were rebuffed by the citizens as being un-Islamic. It would be the crucible of war that would open the door for a more radical form of Islam once again. "Islam in this radical form arrived in Chechnya precisely when more powerful means of mobilizing were needed. The ordeals of war—fear, losses, and the horrors of fighting—were weighing heavily on people, and the Chechen combatants needed symbols to distinguish themselves from the enemy, as well as to build solidarity . . . The references to religion helped justify the sacrifices being made for the 'holy war in the name of Allah.'"[25]

Once Khattab came to Chechnya, he soon demonstrated the fighting abilities of his Arabs and gained prominence after Shamil Basayev declared Khattab as his brother.[26] Basayev, the self-styled Che Guevara of the Caucasus, was one of the most influential Chechens throughout

---

25. Tishkov, 172.
26. Brian Glyn Williams, "The Chechen Arabs; An Introduction to the Real Al Qaeda Terrorists From Chechnya," *Terrorism Monitor* Vol. 2, Issue 1, January 15, 2004, 2.

the entire conflict. He was one of the primary field commanders of Chechen forces during the first war, a candidate for president in the interwar period, appointed secretary of state by President Maskhadov, the planner of the Nord-Ost and Beslan terrorist attacks (among others), and was the de facto military leader of the Chechen insurgency until he was killed by Russian troops in a special operation in July 2006. He started off the war thumbing his nose at the Wahhabis, but later obviously came to some sort of agreement with Khattab. If Basayev (almost all sources indicate he was Naqshbandiyya, but a confidant states confidently he was Qadiriyya)[27] did not convert to radical Islam, then at least he adopted the rhetoric and trappings in order to manipulate those symbols for his own benefit—taking the title of "Emir Abdallah Shamil Abu-Idris" starting in 2003. Basayev knew that religion could be used as an ideology, and personal beliefs, however strong, would have been secondary to what the situation demanded at the time.

Khattab and his International Islamic Brigade (modeled after Azzam and similar units created in Bosnia) were an extremely effective fighting force during the first war and immediately gained the respect of the Chechens. Although he was Saudi by birth, Khattab nonetheless earned the nickname "the Lion of Chechnya," no small feat for a culture that prides itself on its warrior ethos. Khattab brought immense financial resources and international support to the Chechens when the West would not provide it.[28]

The literature regarding Khattab's radical Islamic ideology is substantial, and there is no question that he fell squarely into the ranks of the contemporary radical Islamist movements. He is mentioned in a declassified Defense Intelligence Agency document as one of the nucleus members of Al Qaeda and a friend of Osama bin Laden.[29] This report is derived from a handwritten document—supposedly written by Al Qaeda

---

27. "сто процентов"—100 percent positive, says a former confidant and communications officer for Basayev during the first war.
28. Khattab is credited by many as being the one who "introduced" the Chechens to guerrilla and mountain warfare, and even those who didn't like Khattab's religion still thank him for "teaching them how to fight." But the assertion is shortsighted; guerrilla and mountain warfare has always been a central element to Chechen insurgencies. The conduct of the 1994 war was consistent with historical patterns. Khattab may have "reintroduced" this type of fighting to those that had fought in the Soviet army, but the Chechens would have rediscovered it on their own even without Khattab. It is more likely that Khattab's influence was purposely overstated and used as propaganda by some Chechens in order to justify bringing in the outsiders with their strange new religion.
29. Declassified DIA intelligence report NC 3095345, October 16, 1998, 3 (obtained through the Freedom of Information Act). It is important to note that no evaluation of the information detailed in the report is included in the declassified version; and anyone who deals with intelligence will tell you that text without context is pretext. It is entirely possible that this document was passed to U.S. Intelligence by the Russians in order to bolster the evidence linking the Chechens with Al Qaeda.

members themselves to detail their activities. It outlines the goals of the organization as well as principal members and associations and "orders" for the types of activities the groups should be conducting. It states that bin Laden sent Khattab to Chechnya in 1995 to set up training camps for international terrorists, and that in order to attain the goal of establishing a worldwide Islamic state, they would use the means of "terror, ethnic cleansing, latent penetration and control over nuclear and biological weapons. Further, radical Islamic regimes are to be established and supported everywhere possible, including Bosnia, Albania, Chechnya, Dagestan, the entire northern Caucasus . . . cells are to be created among Moscow and St. Petersburg Muslim-Chechens . . . training camps are to be established in Chechnya."[30] It goes on to say that specific attention should be given to Chechnya—since it is regarded as an area unreachable by the strikes from the West: "[M]ilitants will be used in the interest of the 'Armed Islamic Group' and 'Muslim Brothers,' and for spreading terror in the Central Asian Republics, Crimea and Russia . . . financial crises [are] to be used for creating disorder, and new strikes and kidnapping conducted for the purpose of provoking a unified uprising against Russia, and creating an Islamic State of Northern Caucasus."[31]

However, some scholars show evidence that, although Khattab knew and respected bin Laden, Khattab was a *rival* to bin Laden and, therefore, was never part of Al Qaeda. They cite proof that Khattab's Islamic Battalion never signed bin Laden's 1998 World Islamic Front for *jihad* against Jews and Crusaders, that Khattab tried to convince bin Laden to join *his* organization, that Khattab always vehemently denied he worked for bin Laden and Al Qaeda, and finally that Ayman al-Zawahiri did not join Al Qaeda until his attempt to link up with Khattab in Chechnya failed. Al-Zawahiri was arrested by the Russians during his crossing from Azerbaijan, held for six months, and released. He made his way back to the Middle East and soon thereafter sublimated his own Egyptian organization into AQ, becoming AQ's number two and most important spiritual leader.[32]

Khattab gained respect and influence within the ranks of the Chechen insurgency through his military success, by providing millions of dollars and steady employment with good pay to his fighters, by establishing a foothold for more radical Islamic ideologies to take root, and for introducing extreme forms of violence into the conflict. Khattab was filmed executing a Russian prisoner of war and one source even states he was filmed beheading a POW with his own knife.[33]

---

30. Ibid., 4.
31. Ibid., 5.
32. Williams, "Allah's Foot Soldiers," 164–168.
33. Paul Murphy, *The Wolves of Islam, Russia and the Faces of Russian Terror* (Washington, DC: Brasseys, 2004), 32–44.

Once established, the radicals, led by Khattab, began to make their presence felt and made contact with Wahhabi enclaves in Dagestan. Through Khattab's own example, the fighters around him were influenced to forsake their traditional Sufi practices for the more pure forms espoused by Wahhabism. Longtime observers of the Chechen-Russian conflicts will immediately recognize that this was exactly the same methodology employed by Sheik Mansur in the 1700s and adopted by almost every insurgent leader since then. Khattab has often been described as trying to force Wahhabism on the Chechens in an effort to radicalize them, but some Chechens say that it was just the opposite:

> Khattab was more about fighting Russians, only fighting Russians and then training those who wanted to be trained. If you asked Khattab something about religion he would tell you 'Khattab is a fighter, Khattab is a mujahid, Khattab is not a mullah. Go ask a mullah, I am not a mullah,' because he did not want to be seen as biased towards one side. And if you told your religious views, people would automatically ally you with those people [the radicals]. So he kept out of religious disputes, everything. He was afraid to make a move in Chechnya because the Chechens are wild people and we don't want to be bossed around by a foreigner.[34]

As Khattab continued to have military success, he established training camps for his soldiers and spread money throughout Chechnya to gain additional followers. More importantly, Khattab began to have an influence on the other important Chechen commanders—most notably Shamil Basayev—who commanded major combat units. Many began to espouse more radical Islamic traditions. Soon, major figures in Chechnya had turned to Wahhabism, which they believed would ensure a better mobilizing ideology for the war of independence and would guarantee an uninterrupted flow of hard currency from Islamic sources abroad.

There have been numerous reports about the ties between Al Qaeda and the Chechens, as well as peripheral evidence—the fact that Basayev added a string of Islamic names and titles to his own, and the fact that he and his operatives used slogans of Osama bin Laden verbatim—to support the idea that Basayev had more in mind than just an independent Chechnya. However, it is also true that despite Basayev's tremendous influence on the insurgency and his often de facto leadership, it wasn't until after Basayev's death that the Caucasus Emirate was declared.

Regardless of Basayev's personal motivations or religious beliefs, there is overwhelming evidence to prove that there were Islamic Fundamentalists (Salafists) in Chechnya, that they were involved in the fighting,

---

34. Personal interview with member of Basayev's staff.

that they brought in funds from Islamist sources, that they set up training camps in Chechnya, and recruited jihadists from all over the region. There are indications that there are still Salafists and foreign fighters involved with the Chechen insurgency today, although their numbers are significantly smaller than they were during the 1990s and early 2000s.

However, with Khattab and Abu Ali Walid now out of the picture, those ties are not as strong as they once were—although they were replaced by more Salafists.[35] Nonetheless, many observers argue that the Salafists' (and Al Qaeda's) influence on the insurgency has always been exaggerated, and that Basayev's true motivations were more nationalistic than religious. A reporter who spent time with Basayev shortly before his death said: "Basayev's simple ideology is based on the renunciation of Russia, which he calls 'Rusney.' Basayev laughs as he admits he masterminded the terrorist act in Beslan, acting on the noblest of motives. He accuses the regime (Russia) of hypocrisy, brutality, and deception."[36]

And so if Basayev, one of the most infamous terrorists in history and a man revered by many Chechens, had an unclear and fuzzy relationship with Islam, it is no surprise that many of the rank and file Chechens would have been in a similar situation. It is often in times of great stress (like war and repression) when people turn to religion in order to make sense of their lives—which now seemed beyond their control. Tishkov makes mention of the moral vacuum that Khattab stepped in to fill when he quotes testimony from a former Communist who later became a sympathizer of the radicals:

In this war, religion is used as an ideological weapon by unscrupulous people . . . one cannot be a true believer and have no morals. Unfortunately, there were many such people among our clergy [Sufis]. Dudayev intimidated those who under the Soviets had cooperated with the secret services . . . Out of their number, he formed a kind of public council—the Mehk-Khel—which became notorious for ransacking all the government stores and lining their pockets with bribes. In the end, the head of that council got a bullet in his mouth. But the corruption among that part of the clergy grew worse. To be fair, we must add that in protest against the corrupt clergy there emerged a religious association called Jamaat (accord) which proclaimed the principle of moral purity, gazavat (holy war), and a return to the original pure Islam. Similar to them were the Wahhabites, who rejected the people's religion—Sufi Islam. That movement is still in the making, and I do not know where it will lead us. The interesting thing

---

35. Andrew McGregor, "Chechnya: Amir Abu Ali Walid and the Islamic Component of the Chechen War," *The Central Asia—Caucasus Analyst*, February 26, 2003.
36. Vadim Rechkalov, "Armiya Basaeva. Pochemu spetzsluzhbi ne mogut poimat' Shamilya Basaeva. Prichina nomer pyat," *Izvestia* (Moscow), December 10, 2004.

is, you might expect the clergy's corruption to make the people turn away from religion, but instead they were still reaching for Islam, all over the country.[37]

The "corruption" he refers to is the public perception that all official religious authorities produced during Soviet times were members of the KGB—and now still serve the FSB. The reasoning for such perception is that, in a state that publicly banned religion and considered it antithetical to Communism, the only way someone was allowed to study at an officially sanctioned religious school and become a church or mosque official was to be a member of the secret services. The fact that the fifth chief directorate of the FSB is still responsible for monitoring religious activities, and that there are documented cases where religious leaders were proven to have been working for the KGB, provides "evidence" for those who wish to believe that *every* official clergyman was a member of the secret services.

The former patriarch of the Russian Orthodox Church, Alexy II, was born in Estonia and after the fall of the Soviet Union, the Estonians claim they found Alexy's KGB service file—even indicating he received a certificate of honor in 1988 for 30 years of service. The Anglican Church has also claimed to have examined these documents and found the accusations to be true.[38] The Chechens firmly believe that the Chechen Grand Mufti, Akhmad Kadyrov, was a KGB agent and used his position to further his own influence—and later to sow strife and discord in the Dudayev and Maskhadov governments. For as Vladimir Putin, the man who put Kadyrov in power and the former head of the FSB has said himself, "There are no former [FSB] agents." There is also the alarming fact that currently 78 percent of Russia's leadership has links to the FSB—26 percent of them by their own admissions and the rest by obvious "holes" in their resumes.[39]

It is important to remember that the "truth" of such accusations is largely insignificant, because perception is more important than reality. In a country where the majority of the citizens believe that their government and the secret services are capable of such a thing, a large group

---

37. Tishkov, 171.
38. Multiple sources, including Yevgenia Albats and Catherine A. Fitzpatrick, *The State Within a State: The KGB and Its Hold on Russia—Past, Present, and Future* 1994, 46; Seamus Martin, "Russian Patriarch was KGB Agent, Files Say," *The Irish Times*, September 23, 2000, http://www.catholicculture.org/news/features/index.cfm?recnum=13868. The patriarch, the Russian Orthodox Church, and the Russian government all categorically deny any such association.
39. Francesca Mereu, "Putin's Presidency Boosted Power, Prestige of KGB Successor," *The St. Petersburg Times*, February 12, 2008, available at http://www.sptimesrussia.com/index.php?action_id=2&story_id=24993.

of people will continue to believe what they want to believe even if presented with ironclad proof of the opposite. However, the idea that the Sufi Kadyrov may have been involved with the FSB doesn't mean that Wahhabism was the answer for the majority of the Chechen population, and the introduction of this more fundamental form of religion caused deep rifts in the population. Although the Vainakh felt as though they were good Muslims, the fundamentalists claimed the moral high ground because of their increased level of Islamic education and the possible "contamination" of the clergy by the FSB.

RELIGIOUS DISCORD OR BRILLIANT FSB PLANNING?

There are many who believe that Russia never planned to stand by the Khasavyurt agreement, and the FSB used the period between wars to "prep the battlefield" for the next round. According to this theory, the reason that Russia never followed through on its promises to provide monetary aid to Chechnya for rebuilding was to continue to spread instability in the region and weaken Maskhadov's government. While the Russian army was going through massive restructuring and ideological reorganization with a shift toward greater understanding of coalition and joint warfare, many believe that after 1996, the FSB was now using Kadyrov (the grand mufti of Chechnya) to sow dissent among the people and to *provide a counter-ideology* to the conflict so that when the time came, the people would see Kadyrov as a viable leadership alternative to Maskhadov. Those that hold the "FSB destabilization theory" also remind us that:

> In the year 2000 there was a TV debate on NTV between Kadyrov and Gantimirov [pro-Russian Chechen from 1990 and former Kremlin-appointed mayor of Grozny]. The anchorman asked Gantimirov 'why don't you want to work with Kadyrov?' Gantimirov said 'because during the first war Kadyrov called on every single Chechen to kill 160 Russians.' The anchorman asked Kadyrov how he would comment on that and Kadyrov said 'you know what? Mr. Putin knew what I was doing in Chechnya before, during and after the first war and that's why I'm now the head of the administration.[40]

Many people believe that the religious differences that were emphasized by Kadyrov were simply part of the FSB strategy to split the Chechens and present the Wahhabis as agents of foreign governments and representatives of a form of Islam that was not traditionally rooted in Chechnya. These people believe that Kadyrov was always on the side of the Russians

---

40. As related by Said X.

and realized that, although previously not in a position to take power for himself, with the backing of the Russians, he could become the most powerful man in Chechnya if he brought Chechnya back into the Russian Federation. The other version is that Kadyrov (and the Yamadayev clan) were truly for Chechen independence, but when presented with the increasing influence of extremist Wahhabi ideology antithetical to traditional Chechen values, the chief mufti of Chechnya decided that it would be better to maintain Chechnya for the Chechens instead of changing their religion (and cultural heritage) to meet the demands of this "new" religion.

And the truth? Irrelevant—at least as far as determining the efficacy of the counterinsurgency strategy. If the FSB did actively plan and support such an ideological shift, if they had the strategic foresight to tell their "agent" to work his way into Dudayev's and Maskhadov's confidence (Kadyrov was a mid-level religious authority at the beginning of the first war), broadcast to the Chechens to kill as many Russians as possible to maintain his "deep cover," and then later foment a split— then it was one of the greatest intelligence operations of all time, and it should be studied by every intelligence academy in existence on how to foment insurrection.

If, however, the FSB did not plan and coordinate such activity, and Kadyrov merely came to his decision to defect to the Russian side on his own, then the FSB was still smart enough to move quickly and co-opt him at the most critical point in time. As in most cases, the truth probably lies somewhere in the middle, and it's important to remember the fourth ideology extant in Chechnya at the time: Kadyrov wanted power, he did not want to lose his authority (religious or otherwise) to another group that was ascendant in power, so the enemy of his enemy became his friend—Chechen independence be damned—or, as he said, Chechen independence *because* of his actions.

And yet, despite their differences, during the first war, Salafi and Sufi fought together and for the same goal. As is the case in all insurgencies, there are separate groups motivated by different goals who will come together to fight a common enemy. Many of the Chechen leadership during the first war turned to the Salafists, but not all of them; two of the main commanders—Dokku Umarov (the current leader of the insurgents) and Lechi Dudayev—remained Sufi, yet were always on good terms with Basayev and Khattab.[41] Religion is important as an ideology during the fighting to rally the people to the cause and to give their actions moral authority and legitimacy.

---

41. Yet Dokku Umarov, a secularist, would undergo his own religious transformation in 2005 and declare the formation of the Caucasus Emirate.

Individual sects do not fight amongst themselves while the common enemy still remains. However, those rifts start to become apparent once victory has been achieved (or when it appears that victory will be achieved) as the separate groups begin to vie amongst themselves for power and resources. So during the first war, the strictly religious arguments were not particularly important or significant; however, *after the war*, the effects that the radicals would have on the political landscape would be profound; the historical and cultural splintering of the Chechens would once again return and the battle for *shari'a* would now be fought *between the Chechens* instead of against the Russians, and the idea of who was "us" and who was "them" would shift dramatically.

THE INTERWAR PERIOD 1996–1999

President Dudayev had been killed during the first war, and when Vice President Yandarbiyev assumed power, he decreed Soviet and Russian laws invalid, abolished secular courts, and created a *shari'a* court. Although his term was short, Yandarbiyev quickly stuffed key government and military positions with Salafists. However, after the Chechens signed the Khasavyurt treaty with the Russians in August 1996, a general election was held and the overall military commander during the war, Aslan Maskhadov, was elected by a wide majority. Maskhadov was in a precarious position, as he now had to try to build a government and maintain the peace when he was surrounded by former fighters who wanted a share of political power (and the ability to control resources) and who would use Islam as a means to take it.

Maskhadov had come to power as a representative of Sufism, but he inherited a government of Salafists. He had to immediately come to an agreement with them in order to neutralize them as a possible opposition, as they were some of the best-known commanders and controlled the largest number of fighters. Moreover, between 1997 and 1999, the number of Salafi-jihadists coming into the country continued to rise with 45 percent of Arab fighters flocking to Chechnya during the period. Recent research shows the percentages as: 59 percent Saudis, 14 percent Yemenis, 10 percent Egyptians, 6 percent Kuwaitis, and the remaining percentage from various Arab countries.[42] These Salafists also received money directly from Qatar, Kuwait, Jordan, Egypt, Saudi Arabia, and other transnational groups, so they were able to pay good salaries (and give status) to young Chechens in a region where unemployment was close to 80 percent. According to the intelligence report quoted earlier, it was during this

---

42. Murad Batal al-Shishani, "The Rise and Fall of Arab Fighters in Chechnya," paper presented at the Jamestown Foundation conference, September 14, 2006, and cited in *Terrorism Monitor*, VIII, 27, July 8, 2010, Jamestown Foundation, Washington DC.

period between wars that bin Laden "met with representatives of Movladi Udagov's [sic] party 'Islamic Way' and representatives of Chechen and Dagestan Wahhabists . . . they settled the question of cooperation—agreeing to exchange financial supplies to Chechen militants . . . and a direct route has been established to Chechnya . . . Abu Sayaf coordinates this traffic of 'volunteers,' as well as drug trafficking, working as a representative of bin Laden in the Chechen Foreign Ministry under the protection of Movladi Udagov."[43] Udugov is one of the most prominent ideologues of the insurgency, formerly first deputy prime minister of the Chechen Republic of Ichkeria and head of the Analysis and Information Service of the Caucasus Emirate; he is also often accused of working for the FSB.

But by making concessions to them, Maskhadov allowed the Salafists to build their own alternative hierarchy within Chechnya that would eventually contend with him for power and precipitate a second war with Russia. Maskhadov was doomed to failure from the beginning, as he did not have the means to demilitarize the insurgency groups without asking for help from Russia—which would have meant the loss of all credibility for his government. Unlike the Dayton Accords which brokered a peace deal for Bosnia, the Khasavyurt Accord *did not* have a clause requiring the expulsion of volunteer Arab fighters as a condition for peace. Because there was no lever for the Chechens to rid themselves of the radicals (and because Khattab would have only gone into Dagestan to be with his wife's family even if there was), in the end "the nascent nation-state was never able to disarm its erstwhile defenders and achieve the primary condition of statehood—monopolization of the means of violence."[44]

But the majority of Chechens did not want to see the Salafists take power and even if Maskhadov had wished for *shari'a* himself, he was struggling to keep the populace united. Opposition rallies in Grozny during 1997 and 1998 accused Maskhadov of having surrounded himself with "Wahhabis" and opposition members in the government passed resolutions demanding that he drop his "Wahhabite" ministers. Maskhadov bowed to the demands of the opposition and fired some Wahhabi ministers, but then the Wahhabis staged huge protests of their own—especially in Urus-Martin, which had essentially become a "Wahhabi" stronghold that secular authorities avoided. Maskhadov's followers suggested raiding the Salafist headquarters in the city to reduce their power base, but Maskhadov demurred, fearing a full-blown civil war.

Georgi Derluguian states that the encroaching fundamentalism was disastrous for the majority of Chechens who had reaped the benefits of

---

43. Declassified DIA intelligence report NC 3095345, October 16, 1998, 5.
44. Georgi M. Derluguian, "Che Guevaras in Turbans," *New Left Review*, 237, October–November 1999, 5.

Soviet education and social structure. Derluguian refers to it as the new "Dark Ages" and says, "It is indicative that the propagation of new Islamic piety spread only on the social and political fringes of Chechnya, particularly among the rural young males."[45]

And finally, there was the problem of peace. For men who are skilled fighters, living in a peaceful but poor country is not a good personal economic choice—and as indicated earlier, at some point the conflict always becomes about power, money, and influence. Considering that the *teips* had always constituted a latticework of internal fault lines within Chechen society, the additional influence of an outside ideological group that had money and ties to other nations, and who promised to give prominence to those who joined it, only further deepened those rifts. Clan leaders who felt left out and unappreciated by the new government went back to their mountain villages and refused to acknowledge Maskhadov's government—instead claiming that they recognized only the supremacy of Allah.[46] These groups were ripe for subverting—as are all "junior" leaders of any insurgency movement who are not big beneficiaries in the new regime. Maskhadov attempted to use a personal appeal to bring these commanders, who had once been united against Russia, back into the greater Chechen society, but to no avail.

Maskhadov also had to deal with Salafists who were kidnapping civilians for ransom—which turned Chechnya into a lawless, criminal state. There are numerous sources that describe those events in detail, so it won't be discussed here, but it is important to not underestimate the abysmal state of affairs. When three kidnappers were apprehended in February 1999, they claimed that they were not guilty because a *fatwa* issued by Abd ur-Rahman (a Saudi, military commander and "spiritual leader of Wahhabis" in Chechnya) had approved the kidnappings and payment of ransom.[47] It had been this same Abd ur-Rahman that was involved in the 1998 Gudermes clash between Sulim Yamadayev's forces (Kadyrov's ally) and the Salafists in which between 50 and 100 Chechens killed each other. As a result of that four-day conflict, Maskhadov was finally able to take strong action. He declared the Wahhabis to be extremists working to seize power and officially banned "Wahhabism" for bringing the Chechens to the brink of civil war. He deported many Arabs and other "internationals" and ordered Khattab to leave the country. He disbanded Salafist organizations and stripped Chechen radicals of their rank.

45. Derluguian, 10.
46. Emil Souleimanov, "Chechnya, Wahhabism and the Invasion of Dagestan," *Middle East Review of International Affairs* Vol. 9, No. 4 (December 2005), 50.
47. Vahkit Akiev, *Religious-Political Conflict in the Chechen Republic of Ichkeria* (Stockholm: CA & CC Press AB, 1998), available at http://www.ca-c.org/dataeng/05.akaev.shtml.

However, Basayev and Vice President Arsanov (a Salafist) felt that Maskhadov had gone too far and pointed out that Khattab and other Arabs had not taken part in the conflict and didn't meddle in Chechen politics. Under their influence, Maskhadov relented and did not take collective action against all the Salafists. Eventually though, the Salafists were too powerful and in February 1999, Maskhadov declared *shari'a* to be in effect—and with it, Maskhadov put himself out of a job: the decree of *shari'a* meant that all constitutional activity was void—including his own election. A Shura council would rule the country; Maskhadov and Basayev each called his own, and both declared themselves to be the leader of Chechnya.

EXPORTING THE REVOLUTION

There was another divisive issue among the ChRI leadership—whether or not to take the fight into Dagestan and liberate their traditional allies now that they had achieved their own independence. Khattab may not have been involved in Chechen politics, but he was "... a member of the roaming brotherhood of jihadi paladins that continued to wage holy war on behalf of front line Muslim groups long after the 'divine' victory over the Soviets in the Afghan jihad of 1979–1988. In the aftermath of the Soviet defeat, Khattab and other members of the Afghan alumni swore an oath to the patron saint of the international jihad movement, Abduallah Azzam, to continue the defense of other threatened Muslim groups across the globe."[48] Western Dagestan was one of those places. In addition to the long history that Chechnya and Dagestani Avars shared fighting against the Russians, there was also the fact that Khattab had married a Dagestani woman, and so felt a religious duty to liberate Dagestan now that they had achieved success in Chechnya.

Khattab was not the only one calling for the invasion of Dagestan. Basayev had stated that the long-term economic success of Chechnya was dependent on reviving the old *Imamat* of Chechnya and Dagestan that had been established by his namesake, the first Shamil. And in April 1999 "at the Congress of the Peoples of Chechnya and Dagestan, Shamil Basayev vowed to invade Dagestan."[49] A month earlier, Basayev had called a "Commander's Council," which had elected Basayev as the leader of the Mekh-Khel, and declared itself the highest authority

---

48. Williams, "The Chechen Arabs," 1.
49. Enver Isriev and Robert Ware, "Conflict and Catharsis: A Report on Developments in Dagestan following the Incursions of August and September 1999," *Nationality Papers* 28, 3, September 2000, 87.

in Chechnya—meaning the majority of the fighters now supported Basayev.

Maskhadov believed such a move would be suicidal for Chechnya and rejected out of hand any and all suggestions to invade Dagestan. However, he was not the master of his own country, much less of Basayev or Khattab, and they continued to train radicals in their camps and participate in Islamic conferences with Salafists from Dagestan. It made Maskhadov's attempts at peacekeeping and maintaining order extremely tenuous, as those opposed to him personally (or to his refusal to take the insurgency into Dagestan) simply refused to honor agreements Maskhadov made with the Russians, and engaged in violence and terrorism to sabotage efforts at reconciliation.[50] It would be this final issue between the Salafists and Maskhadov that would prove the ChRI's undoing.

THE END DRAWS NEAR

Chechnya had become a lawless state caught between competing power structures and ideologies, and to say there was a lack of government control would be a gross understatement. None of the militias had disarmed, and although Maskhadov had attempted to outlaw Wahhabism, his only "real" ally in government at the time had been the chief mufti of Chechnya, Ahmed Kadyrov, and some of the Sufi militia commanders like the Yamadayev clan (although the Yamadayevs were also guilty of kidnappings and ransoms).[51] Whether Kadyrov was biding his time until he could have the Russians come in and assist him in taking power for himself, or whether he was truly concerned about the power of a non-Chechen form of Islam, Kadyrov was outspoken in his criticism, which put him in a very good position.

Many Chechens say that Kadyrov and the Yamadaevs sold out Chechen freedom for personal power and that religion had nothing to do with it. However, if there wasn't so much violence tied to the Kadyrovs, one might have been able to say that the Qadiriyya Grand Mufti of Chechnya had followed in the footsteps of Kunta-haji and offered the Chechens a way out of fighting and a way to live peacefully with the Russians—and this time the Russians supported him. Regardless, Ahmed-haji Kadyrov's choice to side with the Russians at the beginning of the 1999 war gave the Kremlin the critical levers that it lacked in the past—a legitimate counter-ideology that the Chechens could understand and support, and a respected leader who could articulate that ideology.

---

50. Hafez, 143.
51. Unless one believes that Kadyrov was working for the FSB and fomenting instability so that Russia could claim that Chechnya was a lawless "black hole" and required Russian troops to intervene to stop the civil war.

It has been said that Maskhadov never really had a chance to make the Chechen Republic of Ichkeria work because he was never allowed a chance by the radicals—who would never accept a government that was not based entirely on the *shari'a*. It was a classic case of different factions within an insurgency splitting along their normal fault lines and beginning to vie for political power once their common enemy disappeared. This is common in most insurgent movements (except for Communist campaigns that build a cadre over many years), but was more easily exploited in a place like Chechnya where the societal fabric was already scored by innumerable clan affiliations. Regardless of what he personally believed as a Sufi Muslim, the institution of *shari'a* would have meant a loss of power for Maskhadov personally and an invitation for the Russians to come back in.

Ironically, in the end, the group that gave Maskhadov the most trouble during his administration gave him the most support once the Russians invaded again in 1999. For the Salafists, the most important thing was to establish the *shari'a*—which as history has demonstrated, has been one of the main reasons for fighting against the Russians for the past 300 years.

However, what had previously been the role of conservative Sufi Islam in the past had now become the role of radical Salafist Islam. That role changed throughout the course of the first war from an initial infusion of much-needed fighters and cash, and culminated in a parallel hierarchy of power during the interwar period that prevented the government unity that was essential for the fledgling ChRI to become a viable state. Despite the fact that the Russians had already made the decision to reinvade Chechnya before the incursion into Dagestan,[52] a strong case can still be made that the radicals caused the second war, partly because they themselves did not honor the Khasavyurt agreement and vowed before the start of the second war to liberate Dagestan, and partly because their presence was framed as "anti-Chechen" by elites both within Chechnya and Moscow.

Had Chechnya been able to "get its act together" like the Baltic countries did after the breakup of the Soviet Union, it would have been far more difficult for the Russians to renege on the Khasavyurt Accord. But the internal fight for power that turned Chechnya into a lawless country and the inexorable advance of Salafism provided at least some of the motivation for the Russians to consider the reinvasion in the first place, while the attack into Dagestan—Russian Federation territory—gave them clear legal justification to do so.

Russia was not blameless in this drama; Matthew Evangelista lists many ways that the Russian government did not fulfill its obligations,

---

52. Former Russian Prime Minister Sergei Stepashin, as quoted by Sergei Pavosudov, "Bloka OVR voobsche moglo I ne bit,'" *Nezavisimaya Gazeta*, January 14, 2000.

failed to make necessary and promised payments to Chechnya, and generally worked at cross purposes with Maskhadov. As a direct result of Moscow's actions during the first war, all factories and processing plants had been bombed and remained inoperable, mines laid by the Russians covered 15 percent of the republic's cultivatable soil, and 60–70 percent of the housing had been damaged or destroyed—all of which Moscow had agreed to take care of and did nothing about. Evangelista also makes a strong point that if the Russian government had been more supportive of Maskhadov, he might have been able to exert more control over the radical elements (as well as the criminal elements) that were tearing the country apart.[53] But that assumes that Russia felt it was in its best interests to help Chechnya maintain its independence—and the Kremlin has never believed that.

Russian efforts to bolster Maskhadov would have only helped him deal with the problems that were already extant—the radical groups that were competing with him for power. In other words, Moscow could have (and according to their own signed agreements, *should* have) helped Maskhadov treat the disease—and therefore Moscow is culpable for withholding the medicine. But the Kremlin, although a contributor, was not responsible for the internal disease that destroyed the organism from within.

---

53. Evangelista, *The Chechen Wars*, pp. 74–95.

CHAPTER 7

The 1999 Chechen War

Everything came to a boil in 1999. Chechnya was clearly suffering from a lack of government control, there were competing power blocs, the people were still vulnerable and suffering from the first war, nothing had been rebuilt, there were no jobs, there was no economy, and the Russians were in the process of completing their plans to invade. There are many who argue that Russia was drawn into another conflict in Chechnya in order to secure the borders of this lawlessness region. They also argue that the Dagestan incursion and the Moscow bombings were precipitous events that drove Russia over the edge and necessitated an invasion of Chechnya. There is some truth to that assertion; nonetheless, there is also sufficient evidence to suggest that Russia was planning to reinvade Chechnya before those events transpired. In addition to the extensive MOD (Ministry of Defense) training and preparation, the sealed border, and other activities by the Russians to prepare their way, there is an actual admission by Russia's prime minister.

Less than four months after the start of the second war, Sergei Stepashin, the former director of the FSB during the first Chechen War and prime minister of Russia during the interwar period stated: "Regarding Chechnya, I can say the following. The plan for [military] action in this republic has been under development since March [1999]. We planned to move out and reach the Terek [river] by August or September. This would have happened even if there hadn't been explosions in Moscow. I actively led the work in strengthening the border with Chechnya in preparation for the offensive. As such, Vladimir Putin hasn't opened [started] anything new. You can ask him yourself about this. At that time he was the director of the FSB and had full knowledge of all the information."[1] But then Shamil invaded Dagestan, and everything changed.

---

1. Sergei Pravosudov, "Bloka OVR voobsche moglo I ne bit,' " *Nezavisimaya Gazeta*, January 14, 2000.

THE INVASION OF DAGESTAN

The facts of the August 1999 invasion of Dagestan are, like many events in 1999, fuzzy; different sources say different things, participants on both sides claim the other started it, some claim Basayev and Khattab led the initial invasion while others say that Basayev waited to respond until asked to, and both sides say the FSB was pulling strings behind the scenes. What is generally accepted is that a form of Salafism entered Dagestan *before* it made its way into Chechnya. This "Wahhabism" was initially well received in Dagestan and became a major force in the early 1990s. However, clashes soon broke out between the new Wahhabis and an alliance that formed between the secularists and the ensconced Sufi hierarchies. Armed clashes between the groups began in earnest in 1997, and the Dagestani government responded with an effort to discredit the Wahhabis and their ideology which culminated in a law called "On the Fight Against Islamic Fundamentalism."

At the invitation of Zelimkhan Yanderbiyev, Bagauddin Magomedov, the Avar Wahhabi leader, fled Dagestan and came to Chechnya with several hundred families and established ties with the Wahhabis. In 1998, a village in Dagestan declared itself to be an independent Wahhabi republic despite pressure from the local government not to do so. The response from the Russians, while sufficient to keep the movement from spreading, was nevertheless far less drastic than anticipated and the local government was not able to dislodge Wahhabi control over the village; Prime Minister Stepashin eventually granted limited autonomy to the enclave. This first small step combined with Khattab's increasing material support (transport of weapons from Chechnya into Dagestan), Basayev's public support ("[We] will not allow the occupying Russian army to wreak any havoc in the land of our Muslim brethren"), and the virtual unification of Dagestani and Chechen Wahhabis would indicate in hindsight that something was being planned for Dagestan.

In January 1999, Khattab formed a new unit, the "International Islamic Regiment," comprised of foreign volunteers and began training in earnest; Khattab had conducted a "probing" attack against Russian units in late 1998 in order to determine their effectiveness, and found the Russian response to be anemic. It was probably the lessons drawn from this engagement that encouraged Bagauddin Magomedov, now the self-proclaimed (but Chechen supported) emir of the Islamic *Jamaat* of Dagestan (in exile), to start thinking about returning to Dagestan with his supporters. In April 1999 he called for volunteers to "take part in the jihad" and do their part in "liberating Dagestan and the Caucasus from the Russian colonial yoke."[2]

---

2. Emil Souleimanov, "Chechnya, Wahhabism and the Invasion of Dagestan," *Middle East Review of International Affairs* Vol. 9, No. 4 (December 2005), 62.

We now reach the first point of contention among analysts who argue that one side or the other was planning an invasion and the other side was merely responding to the threat; this is also the point where conspiracy theories begin to muddy the waters even more. What is clear is that, according to the Russian prime minister at the time, the Russians began plans in March for a reinvasion of Chechnya that would see Russian troops occupying the northern third of Chechnya (Yermolov's traditional Caucasian line) by "August or September" 1999. It is also clear from their own published statements before the war that the Islamists intended to establish an *imamate* that would encompass the entire North Caucasus.[3] So it was a race. The radicals, whether they had good intelligence or merely believed the Russians would invade soon, made statements at the time indicating that they knew the Russians had plans to attack, and began making plans to invade Dagestan before the Russians could stop them.

Based on the available evidence, it seems pretty clear that both sides knew that there would be a Russian assault before too long and both sides were preparing for it—the large-scale Russian joint services military exercises in neighboring North Ossetia and the tight seal around the Chechen border being the strongest indicators. Additionally, one cannot overlook the fact that the Russian Special Services are extremely skillful, and one of their basic missions is to foment unrest and insurgency. In some cases this unrest can be used to create conditions allowing Russia to "intervene" in a conflict while maintaining sufficient plausible deniability.[4]

President Maskhadov still clung to the hope that a new war could be avoided. However, Basayev, being the realist, saw the writing on the wall, and whether his actions were pre-emptive (as some have speculated), provocative (as the Russians claim), or defensive (as Basayev and other Chechen fighters claim), he began to make preparations for what he considered an inevitable invasion.

Regardless of intentions, at least some of the Chechen warlords believed their long-term survival was dependent on getting Dagestan involved in any future conflict with the Russians. Dagestan and Chechnya had a shared history of fighting the Russians, they were cultural "cousins," their economies were virtually identical in terms of being the absolute worst in the Soviet Union (and later Russia), and there was the new "Wahhabi" factor. Whether it was to further the expansion of Wahhabism, to reestablish the Mountain Republic, to gain a foothold on the Caspian Sea that could facilitate the transshipment of petroleum

---

3. Charles W. Blandy, *Chechnya: a Beleaguered President,* Conflict Studies Research Center, No: OB 61, August 1998.
4. Many aspects of the situation before the 1999 Chechen War bear striking similarities to the build up to the 2008 Russo-Georgian war.

products from Central Asia to the West, or to simply broaden the conflict and exponentially increase the difficulty for Russian forces once the fight started again, from the Chechens' point of view, getting the Dagestanis involved was strategically sound—especially as many of those same Chechen warlords didn't believe that Russia would ever make good on its promises to rebuild Chechnya or allow it to stay independent.

The actual plans for the Dagestan invasion are unknown, but a standard "start an insurgency plan" would look something like: (1) support a large group of people inside of Dagestan that want to secede from the present government for ideologically and politically defensible reasons (religious differences for example); (2) arm, equip, and train those people; (3) create a "situation" within Dagestan where the authorities would respond in a dramatically harsh way, requiring the Chechens (or other ideologically minded "patriots") to rush to the aid of their brethren (with battalions of secretly well-trained zealots like Khattab's Islamic battalion); (4) spin the conflict to the international media in such a way as to show the secular Dagestani government was repressive and attempting to crush the people for religious reasons; (5) portray the Chechens as heroes so that when the inevitable Russian reinvasion of Chechnya came, the Chechens could frame the conflict as one of religious persecution and retaliation, thus gaining the support of the West and the Middle East. If large-scale support could be gained from either the West or the Middle East, the world community would apply pressure to Russia to stop attacking its own citizens, while the combined populations of Chechnya and Dagestan would be too much for the Russian army to handle—ensuring continued survival for Chechnya and "independence" for Dagestan, who would now join as a junior partner with Chechnya in some sort of Islamic Mountain Republic.

The actual events were very similar to what was outlined above, giving credence to the Russian claim that the Dagestani invasion was planned in advance. At the beginning of August, some of Magomedov's "patriots" re-entered Dagestan and took over a number of villages, killing a few Russian ministry of defense soldiers during skirmishes on the border. A week later, Basayev and Khattab led the Islamic Brigade (approximately 1,500 fighters, mostly Dagestanis, but with Chechens and foreign Wahhabis as well) into Dagestan and occupied more Wahhabi villages in Dagestan. On August 9th, Sergei Stepashin was sacked as Russian prime minister and replaced by the FSB chief, Vladimir Putin. The next day the Dagestani invaders declared the areas they had taken over to be the independent Islamic State of Dagestan, and a small war began. Luckily for the Russians, the anticipated general uprising of the Dagestani people necessary for the success of the operation did not occur. Instead, many Dagestanis viewed their returning countrymen as aggressors and religious

fanatics who were better off staying in Chechnya, and they perceived the Chechens and foreigners as opportunists with territorial
ambitions.

With the help of a ferocious Russian air and artillery campaign
(including the first use of fuel-air explosives and scatterable mines in the
region) that presaged the tactics that would level Grozny within the next
two months, the local authorities mobilized and fought off the invaders
in a delaying action until regular Russian forces arrived. The combined
forces soon drove the invaders out of the mountains. In late August,
Prime Minister Putin flew down to Dagestan to oversee the last push to
drive all the Wahhabis out of Dagestan. The Chechens responded by
launching another offensive intended to divert the Russians, and on September 4th, as the Russians were struggling to eradicate the last vestiges of resistance from the "autonomous" Wahhabi enclaves, a car
bomb detonated outside a five-story apartment complex housing Russian border guards and their families in Buynaksk, Dagestan—
killing 64 and injuring another 133 in what is generally referred to as
the first of the "Moscow apartment bombings." By mid-September all
the invasion forces were pushed back into Chechnya, and the die for
war was cast.

President Maskhadov strongly condemned the Dagestan attack in an
attempt to stave off a Russian invasion, but to no avail. Although already
planning to reinvade anyway, the Dagestan incursion—in conjunction
with three more suspicious apartment bombings in Moscow that were
blamed on the Chechens—accelerated Russia's plan to invade Chechnya
and provided the justification to exceed the original intent which had only
called for occupying the areas north of the Terek River. Maskhadov
regarded the Russian invasion as a violation of the Khasavyurt agreement,
and for Maskhadov, there was no choice but to fight to retain Chechnya's
independence; for the Salafists, living under Russian rule was unthinkable,
they would fight until the end.

There are quite a few reputable sources that claim the FSB or the GRU
or both were instrumental in "creating" the Dagestani war, and now is as
good a time as any to discuss why examining the "conspiracy theories" is
important. If the Russians *did* create the conditions through active measures, then those active measures and their repercussions yield important
lessons for COIN practitioners (both good and bad). And if the Russians
didn't engage in active destabilization measures, they nonetheless used
the actual events to their advantage in order to create the conditions for
success—which requires even closer scrutiny—because then the Chechen
actions become a list of "what not to do." Unless one is looking to assign
blame, the facts are not as important as how those facts are framed and
packaged—and perception can be manipulated. How the Russians framed
the facts (and for what purpose) is important for understanding the COIN

campaign because the Russians obviously learned from the first war and made positive steps to prepare for the second.

Many people want to discount the conspiracy theories as unbelievable, but this approach is egocentric and not based on actual capabilities. U.S. Special Forces were designed and trained to foment insurrection and conduct sabotage in order to liberate nations from Communist rule; to insinuate that the Russian special services are not capable of conducting the same types of activities would be an insult. Some special operations forces, the Russians included, have a mission to shape the operational environment for follow-on forces in such a way so that the government they support will have plausible deniability. There is no evidence to prove the Russian Special Services were involved in fomenting unrest in the Caucasus, but then, if they conducted their mission properly, there wouldn't be any. U.S. forces and agencies are prohibited by law from conducting certain types of activities for moral, ethical, and cultural reasons; not all countries share U.S. ideals, and not all governments place the same restrictions on their special services. One cannot assume that other governments will act the way we want them to, or to act the way that we would in a similar circumstance. To make these assumptions would be counterproductive and violate one of the cardinal sins of counterinsurgency—egocentric and socio-centric thinking.

Conspiracy Theory #1–Wag the Dog in Dagestan

There are many who believe the invasion of Chechnya in 1999 had as much to do with the elections in Russia as it had to do with anything else. Duma elections were scheduled for December 1999 and presidential elections were to follow in June 2000. In late 1999, the Russian newspaper *Moskovsky Kossomolets* published recorded telephone conversations that it claimed were between Boris Berezovsky (one of the billionaires created by President Yeltsin) and some rogue Chechens. They reportedly discussed a possible invasion of Dagestan and setting bombs in Moscow to create enough chaos to justify suspending the elections if things were going bad for Yeltsin, or ride the wave of popularity if things were going well. The Chechen identified in the conversation (Movladi Udugov, a staunch Salafist, ideologist, and propagandist) allegedly wished for the Russian military response to topple Maskhadov's secular government so that the Salafists could create a new Islamic republic that would be friendly to Russia.[5] On October 12th, the editor of another Russian newspaper, *Nezavisimaya Gazeta*, asserted in a front-page article, "It is absolutely obvious that the Chechens have been lured into Dagestan. This

---

5. Alex Goldfarb, with Marina Litvinenko, *Death of a Dissident: The Poisoning of Alexander Litvinenko and the Return of the KGB* (New York: Free Press, 2007), 216.

was clearly an operation planned by the Russian secret services (quite separate from the blowing up of apartment blocks in Russia), and moreover sanctioned at the very highest political level"—in other words, quite a few believe that the war was started to give Yeltsin a bump—the classic "wag the dog" theory. The journalist Anna Politkovskaya—assassinated in 2006 outside her Moscow apartment—resolutely believed that the Russian secret services engineered the Dagestani invasion.

The Moscow Apartment Bombings

Conspiracy theories also continue to swirl around the spate of bombings that began in August 1999. Part of the reason that the conspiracy theories persist is because of major inconsistencies in the official Russian explanations of the events, the denials of the Chechen terrorists themselves (who claimed the rest of their terrorist attacks both before and after the Moscow bombings), and the research of respected analysts and observers.

The facts: On August 31st, a bomb exploded in a Moscow shopping mall killing one and injuring 40, and on September 4th, a military apartment block in Dagestan was bombed. On September 4th, a military apartment block in Dagestan was bombed. Two Moscow apartment buildings were bombed on the 9th and 13th respectively, and another apartment building was bombed in Volgodonsk on the 16th; almost 300 people were killed and hundreds more injured. All the bombs had the same "signature"—RDX and timing devices expertly placed in order to destroy the weakest structural elements of the buildings at a time calculated to cause the most casualties (5 A.M. for the apartment buildings). The majority of these bombings occurred during the Dagestan invasion discussed previously.

On September 15th, Vladimir Putin announced that the terrorists responsible for the attacks were hiding on Chechen soil and demanded that the Chechens hand over the suspects; the Chechens vehemently denied any involvement or that they were harboring suspects. All Russian cities were put on high alert for suspicious activity, and on September 23rd police in Ryazan arrested two suspects who had placed sacks of white powder and (what appeared to be) detonators in the basement of an apartment building in Ryazan; the three men turned out to be FSB agents from Moscow. Explosives experts from the local FSB were brought in to defuse the devices, and, using well-maintained technical equipment, confirmed that they were constructed of RDX, had working detonators, and were similar to the bombs used at the other locations. Soon after, FSB headquarters in Moscow claimed that it was not a real bomb, and the entire incident had been a training exercise. Later, one of the arrested FSB agents (the one who had rented the basement and was seen emplacing the sacks) was killed in Cyprus in a hit-and-run car accident that was never solved. A former KGB agent-turned-lawyer who was investigating the case independently on behalf of the victims was arrested and convicted by a secret tribunal, and four more people investigating the FSB's possible involvement were killed under mysterious circumstances—including a member of the Russian Duma and journalist Anna Politkovskaya. The official FSB investigation was completed in 2002. It named al-Khattab and an associate, Abu Omar al-Saif, as the trainers and a Karachi businessman as the mastermind behind the bombings. In 2004, a sequestered Moscow court sentenced two members of a Karachai-based pro-Chechen Wahhabi group for emplacing the bombs. Significantly, the FSB investigation did not implicate the Chechen government or Maskhadov—although Russia would invade Chechnya because of its alleged involvement.

Although there are many who do not believe the official Russian version is accurate and continue to investigate,[6] what is more important is how "the Russian leadership exploited the tragedy of the bombings for political purposes" in order to justify the attack into Chechnya.[7] If Moscow was to be successful in a second war, it needed to have the national will behind it; so not only did the Kremlin need to show that the current government in Chechnya was illegitimate (counter-ideology), it also needed to demonstrate to its own citizens and the army that its actions were legal and therefore legitimate. What is irrefutable about the Moscow apartment bombings is that Prime Minister Putin declared that the Chechens were responsible for the terrorist attack before a full investigation was completed. This was a clear example of "elite framing"—designed to construct an interpretation of events in such a way as to build upon the earlier case of the Dagestan incursion and demonstrate to the Russian people that Russia's vital interests were at stake.

As for President Maskhadov, although he maintained that the bombings were a set-up by the FSB in order to win public support for a new invasion, he nevertheless offered to crack down again on the Salafists and renegade warlords in Chechnya in a futile hope to keep the Russians from invading. The Russians had already begun an air campaign

---

6. The best piece to date is Scott Anderson's "None Dare Call It Conspiracy," *Gentleman's Quarterly*, September 2009, 246–251, 311–313. This article was aggressively suppressed by Condé Nast after initial publication. Internal directives banned the article from the magazine's Web site, prohibited reprinting it in other Condé Nast magazines abroad, stopped any U.S. editions from being sent to Russia, and didn't advertise the article in any way. Available at http://groups.yahoo.com/group/chechnya-sl/message/57980.

7. *The Crisis in Chechnya: Causes, Prospects, Solutions*, Princeton University Conference Summary, March 3–4, 2000, p 3.

in Chechnya as part of the defense of Dagestan, bombing suspected rebel positions along the border. But by mid-September, the Russian air force was conducting bombing raids deep into Chechnya. By the time the ground offensive began, hundreds of civilians had already died and close to 100,000 Chechens had fled the country—most of them to neighboring Ingushetia.

Maskhadov appealed to the Russians, the European community, and even NATO, but by this time, the Russians refused to speak to him. On October 1st, Prime Minister Putin declared Maskhadov and his government to be illegitimate based on Maskhadov's own actions in declaring *shari'a*, resulting in the illegal dissolution of the Chechen parliament. The Chechens prepared for the inevitable invasion, and many of the former warring factions once again flocked to Maskhadov and pledged their allegiance.

THE COUP DE GRÂCE

Once the Russians began their ground attack into Chechnya in October 1999, they moved quickly to their originally planned "limit of advance" (the northern bank of the Terek), rolling over the lowlands and upper third of Chechnya within five days. Maskhadov was alarmed, but felt that his combined forces could stall the Russians long enough for him to broker a peace deal with the Russians, and to lobby the international community to force Moscow to accept.

Ahkmed-haji Kadryov took a different view. The chief mufti of the Chechen Republic of Ichkeria, who under Dudayev had officially declared *gazavat* against the Russians during the first war, had strongly condemned both the initial Wahhabi incursion into Dagestan and the subsequent invasion of Khattab's Islamic Brigade. Now, with the Russians on the other side of the Terek River, Kadyrov publicly called for the Chechens *not to resist*. Maskhadov promptly fired him as mufti and branded him Public Enemy Number One. Whether he had previously made arrangements with the Russians or not, Kadyrov, along with the Yamadayev clan, switched sides and joined Bislan Gantimirov (the former Russian-appointed mayor of Grozny), and the Khakievs (from the northern part of Chechnya), another powerful group that had always been allied with Russia against a coalition of Maskhadov's remaining secularists and the radicals.

ADVANCE INTO THE CENTRAL VALLEY

On October 12th, the Russians crossed the Terek, but they were a very different force that had entered in 1994. Despite some lingering problems, the Russian army demonstrated that it had learned and applied many lessons from the earlier conflict.[8] This time the Russians brought close to 100,000 men (four times as many troops than they started with in 1994), and they didn't immediately attempt to seize Grozny for a quick victory in a *coup de main*. This time they moved methodically through the central valley, conducting a thorough "artillery preparation" on each village before sending in troops. Much has been written about the tactical differences between 1996 and 1999 and their very significant impact on the war, but to be honest, the Russians were merely catching up to the times in terms of secure communications equipment, improved air-ground coordination, better staff planning, advanced munitions (fuel-air explosives and flame-throwers), operational security (OPSEC), better use of infantry task forces in urban terrain, etc. The most significant change they made was improved intelligence; now that they had Chechens fighting on their side, they had access to the same information about routes and terrain that their enemy had, and "their" Chechens were able to get updated information on enemy locations and intentions from the local population that the Russians had been unable to get in years past.

At an operational level, however, besides bringing in more troops and not trying for the "quick win," there was very little about this method of "destroy, clear, move on" that was different from historical marches through the valley—an enemy-centric, purely military operation designed to minimize federal casualties while enforcing or coercing civilian compliance. The Russians moved into position and gave ultimatums to the civilians to surrender; if they didn't, the Russians employed heavy artillery and air assets to reduce the structures, and only later would they send infantry in to secure the area. The justification for these attacks was that the villages were harboring international terrorists. The Russian defense minister Igor Sergeyev stated that the Russian plan was to take Grozny by the middle of December after six to seven weeks of continuous bombing.[9]

Now that the Russians had local Chechens to assist them, they were able to bypass the ChRI positions around Grozny and seize key terrain quickly—and with far fewer casualties. As the Russians began bombing Grozny using rockets and heavy artillery, President Maskhadov declared *gazavat* and martial law, calling on all Chechens to defend their homeland. The civilians began streaming out of the towns and cities toward Ingushetia, the numbers reaching the hundreds of thousands. Many of the fleeing civilians were killed as the Russians started using short-range

---

8. For a detailed analysis of tactical operations lessons learned and application in the battles for Grozny, see Olya Oliker, *Russia's Chechen Wars 1994–2000* (Santa Monica, CA: Rand, 2001), and Lester Grau and Timothy Thomas, *Russian Lessons Learned From the Battles For Grozny*, Foreign Military Studies Office (Fort Leavenworth, KS), originally appearing in the *Marine Corps Gazette*, April 2000.

9. Ib Faurby and Marta-Lisa Magnusson, "The Battles of Grozny," *Baltic Defense Review*, 2/1999, 86.

ballistic missiles in Grozny and even hit refugee columns stopped at the borders.

On November 12th, Kadyrov arranged for Gudermes, the second largest city in Chechnya—and perhaps the most significant in terms of key terrain because it serves as the gateway to the central valley—to voluntarily accept Russian troops; and Maskhadov's defense plans literally crumbled before his eyes. In return, Putin would later appoint Kadyrov as acting head of the Chechen administration in 2000, and help him get elected president in 2003. In exchange for their defection, the Yamadayevs were given assorted gifts as well—including awards of the "Hero of Russia"—the nation's highest award (equivalent to the U.S. Medal of Honor) to three of the Yamadayev brothers—the only family in the history of Russia to have achieved such an honor. The eldest, Ruslan, was made a member of the Russian parliament, while Sulim was given command of the East (Vostok) Chechen Battalion of the GRU (the military Main Intelligence Directorate, also the parent organization of Spetsnaz military special forces).[10] Khakiev was given command of the Zapad (West) GRU Battalion composed entirely of northern Chechens who remained loyal to Moscow during the first war. The appointment of the Sufi chief mufti as the new leader of Chechnya by President Putin was the shrewdest move of the entire second war and the turning point for the Russians.

THE THIRD BATTLE OF GROZNY

By December 4th, the Russians had surrounded Grozny, and following an artillery preparation that left Grozny looking like Berlin in 1945 (the United Nations shortly thereafter declared it the "most destroyed city on earth"), and a leaflet campaign that warned any remaining residents to flee, the Russians began their ground offensive using the Chechen militias to spearhead the attack.[11] Unlike the 1995 assault on Grozny, the Russians had taught their soldiers some basic MOUT (military operations on urban terrain) techniques, developed new tactics based around a new combined arms configuration called a "storm detachment," and worked

---

10. Ahmed-haji Kadyrov was assassinated by a bomb in 2004 by the insurgents, and his son, Ramzan, is now president. Dzhabrail Yamadayev, the eldest brother and first commander of the Vostok battalion, was killed in a bomb blast as well (although the insurgents deny responsibility for his death and claim that it was carried out by Kadyrov in order to consolidate power). Ruslan was assassinated in Moscow in September 2008 on his way to a meeting with President Medvedev—allegedly to talk about the ongoing power struggle in Chechnya. His brother Sulim took over the Vostok battalion and had had numerous clashes with the younger Kadyrov before he was assassinated in Dubai in April 2009 with a golden gun.

11. Rupert Wingfield Hayes, "Scars remain amid Chechen revival," *BBC News*, March 3, 2007, available at http://news.bbc.co.uk/go/pr/fr/-/2/hi/programmes/from_our_own_correspondent/6414603.stm.

methodically from one sector to the next, not even attempting to push forward into the city until they had established a strong foothold.[12] They employed significant artillery and aviation support, including fuel air explosives, SCUD, and SS-21 Scarab missiles to wear down the fighters and reduce the buildings that they used for cover and defense. The Russians conducted aggressive reconnaissance throughout a given sector to identify potential Chechen strongholds and relayed coordinates to fire control centers. Missiles and high explosives were used to penetrate basements and bunkers, and in so doing denied the Chechens their previous advantage of defending on home terrain. In many ways it was similar to the deforestation campaigns of the 1800s: deny the Chechens a place to hide or fight from.

This effort did not represent an improvement in the Russian counter-insurgency techniques; rather, as was mentioned previously, this was a dramatic improvement on the Russian Army's doctrine on fighting in urban terrain and was based on revisiting the lessons of the Red Army during WWII. After recon and artillery prep, sappers cleared lanes, the Chechen militias and Russian Spetsnaz would move through the lanes supported by snipers and take control of key hubs. These hubs were then interconnected in order to provide mutual support and Russian infantry was able to move out from the hubs in storm detachments supported by tanks and APCs to reduce remaining pockets of resistance. The storm detachments were given more lethal weapons (especially flamethrowers), which were effective in keeping the Chechens from "hugging" the advancing Russian forces as they had done in the 1994 war. Nonetheless, it was still brutal because house-to-house combat is always hellish; moreover, the Russian army's predilection for "recon by drawing fire" is enough to make any young soldier lose his nerve in addition to his life.[13] The Chechens gave ground but later retook lost areas once the Russians had moved on, meaning that the Russian rear areas and mutual-support avenues were never really secure. Eventually the battle became a snipers' war, turning the few remaining tall buildings into key terrain and sometimes having snipers from both sides occupying different floors of the same building.

The battle raged back and forth, as the Chechens seemed to miraculously find ways to keep their supply lines open and bring in fresh

---

12. See Oliker, *Russia's Chechen Wars 1994–2000*, for a good analysis of the Russian MOUT campaign.

13. A recon tactic personally observed by the author and even used by elite Russian forces like the airborne: a squad sends its two youngest soldiers ahead in the hopes that they will "draw fire" from the enemy. The rest of the squad will then attempt to locate the source of the incoming fire and lay down suppressive fire in an attempt to get the decoys out. Once out of "danger close" artillery range, the Russians will then attempt to use mortars and other indirect fire on the enemy.

fighters. In early January the Chechens mounted counterattacks outside of Grozny to retake territory, open fresh supply lines, and ambush Russian convoys and rear-echelon troops. By then, the Russian plan was beginning to unravel, and the support of the Russian people was beginning to wane; the Russian press began to break ranks with the government (as well as soldiers' mothers groups and returning Russian officers) and began to dispute the official Kremlin reports on casualties and conditions.

The campaign was also taking a toll on the Chechens, and whether or not there was any Russian involvement, Ruslan Gelayev (aka the Black Angel) unexpectedly withdrew his force of approximately 1,500 from Grozny without orders, leaving the rest of the Chechen forces open to attack.[14] With Gelayev's forces gone and the rest of the Chechens encountering increasing casualties and dwindling supplies, the order was given to evacuate Grozny at the beginning of February. The Russians claimed that they "set up" the Chechens through a special services operation where they offered the Chechens a route with safe passage for $100,000, but in an elaborate double-cross the Chechens were purposely directed into a gauntlet—a minefield covered by Russian artillery and direct fire. The evacuation became a massacre. During a violent snowstorm, many Chechens sacrificed themselves and cleared a path through the minefield by running across it under fire. A survivor wrote, "We had to walk on our dead comrades to avoid stepping on unexploded mines."[15]

At first the Russian high command didn't realize that the Chechens were escaping, evidently not believing their ruse had worked. But once

---

14. "The Rebel Who Rides to Moscow's Rescue," *The Moscow Times*, October 2, 2002. This article asserts that Gelayev may have been working for the Russians, as in critical situations, Gelayev and his forces would make a move that assisted the Russian cause. Available at http://www.moscowtimes.ru/article/908/49/243201.htm. Following the precipitous exit out of Grozny, Maskhadov demoted Gelayev from brigadier general to private and forbade him from "defending the motherland" in the future. Gelayev would go on to fight against some of his former comrades, cross into the Pankisi Gorge (Georgia) with about 800 Chechens and 80 foreign fighters, and later side with Yanderbiyev against Maskhadov. He eventually left the Pankisi Gorge and supported Maskhadov again after the U.S. GTEP mission began to mature and Georgian forces moved into the region. Georgian President Shevardnadze consistently refused to give up Gelayev to the Russians, referring to him as a "noble man," although it may have been because Gelayev attacked Abkhazia in 2001 on behalf of the Georgians. Gelayev's ideology was profiteering: power and money. Considering that he parlayed with all sides at one point or another, it is not inconceivable that the Russians bought him out in 2000.
15. Marcus Warren, "Rebels March Over Mines to Save Their Comrades," *The Telegraph*, February 6, 2000, available at http://www.telegraph.co.uk/htmlContent.jhtml?html=/archive/2000/02/06/wchec06.html.

they realized their mistake, they attempted to interdict the fleeing Chechens by destroying the villages along the Chechen route of march. On
February 4th, in one of Russia's best-documented human rights abuses,
without warning the population or giving them a chance to evacuate,
the Russians bombed the village of Katyr-Yurt with 500-pound general
purpose (non-precision) high-explosive bombs for approximately eight
hours (generally referred to as carpet bombing), because some of the
fleeing Chechens had taken refuge in the village. Later, as civilians
attempted to flee, the Russians bombed and strafed the columns of
cars resulting in 363 civilian casualties. Nonetheless, despite their heavy
losses (about 600 alone during the break-out), the bad weather, and the
determined effort by the Russians to annihilate them, the majority of the
fighters made it into the Argun and Vedeno gorges where they dispersed and began a guerrilla warfare campaign against the Russians
from the Southern Mountains.

The Russians cautiously began clearing Grozny, but had to be careful
of booby-traps, their own unexploded ordnance, as well as "stay-
behind" saboteurs and snipers that remained to keep the Russians off
balance. This forced them to keep a large contingent of soldiers to garrison and secure Grozny—soldiers that could not then be used in offensive operations against the guerrillas. This group of "force multipliers"
(between 500 and 1,000) hid in tunnels and basements by day and
emerged at night to plant IEDs or snipe at Russian positions.

GUERRILLA WAR

Despite the military's announcement at the end of February that the
"counterterrorism" operation was over and that all that remained was
to round up a few "splinter groups," the guerrilla warfare campaign has
continued with varying degrees of success and intensity until the present
day. I have divided up the present guerrilla campaign into four periods:
Bez Predel (a savage Guerrilla War, Feb 2000–May 2002), Basayev's War
(the Terrorism Phase, May 2002–October 2005), the latent and incipient
phase (October 2006–December 2007), and the Caucasus Emirate Phase
(December 2007 to the present).

Bez Predel (without limits)

Immediately following the evacuation of Grozny, fighting started in
lowland areas accessible from the mountains, and was characterized by
large-scale attacks. Newspaper reports and official Russian press releases
tell the story of the first few months: "84 Russian paratroopers killed in
fighting," "400 Chechens killed in the last few months," "24 Special Police

killed in ambush," "22-vehicle convoy ambushed," etc. The Chechens focused exclusively on legitimate military and government targets, and despite Moscow's claims that they were fighting terrorists, at this point the conflict was still a clear guerrilla versus government battle that focused on ambushing regular government forces and even occasionally saw large Chechen units engaging in Phase III-types of maneuver warfare (such as Gelayev's two-week defense of Komsomolskoye in March).

In May 2000, newly elected Russian President Vladimir Putin established direct rule in Chechnya and appointed Akhmad Kadyrov as the interim head of the government. The process of "Chechenization" continued, despite the average monthly loss of 200 Russian troops. In June, the first "black widows" attacked, as two female suicide bombers detonated a truck bomb at the Russian commander's headquarters in Alkhan-Yurt, killing two soldiers. The next suicide bomber struck a few days later and then the attacks continued to escalate. During one 24-hour period in July there were five suicide attacks that killed 26 police and injured more than 150. The use of suicide bombers would steadily increase in Russia until the Iraq War began—when it is assumed that the majority of prospective suicide bombers went to the Middle East. Throughout the rest of 2000, there was an average ten guerrilla or suicide bomb attacks per month on Russian forces, while Russian counterguerrilla forces conducted just as many if not more major operations of their own (as of November 2010, there is at least one insurgent attack *per day* in the North Caucasus). More Chechens began to defect to the Russian side as the pro-Moscow Chechen contingent began to establish itself in Grozny. The prospect of living and fighting in the mountains for the foreseeable future did not sit well with many Chechens who began to long for their homes and peace. In Grozny, Doctors without Borders stated: "The war . . . has entered a new phase. The Russian forces have transformed Chechnya into a vast ghetto. In this ghetto, terror reigns . . . every civilian is a suspect and freedom of movement is denied. Each and every checkpoint is a 'Russian roulette' which puts their lives at stake."[16]

Even the Russians called this period *bez predel* (without limits). Analysts claimed it came from a desire for revenge combined with the hardships of the war—and the government's reneging on its promise to pay the soldiers higher amounts of combat pay. Certainly those reasons contributed to the problem, but the savagery was really a manifestation of the core problem of the Russian military establishment—a lack of professionalism at the non-commissioned officer and enlisted ranks. And as bad as it was in the lower ranks, it was further compounded by Russian officer complacency or even complicity; it was often the officers who pocketed the extra

---

16. Scott Peterson, "Heavy civilian toll in Chechnya's 'unlimited violence,'" *The Christian Science Monitor*, December 11, 2000.

money that the soldiers were supposed to get and who didn't bother to attempt to discipline their soldiers or maintain any sort of order. The institutional acceptance of the *dedovshchina* (hazing and torture of Russian recruits that routinely resulted in up to 10 percent casualties per year) among the lower ranks had taught them how to be cruel to each other, and now they were free to take it out on the civilians. Officially, more than 10,000 Chechens were arrested in the first five months, and even pro-Moscow Chechens who worked for the Kremlin-backed government (many had previously been held hostage by the insurgents) said, "People are being exterminated by federal forces—that is the truth . . . Troops catch everybody, military or not—they just disappear . . . it's like the extermination of the nation."[17] This unprofessionalism and corruption is a big part of the reason that the insurgency continues on to this day. Insurgencies will not stop until the people believe that they have more to fear from the insurgents than they do from the government. As in past Chechen campaigns, the Russians were once again sowing the seeds for further conflict even as they believed they were on the cusp of putting an end to it.

---

17. Ibid.

CHAPTER 8

The Russian Counterinsurgency Campaign 1999–2005

As discussed previously, the bulk of military scholarship on the Chechen COIN effort actually addressed subsets of COIN operations: counter-guerrilla ops, military operations in urban terrain (MOUT), etc. However, it is now time to also examine the actual Russian counterinsurgency strategies because, just as the Russians made improvements in their tactics, techniques, and procedures at those tactical levels, they also made significant changes to their COIN approach.

Designing and planning a COIN strategy is extremely difficult and subject to constant reevaluation and changes based on successes and failures; hence, trying to tease apart the process and discover all aspects of the Russian COIN plan is difficult, especially as the architects of the campaign haven't published anything detailing the initial design or subsequent planning and staffing processes. Nonetheless, if overlaid with a COIN framework, it is possible to identify important aspects of the plan based upon public statements and the actions of participants. It is tempting to simply take the new U.S. Counterinsurgency Field Manual (FM) and apply that framework to the Russian campaign like a "Monday morning quarterback" and give the Russians "thumbs up" and "thumbs down" for how well they executed the primary tenets listed in the FM. But after a preliminary analysis of the campaign using that manual, it is obvious that U.S. doctrine is not the proper yardstick with which to evaluate the campaign, because frankly, using the U.S. manual as a metric, the Russian COIN campaign earns failing grades in most respects.

Yet, the Russians have had some success—and in April 2009, the Russians (as well as most observers, journalists, and intelligence agencies) declared the "counterterrorism" mission in Chechnya over—despite the fact that the Russians (according to U.S. doctrine) did many things "wrong." The

Russians even claimed that their doctrine was superior to U.S. doctrine and that their "departure" from Chechnya during a period of U.S. build-up in Afghanistan was clear evidence of it. Six months later it was obvious to everyone that the insurgency was far from over—but that doesn't necessarily mean that it was because the Russians hadn't used the West's "population-centric" approach—because Chechnya *did seem* quiet; it was the neighboring republics of Ingushetia and Dagestan that had an increase in attacks. To discern the effectiveness of the Russian campaign, it is necessary to go beyond "tactics" and look deeper into the principles of warfare to see how the Russians have strategically designed their COIN campaign.

The new U.S. counterinsurgency manual begins the discussion of COIN plans by talking about the relationship between "designing" and "planning," and it's an important point for our departure as well. The manual states: "When situations do not conform to established frames of reference—when the hardest part of the problem is figuring out what the problem is—planning alone is inadequate and design becomes essential. In these situations, absent a design process to engage the problem's essential nature, *planners default to doctrinal norms; they develop plans based on the familiar rather than an understanding of the real situation*" [italics mine].[1]

The traditional form of combating the Chechen insurgency has largely been exactly that, reverting to "doctrinal norms" and attempting to modify them to meet the need instead of analyzing the real problem. In the past, the Russians have tended to define "the problem" as: "The Chechens are resisting Russian rule and attacking us." Intuitive responses to such a problem statement would be, "Stop the Chechens from attacking us," and related plans would tend to be coercive. Viewing the situation through contemporary "Western" military tradition and applying a thorough and iterative design process would yield a different problem statement, something more like: "A significant portion of the Chechen population desires self-rule." This brings to mind a completely different way of looking at the conflict, resulting in different strategies—more along the line of "changing minds." In 2003, the chief spokesman for the Russian government, Sergei Yastrzhembskii, perhaps best summed it up when he said, "Some Western politicians have been remarkably persistent in trying to discuss 'alternative' means of *resolving the Chechen problem*. Yet all of these proposals, upon closer inspection, boil down to the same thing—negotiations with terrorists. That path, needless to say, is a dead end" [italics mine].[2] And less than two months after the start of the 1999 offensive at an international summit in

---

1. U.S. Army Field Manual 3–24, *Counterinsurgency* (Washington, DC: U.S. Government Printing Office, 2006), 4–2.
2. Andrei Pilipchuk, "Stereotip 'chernoi dyry,'" *Krasnaya zvezda* (Moscow), No. 12 (December 2003), 37.

Istanbul for the Organization of Security and Cooperation in Europe (OSCE), President Yeltsin angrily told the leaders and representatives from 54 countries, "You have no right to criticize Russia for Chechnya. There will be no negotiations with bandits and murders."[3]

Although the consistent use of the words "terrorists, bandits, and murders" by the Russians is a method of framing the conflict, it would be counterproductive to ignore the argument and simply write it off as elite framing. Words are important; the Russians *meant* what they said, and if we take them at face value and carefully look at all the statements the Russians have made about the conflict, we are able to see exactly how the Russians defined the problem: "There are certain undesirable elements (bandits and murderers) in a Russian territory, and they are causing political instability at the national, international, and local levels; moreover those elements are influencing the people of that region to assist in that instability." This problem statement falls somewhere between the Western and Stalinesque examples listed above, and corresponds roughly to the strategies that the Russians have thus employed: an intense information operations (IO) campaign aimed at the national and international audiences (because as far as the Russians were concerned, those two audiences posed a greater threat to the Russian government than the Chechens ever did) and a combination of coercion and "changing minds" at the local level (an enemy-centric approach).

ENDS, WAYS, AND MEANS

Strategic design, however, is based upon more than simply identifying the problem and then dealing with it in the best manner possible. All strategy must start with addressing the basic concepts of "ends" (clear concise objectives), "ways" (broad courses of action), and "means" (resources available). If the Russian "ends" were to rid themselves of the instability caused by "terrorist" groups in Chechnya, they could not design a *way* of dealing with that problem until they took a hard look at the *means* available with which to achieve those *ends*. And it is by looking at the *means* that the resultant Russian *ways* become apparent.

Just as Soviet military doctrine was based upon Soviet *means* in order to come up with broad courses of action designed to exploit unique Soviet advantages (most notably their vast population), so was the 1999 Chechen campaign based upon those same principles. In broad terms the Russians still had the advantages of a large military force, some

3. Michael R. Gordon, "Summit in Turkey: The Overview; Yeltsin and West Clash at Summit Over Chechen War," *The New York Times*, November 19, 1999, available at http://query.nytimes.com/gst/fullpage.html?res=9C03E6D8173CF93AA25752C1A96F9 58260&sec=&spon=&pagewanted=all.

advanced technology, large weapons platforms (aircraft, helicopters, artillery, tanks, missiles), complete air superiority, the ability to project military, economic, and political power, a large geopolitical footprint with analogous influence, and a group of nations that had strategic partnerships with Russia for many years. Because this was an "internal" problem for Russia, it was also able to draw upon other resources that the United States would not utilize in such a conflict: robust and efficient intelligence services that were legally allowed to operate within the confines of the Russian state (FSB, GRU, SVR, and others), a national police force equipped with heavy weapons platforms, and, critically, an increasing ability to control the press.

What the Russians *did not have* in early 1999 was a large number of professional soldiers that were capable of executing a major shift in mission focus (from combat to "protection"), a secure international border that would allow the Russians to even consider retooling a portion of their military force to conduct COIN operations like the West does, a budget capable of purchasing the kinds of precision weapons, protective gear, and training to conduct a major retooling, an NCO corps capable of "mission command" type orders, a system of training recruits that didn't rely on brutality and hazing, a robust economy that could support increased spending on economic and infrastructure projects necessary for reviving the Chechen nation and reducing the vulnerable population, cutting-edge equipment that would provide a marked advantage to counter-guerrilla operations, international and Russian population support for a renewed conflict, well-trained, well-paid, and incorruptible police forces, or a concrete and inviolable rule of law.

I can speak on much of this with considerable authority as, when the 1999 Chechen campaign kicked off, I was with the Russian 13th Tactical Group (Airborne) who were (arguably) the best trained and most prepared Russian unit to conduct a Western-style "population-centric" mission—and we were in Kosovo. And despite the additional training that the 13th TG had been given for exactly the kind of operation that Chechnya was shaping up to be, *none* of the highly trained soldiers or officers assigned to the Kosovo mission were reassigned to go to Chechnya—meaning that those who did go to Chechnya were even less prepared to conduct that mission than those who had at least a modicum of training.

President Putin himself defined the problem in terms of a "lack of means" as recently as 2004 when responding to the Beslan terrorist attack. Clearly shaken and upset by what had happened (keeping in mind that Beslan was the third major terrorist incident leveled at the Russians within a week: two downed aircraft and a subway bombing preceded Beslan), Putin himself criticized the corruption in Russia's judiciary system, the inefficiency of law enforcement, and the lack of government resources that Russia had to deal with the problem because of the difficult and slow transition to capitalism. Russia's option was to play the hand it was dealt—and it wasn't much. And so Putin, in a rare acknowledgement that the Russians had earlier failed to properly identify the problem, stated: "We have to admit that we failed to recognize the complexity and danger of the processes going on in our country and the world as a whole."[4]

If we then look at what the Russian "means" consisted of at the end of 1999 and apply it toward the problem, one can easily see why the Russians would tend to focus on activities that best utilized their assets. However, at a strategic and operational level, the Russians realized that despite the fact there were problems at the tactical level which the Chechens exploited in order to achieve some spectacular successes; the Russians actually won most of the battles between 1994 and 1996. Nonetheless, they lost the war at the strategic level because they lost the support of the Russian people—and the international community had been highly critical of their operations.

If one were to ask the generals at the end of the first Chechen War why they "lost" the first war, they would respond that they were simply not given enough time to finish the job, and that they were on the brink of breaking the insurgency when the Russian government caved in to public opinion and signed the Khasavyurt agreement. The Russian military, although acknowledging that there were improvements to be made, believed the main impediment to success was a lack of national will to do what needed to be done in Chechnya. Therefore, if one observes the actions of the Russian government prior to the invasion in 1999, one can see that the Russians viewed winning a "hearts and minds" campaign to be critical to their success, but it was the "hearts and minds" of the *Russian* population—not the Chechen one—which is completely contrary to the vision espoused by Western military thought.

By recognizing that critical point, and by examining the actions and statements of the Russian government, it is possible to discern the following COIN strategies used by the Kremlin to regain Chechnya (from most to least critical):

1. A "shaping operation" to physically disrupt the Maskhadov government's control (break initiative and momentum). This was accomplished through a combination of economic stranglehold, effective capitalization of the ChRI government's inability to establish an effective society (or active FSB destabilization programs, or a combination of both) to create a vulnerable population. In combination with the physical program, there was also an aggressive information operations (IO) campaign designed to set the conditions for success utilizing the Salafist and foreign presence to *re-frame the conflict* so that

---

4. President Vladimir Putin's televised speech at the Kremlin, September 4, 2004, translated by the *New York Times*, available at http://www.nytimes.com/2004/09/05/international/europe/05rtext.html; accessed on February 8, 2008.

the *Russians became the guarantor of authentic Chechen culture and Sufi* Islam and thus became the lesser of two evils.

2. An IO campaign to gain and maintain the Russian national will by using the Dagestan attack and the Moscow bombings to frame the situation as one of national survival. Although #1 had to be accomplished first, this IO campaign was the Russian Main Effort (ME).

3. Disrupt the Chechens' relations with the international community by revealing the actual situation on the ground regarding lawlessness and kidnappings (some have suggested the FSB actively support kidnappings in order to reduce the international presence), as well as limiting access to independent journalists and international NGOs in the area.

4. Direct military action against the insurgents and terrorists using improved military coordination, training, and equipment along with new tactics and weapons designed to deal with urban combat. This later turned into a counter-guerrilla campaign once the Chechens retreated to their mountain strongholds.

5. An aggressive "outreach" campaign aimed at establishing ties with the international community that would reduce international support for the Chechens. This was supported by an IO campaign designed to justify Russian actions as a counterterrorism operation necessary to restore order, constantly stressing that it was a Russian "internal affair" that didn't merit international interference.

6. Gain support of the Chechen population through a number of means, the most important being to establish governance by establishing an authentic Chechen religious figure that was able to frame the "us against them" conflict as being "Chechens against Wahhabists" instead of "Chechens against Russians." Longtime Russian analysts refer to this phase as the "Chechenization" phase, while COIN practitioners would recognize this phase as initiating Lines of Effort (LOE).

7. And finally, beginning sometime around 2003—when the Chechens aggressively began using terrorism—the Russians added an additional defensive counterterrorism (C/T) strategy designed to prevent the Chechens from disrupting or eroding Russian national will. Although not dissimilar to strategy #2, which was designed to gain and maintain the national will (an offensive effort), the terrorist onslaught that the Chechens directed against the Russians required an additional defensive strategy aimed specifically at disrupting the new Chechen terrorist offensive. Although often criticized, the Russians demonstrated an iron will by refusing to give in to any terrorist demands. Those close to Shamil Basayev stated that after the Beslan School attack, Basayev swore off terrorist attacks because he believed that if the Russians could not be swayed by the deaths of hundreds of children, they would not be swayed by anything. An active IO campaign was an integral part of this strategy to prevent the Nord-Ost or Beslan terrorist attacks from swaying public opinion, as well as "defensive" measures to control all information coming out of those attacks, by classifying and restricting access to information after the facts and closing official investigations quickly.

Figure 8.1 highlights this campaign (the first six strategies) and the relationship between actors. There are two striking conclusions that are immediately clear from analyzing strategic design in such a way: first, it shows

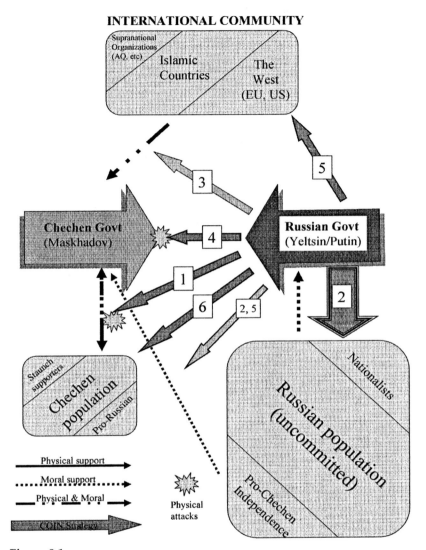

Figure 8.1

very plainly why a counterinsurgency campaign cannot be primarily a military campaign and must be a government campaign. It is obvious that the Russians understand that the military is not—and cannot be—the manager of such a plan, because ultimately, what was at stake was political power. Second, the Russian COIN campaign would appear to turn "Western" COIN theory upside down and, if not presenting a completely different COIN theory, then to at least present a dramatically different ranking of priorities (#6 on the chart is #1 for the population-centric approach). U.S. doctrine argues that the first and most important thing for successful COIN is to provide security to the inhabitants while working toward establishing legitimacy of the government.

Although the Russians include security in their plans, real security for the populace of the North Caucasus has been a low priority, and the ugly truth is that the population fears the government forces more than it does the insurgents; the current strategy is remarkably similar to historical ones—the central tenet being to coerce acceptable behavior through fear.

And why did the Russians place such a low priority on population security? Instead of trying to completely re-tool their enlisted system and teach their soldiers many new tasks as well as developing special units designed to try and win the population over, the Kremlin identified the greatest threat as *external support* for the Chechen insurgency and have thus focused their efforts on cutting off that support and preventing and discouraging future support from both inside of Russia and from other countries. The idea is that, given sufficient time, if the insurgency is not allowed to grow, then the situation in Chechnya will gradually improve and the insurgency will simply die out. And regardless of what the West believes is the "right" or "moral" course, this is what Russia considers its most efficient "way," as its military establishment is in the midst of an effort to improve basic combat effectiveness and deal with deficiencies observed during the recent war with Georgia. Chechnya is not strong enough to survive on its own, so according to Russian thinking, if Russia is able to cut off external support, then at least the North Caucasus insurgency will not get big enough to cause any major problems or threaten the survival of the current administration.

RUSSIAN COIN STRATEGIES

Chapters 6 and 7 already discussed the Russian efforts to disrupt Maskhadov's control during the period leading up to the 1999 invasion (campaign #1). The 1999 invasion itself, although widely viewed as the first step in regaining Chechnya and critical in setting the conditions for future operations was, in reality, the penultimate step of breaking the Maskhadov government's control.

Strategy #2: Gain and Maintain the National Will

When the Russians began planning for a reinvasion of Chechnya, their military planners would have started by analyzing the different groups (sometimes referred to as "stakeholders") within a population in order to determine their characteristics, networks, motivations, and how to influence them. There were three basic stakeholder groups and three special ones within the Russian population that needed to be addressed. At a minimum, Russian society consisted of a group of committed nationalists who had very harsh views on dealing with the Chechens and did not need any prompting from the government to convince them of the need to retake

Chechnya regardless of cost. There was also a very liberal group who believed in granting the Chechens their independence—and changing the minds of this group would be very difficult. The largest, most exploitable, and therefore most important group was the majority of the Russian population which was uncommitted, but had supported ending the conflict in Chechnya in 1996 in order to stop the bloodshed. There were also three specific subgroups that merit attention—the army, the ministry of internal affairs troops, and the special services (not indicated in Figure 8.1).

The special services (FSB, SVR, Spetsnaz etc.) did not need a lot of convincing to go back into Chechnya. Having been eviscerated during the first war and renamed the FSK, the FSB was now resurgent, and its most recent director—Vladimir V. Putin—had recently been appointed as the prime minister. As discussed earlier, the FSB had not been idle from 1996 to 1999, and with Putin at the helm, they understood that they would get all the support they needed.

As for the army and the police (ministry of internal affairs—MVD), considering the great number of casualties they suffered during the first war and the overwhelming public support for getting out of Chechnya in 1996, if Russia wanted to go back into Chechnya in 1999, it was going to be necessary to prepare the army and the MVD to go back into that fight. The Russian ministry of defense (MOD) and the MVD had spent a lot of time and energy developing new strategies for coordination at the joint staff level, running numerous combined exercises near the Chechen border—near terrain they would actually fight on, and developing new tactics for urban operations, but if they were going to go back in, they wanted their government to act legitimately. And if the Russian government was able to make a legal case for the military, it would go a long way toward convincing the uncommitted general population as well.

The Legal Foundation for Invasion

Russia had been careful not to grant any constitutional independence in either the 1996 Khasavyurt Accord or the 1997 treaty, and they now used a multi-pronged approach for their legal justification. They claimed that it was Maskhadov who had first broken the Khasavyurt agreement, that he consistently violated the Chechen constitution and finally, he ignored his own criminal code by allowing extremists such as "Khattab, Basayev, and Raduyev" to remain free in Chechnya.[5] Remember, there

---

5. See the official statement of the Russian ministry of justice, *Pravovaya otsenka deistviy organov vlasti v Chechenskoy respublike*, October 12, 1999, and Colonel-General Yu Demin, "Zakon na storine federalov," (the Law is on the side of the federal forces), *Nezavisimaya Gazeta*, October 13, 1999, and Steven J. Main, "Counter-Terrorist Operation in Chechnya: On the Legality of the Current Conflict," *The Second Chechen War*, ed. Anne Aldis (Shrivenham, UK: Crown Copyright, Strategic and Combat Studies Institute, 2000), 21–22.

has to be both a "competing" ideology (one that is directed at the populace to further the COIN campaign) as well as a "counter" ideology
(directed at the insurgents' ideological claims) and these ideologies had
to play to many different audiences—both in Chechnya (as there were
also differing stakeholders in Chechen society, some of whom supported
the Russians) and in Russia. During the first war, the Russians lost the
information war—the Pervomayskoye incident being the worst example:
despite the fact they were combating a full-blown terrorist hostage situation, the Russians ended up looking like the "bad guys," while Russian
citizens called the terrorists "their saviors." Pervomayskoye could not
be repeated, so at the outset of the new conflict, the Russian information
campaign was waged to both de-legitimize Maskhadov while legitimizing their own actions. Thus, the argument was framed as a need to fight
terrorists who were attacking the Russian homeland as well as an opportunity to "save" the people in Chechnya who were being terrorized by
their own "illegitimate" government.

The "international terrorist" part was critical, for if Russia reinvaded
Chechnya, and if it used the army to do the fighting, *it would be granting a
"de facto" legal recognition of Chechen sovereignty.* After all, if Chechnya was
still a part of Russia, then it should be a matter *solely* for the police and interior ministry troops—and as the first war demonstrated, many senior
army members balked at the idea of declaring war on their own people.
If, however, the issue was one of dealing with *international* terrorism,
where the threat was directed to "undermine the foundation of the state,"
then a counterterrorism operation involving military forces (and their
associated heavy weaponry and firepower) was entirely within the scope
of the Russian constitution and was covered explicitly by the new Russian
counterterrorism law that had been passed in 1998.

This effectively brought the threat to the average Russian who, seeing
their own security threatened by a "rogue, lawless republic," would now
see the need to take care of the problem for both their own sake and the
sake of the people within Chechnya who were suffering from an illegitimate government. Russia was able to both take care of its own problem
with terrorists attempting to destabilize Russia and, in so doing, also conduct a humanitarian mission to save the people of Chechnya who longed
for peace and stability. Moreover, it convinced the uncommitted Russian
population to support the war (and the soldiers), and it was effective in
mobilizing those pro-Russian groups that lived in the North Caucasus
region.

Strategy 3: Disrupt Chechnya's External Support

The Russians not only fought the insurgents by "following the money"
and shutting off the flow of weapons, fighters, and cash, but also used

other methods to cut off external support to the Chechens and isolate them psychologically. One of these was to limit the international presence in Chechnya, most notably the non-governmental organizations (NGOs) and the independent press. As discussed earlier, following the signing of the Khasavyurt Accord and during the administration of the independent Chechen Republic of Ichkeria, Chechnya turned into a morass of lawlessness, and kidnappings were commonplace. Many of the kidnappings and some of the killings were directed at international aid workers and journalists, making life extremely dangerous for them to assist Chechen refugees and those who had lost their homes and families.

Because the humanitarian aid groups were consistently distributing food and supplies, and providing shelter in areas outside Grozny where the press didn't often venture, the NGOs provided the press with more sets of eyes. Aid workers consistently gave journalists reliable updates on Russian civil and human rights violations, and publicized those violations through their own organizations. However, once these workers began to be targeted by groups led by Raduyev and the Yamadayevs—they began scaling back their operations. And when Vincent Cochetel, the regional director for the United Nations High Commission for Refugees (UNHCR) was taken hostage in 1998, most aid groups left Chechnya entirely.

The situation became so bad that there was not a single expatriate aid worker living in the region when the Russians invaded in October 1999 and more than 150,000 people became refugees and needed help. However, when aid workers tried to return to Chechnya, the Russians refused to let them back in, as they could justifiably argue that letting civilian aid workers into an active war zone would put them in danger.

The lesson here is that protecting the lives of anyone who criticizes your enemy should be a critical task—and anyone that threatens them should be quickly dealt with. Interestingly enough, Basayev reputedly offered to take care of the kidnappers during the 1996–1999 interim period, but Maskhadov stayed his hand because such actions would have been against the law, contrary to the constitution, and more importantly, likely to start a civil war.

This is yet another example that reinforces the idea that an essential part of national power is the rule of law—a functioning legal system—for without one, the government cannot be considered legitimate. Anyone seeking to destabilize a government (insurgents or counterinsurgents) can exploit the inability of the government to safeguard its citizens and portray the sitting government as illegitimate. Remember, at this point, it was really the Russians who were the insurgents and it was the democratically elected ChRI that should have been conducting COIN. What is beyond doubt is that the Russians used the lawlessness of Maskhadov's government to their advantage, not only to restrict the flow of international journalists and aid workers into Chechnya, but for other IO campaigns as well.

Conspiracy theories also surround the issue of kidnappings, and many believe that, at a minimum, Russian special services took advantage of the kidnappings not only to drive the foreigners out, but also to further destabilize Maskhadov's government by agreeing to pay enormous ransoms, and pay the money directly to the kidnappers, thus encouraging the practice. Regardless of whether the Russian special services were involved, the effective result was the same.

What is known for sure is that huge ransoms were paid to the kidnappers (sometimes by the Russian government itself), and that paying ransoms was inconsistent with the "we will not negotiate with terrorists and criminals" stance that the Kremlin adopted at Pervomayskoye and for all terrorist attacks after 1999. Additionally, the fact that Maskhadov's government was usually bypassed in all the kidnapping negotiations made it virtually impossible for the Chechen government to even attempt to negotiate for the release of the hostages, involve state institutions, or maintain any semblance of legitimacy.

Strategy 4: Direct Action

Although the Kremlin and North Caucasus regional governments exclusively refer to them as counterterrorism operations, most of them are counter-guerrilla operations. The 1999 invasion, which was a full-scale military operation, can only be referred to as a counterterrorist operation in the broadest possible sense and only insofar as it could be argued that Chechnya was being used as a base for terrorists—much as the United States invaded Afghanistan to prevent that country from being used as a base for Al Qaeda.

That is not to say that there were not terrorists operating in Chechnya in 1999, there were—but as discussed in earlier chapters, the terrorist cells were a part of the overall insurgency campaign. As of August 2010, there is still a heavy military presence in the North Caucasus and it is still growing. However, a significant number of *counter-guerrilla* operations (termed counterterrorism operations) are carried out by members of the ministry of internal affairs (MVD) rather than the Russian army. The current situation and array of forces will be discussed later.

Strategy 5: Establish/Strengthen Relations with the International Community

Strategy #3 was "defensive" in nature and sought to sever the significant ties that the Chechens had established with the international community. Strategy #5 sought to fill the void by increasing the Russian presence in the geopolitical sphere, making it more difficult for the Chechens to get aid from foreign governments because those governments would not want to disrupt their "new and improved" relations with Russia. Russia was beginning to emerge from the economic hardships it had endured during the 1990s, and as its ability to control natural resources and engage in trade increased, so did its stature in the world.

Russia, always an expert in the geopolitics game (and with a permanent seat on the UN Security Council), began reasserting itself with countries where the Soviet Union had once wielded considerable influence. Although this had limited success with Europe and the United States, two Yeltsin-era "boogeyman" stratagems continued to work for a short time: terrorists and Communists. The first boogeyman allowed the Kremlin to demand that the West give Russia a free hand in the Caucasus because in 1999, Russia was the frontier and was single-handedly holding back Islamic extremism and instability emanating from those regions.[6] The second was the "Communist boogeyman" threat: Ask for help from the West in order to keep Russia from collapsing—or the Communists from taking over. A third and compelling reason was the very real suffering that the Russian people had experienced from the waves of terrorism.

It is important to remember that in 1999, Russia was still in a precarious situation and there was a very real chance that Yeltsin's democratic government would not survive the elections. The Communists were still strong in Russia at the time and were constantly criticizing Yeltsin's handling of the situation. The last thing the West wanted was for the Communists to take Russia back—and as such, they were willing to bargain. So when world leaders heavily criticized Russia's action in Chechnya and forcefully called for an end to the bombing, Russia dropped its opposition to U.S. policy in Iraq in exchange for not bringing the issue of Chechnya to the UN Security Council.[7] Overtures toward the West moved slowly, but the process was helped immeasurably after the 9/11 attacks in the United States and the subsequent War on Terror that President Bush initiated soon thereafter. The budding relationship between newly elected presidents Bush and Putin meant that Russia received a significant amount of intelligence from the United States, public validation that the Chechens were using the Pankisi Gorge in Georgia as a sanctuary, and a subsequent 2002 U.S. Special Forces mission to eliminate that external support, as well as increased cooperation on counterterrorism issues across the board.

Following the Dubrovka Theater terrorist incident in 2002, the Russians lobbied heavily to have the entire Chechen insurgency designated as a terrorist group, and the United States, possibly seeking support for its own actions in Afghanistan and possible action in Iraq, acceded to the Russian

---

6. Vladimir P. Lukin, "Remaking Russia: Our Security Predicament," *Foreign Policy* 88 (Fall 1992).

7. Gordon, "Summit in Turkey."

request and three Chechen insurgent subunits were designated by the United States as "terrorist organizations with links to Al Qaeda": the Riyadus-Salikhin Reconnaissance and Sabotage Battalion (aka the Battalion of Shaheed Suicide Bombers), the Special Purpose Islamic Regiment, and the Islamic International Brigade. However, even while the U.S. State Department was putting these groups on the list of international terrorist groups and seeking to seize their assets, Richard Boucher, the DOS spokesman said, "The broader conflict in Chechnya cannot be resolved militarily and requires a political solution."[8]

Although the West was important, it was the Middle East where the Russians got the most support. Once the United States began projecting influence into the Middle East after the first Gulf War, an old Soviet ally—Iran—began to look to Russia to help maintain its own position. For their part, the Russians were initially concerned that Iran might attempt to export their own (Shi'a) version of Islamic revolution to Muslim republics within Russia, but once the Kremlin saw that Iran was willing to cooperate to end the civil war in Tajikistan, the Russians realized the potential for a strategic regional partnership. Thus Russia has remained friendly with Iran and helps to maintain the balance of power in much the same way it did throughout the Middle Ages when the region was controlled by the three great powers in the region—the Russian, Ottoman, and Persian empires.

As for the Sunni Arab countries, energy prices have stopped them from interfering in Chechnya or seeking greater influence among the Muslim populations. The Sunnis depend on Russia to maintain its hold on natural gas to keep prices where OPEC needs them to be, and Europe needs to buy the petroleum products. In a historical context, this merely puts Chechnya in the same spot it's always been in, too small for any of the traditional religious "allies" to risk their more important relationship with Russia. Even in early 2000, Russia was demonstrating that it was still a superpower in the energy sector. It had, and still has, the world's largest natural gas reserves (33 percent) and cut deals with its former Soviet republics to be the primary agent for transporting another 23 percent—giving Russia the ability to control up to 55 percent of global reserves. Currently, Russia provides 40 percent of all natural gas consumed in Europe, and is expected to reach 75 percent by 2026. Russia also has the world's second largest coal reserves, and the eighth largest crude oil reserves. It is the world's second largest oil exporter and was the number one producer in 2006.[9]

8. Steven R. Weisman, "Threats and Responses: Terror links; U.S. Lists 3 Chechen Groups as Terrorist and Freezes Assets," *The New York Times*, March 1, 2003, available at http:// query.nytimes.com/gst/fullpage.html?res=9C05E3DB103CF932A35750C0A9659C8B63.
9. U.S. Energy Information Administration, *Russia Country Analysis Brief*, available at http://www.eia.doe.gov/emeu/cabs/Russia/Background.html.

Saudi Arabia had been one of Chechnya's most important sources of external support, both financial and moral—and it had been the most severe critic of Russia's actions in the Caucasus against Muslims; however, that support to the Chechen insurgents largely dried up. In addition to its growing influence as an energy exporter, Russia also assuaged Saudi Arabia by requesting observer status in the Organization of Islamic Countries (OIC), and demonstrated that it attaches great importance to issues in the Muslim world, which it takes into account regarding policies toward the Middle East, the Israeli-Palestinian conflict, and other regional issues.

Where Russia made some of its shrewdest moves, however, was with its traditional archenemy, Turkey. Early in the Yeltsin presidency, the Russians were concerned about Turkey establishing itself among the Central Asian republics and their resurgent "Turkic" nationalism. Later, Turkey consistently supported the Chechens—albeit quietly—especially as Turkey has large diasporas of North Caucasian Muslims, the descendents of the deportees from the 19th and 20th centuries. Those diasporas have a powerful lobbying group within Turkey and have exerted considerable influence on the Turkish government to support their cousins as much as possible. Considering that Turkey has been a member of NATO for the last 40 years and a traditional enemy of Russia for 400 years prior to that, this kind of support was to be expected. However, the geopolitical situation has changed, and Russia has taken advantage of it to slow down, and in some cases to completely shut off, what was once the greatest source of external support to the Muslims in the North Caucasus. As Turkey has been shunned by many of the "old European" nations in its bid to become a member of the European Union, Russia stepped in to begin a relationship with Turkey that benefits Russia in many ways.[10]

Russia has been supplying intelligence and support to the Turks in their own battles against terrorism. Whereas the Soviet Union used to support the Kurdistan Workers' Party (PKK; based on revolutionary Marxist-Leninism), Russia has been quietly using its old KGB files to give information to the Turks to stop the PKK. Considering that since its inception in 1984 the PKK has killed over 5,500 Turkish civilians in hundreds of attacks, much of Turkey's political landscape has been shaped by the fight against the PKK. Correspondingly, in a very simple sense, Turkey considers those countries that help the PKK as their enemies and those that help them against the PKK as friends. Russia has taken advantage of gaps in the once strong relationship between Turkey

---

10. Some European countries are strongly resisting Turkey's accession into the EU because of its vast population and because it's Muslim. If Turkey becomes a member of the EU, it will immediately become one of the most powerful countries (with the highest number of votes in the EU) while being simultaneously one of the poorest.

and the West, as the U.S. presence in the Kurdish areas of Northern Iraq following the 1991 war (Desert Shield/Desert Storm) had essentially provided a safe haven to the PKK. U.S. ambivalence and European exclusionism has turned a once-strong ally into a country where the Turkish prime minister publicly encouraged citizens to attend a movie where the villains were U.S. soldiers and army doctors harvested the organs of Iraqi prisoners. In a country where the majority of the population used to support the United States, now books about a fictional war between the United States and Turkey top the best-seller lists. And as the West's influence with Turkey wanes, Russia has quietly, but increasingly, stepped in to fill the gap—and the stepped-up cooperation has resulted in greater Russian influence throughout the entire region.

Looking beyond Chechnya for a moment and thinking about the larger picture, as far as geopolitical posturing is concerned, Russia doesn't really mind a little instability in the North Caucasus—especially if the Kremlin knows that neither Turkey nor Iran are fomenting it. A little instability makes it easier to justify keeping large military forces in the region where it can project power into the rest of the Caucasus and remind Azerbaijan, Georgia, and Armenia that they fall squarely within Russia's declared "sphere of influence."

Strategy 6: Gain Support of the Local Population

The initial Russian military strategy (#4) for reinvading Chechnya in 1999 called for a heavy bombardment designed to crumble the resistance while simultaneously choking any external support with a military and economic blockade. The second stage of the plan called for the methodical establishment of Russian-controlled "safe" areas within Chechnya where life would be allowed to follow a normal routine with functioning schools, hospitals, and trade; control of those areas would eventually be turned over to local authorities in what would come to be known as the "Chechenization" process. The Kremlin did not put much effort into designing a plan for gaining the support of the locals in 1999, because there were already some Chechens who supported the Russians and those Chechens convinced the authorities that the rest of the population was tired of war and would quickly succumb. Therefore, the Russian general staff envisioned the whole republic just falling into their hands by the spring—in time for the run-up to the presidential elections. It didn't happen, and examining why it didn't happen is instructive for the Chechen conflict in particular and COIN warfare in general.

The Chechen "hearts and minds" strategy of the initial 1999 Russian campaign was clearly the lowest priority for the Russians in terms of where they wanted to allocate resources (this itself is illustrative), and by current Western doctrinal standards, completely backwards. Frankly, the Russians felt that a "hearts and minds" strategy would yield the slowest returns, which is why it was so low on their priority list. In current U.S. military doctrine, this phase is referred to as employing "lines of effort" or "lines of operations," which is merely a way of conceptualizing programs that increase the government's legitimacy utilizing the elements of national power—diplomatic, economic, informational, military—also cultural and legal. The purpose of such capacity building is to change the minds of the majority of the population from passively supporting the insurgents to actively supporting the government.

Current Western COIN theory posits that the most important aspect of this process is to establish security for the local population and to provide for their basic needs. This in turns starts a virtuous cycle where the population, now seeing the increased benefits of government control, begins to quietly provide information to the authorities about the insurgents—who now threaten their newly established security and better living conditions. The increased volume of intelligence aids the authorities, who use it to capture more insurgents and create even more security; this creates what I refer to as the "security-intelligence cycle." The Russians, for their own reasons, do not place the same emphasis on the security aspect because they simply do not have the means to do so. Crippled by an endemic and pervasive disregard for the law that even Russian President Medvedev referred to as "legal nihilism," coupled with young, conventional forces that can't be reoriented for counterinsurgency, and local law enforcement personnel that owed their livelihoods (and often their lives) to a regional patron, the Russians could not (and still cannot) initiate the security-intelligence cycle that would actually lead to long-term peace and stability in the region.

The Chechenization process has evolved significantly since 1999 and become a multi-faceted, robust effort. Regardless of how this strategy has increased in importance, in 1999, there was no plan to engage the population using the economic and security elements of national power; the Russians did, however, aptly apply the other two: political and informational. If there is one counterinsurgency lesson that can be learned from the Russians, it would be their emphasis on the political process and the Russian method of "divide and rule."

By giving power to different groups and splitting the Chechen population by playing up the religious differences between the "traditional form of Caucasian Islam" and the "dangerous radical foreign Wahhabis" as early as 1999, the Russians provided an alternative ideology to the beleaguered vulnerable population of Chechnya and promised them a way out of fighting another devastating war. Moreover, the Kremlin-supported Chechens could claim greater legitimacy than the ChRI because they promised to maintain Chechen Sufi traditions and Chechen leadership in the area; Jordanian Salafists ran a *shari'a* court during Maskhadov's administration, which was not in keeping with Chechen tradition. Thus Chechenization transformed the conflict from a rigid inter-ethnic war (Chechnya fighting Russia for independence) into a civil war between Chechens with differing ideologies. If one thinks of a hydra, the oft-used metaphor for insurgencies, then Chechenization was designed to get the heads fighting among themselves rather than attacking Russia.

This is still an "enemy-centric" approach, because both the enemy-centric and population-centric approaches require a combination of the two basic strategies of COIN—coercion and changing minds; the difference lies in which strategy is given priority. The Russian plan in 1999 was a "carrot and stick" approach where the emphasis was still on the stick, but the population was given the choice between having at least a few small carrots and a little less stick or no carrots and lots of stick. This strategy can work—as long as there is consistent movement toward more carrots and less stick; regrettably, that has not been the progression in the North Caucasus.

While he was in power, Maskhadov had correctly identified that he was dealing with a budding insurgency within Chechnya; unfortunately for him, he neglected to occasionally look over the other shoulder. While he was busy dealing with the Salafists, his erstwhile ally, Kadyrov, had managed to snatch his independence away. The four prerequisites for insurgency (lack of government control, available leadership, vulnerable population, and ideology) had been extant not only in pre-war Chechnya, but in post-war Ichkeria as well, and either through expert Russian planning or capitalizing on Chechen mistakes (or a combination of both), the Russians were able to "steal the insurgency" from the insurgents by splitting the Chechens along religious and clan ties and co-opting large groups that desired more power for themselves.

Unfortunately for the Russians, the population did not fully support the Chechen leadership that they chose to head the administration. The Kadyrovs and Yamadayevs (and to a lesser extent the Khakievs) were now responsible for the critical task of providing security to the population, but as those groups were nothing more than private militias with a badge, their abusive methods of trying to obtain information had the opposite effect on the "security-intelligence cycle," failing to bring passive supporters of the insurgency over to their side in the short term. The high-profile bomb attack that killed President Kadyrov in 2004 (which could not have been accomplished without the assistance of "passives" and "neutrals"), should be ample evidence of that.

This is not to say that the Russians have not paid attention to the Chechen "hearts and minds" campaign; they have, and it has evolved considerably since this inchoate, under-emphasized, and non-resourced strategy was launched as part of the 1999 invasion. That metamorphosis will be examined in detail later, as it has since become a far more important part of the overall campaign and, from 2005 to 2008, contributed to reducing the level of violence in Chechnya.

Strategy 7: Counterterrorism—Prevent Terrorism from Eroding the National Will

Although not anticipated at the beginning of the 1999 campaign in Chechnya, the need for an additional defensive strategy to maintain the national will of the Russians under an unprecedented onslaught of terrorist attacks soon became apparent. Although strategy #2 was sufficient to gain the support of the general Russian population for reinvasion of Chechnya, it was not sufficient to maintain the national will once the Chechens started attacking Russians in their own homes.

Soon after the 1999 invasion, some Chechens—Shamil Basayev being the most outspoken and active—realized they had little chance against the overwhelming Russian forces. Sensing that they had lost support from the international community (or that any support from the West would be insufficient to effect real change), they began a terrorism campaign against the Russian people in order to convince them that the cost of taking Chechnya was too high. And so, without the approval of President Maskhadov, Shamil Basayev changed the nature of the conflict and moved it from a classic guerrilla war (referred to earlier as Bez Predel) and added another dimension—an urban terrorism focus—which would characterize the conflict from 2002 until Basayev's raid on Nalchik in 2005. For all intents and purposes, by 2003, this terrorism campaign would become the insurgents' main effort, as the Chechens also came to realize that the center of gravity for the Chechen conflict was the *Russian* population, and without the support of the international community, the only real hope for independence lay in breaking the bond that the Putin administration had established with the people.

Whether or not the Chechens were involved in the 1999 Moscow apartment bombings now became superfluous, as Chechen and foreign terrorists tried to blow Russia apart from the inside, attacking military, government, and civilian targets, killing over 1,000 people, and injuring thousands more by the end of 2004.[11] Chechen demands were always the same—Russian military forces must leave Chechnya and abide by the two earlier agreements it had signed. Despite the fact that there were also attacks on government and military forces, the Chechen "main effort" was the Russian national will; it was a Chechen campaign to create fear in the minds of average Russian citizens, to create a schism between the people

---

11. Although in his demand letter for the Beslan School attack, Shamil Basayev wrote to President Putin, "We are not related to the apartment bombings in Moscow and Volgodonsk, but we can take responsibility for this in an acceptable way." View the note at http://www.pravdabeslana.ru/zapiska.htm. One of Basayev's associates verified the handwriting is Basayev's.

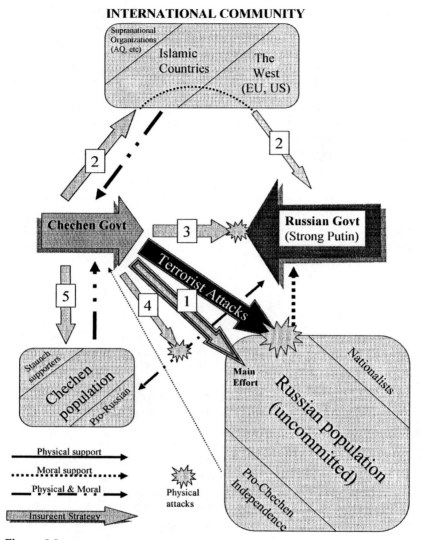

Figure 8.2

and the government that would encourage them to protest to stop the war like they had in 1980 (Afghanistan) and the Chechen campaign in 1994.

This change in Chechen operational approach demanded that the Russians modify their overall COIN strategy and add an additional campaign to their original six—namely, an integrated C/T strategy that would prevent Chechen terrorism attacks in the Russian heartland, and more importantly, *prevent the public from being affected* by the attacks when they couldn't be stopped.

This new effort employed three out of four elements of national power (diplomatic/legal, military, and informational). It emphasized legal and governmental efforts to increase the "ways" and "means" with which the government could fight the terrorists and employ a sophisticated information operations (IO) campaign that included new narratives and even more control of information. Essentially, when things went well for the Russians, it was reported extensively and when things didn't go well, no one was allowed to talk about it. There was also a renewed kinetic effort to kill insurgent and terrorist leadership.

The fact that an "additional" C/T strategy was added to the overall COIN campaign should further reinforce the idea that terrorism was being used as a tactic by components of the Chechen insurgency. Notice that the Russians did not stop using the previous six strategies (as needed) even while focusing on counterterrorism. Moreover, the C/T strategy had elements that evolved from earlier COIN versions.

A CZAR IS BORN—SINGLE EXECUTIVE AUTHORITY AND SUBORDINATION OF THE NATIONAL WILL

Dr. Kalev Sepp (former assistant U.S. secretary of defense for special operations, a former Army Special Forces officer and a contributor to the current U.S. Counterinsurgency Field Manual) talks about the need for exceptional leadership during an internal war and lists the empowerment of a single executive authority as a best COIN practice. He writes, "Emergency conditions dictate that a government needs a single, fully empowered executive to direct and coordinate counterinsurgency efforts. Power-sharing among political bodies, while appropriate and necessary in peacetime, presents wartime vulnerabilities and gaps in coordination that insurgents can exploit." He gives examples where chief executives who had overwhelming popular support, and who had given themselves exceptional authorities to prosecute the fight against terrorism and insurgencies, had proven successful. And although many criticized President Putin for his continued consolidation of power through his "power vertical" process, intentionally or not, he closely followed the example of Peruvian President Alberto Fujimori who had great success against the Shining Path in his country in the early 1990s.

By the time President Putin was elected to a second term by over 70 percent in March 2004, there were no longer any restraints on his executive powers. His turnaround of the economy and his willingness to take on the oligarchs (and other beneficiaries of the Yeltsin-era, Western-style, free-market economy) gave him the overwhelming support of the average Russian—who had suffered during the preceding ten years. And with that mandate, the president circumvented the problem of national will by simply taking it back from the people and wielding it as the czars had done in the past. The opposition had been eviscerated, and even so, who would have argued about the need to put the nation on a war footing. Putin simply became the "war leader" and everyone rallied around him. And by then it was evident that the Kremlin no longer needed to worry about public opinion, because by August 2004 "the Kremlin no longer care[d] about public opinion"; Putin's will had become the public's opinion.[12]

Almost immediately after the Dubrovka Theater terrorist attack in 2002 (850 hostages were taken and at least 130 died from the gas that the Russian Spetsnaz pumped into the building before their assault), the Russian government passed more laws on terrorism which further restricted the press and non-governmental organizations. This demonstrated another feature of their counterterrorism strategy—using each major attack as justification for modifying or changing Russian laws to make it easier for the government to control civil society.

Russian counterterrorism laws are now so restrictive that essentially any individual, organization, or news outlet that doesn't conform to the government-approved narrative can be prosecuted for inciting "extremist" views. Moreover, they mandate that the Russian security services have the right to monitor all Internet, phone, and mobile communications without advising the providers or users. President Putin used his extraordinary powers to suspend the popular election of governors so that he could appoint trusted associates to carry out his reforms. And regardless of what it did for Russian democracy (which many Russians themselves don't consider to be particularly important), the president's consolidation of power and creation of laws that increased "ways and means" had a decisive effect on the terrorism campaign—and Beslan would prove it.

One of the paradoxes of insurgency is that if the guerrillas don't lose, they win. The idea is that a government must do more than simply win battles to succeed; unless the insurgents are completely destroyed (or join the political process), they will continue to fight—and thus, they are winning. However, as Beslan proved, the best practices approach of a single empowered executive stripped away the Chechen advantage and turned the paradox on its head. With hundreds of childrens' lives at stake, Putin's iron refusal to negotiate with the terrorists forever shattered the idea that if the Chechens kept trying, they could eventually find a lever that would convince the Russians that the war wasn't worth the effort—a crushing blow to Chechen morale that forced the insurgency to retreat back to a Phase I latent and incipient phase. Putin was able to turn one of the insurgents' natural advantages against them and after Beslan, it became generally accepted that if the *insurgents couldn't win they would lose*—because the

12. Yevgenia Albats, "The Kremlin Shows Its True Face," *The Moscow Times*, Monday, August 2, 2004, 8.

enormous size and power of Russia would slowly but inexorably crush them.

The ensuing loss of morale, along with the increased kinetic effort to decapitate the insurgency and the terrorist cells of their leadership, forced the insurgency into a rebuilding phase and convinced many fighters to give up and seek employment with the pro-Russian government, which further accelerated the downward trajectory of the insurgency until late 2007.

It took a major reorganization of the insurgency to reverse this trend. However, despite the fact that insurgent operations increased 122 percent in Chechnya alone from 2007 to 2008 and another 35 percent in the period before the Russians officially declared the counterterrorism operation "complete" in April 2009, few experts still believe the insurgents are capable of winning without substantial external support.[13]

THE HIGH VALUE TARGET CAMPAIGN

Although the Russian COIN campaign had always had a heavy kinetic focus (conceptualizing the entire conflict as a counter-guerrilla campaign), when the Chechens upped the ante by increasing terror attacks on Russian civilians, the Russians responded by giving the Kadyrovtsy free reign in Chechnya proper and focusing the efforts of the FSB and Spetsnaz on eliminating insurgent and terrorist leadership—referred to as high-value targets (HVTs). Historically, focusing on HVTs is not a "best COIN practice" and is generally counterproductive—often indicating that a government is resorting to desperate measures in an attempt to blunt a mature insurgent movement. The success a government has in killing HVTs (and there will always be some) tends to make the government believe that its kinetic approach is a "magic bullet" and lowers the incentive to address the root causes that will actually lead to long term results. Nonetheless, as Dr. Steven Metz of the Strategic Studies Institute of the U.S. Army War College writes in a recent paper, high value targeting can have "strategic effects under certain conditions, in certain ways." Dr. Metz posits that for insurgencies that devolve into terrorism or low-level guerrilla activity with little or no chance of seizing control of the state (which is where the Chechens were in the mid-2000s), and the government deems the "threat management" to be acceptable (which the Russian government does), then a "relentless, extensive, and protracted" high value targeting campaign may have value—especially if a government is willing to go outside of its borders (which Russia is) because it erodes the value of sanctuary.[14]

---

13. North Caucasus Incident Database; overall figures for each region are presented later.
14. Steven Metz, "The Dynamics of High Value Targeting in Counterinsurgency," *Strategic Studies Institute* (U.S. Army War College), draft, presented July 17, 2008, to the Insurgency Strategy Board at the Washington, DC, Office of the RAND Corporation.

And so, while allowing Kadyrov and his Chechen security forces the freedom to maneuver at the local level, the Russian special services were told to "take the gloves off"—especially following the terrorist attacks on Dubrovka and Beslan. President Putin stated publicly the necessity of defending the interests of Russia anywhere throughout the world by attacking terrorists preemptively—and on the territory of other countries if need be.[15] This directive was accomplished with alacrity—primarily by the FSB's Special Purpose (Spetsnaz) Directorates A and B, operating from a Spetsnaz center created just before the second war and given a permanent base in the North Caucasus. The commander of the FSB's Directorate "A" (better known as "Alfa" Group) and deputy chief of the Oznaz (Spetsnaz) center, Major General Vladimir Vinokurov, related that after the 1994 war the Russian government decided that a powerful, concentrated force under single leadership had to be established in the North Caucasus. He goes on to say that although the will to eliminate "terrorist ringleaders" had always been present, there had not always been the capability or opportunity to do anything about it, but that after the Dubrovka Theater and Beslan attacks "it was our personnel who neutralized Raduyev, Barayev, Abu-Umar, [Shamil] Basayev, and Maskhadov." When asked if special operations were conducted outside of Russia's borders, he replied, "Our personnel are prepared to also resolve such tasks, including outside the borders of the Russian Federation."[16]

True to their word, the Russians went after the terrorists wherever they were located in a "relentless, extensive, and protracted" campaign designed to deny them sanctuary. Soon after Beslan, the FSB assassinated ChRI President Maskhadov, who had begun taking greater risks in the hopes of communicating with President Putin and putting an end to the conflict and the killing. But despite Maskhadov's genuine desire for a peaceful solution with Russia, he now represented a regime that Moscow could never do business with—and as one of the top two HVT's, he was targeted and killed. As for HVT #1, Shamil Basayev, he maintained vigilant security—aware of the bounty on his head—but even he was eventually found and killed. The official version is that the FSB bribed one of Basayev's inner circle to plant a radio detonator in a truck full of explosives that Basayev was transporting—ostensibly to disrupt a G8 conference in St. Petersburg.

Although Spetsnaz has claimed assassinating HVTs within Russia, operating in other countries is another matter. Although there is little in the

---

15. "Putin: Rossiya gotovit' udari po terrori'stam," Lenta.ru, available at http://lenta.ru/terror/2004/09/17/putin/; accessed on March 10, 2010.
16. Tatyana Kuznetsov, "Our work is most often done away from the camera," *Argumenty I Fakty*, April 23, 2008, BBC Monitoring, "Popular Russian Weekly Interviews Deputy Chief of FSB Special-Purpose Centre."

way of proof, it appears that the FSB followed the president's directive and began a "mop-up" campaign outside of Russia in early 2004. It started in Qatar with the assassination of Zelimkhan Yanderbiyev, the second president of the Chechen Republic of Ichkeria. Yanderbiyev had been one of the earliest Islamist ideologues and after losing to Maskhadov in the election, he traveled to Pakistan and other Muslim countries to obtain support for the Chechen cause. He raised money for Al Qaeda and directed funds to the Chechen terrorists who conducted the Dubrovka Theater attack. Yanderbiyev was later listed by the United Nations as a terrorist, and Russia tried unsuccessfully to have him extradited from Qatar. He was assassinated by a car bomb in February 2004, and three Russians were arrested a week later. The fate of the three Russians accused of the crime is of some interest, as it would be the only time that Russians would ever be arrested for what I refer to as their "zachisti iz granitzi" operations (mop-ups beyond the border).

The first of the three accused was released due to his diplomatic status, but the other two were charged with the assassination. Moscow stated that the two were intelligence agents sent to Qatar to collect information about global terrorism and claimed their detention was illegal. They were tried and sentenced to life imprisonment; the judge stated that they had acted on orders from Russian leadership. The verdict severely strained relations with Moscow and in December 2004, Qatar agreed to extradite the prisoners to Russia where they would serve out their sentences. They returned to a heroes' welcome in Moscow, disappeared from public sight, and the Russian authorities later admitted that they were not in jail because a sentence handed down in Qatar was irrelevant in Russia.[17]

Although the Russians didn't deny their involvement in Yanderbiyev's assassination, whoever has been conducting the assassination campaign since then has maintained plausible deniability. Although no proof exists, many veteran observers believe that a number of unexplained deaths have been perpetrated by the Russian special services (or the Kadyrovtsy) in accordance with President Putin's statement, indicating a protracted campaign that is still ongoing. Beginning in the fall of 2008, a spate of high-profile extra-territorial assassinations of Kadyrov opponents proceeded at a rate of about one per month. The list included: Gaji Edilsultanov (an insurgent "colonel" shot dead in Istanbul); Ruslan Yamadayev (former member of parliament, Hero of Russia and the eldest of the Yamadayev clan) who was killed in Moscow on his way to a meeting with Russian President Medvedev; Islam Zhanibekov (former Chechen field commander); Umar Ismailov (a former Kadyrov bodyguard who had accused the younger Kadyrov of torture and murder to the European Court of

17. Sarah Rainsford, "Convicted Russia agents 'missing,'" *BBC News*, February 17, 2005, available at http://news.bbc.co.uk/2/hi/europe/4275147.stm.

Human Rights and the *New York Times*) who was killed in Vienna; Musa Atayev (Dokku Umarov's cousin and deputy outside of Chechnya) killed in Turkey; and finally, just before the official end of the counterterrorism campaign in Chechnya, Sulim Yamadayev, the former commander of the Vostok battalion, Hero of Russia, and Kadyrov's main challenger for power in Chechnya was assassinated in Dubai.

Although nothing can be proven, what is most significant about these killings is the frequent use of the "Groza" pistol, which was developed specifically for the FSB Spetsnaz groups. Using a "signature" weapon would be a mistake if one wanted the murder to go unnoticed: the only logical explanation is that Russia and the FSB are sending a clear signal to the insurgents, the countries where Russia's enemies reside, and the rest of the world, to let them know that if you work against the interests of Russia, then the FSB will get you.[18] In the case of Sulim Yamadayev, a golden gun was used and left at the scene—reportedly smuggled into the country via diplomatic pouch by one of Kadyrov's cousins.

Again, one could claim that these are all conspiracy theories, but even if each killing was conducted by a different person with a different agenda, the result is still the same: the Chechen underground living outside of Russia firmly believes in the existence of a special program designed to eliminate them.[19] A recent Radio Free Europe/Radio Liberty report quoted prominent Chechens who stated that they had received threatening phone calls warning them to come home or else—and there are reasons to believe that they are telling the truth. After two years of providing confidential reports to the European Court of Human Rights and a series of secret interviews to the *New York Times* detailing the abuses he witnessed, Umar Ismailov (Kadyrov's former bodyguard) finally agreed to allow the *New York Times* to publish his story—as well as the transcripts of the written legal complaints he had submitted to the European Court against the Russian government. On January 9, 2009, after independently researching Mr. Israilov's claims, the *New York Times* decided to go public with the story and asked the Russian government for an official statement regarding Israilov's claims. The Russian

---

18. The actual nomenclature of the weapon is the MSP. The MSP is one of the very rare, truly silent pistols, as the only sound it makes is the click of the firing pin. It uses a specially designed cartridge that traps the gasses inside, so it doesn't require a silencer and is very small and compact. It is a derringer-type weapon without extractors or ejectors (ensuring that no shell cases are left at the scene), and is only effective as an assassination weapon at close range. There is also the newer PSS, which fires a full clip as opposed to the MSP, which only has two rounds.
19. Prague Watchdog, the "mop-up" of Europe (interview with Magomed Ocherhadji), March 6, 2009, available at http://www.watchdog.cz/index.php?show=000000-000004-000001-000256&lang=1#; accessed on March 8, 2009.

government declined to comment, stating it would be imprudent to discuss "rumors." On January 13, 2009, outside of a market near his home in Vienna, Austria, two men approached Israilov and shot him multiple times; he died soon after.[20]

THE COUNTERTERRORISM INFORMATION OPERATIONS (IO) CAMPAIGN

Whether there is an active policy on the part of the Russian government or whether Kadyrov's critics have coincidentally met with random acts of violence common in all large cities, the result has been the same—people are afraid to talk and so very little information gets out of the Caucasus. Moreover, the journalists themselves are restricted and those allowed into the area are afraid, so what little does get out of the region is often self-censored. By 2004, the average Russian knew very little about what was really going on in the Caucasus—except that there were terrorists in the area who were attacking their sons serving in the military. This was an important part of a concerted IO campaign that reinforced the "foreign invader/terrorist" construct and introduced the new IO theme of "Chechens are Russians, and Chechnya is part of Russia."

IO #1—From Bandformirovanniya to Terrorists and Wahhabists

Although it had been part of the narrative since the mid-1990s, the "internationalization" of the conflict now became the marquee item, moving from a supporting role to the star performer. This narrative was directed both outward to the international community as well as inward to the average Russian, becoming a justification for every conceivable type of security activity. Whereas President Yeltsin had classified the insurgents at the beginning of the 1999 war as "illegal bandits," once the terrorism campaign began any previous associations of the insurgents to bandit groups (bandformirovanniya) disappeared from the Russian narrative and all the "bandits" were transformed into terrorists and Wahhabists. But even in the shadow of 9/11 and the War on Terrorism, there was something worse than being a terrorist, something even more deeply rooted in history and the fear-producing region of the Russian psyche, the "foreign invader." And because no

---

20. For a full accounting, see C. J. Chivers, "Slain Exile Detailed Cruelty of Chechnya's Ruler," *The New York Times*, January 31, 2009, available at http://www.nytimes.com/2009/02/01/world/europe/01torture.html?ref=world; accessed on February 1, 2009.

lie works so well as one based partially on truth, by simply combining the two parts and emphasizing those elements of the truth that best fit the construct, almost overnight the Russians re-branded the Chechen insurgency as a terrorist organization hell-bent on invading the mother-land and destroying her from within; the age of the "foreign terrorist" had begun.

This IO campaign has been particularly effective, and there has not been a Russian government statement for the past few years that doesn't allude to the foreign terrorists operating on Russian soil; any references to "separatism, separatists, insurgents," or any other impartial but doctrinally correct term is assiduously avoided, and any opportunity to link "inter-national" to the North Caucasus conflict is aggressively pursued, even when the references are specious or outright lies.

As already mentioned, the summer of 2004 was a turning point for the conflict, and it is illuminating to examine one of President Putin's statements about two Russian planes brought down by suicide bomb-ers, resulting in 90 deaths, the week before Beslan. Although Putin admitted that any link to Al Qaeda had yet to be proven when refer-ring to the two Chechen women who detonated explosive belts while airborne, Putin nonetheless stated, "The fact that one of the interna-tional terrorist organizations linked with Al Qaeda has claimed respon-sibility for the explosions on two planes once again confirms the links between destructive elements in the territory of Chechnya and interna-tional terrorism."

And the "international terrorist organization" that claimed responsibil-ity? The Chechens. We can't really call the president a liar because in truth, the Russians had already branded the Chechen insurgency as a ter-rorist organization, the United States and the United Nations had already branded certain units of the insurgency as "terrorist organizations," and there were individuals sent from Al Qaeda to assist the Chechens. So in truth, the "international terrorist organization with links to Al Qaeda" that President Putin was referring to was in fact the Chechen insurgency led by Maskhadov and Basayev.

This was a prime example of the new "foreign terrorist" construct and it was nothing more than a skillful manipulation of words by the presi-dent to paint the perpetrators as the worst kind of terrorists. It was imper-ative that it wasn't just "Chechens" who were responsible, because then a segment of the Russian population might be swayed to give in to the Chechen demands. By making the adversaries a group of religiously crazed zealots who would stop at nothing, any discussion of agreeing to Maskhadov's repeated pleas to sit down and discuss an end to the hostil-ities was squashed before they could even arise. The Russians had already bargained with Chechens—but no one could expect them to negotiate with international terrorists.

IO #2—Chechnya *is* Russia

There is another reason Putin didn't say "Chechens" in his statement, instead using the words "destructive elements in the territory of Chechnya." In addition to unveiling the improved "international terrorist" construct, this statement is also emblematic of another Russian IO campaign: "Chechnya is no longer the problem, Chechnya is Russia." It was critical to divorce Kadyrov's "new" Chechnya, which was filled with heroic Chechens who protected the motherland from foreign terrorists and fielded championship soccer teams from the "outsiders" who were corrupting the good people within Chechnya.[21]

Although linked to the earlier "Chechenization" of the conflict which emphasized the difference between "good" and "bad" Chechens, this new campaign began in October 2003 immediately after the Chechens "elected" Akhmad Kadyrov as president. Putin, flanked by German Chancellor Gerhard Schroeder and French President Jacques Chirac, held a news conference and stated that the "Chechen people made their choice by voting for preserving a position in which Chechnya is an inseparable part of Russia." Not only did the two Western leaders not dissent (despite the international agencies who declared the elections unfair, the Council of Europe who called it a "farce," and the U.S. State Department's official statement that the election was "seriously flawed and did not meet international standards"), Chirac went so far as to state that "no one can contest Russia's territorial integrity" and that elections had taken place "in conditions that we cannot contest."[22]

The "Chechnya is Russia" campaign was in full swing by August 2004, a few months after Kadyrov's assassination, just before Beslan, and at the height of the Chechen terrorism campaign. It canonized Kadyrov as "the best Chechen in Russian history" using spin doctors to manipulate his legacy in much the same way they did for Lenin. Press releases announcing the inauguration of a Moscow street named after Kadyrov lauded him as the "main politician of all nations and all times" and in so doing constructed an ideology for the Russians (and secondarily for the Chechens) that Chechnya is an integral part of Russia. Work also started in August on a feature film on Kadyrov, and monuments were erected to his memory in Chechnya and in other parts of Russia.

In the film, *Akhmad Kadyrov, the Last Parade of the Victor*, President Putin is shown numerous times praising Kadyrov and (allegedly) relating their

---

21. "Putin links Chechen fighters to international terror," *The Associated Press*, August 31, 2004, also available at http://groups.yahoo.com/group/chechnya-sl/message/39726.

22. C. J. Chivers, "Kremlin's candidate wins Chechnya vote, Election marred by allegations of fraud," *International Herald Tribune*, August 31, 2004, available at http://www.highbeam.com/doc/1P1-98552089.html, and Andrew Jack, "Kremlin candidate wins Chechnya election," *The Financial Times*, August 29, 2004.

first meeting. Putin says, "What was especially important for me is that I understood that Kadyrov understands the erroneousness of the whole idea of separatism and believes that it is impossible to build a future, a happy future for his people and for Chechnya, outside of the Russian Federation."[23] After Kadyrov's assassination, Putin interrupted his vacation and traveled to Chechnya to visit Kadyrov's grave on what would have been his birthday. It is important to keep in mind that President Putin had just been re-elected with 71 percent of the vote, and his approval ratings had climbed even higher since then. Putin was so popular that a Russian pop group scored a number one song in Russia entitled "I want a man like Putin."[24] Therefore the association with Putin made Kadyrov, and all the rest of the "good Chechens" who thought like Kadyrov, a group that the Russians needed to protect against the "foreign terrorists."

After all, if the insanely popular Putin said that Kadyrov was a hero and that Chechens were good, then of course they were good. And to drive the point home, that same month in 2004, the Chechen professional soccer team (FC Terek-Grozny) was sent to play in the prestigious European Football Association Championship tournament (EUFA Cup) representing Russia—and beat Poland in the first round. Despite the fact that the team rarely spent time anywhere close to Grozny (there was no stadium in Chechnya), and its players were almost exclusively ethnic Russians, the Terek club quickly became the darlings of the average Russian because it was the first Division I team in history to win the Russian cup.

The goal of this IO campaign was to convince the average Russian—the center of gravity for both the Russian and Chechen campaigns—that the "Chechens" were no longer the problem, and whenever attacks occurred, they were committed by international terrorists. This counter-ideological theme undercut the insurgent narrative that said, "Chechnya can never be part of Russia because Chechnya has a separate people, culture, and religion. We insurgents are part of the people, but you Russians are totally different, so let Chechnya go its own way because both of us are better off as separate entities." This had been a highly effective narrative during the first war and quite a few Russians still adhere to this point of view.

With this new narrative, the Russians were not only preventing the insurgents from splitting the Russian population, they were also presenting a counter-ideological argument that separated the insurgents from their mass base in Chechnya. When the perpetrators of attacks turned out to be native Chechens, then it was because their minds had been subverted by the foreign influence of Salafism, because *true* Chechens

---

23. "Putin Compliments Akhmad Kadyrov," *RIA Novosti*, August 23, 2004, available at http://groups.yahoo.com/group/chechnya-sl/message/39506.
24. Watch it on YouTube at http://www.youtube.com/watch?v=gncW1zqMFgs.

acted like Akhmad Kadyrov, *true* Chechens understood that Chechnya was a part of Russia, and *true* Chechens now represented Russia on the world stage in sports. These two IO campaigns would prove critical in dealing with the upcoming Beslan tragedy that would unfold in another two weeks. They would also be important for laying the groundwork for the eventual assumption of Ramzan Kadyrov, then 27, to take over the presidency of Chechnya once he reached the minimum age of 30. Ramzan was not only the son of the martyred Chechen leader, but also, not coincidentally, the overseer and manager of the victorious Terek-Grozny football club which had raised the prestige of Russia in Europe and garnered the appreciation of every Russian.

IO #3—Control Information

Keeping the lid on events in Chechnya was relatively easy, as security forces and government ministries were able to control access to the area because all of Chechnya had been officially declared a counterterrorism operation (CTO) zone. This allowed the government to completely shut out any and all journalists. Thomas de Waal wrote, "The official Russian position is more or less as follows: Chechnya is a front in the international war on terror and our policies there deserve unreserved western support; however, it is a domestic political issue and no international organizations can be involved. The situation is getting back to normal; but it is still too dangerous for journalists or human rights workers to be given free access."[25] Today, even after the CTO has been lifted, the reporting situation in the North Caucasus still remains roughly what it was like during the initial 1999 Russian campaign. Reporters Without Borders ranks Russia as one of the most dangerous places in the world for journalists, and any one of their annual reports documents attacks on correspondents and media outlets.[26]

However, despite the relative ease in which the Russians were able to control the news coming out of Chechnya in early 2000 (strategy #3), it was far more difficult to ignore the suicide bombings and other terrorist attacks occurring in the rest of Russia—which is precisely why terrorism is so effective. Unable to make the average Russian feel the pain of war, and with Budennovsk and Pervomayskoye as examples of how to influence Kremlin policy, the Chechens began committing large-scale terrorist attacks outside of the North Caucasus to turn public sentiment against the war and force the Russian government into negotiations.

Although the Dubrovka Theater incident had received the most media coverage in the West to that point, Moscow had been under siege for

---

25. Thomas de Waal, "Europe's darkest corner," *The Guardian*, August 30, 2004.
26. "Russia–2008 Annual Report," Reporters without Borders, available at http://www.rsf.org/article.php3?id_article=25500&Valider=OK.

some time and during one week in August 2004, the terrorist death toll *in Moscow alone* reached more than 100, sparking public recrimination and demonstrations about the government's ability to protect its citizens against the "terrorism onslaught."[27] Basayev thought the Russians were ready to crack, so he planned the most horrific terrorist attack in history to force the Russians out of Chechnya.

THE BESLAN SCHOOL TRAGEDY—EXEMPLAR OF THE COUNTERTERRORISM CAMPAIGN (#7)

Just a few days later at the beginning of September, over 1,300 children, parents, and teachers were taken captive at Beslan (North Ossetia) on the first day of school by Chechen and Ingush terrorists of the Riyadus-Salikhin Reconnaissance and Sabotage Battalion of Chechen Matryrs—a group belonging to Shamil Basayev who was (ostensibly) an independent warlord at the time. They demanded the Russians leave Chechnya; the Russians said they would not give in to terrorist demands (but publicly claimed the terrorists hadn't made any demands), and a tense standoff ensued. Two days later something exploded in the gymnasium that set off a deadly chain reaction. Some claim they saw the Russians fire an anti-tank missile into the gym to initiate an attack while others claim a terrorist was careless and allowed an explosive charge to go off accidentally.

Regardless of how it started, once the explosion went off, the Russians fired on the gym and began an ill-coordinated assault; the terrorists fired back. The resulting fires detonated some of the terrorists' explosives; the gymnasium roof collapsed and a battle raged on for hours with civilians—mostly children—caught in the crossfire. More than 1,000 people were injured and over 400 were killed—at least 186 of them were children. The Russians later revised the number of dead to 334, but close to 200 people remain missing or unidentified and are therefore not counted as part of the official death toll. All three of the Russian Spetsnaz assault commanders were killed as well as a number of their men.[28]

If one were to try to pick the exact date that the conflict turned dramatically in favor of the Russians, it would be September 1, 2004, but it was not, as many have suggested, that the Chechens lost the engagement as much as the Russians won—despite the incredibly high casualty rate. Although it will sound callous to speak about the Russians "winning"

27. Anastasiya Berseneva, Irina Masykina, and Aleadnsr Rybin, "Sostayanie krainei tyazhesti: Informatsiya o vzryve u 'Rizhskoi' poka skudna I protivorechna," *Novye izvestiya* (Moscow), September 2, 2004, 3.

28. John Dunlop presents a compelling case that the Russians initiated the attack and caused the first explosions in "The September 2004 Beslan Terrorist Incident: New Findings," *CDDRL Working Papers*, Number 115, July 2009, Center on Democracy, Development, and the Rule of Law, Stanford University. Available at http://cddrl.stanford.edu/.

Beslan when 186 school children were killed, keep in mind just how remarkable it is that President Putin managed to stay in office and the Russians were able to hold onto Chechnya at all, given the enormity of the loss and the impact on the Russian psyche. The Waco, Texas, siege of 1993 is the closest example that we've had in the United States, and federal authorities negotiated for 51 days in an attempt for a peaceful settlement before the ATF began pumping in tear gas to end the siege. The majority of the fatalities were caused by the fires set by the Branch Davidians themselves or from "mercy killings" from their own members. Nonetheless, the lawsuits and investigations went on for years and dramatically changed the way operations were conducted in the United States. No such process has been conducted in Russia over Beslan—in fact, the opposite has occurred. And it was the overall counterterrorism campaign outlined above that not only allowed the Russians to survive Beslan, but to emerge from it almost completely unscathed.

Control Information—Stop the Terrorists
from Spreading Their Message

Once the terrorists seized the school, the Russians moved quickly to take control of the situation, deploying huge numbers of military and police to seal off the area and prepare for an assault, while Kremlin officials quickly moved in to take over from the locals. Immediately designating the area as a counterterrorist operation, the Russians were legally able to control press access, and in cases where it would have been politically imprudent to deny access outright, the FSB found ways to prevent non-approved journalists from reaching their destinations. When Radio Free Europe/Radio Liberty journalist Andrei Babitsky attempted to enter Russia to cover the story, he was arrested for trying to smuggle explosives into the country. When that ruse didn't work, two men approached him in the airport and then started to fight each other. The police intervened and Babitsky was arrested with the others for fighting. Russian journalist Anna Politkovskaya fell ill and lost consciousness on the plane enroute to Beslan after getting a cup of tea from the stewardess; the subsequent diagnosis showed she had ingested poison.

Reporters who did make it to Beslan had to work under tough security restrictions; the authorities might not be able to control what actually happened, but having learned from Pervomayskoye, they took a page from their Communism past and re-learned how to control the narrative of events so that the official statements *became* the truth. The 2004 Beslan attack showed just how far the Russians had come, and an Organization for Security and Co-operation in Europe (OSCE) report details a well-practiced Russian system for controlling the press. The report states that the Russians were so effective at manipulating

the press that distraught mothers and fathers physically attacked journalists for reporting gross inaccuracies about the actual situation.

The reporters, who had no independent access, were unable to do
anything but relay what Russian officials told them—but in so doing,
they provided a sheen of legitimacy to the prepared statements. Negotia-
tors were forbidden from disclosing the terrorists' demands as well as
the number or nationality of the terrorists; local doctors had their cell
phones confiscated so they could not report on the severity of injuries;
family members were prevented from visiting the injured in the hospital, and those who escaped the terrorists were prevented from talking to
journalists.[29] What is most remarkable about the OSCE report is that it
got published at all—considering that Russia is a powerful member of
the OSCE.

As part of the overall media campaign, specific instructions were issued
to the media about what could and could not be said. As a result, President Putin's name was not mentioned in any of the reports regarding
Beslan, effectively cutting off discussion of any relationship between the
president's policy toward Chechnya and the actions of the terrorists,
whose only demand (independence for Chechnya) was never released to
the public. To minimize the effect of the school seizure on the rest of the
Russian population and prevent them from calling for actual negotiations,
the number of hostages (1,100—777 of them children) was consciously
misrepresented to the media as one-quarter the actual number.[30]

Shamil Basayev, who was not with the terrorists at Beslan, personally
wrote the Chechen demands to President Putin; and despite the fact
that the demand note was given to the president of Ingushetia (the chief
negotiator)—who turned it over to the authorities—neither the note nor its
contents were released to the public. This served to keep the myth of the
"international terrorists" alive and distance the Chechens from the attack
altogether. In the note, Basayev wrote: "The Chechen people are conducting a national-liberation struggle for our Freedom and Independence, for
our self-preservation, and not to destroy Russia or to humiliate it. Being
free, we would be strong neighbors. We offer you peace, but the choice is
yours."[31] The demands were to recognize the independence of Chechnya
and Russian troop withdrawal—to restore the Khasavyurt Accord.

---

29. Miklós Haraszti, "Report on Russian media coverage of the Beslan tragedy: Access of
    information and journalists' working conditions," Organization for Security and Co-
    operation in Europe (OSCE), official report dated September 16, 2004, 1–13.
30. Ibid., 3–7.
31. Shamil Basayev's handwritten note. See http://www.pravdabeslana.ru/zapiska.htm;
    accessed on December 7, 2008. This note, listed as court exhibits 193 and 194, was pre-
    sented on January 19, 2006, at the trial of Nur-Pasha Kulayev, the only terrorist that
    was taken into custody by the Russians. Ingushetian President Aushev verified this
    was the note he received from the terrorists.

However, Kremlin information control prevented the terrorists from using the hostages as bargaining chips and mobilizing the uncommitted Russian population (the center of gravity) from rising en masse to force the government to save the children. Considering that a majority of the Russian people had originally supported the Khasavyurt agreement, and the fact that culturally, Russians place a very high value on children, it would be reasonable to assume that such a demand would have resonated with a large part of the population. However, because of the lockdown, the public didn't know about the note, that the attack was related to the Chechen insurgency, or that large numbers of children were being detained. As far as they knew from the "independent" journalists reporting from the scene, a small international terrorist situation was developing in North Ossetia for which nothing could be done because the terrorists made no demands.

Deny the Insurgents Any Legitimacy

In addition to keeping terrorist demands unreported, the Russians prevented Aslan Maskhadov from coming to the scene and mediating. Maskhadov, who did not condone the terrorism waged by his fellow countrymen, had tried to mediate at the Dubrovka Theater incident as well. The Russians were afraid that if Maskhadov was allowed to talk to the terrorists, he might be successful in negotiating a peaceful resolution. And although that would have been good for the children being held hostage, it would also give legitimacy to Maskhadov's position as the president of the Chechen Republic and put a human face on the insurgency again. In order to maintain the "international terrorist" construct, Maskhadov was not allowed to intercede on behalf of the hostages.

The IO Counterattacks

As discussed earlier, the two pillars of the Russian counterterrorism IO campaign were to constantly present the specter of the "international terrorist" and to never mention that Chechens were involved (because Chechens were good—or at worst—misled). Again, Beslan provides the perfect case study. Prior to September 3rd, when Russian special forces assaulted the school and the shootout began, the Russian government had been releasing reports to foreign news agencies, especially those with close Russian ties, to bolster the "international terrorist" theme. On September 3rd, the Sofia News Agency published a report entitled "Al Qaeda Financed Seizure of Russian Hostages."[32] President Putin went on the air and blamed the crisis on the "direct intervention of international terrorism" and days after the start of the crisis, the president's aide still denied any Chechen involvement saying, "They were not

---

32. Http://www.novinite.com/view_news.php?id=38832; accessed on December 6, 2008.

Chechens. When I started talking to them in Chechen, they answered 'We do not understand.' "[33]

Once the assault had begun, the Russian press was already broadcasting that out of the 20 terrorists killed during the shootout, "10 of them turned out to be natives of Arab countries and 1 was a black man."[34] Analysis in 2008 showed a very different story;[35] the reported "black man" from Africa turned out to be a native Chechen,[36] and the only international terrorists turned out to be two British-Algerians. The rest of the terrorists were all homegrown—the overwhelming majority coming from Chechnya (12) and Ingushetia (16). Later, numerous reports in the Russian press pointed out the conscious inaccuracies that the government had broadcast; *Moskovskii Kossomolets* ran a week-long series entitled "Chronicle of Lies," and other Moscow dailies like *Izvestia* and *Vedomosti* also ran exposés. The result was that some editors were "resigned," while President Putin lashed out at anyone who tried to link the attack with his Chechen policies and said that no one had a right to tell Russia it should negotiate with child killers.[37]

The other reason to not release the identities of the terrorists was to keep ethnic unrest and violence from escalating between the Ingush and the North Ossetians. The single terrorist captured by the Russians, Nur-Pasha Kulayev, reportedly told the Russians that the school in Beslan was chosen specifically to foment unrest between those two regions, to reignite the historical grievances over the Prigorodnyi region, and to drag Ingushetia into the greater regional insurgency. It is probable that the Russians identified this threat early on and attempted to downplay the "separatist" angle, as it was obviously part of Basayev's plan. Shamil Basayev's own account states that he sent "12 Chechen men, two Chechen women, nine Ingush, three Russians, two Arabs, two Ossetians, one Tatar, one Kabardinian and one Guran" (another ethnic group that lives in Russia).[38] By refusing to release

---

33. *Na etom etape' mi dolshni bit' bditel'nie,* Radio Mayak, September 8, 2004, transcript available at http://old.radiomayak.ru/schedules/6852/17139.html.
34. "International Terrorist Gang Headed by Militant Thought Dead," *MosNews* carried by *NTV*, September 3, 2008, available at http://groups.yahoo.com/group/chechnya-sl/message/39878.
35. Ella Kesaeva, "Terroristi-agenti, Neizvestnie podrobnosti beslanskoi tragedii," *Noyava Gazeta,* November 20, 2008, http://www.novayagazeta.ru/data/2008/86/00.html; accessed December 6, 2008.
36. Haraszti, 3.
37. Jeremy Bransten, "Russia: Putin Rejects Open Inquiry Into Beslan Tragedy as Critical Voices Mount," *Radio Free Europe/Radio Liberty,* September 7, 2004, available at http://www.rferl.org/content/article/1054719.html.
38. As quoted by Timur Aliev, Aslanbek Dadayev, and Ruslan Zhadayev, "Confusion Surrounds Beslan Band," *Institute for War and Peace Reporting,* Caucasus Reporting Service, No 254, September 23, 2004, available at http://www.iwpr.net/index.php?apc_state=hen&s=o&o=p=crs&l=EN&s=f&o=159655.

the identities or reveal the presence of a "demand note" until forced to disclose it during Nur-Pasha Kulayev's trial, the Russians could continue to keep hammering the "international terrorism" IO theme; and by the time the truth came out, the campaign had already achieved its objective and no one really paid attention.

Don't Blame Us, YOU Are Harboring Terrorists

The fallout from the Russian assault was tremendous once the enormity and horror of seeing so many dead and injured children began to manifest itself in the minds of the Russians. But remarkably, blame and anger were directed at *local and regional* law enforcement and government organizations; the central government was largely spared from recriminations. Although human rights groups and liberals called on the government to negotiate with the Chechens, there were no large-scale demonstrations to stop the war as there had been prior to the Khasavyurt Accord. How did the Russians accomplish this?

After Beslan was over, the IO campaign went on the offensive in order to deflect any criticism of Russian actions. During the assault, the Russians used tanks and flamethrowers and some human rights organizations claim that up to 80 percent of the hostages were killed by indiscriminate Russian fire. When the European Union demanded an explanation for the bloodshed, the Kremlin "bridled" at the question and denounced it as "blasphemous." The Russian foreign minister went on to say, "I do not want to suspect him [Dutch Foreign Minister Bernard Bot] of siding with such activists as Akhmed Zakayev, who found a soft spot in London and disclosed today that the Russian government was to blame for the tragedy in the [sic] North Ossetia. The explanations must be demanded from the EU countries, where such terrorists as Zakayev entrenched themselves."[39]

The Russians made it less complicated for themselves by tightly controlling the information during the crisis, making it much easier to place full blame on the terrorists afterwards. Because the truth is—regardless of how one analyzes the effectiveness of the Russian hostage rescue operation, the wisdom of using heavy weapons when children were involved, of which side initiated the explosion that triggered the assault, and what the Russians did or didn't do to find a peaceful resolution—the incident occurred because terrorists seized a school. The horror of taking school children as hostages had been a hideous fourth-quarter gamble that failed, and the horror of such an attack gave the Russians virtually unlimited support from the international community.

---

39. "Minister Lavrov: The Netherlands' demand seems blasphemous," RIA Novosti, September 4, 2004, http://groups.yahoo.com/group/chechnya-sl/message/39913.

Basayev would later say that he couldn't believe the Russians wouldn't negotiate to save their children; he guessed wrong. Some conspiracy theorists say that the Russians had nothing to lose by assaulting because any dead children would be blamed on the terrorists, and such a heinous act could never be justified.

Whereas the West had been speaking out against human rights abuses in Chechnya before September 2004, Beslan silenced any and all criticism. President Bush called Putin to say that they were standing "shoulder to shoulder in the fight against international terrorism." "No cause can justify such wicked acts of terrorism," read a message from British Prime Minister Tony Blair. "My thoughts, and the thoughts of the British people, are with you and the Russian people at this difficult time."

President Putin then called for a meeting of the UN Security Council, which subsequently issued a statement condemning the attacks as a threat to international peace and security and put Russia on the front lines of the War on Terrorism. Defense Minister Sergei Ivanov told reporters that international terror networks had declared war on Russia, taking the United States out of the role of "most aggrieved" and principal target of AQ.[40] The official U.S. statement read, "The blame for the tragedy lies squarely with the terrorists. There is no cause that can justify these kinds of terrorist acts."[41] If President Putin had been losing domestic support before Beslan, this most heinous of attacks put him firmly back in the driver's seat and cemented his position—and with that renewed mandate, he took decisive action.

---

40. Simon Saradzhyan, "Attack Creates Dilemma for Putin and U.S.," *The Moscow Times*, September 2, 2004, 1, official statement at http://groups.yahoo.com/group/chechnya-sl/message/39829.

41. State Department Spokesman Richard Boucher, U.S. Department of State, Daily Press Briefing Index, Friday, September 3, 2004, 12:40 P.M. EDT, available at http://www.globalsecurity.org/military/library/news/2004/09/mil-040903-usia01.htm.

CHAPTER 9

The Rise of the Caucasus Emirate: 2005 to the Present

Although some claim that it was the death of Basayev that led to a dramatic downturn in terrorist attacks within Russia, the nature of Chechen attacks after Beslan demonstrates that it was actually the Russian response to Beslan that stopped the terrorism. In a 2005 interview with the BBC (which subsequently aired on ABC's *Nightline*), Basayev stated his incredulity that President Putin did not consider bargaining with him when the lives of children were at stake.[1] It was the realization that Putin would not negotiate under any circumstances, coupled with the fact that the Russian population would not turn on their government, that finally changed the nature of the conflict. Shamil's urban terrorism strategy was beaten by Putin's iron will, his reorganization of the government to give him more executive authority, and his ability to control information—but at a great cost to Russian society. What should have been a crushing blow for the Russians (given how they mishandled Beslan), turned out to be the end for Basayev and his way of war.

Although Basayev goes on to state in the interview that he considered the Russian population responsible for the conflict because they supported the war (and thus appeared to condone future attacks against the Russian population), the number of attacks—both terrorist and insurgent—dropped sharply after Beslan. And even though civilians were killed in Basayev's last major attack, the October 2005 Nalchik raid (the capital of the Kabardino Balkaria Republic), the raid was directed exclusively at Russian security forces and their buildings.

After the death of Basayev in July 2006, terrorist attacks largely disappeared, because Maskhadov's successor, Abdul-Halim Sadulayev (who

---

1. See excerpts of the interview at http://www.siberianlight.net/shamil-basayev-abc-interview-video/; accessed February 8, 2009.

only lasted a year before he was killed), and the current leader, Dokka Umarov (a long-time Chechen insurgent who commanded large detachments in both wars), publicly stated that the insurgents would only target legitimate government and military targets—and for the most part, that is what they did for three years—three critical years that gave the insurgents a chance to regroup and the Russians a chance to try something different.[2]

A SIGNIFICANT CHANGE IN THE
OPERATIONAL ENVIRONMENT

As mentioned earlier, 2004 was a watershed year for the Chechen insurgency in many ways. But it would be Akhmad Kadyrov's assassination in 2004 that served as the catalyst for two additional events that brought about a re-conceptualization of the "hearts and minds" campaign, forced the insurgency into a latent and incipient stage, and appeared to bring peace from 2005 to 2007. First, the death of Ahkmad-haji Kadyrov cleared the way for his son, Ramzan Kadyrov, to eventually take over as president of Chechnya. The younger Kadyrov, often referred to in the press as sadistic, young, impetuous, obsequious (to Putin), and stupid, has nonetheless proved to have a shrewd grasp of how to use culture and religion to create counter-ideologies and narratives with which to combat the insurgents.

Ramzan understands the Chechens and how to coerce their behavior. Moreover, whereas the elder Kadyrov had made agreements with other powerful families like the Yamadaevs and Khakievs, the younger Kadyrov has striven endlessly to consolidate his power in Chechnya—even calling for the removal of Russian federal troops from Chechnya altogether. Kadyrov understands Chechenization, and since his father's death, he has worked hard to make this policy work.

Another significant event in 2004 brought about by Akhmad Kadyrov's death was the flight over Grozny that President Putin made enroute to Kadyrov's funeral. Multiple reports speak about Putin's very visceral response to seeing first hand the destruction of Grozny and the obvious mishandling of the reconstruction funds. After that flight, Putin got serious about rebuilding Grozny—to the tune of billions of dollars in reconstruction aid. Although much of this money has undoubtedly found its way into the pockets of unintended recipients, billions of dollars have still managed to get into Chechnya. Ramzan Kadyrov has used a good portion of the money to create an economic upturn for Chechnya that, combined with his cultural and religious "reforms," has done much to create the conditions for short-term counterinsurgency success from 2005. In essence,

2. Umarov later changed his stance in 2009 and terrorist attacks have begun again.

because all counterinsurgency campaigns should be iterative in nature, one can view the updates and improvements to strategy #6 as the first real attempt at a "hearts and minds" campaign.

However, as we look at Kadyrov's efforts, it is important to keep in mind that a large part of the reason that the "new" campaign plan seemed to work so well was because of the relative calm in which it was allowed to operate. The U.S. invasions of Afghanistan and Iraq electrified much of the Muslim world and the number of foreign fighters going to Chechnya declined sharply—choosing to fight Americans instead of Russians. By the beginning of 2005, external support (especially money and fighters) to Chechnya had greatly diminished. Moreover, the 2002 U.S. invasion of Afghanistan that toppled the Taliban was a significant blow for the Chechens as it had been Afghanistan's Taliban-led government that had previously provided so much support (money and training)—as well as being the only government to officially recognize the Chechen Republic of Ichkeria.

By March 2005, it looked as if the writing was on the wall for the Chechen insurgency as Aslan Maskhadov was killed and his loss was seemingly catastrophic. His successor, Abdul-Halim-haji Salamovich Sadulayev, did not have the international profile that Maskhadov had, and it appeared as though the insurgency was dead and the only thing left to do was to find and eliminate Shamil Basayev. Moreover, FSB efforts to eliminate high value targets (HVTs) meant that the majority of experienced field commanders were dead (or soon would be); only a few managed to flee abroad. And when the indestructible Shamil Basayev was finally killed in July 2006, the FSB shrewdly offered an amnesty to the remaining fighters, and 300 of them took their offer. The insurgents were tired of the brutal fighting, and with Basayev gone, opposition to the federal forces now seemed hopeless.

But it wasn't only what the Russians were doing; the Chechens actively reduced their profile during the period as Sadulayev worked to reorganize the insurgency during his one-year presidency of the ChRI. The insurgency was gripped by an identity crisis after the crippling loss of Maskhadov. Moreover, there was the need to develop a new insurgent strategy after the Beslan tragedy invalidated Basayev's urban-terrorism-based approach. Sadulayev is credited with refocusing insurgent attacks back to military and government targets and insisting that such attacks should avoid injuring civilians.

Although Sadulayev endorsed returning Chechnya to democratically elected leaders after the end of the conflict, he also called for the region to fall under *shari'a*. As such, Sadulayev was emblematic of the internal crisis that the insurgency suffered from for the next few years—an internal struggle between the "old school" secularists that had fought in the first war and desired Western-style democracy (but who were quickly dying out), and the next generation who tended to gravitate toward the hard-line

Salafists seeking an imamate. Although attacks still occurred during this period, for all intents and purposes, the insurgency reverted to a latent and incipient stage in order to reorganize and thus created an opening for Kadyrov and the Kremlin to revamp the Chechenization process with little interference.

THE CAUCASUS EMIRATE AND THE CURRENT
STATE OF THE INSURGENCY

After the death of Sadulayev in June 2006, the vice president of the separatist Chechen Republic of Ichkeria (ChRI), Dokka Umarov, assumed the presidency and in his first published comments vowed to expand the conflict to "many regions of Russia," and stressed that Chechen insurgents would only attack military and police targets. Umarov then appointed Shamil Basayev as vice president—in the hopes of forcing Russia into a political negotiation, for if they killed Umarov, then Basayev would become the leader of the insurgents. This strategy was short-lived, however, as Basayev was killed the next month. Despite concerted efforts by the FSB to kill Umarov, he managed to escape and began traveling to neighboring republics to meet with local *jamaats* (an Arabic term meaning "assembly") fighting against the Russians in order to consolidate the movement into one unified front. These military *jamaats* were comprised almost exclusively of radical Muslims, and although few in number, they were extremely motivated, highly disciplined, well organized, and provided a much needed infusion of enthusiastic fighters. The *jamaats* began to emerge in the neighboring republics and soon became anchors for additional forces to link up with.

On October 31, 2007, Umarov, who had not been considered an ideologue by any means, shocked the Chechens and Russians by proclaiming the end of the Chechen Republic of Ichkeria and the birth of the Caucasus Emirate. He then declared himself emir and dramatically changed the nature of the insurgency. The insurgency had always contained multiple groups of fighters united against a common foe, but now Umarov took a bold step to sharpen the resistance and give it an ideological footing that would strengthen the resolve of those who had decided to stay and fight. Many of the remaining "secularists" had left the insurgency after Basayev's death, so at this point, Umarov felt he had nothing to lose.

Although initially stating that the emirate considered the United States, the United Kingdom, and Israel as common enemies of Muslims worldwide, Umarov soon retracted his statement and indicated that only those who help the Russians or Israel are their enemies. This move had long been advocated by Movladi Udugov and other ideologues, but had heretofore been rejected by separatist leaders as counterproductive and further splitting their already weakened forces. Umarov himself stated that he had been against the idea of an emirate before assuming the leadership, but that after much prayer and contemplation decided that it was best for the movement.

The new emirate's "borders" roughly encompass the Russian republics—the emirate refers to them as the *vilayahs* (provinces)—of Dagestan, Chechnya, Ingushetia, North Ossetia, Kabardino-Balkaria, and Karachay-Cherkessia. The new emirate was quickly condemned by the Western democratic-leaning vestiges of the Dudayev and Maskhadov eras, most notably the minister of foreign affairs, Akhmed Zakayev, who lives in exile in London and still manages the affairs of the remaining ChRI government in exile. Zakayev called Umarov's declaration a "crime" that undermined the legitimacy of the Chechen Republic of Ichkeria and called upon the remaining separatist commanders to pledge allegiance to his own government in exile in an attempt to isolate Umarov; only three field commanders followed Zakayev's call.

Umarov responded by firing Zakayev and prohibiting any of the fighters to cooperate with infidels or Western countries. Left without any military presence in the region or mechanisms to assert his government's position, Akhmed Zakayev is a leader in name only, yet Zakayev continues his activities and issues official decrees from the government-in-exile to the European Union and the United Nations on a regular basis.

At first glance it would seem that Umarov's declaration would have further split the insurgency, but it does not appear to be the case. Insurgent attacks increased significantly since the end of 2007, but most importantly, the insurgency effectively spread to the point that Dagestan and Ingushetia are now just as unstable as Chechnya. Table 9.1 shows that Chechnya is no longer the only dangerous place in the North Caucasus.[3]

When the other North Caucasus republics are added, the total number of pro-Russian forces that were reported killed in 2009 is at least 332, the total number of injured is at least 636, the total number of insurgent or terrorist attacks directed against pro-Russian forces was a whopping 745—meaning that there were at least two violent attacks per day (bombing, armed attack, etc.) in an area roughly the size of Maine (approximately 35,000 square miles). Keep in mind that the actual casualty figures are probably much higher, as the authorities try to restrict information about Russian casualties—especially in Ingushetia where government officials were prohibited from giving information about attacks. Moreover, once an injured person is transported to a hospital, his ultimate fate is unknown; some surely died from their injuries. However, the government claims it arrested over 500 insurgents in Chechnya alone in 2008, and killed/arrested another 650 throughout the North Caucasus in 2009. This is surprising given that, at the beginning of 2008, Ramzan Kadyrov claimed that there were no more than 70 insurgents left in all of Chechnya. The bottom

3. 2010 statistics (through September) show that Chechnya has now climbed back into the #2 spot. Dagestan is currently #1.

Table 9.1

Totals	Chechnya	Dagestan	Ingushetia
2008			
Attacks vs. Gov't	141	114	346
Police killed	63	51	59
Police injured	85	75	164
Federals killed *	67	3	61
Federals injured *	99	2	57
Insurgents KIA	43	65	59
Insurgents arrested	98	43	13
2009			
Attacks vs. Gov't	152	242	308
Police killed	81	71	66
Police injured	143	139	193
Federals killed *	33	35	33
Federals injured *	57	17	66
Insurgents KIA	166	149	93
Insurgents arrested	127	39	24

* "federals" include FSB, military, border guards, etc.

line is that official figures from the government are disingenuous, so these statistics, taken from independent media reports, should be considered conservative estimates. 2010 is even worse: the average number of insurgent attacks *per week* (through October 1st) in the region exceeds 20.

So, contrary to the official statements, Russia's North Caucasus region has seen a significant increase in attacks over the past three years, and the Caucasus Emirate (CE) is a strong, resilient, and capable guerrilla force. The Russian government officially ended the counterterrorism operation in Chechnya in April 2009, and the government and newspapers marked the occasion as the "end" of the Chechen insurgency; but as the table above shows, this view is extremely shortsighted. To put the numbers in context, during the same period (2008), the United States lost 314 soldiers in Iraq—an area and population five times larger than the North Caucasus. And in Afghanistan, losses for the entire coalition came to 294—and no one is talking about that conflict as being over.[4]

There is a tendency within the Russian government to want to continue to treat the violence in Dagestan and Ingushetia as being fundamentally different from the Chechen insurgency, yet nothing could be further from the truth. It is precisely because the insurgency is able to spread out that it is not necessary to have so many attacks in Chechnya. Mao Tse Tung said: "Enemy advances, we retreat. Enemy halts, we harass. Enemy tires, we

---

4. Icasualties.org, the Iraq Coalition Casualty Count, available at http://icasualties.org/. Keep in mind that the U.S. and coalition data include non-combat fatalities as well, which are not included in the North Caucasus figures.

attack. Enemy retreats, we pursue." It is easier to conduct attacks in the neighboring republics at the moment, so that is where they strike. It is politically expedient to talk about the success of Ramzan Kadyrov within Chechnya itself and to advertise the drop in attacks (in 2006 and 2007) as evidence of some successful policies.

It is wishful and dangerous thinking on the part of the Russians to not view the violence across the entire North Caucasus as being related—*even when nationalists or those alienated by the current regime are conducting the attacks.* If there are secularists who want to espouse a change in government in Ingushetia, do they care if they get weapons and explosives from extremists? Of course not. If anything, the successful attacks of the Islamists demonstrate that the government is vulnerable and encourages others to attack as well—regardless of ideology. Think back again to Chapter 1: throughout history insurgencies have often been coalitions of diametrically different groups united by their common goal of destroying the current government or obtaining their freedom.

The Russians did not even refer to the "Caucasus Emirate" in official statements until February 2010, and ignoring the reorganization of the insurgency was a big part of the reason that Russian soldiers and police suffered such high casualty rates. In order to survive, the Chechens did what insurgents are supposed to do, revert to a Phase I latent and incipient phase, reorganize, and reemerge with a different strategy. During the reorganization period (2006 and 2007) attacks were down, as is natural. However, to claim that the Chechen insurgency was defeated at the beginning of 2009, as the Russian authorities and many journalists did, meant being ignorant of basic insurgency warfare or falling prey to a Russian IO campaign aimed at discrediting the insurgency.

A quick look at Army Field Manual 3–24.2, "indicators of a shift in strategy" will demonstrate that the insurgency was never over; even new observers of the Chechen conflict should be able to identify the "changes in propaganda message content, unexplained pauses in guerrilla attacks, shift of effort between urban and rural efforts, displacement of insurgents from one location to another, and change of focus of attacks."[5] In other words, what the Russians and many journalists (and U.S. intelligence agencies) had described as the Russian victory over the Chechen insurgency was, in fact, a classic case of insurgent reorganization.

The insurgency isn't dead, it's just different—and it has spread beyond the borders of Chechnya; the 1994 and 1999 Chechen Wars have spawned yet another iteration of the 250-year-old North Caucasus insurgency. What the secular democratic movement was unable to achieve—an ideology that transcended nationalism and state boundaries—has been achieved by

---

5. Army Field Manual 3–24.2, *Tactics in Counterinsurgency* (Washington, DC: Department of the Army, Headquarters, 2009), 2–19.

reorganizing the conflict and giving it a greater unifying structure: reactionary traditionalism in the form of conservative Islam. Despite Kadyrov's rhetoric, the insurgent ranks are filled and attacks have risen steadily over the past three years. Even the secularist-Islamist "split" among the Chechens only serves to help the insurgency in the long run.

The official divorce of the two separate elements of the insurgency has left both parties with the ability to seek help and solace from their respective "families," thus giving both sides a better chance to gain resources and support without being tainted by the other. Actively pursuing the secularist agenda in London, Akhmed Zakayev is still able to represent the hopes of European countries that supported the democratically elected Chechen government and, if anything, seems to have gained some additional moral support for his apparent loss. And because the emirate has clarified the insurgency and their message, they have recently gotten some external support from Islamic countries—although nothing near the levels provided in the late 1990s and early 2000s. Make no mistake, if there were ever to be another real opportunity for the Chechens to assert themselves against the Russians in a war of maneuver, the two sides would quickly rejoin for the sake of the common foe. In essence, the "split" has not harmed the insurgency. The greatest fear was that the West would stop supporting the insurgents, but as Umarov rightly calculated, the Chechens lost any support they had from the West after Beslan. Ergo, the emirate has adopted a stance that is not antithetical to the West while actively reaching out to the Muslim world.

ANALYSIS OF THE CURRENT NORTH CAUCASUS INSURGENCY

Before analyzing the changes to the Russian counterinsurgency strategy since 2005, it is necessary to look at how the insurgency changed as well. Some characteristics of the current regime remain unchanged over the past 250 years; in fact, at this point, the insurgency more closely resembles the historical models than at any other point since the start of the recent conflict, beginning in 1994. It is no longer the "Chechen insurgency," it is once again a North Caucasus insurgency.

Ideology

The use of the term "emirate" when identifying one's movement is a dead giveaway that Dokka Umarov and the Caucasus Emirate espouse a *traditional* ideology. The Salafist-inspired ideologues like Movladi Udugov and any foreign fighters are *reactionary-traditionalists*, which is a specific subset of traditionalists (usually espoused by zealots) to reestablish an ancient political system that they idealize as a golden age.

There is a group that was best represented by Shamil Basayev—those who rely on a simple renunciation of "Rusney" and who keep fighting for a variety of reasons: nationalism, revenge for the destruction that the Russians wreaked upon their families and their way of life, a lack of other options, a hatred of the current government and their grip on the region, or those who merely hope to profit from the fighting. Many fighters in Dagestan and Ingushetia fall into this latter category. Fighting still gives young men a sense of purpose and a link to a tradition of resistance; they fight because it gives honor to their forebears who died in the very same conflict. Although it is difficult to categorize this last ideology (the closest would be a hybrid traditional-secessionist-profiteer), it does illustrate the point that ideologies are often vague and contradictory.

Besides the emirate, there is also Akhmad Zakayev's London-based shadow government, which coordinates the remnants of Maskhadov's administration. The official stance of the ministry of foreign affairs of the Chechen Republic of Ichkeria (ChRI) states that "Chechnya's resistance to Russia has always been about a struggle for independence."[6] Further reading of this document shows that secession or independence from Russia is clearly the long-term goal of those associated with Zakayev and the Chechen Republic of Ichkeria. However, given that Russian troops are all over the place and Kadyrov seems to have a firm grasp on the country, the "Ichkerians" seem to understand that outright independence is unlikely in the short term. In the meantime, they continue to espouse a concept called "conditional independence," which would establish a structure in Chechnya similar to what the UN established in Kosovo. As such, the Ichkerian government is clearly *secessionist*; but as mentioned earlier, Zakayev and the ChRI are supported by only four (significant) Chechen units since the establishment of the Caucasus Emirate.

So there is not one single ideology espoused by all the insurgents—rather, different groups have different goals—but the group is united in their desire to get the Russians out. However, this lack of a unified ideology is a weakness that has been exploited by the Russian government in the past.

Strategic Approach

Despite the fact that the Chechens have not yet regrouped into a unified resistance, the other nationalities within the emirate seem to have coalesced into a relatively professional force with some clearly discernable organizational characteristics. As discussed above, the emirate is now operating as a "traditional" insurgency utilizing an identity-focused strategy, using both the existing clan structures as well as the superimposed religious structure of an emirate, complete with traditional Islamic titles and terms. This is

---

6. *The Russian-Chechen Tragedy: The Way to Peace and Democracy*, the Ministry of Foreign Affairs of the Chechen Republic of Ichkeria, February 2003, 25.

markedly different from the strategy employed during the Dudayev and Maskhadov eras, the strategy during those periods being something closer to a mix of "protracted popular-war" and "urban" strategies.

The 1994 and 1999 struggles resembled the French-Algerian model where the "French won on the battlefield but the Algerians won the war . . . the Algerians were able to maintain widespread popular support and wear down French resolve through skillful propaganda efforts at home and abroad, to exploit violent excesses by the French (torture and terrorism) and to pose the prospect of a costly and interminable struggle."[7] Replace "French" with "Russian" and "Algerian" with "Chechen" and one could easily describe the 1994–1996 Chechen War with those same words. However, by 2002 that strategy was no longer working for the Chechens, as Moscow had co-opted a large portion of the population to its side. The deaths of Maskhadov and Basayev further demoralized the insurgency, and overt popular support waned sufficiently to require the insurgency to abandon their once successful protracted popular-war strategy.

The Caucasus Emirate's (CE) strategic approach is "identity-focused" with elements of "urban warfare" and "military-focused" thrown in because it is a rural-based insurgency with strong urban components. This strategy is based on the common cultural and religious identities of the insurgents and makes legitimacy and popular support relatively easy—as it is almost automatically granted by the mass base by virtue of shared identity. Although some effort has been made to garner popular support with non-Caucasian Muslims, the primary means of external support comes from international Caucasian diasporas. This also explains why the CE occasionally attacks civilian targets (rival imams) who threaten the traditions and social structure of their group.

The CE has no use for the shadow government of Zakayev, as it has adopted a traditional Muslim hierarchy—which is also favorable for conducting decentralized attacks throughout the region in both rural and urban areas. This combination ties up significant government forces in the urban areas and provides financial backing, intelligence, and logistics to the rural elements. Perhaps more importantly, the urban component receives better media coverage than the attacks in the mountains and forests, as it is much more difficult to cover up an attack when hundreds of city dwellers can take pictures with their cell phones. Because of historical animosity with Russians, as well as an ethnically homogenous population, underlying cultural and religious differences, and numerous accounts of Russian atrocities, the insurgents have not had to spend much time trying to develop support for their cause among the population, obviating the need for the insurgents to create and frame compelling narratives to justify their actions or to draw supporters to their cause; the Russians have done that for them.

---

7. O'Neill, *Insurgency and Terrorism*, 39.

Estimates on overall insurgent strength vary wildly. I estimate the guerrilla force to be about 500 full-time rural-based fighters and another 600–800 urban-based, part-time insurgents that rally to conduct operations as needed in either urban or rural environments. Platoon-sized elements of up to 30 men operate in the mountains and forests, while smaller cells of five to eight routinely attack targets in the cities and population centers.[8] Although Ramzan Kadyrov stated as recently as July 2008 that the total insurgency now only consists of 60 to 70 *shaitans* (devils), the Russians themselves claimed they captured over 500 insurgents by the end of 2008.

Moreover, if one simply counts the total number of subunits identified through the open press and CE press releases, the CE leadership alone would number close to 50. The number of fighters in each unit varies, but photos of individual groups posted regularly on the Internet generally show between 15 and 20 guerrillas. In a 2008 video of an insurgent group led by Tarhan Gaziev in Chechnya, 35 guerrillas march past the camera in single file; there were more, but the cameraman broke off filming before the last man came into view.[9] Chechen insurgent media sources refer to Gaziev as a commander of southwestern operations. The insurgents appeared strong and well fed, properly equipped, with decent uniform standardization, and some attempt at camouflage. Quite a few carried RPGs and crew-served machine guns. They did not display good tactical dispersion either on the roads or in the forests, but morale appeared high (both could have been a result of the fact they knew they were being filmed). All of them wore beards of varying lengths. Each had what appeared to be a heavy rucksack—as indicated by the care that they took while crossing a relatively small stream in the forest. A cursory assessment is that they appeared to be relatively professional for a guerrilla band—not the kind of thing that a platoon of Russian conscripts with less than two years experience wants to run into.

Organization

The emirate has both administrative and military organizations, with some leaders occupying both positions—especially at the village levels. The military structure is initially organized by "fronts" (or *vilayats*, sometimes spelled *wilayahs*), and corresponds roughly to the existing Russian political boundaries with fronts established in Dagestan, Chechnya, Ingushetia, North Ossetia, and a joint vilayat of Karabino-Balkaria and Karachay-Cherkessia. There are also smaller fronts on the Nogai steppe

---

8. Based on news reports, photos, and videos that the insurgents have posted on the Web and run against various unclassified link analyses.
9. At http://www.chechencenter.com/ under file name of "Mujahadeen Summer 08 Tarhan Group.AVI," posted July 29, 2008; also available on YouTube.

(in Stavropol Krai), as well remote vilayats in the Urals and in the Volga region. Larger and more active vilayats (Chechnya, Ingushetia, and Dagestan) are further broken down. Chechnya has Eastern, Central, and Western Fronts; the fronts are further subdivided into districts or sectors, and some are further subdivided into villages. Although some organizations are known by multiple names, in Chechnya alone there are multiple units organized in Kurchaloy, Vedeno, Nozhay-Yurt, Argun, Gudermes, Shali, Shelkov, Shatoy, Grozny, Darginsky, Urus-Martan, and many others. In addition, there is the Khattab group (aka the Al Ansar Brigade and formerly known as the Islamic International Brigade) and the Riyadus-Salikhin Battalion of Recon and Sabotage (aka Battalion of Shaheed Suicide Bombers).[10] Dagestan and Ingushetia are similarly organized, albeit with not quite as many subunits.

The last good estimate of the auxiliary in 2004 put it at 15,000, but that included auxiliary and underground groups together.[11] This would make the ratio of guerrillas to auxiliary around 10:1—well within the parameters of the usual ratios for insurgencies. Nonetheless, anyone who tacitly supports the insurgents could be called upon to support them and probably will—putting the total number of potential auxiliary at a much higher number. In May 2008, the commander of the combined forces in the North Caucasus, Major General Nikolai Sivak, told the military newspaper *Krasnaya zvezda* (*Red Star*), "The local population either support the militant groups or remain neutral." As such, FSB and police from different Russian regions doing mandatory six-month tours in the North Caucasus do not trust the local police (the majority are former insurgents), because quite a few of them give information to their former comrades (if only to guarantee the safety of their own families), and can be considered part of the auxiliary or at least the "support base." All of the insurgency leaders are well known and involved in the fighting so there is no need for a separate underground organization; a classic "underground" organization would also not be in keeping with Islamic tradition.

The assassination of Sheikh Abu Umar al-Sayaf (the "coordinator" mentioned previously in the declassified DIA intelligence report) in Dagestan in November 2005 was a blow to the underground movement and shut down a significant flow of money from the Arab Gulf. As the *imam* and spiritual leader for the Arabs operating in Dagestan, Abu Sayaf was the main conduit for money coming from *zakat* (religious

---

10. See IntelCenter's Caucasus Emirate Wall Chart, 2008, and the MercyHurst Caucasus Insurgency Analysis Team's Link Analysis (https://caucasus.wikispaces.com/Link+ Analysis), to get a feel for the full scope of the insurgency as well as the messy complexity of their relationships. Neither one is 100 percent correct, but comparing and contrasting the two yields useful insights.
11. Vadim Rechkalov, "Ideologiya Basaeva. Pochemu spetzsluzhbi ne mogut poimat' Shamilya Basaeva. Prichina nomer odin," *Izvestia* (Moscow), December 7, 2004.

tithing) and international Islamic charities. Funds that operated out of the United States were shut down after 9/11 (like the Benevolence International Foundation in Chicago), but other countries still allow those "charities" to operate and send funds to jihadists. Although Abu Sayaf has undoubtedly been replaced and funds still move through the Caspian corridor, increased Russian emphasis on Dagestan and increased cooperation with the Azeris is responsible for moving much of the insurgency's support to the West.

There are no good estimates for the size of the underground outside of the North Caucasus to be found, but it is well known that there are large diasporas operating in many countries, and many within those diasporas support the insurgency. A series of assassinations during the last half of 2008 and early 2009 against prominent emirate figures living in Turkey confirmed that the most influential and important underground group operates out of that country (the North Caucasus diaspora there is estimated to be five million). It is generally believed that the Russian FSB is targeting the Turkish underground group because it is the base of operations for the rest of the Chechen diasporas worldwide.

The February 2009 assassination of Musa Atayev in Istanbul exposed some of the inner workings of the underground by virtue of what *did not* happen after his death. Atayev (Dokka Umarov's cousin) was the deputy chief representative of the emirate outside of the North Caucasus. He controlled the rest of the emirate's representatives abroad and, most importantly, was responsible for funneling money to the emirate; however, his death was not catastrophic for the emirate. This is because the underground abroad is organized in the classic "cellular" form so that the death or exposure of one cell does not cripple the rest of the organization. Atayev's functions were immediately taken up by a mirror cell run by the chief representative (Shamsuddin Batukaev), and Atayev's cell was reconstituted with new individuals, most likely someone else from Dokka Umarov's extended family.[12]

Other Characteristics

In many ways the current insurgency closely resembles what it was like 250 years ago. The cities are more built up, but the environment and geography is the same, and as such, the insurgents are once again fighting a classic Phase II guerrilla war from the mountains and forests against overwhelming Russian forces. During the harsh winters the guerrillas conduct fewer operations in the mountainous, forested regions and there tends to be more urban attacks. It is also easier for Russian forces to find larger

---

12. Mairbek Vatchagaev, "Dokka Umarov Suffers Setback in Turkey," *North Caucasus Analysis*, Vol. 10, Issue 9, March 6, 2009, available at http://www.jamestown.org/single/?no_cache=1&tx_ttnewspercent5Btt_newspercent5D=34677; accessed on March 14, 2010.

groups of guerrillas in the winter, as the lack of foliage, the telltale signs of campfires, and the need to bring in large quantities of food make trails that can be easily followed. Rural and large-scale guerrilla operations increase as the temperature does.

External support in the form of money is provided largely by Chechen diasporas—including Chechen businessmen in St. Petersburg and Moscow, as well as local Chechen citizens. In the past, insurgents claimed to receive funds from Germany, Turkey, and the United Arab Emirates.[13] Although there were clearer ties to international Salafist organizations when Khattab and other prominent Arabs were alive, it would be safe to assume that there is still some money coming from Islamist sources. Russian counterintelligence officers claim that the profits from illegal oil production in Chechnya are also used to finance insurgent operations. In the past the insurgents enjoyed sanctuary with supportive populations in neighboring Georgia and Azerbaijan, but that has largely been eliminated in the past few years. Increased tensions between Georgia and Russia since the 2008 war ensure the Georgians don't give the Russians another reason to invade, although the Kists (Vainakh cousins who live in the Pankisi Gorge) quietly support the fighters. Even though the Kists aren't fighting, they are experiencing a similar type of radicalization of their younger generation, who believe their Sufi elders are neither following Allah's laws nor fulfilling their roles as political leaders. The Azeris are currently working closely with the Russian special services to stop the transit of fighters and supplies from Azerbaijan into Dagestan— especially as the predominantly *Shi'a* Azerbaijan has begun to experience its own problems with extremist Sunni Salafists.

Although the insurgency used to get fighters, training, and moral support from extremist organizations, coalition operations in Iraq and Afghanistan have largely dried up those avenues; instead numerous official government, military, and media reports indicate that the flow of fighters has been reversed and that Chechens have left the North Caucasus to fight in those countries instead of at home.[14]

---

13. Vadim Rechkalov, "Deneg Basaeva. Pochemu spetzsluzhbi ne mogut poimat' Shamilya Basaeva. Prichina nomer tri," *Izvestia* (Moscow), December 9, 2004.
14. The issue of undocumented Chechen "ghosts" is a point of consternation for European supporters of a democratic and secular ChRI. News reports routinely state the presence of Chechens fighting in Afghanistan, but no proof of nationality has ever been provided (like an ID card or the name of a hometown). However, a former interrogator stated that the prisoners themselves told him they were Chechens, and that it was relatively easy to tell the difference between North Caucasus fighters and the local Afghans. It is also generally accepted that Osama bin Laden used Chechens as his personal guards for a significant period of time because he valued their fighting skills.

As of 2010, there is no external state sponsorship of Chechnya and it is evident that there hasn't been for at least five years, although some have claimed that members of the Georgian government provided aid in the recent past. Before Basayev began his campaign of spectacular terrorist attacks, Western countries provided significant external state sponsorship in the form of moral support by criticizing the brutality of Russian operations. Much of that support dried up after 9/11 and the Dubrovka and Beslan terrorist attacks—as the entire Chechen insurgency was then linked to terrorism. Other prominent liberal democracies went silent after natural gas shortages in the winters of 2007 and 2008 demonstrated Russia's ability to bring well-developed economies to their knees.

Even Turkey, with its significant diasporas, has stopped turning a blind eye to the activities of the North Caucasus underground, and under pressure from Russia, the Turks have outlawed fundraising and the transfer of funds to the insurgency. This hasn't stopped the activity, but has made it far more difficult to estimate the amount of money going to the insurgency through Turkey because now the activity is secret. There is no doubt that there are many Muslims who are not pleased with Russia's policy or Ramzan Kadyrov's activities in the region, and they are undoubtedly providing funds to the emirate through its representatives in Turkey. Although likely to cede to the Kremlin's requests to take stronger measures against those that Moscow has branded terrorists, in private, many Turks still see the Caucasus in the same strategic foreign policy context that they have for the past 400 years—a mechanism for expanding pan-Turkism throughout the region.

The stated long-term objective of the Caucasus Emirate is clearly explained on the pro-emirate Web site, "Kavkazcenter.com." Although the emirate has not delineated clear political boundaries, it states that it wants the Russians out of the North Caucasus republics and to establish a *shari'a*-based government. The emirate's short-term tactical objectives are to limit the ability of the regional governments to control the populations by physically occupying areas for periods of time, or by frightening local and federal authorities from establishing a full-time presence in those areas.

They are attempting to obtain the support (or at least the neutrality) of large segments of the population by highlighting the pro-Russian government's illegitimacy, especially in the areas of corruption, violence against innocent civilians, inability to provide basic services, and focusing on the fact that they are not proper Islamic governments. They target government leaders, military, and police commanders in an attempt to physically eliminate them either through death, abdication, or removal (as in the case of President Zyazikov in Ingushetia) and to cause the remaining leaders to constantly fear for their safety, degrading their ability to act against the insurgents. Finally, they are targeting and attacking police and military units in an attempt to reduce their coercive power over the population and to strengthen their own position. In 2009, the CE also began using suicide bombers and terrorist attacks again. The majority of insurgent attacks are focused on legitimate military and police targets, and it appears that the terrorism campaign will be focused on larger cities in order to bring the war into the living rooms of the average Russian citizen and erode popular support for the current Kremlin policies toward the Caucasus.

These objectives are consistent with traditional insurgencies that use an identity-focused approach. Although effective at the tactical level, the lack of engagement with the most important stakeholder group—the Russian population that supports the government's strategy in the North Caucasus—presents the biggest obstacle to strategic long-term success; this may be why Umarov has reversed his early decision to not use terrorism. Although one would be tempted to say that terrorism is not the way to engage with the Russian population, it is prudent to remember that terrorism has worked; furthermore, traditionalists using an identity-focused strategy are generally unconcerned about larger demographics, and tend to focus on their indigenous stakeholder groups who form the mass base that provides them immediate support—and are most likely to be influenced by their narratives and ideology.

The emirate is reaching out to similar communities, like other Islamic states, Al Qaeda, and particularly the Islamic Movement of Uzbekistan (IMU—aka the Islamic Movement of Turkistan, IMT). The IMU operates in the former Soviet republics of Kyrgyzstan, Tajikistan, Turkmenistan, Uzbekistan, and Kazakhstan, and seeks to overthrow those governments and establish an Islamic state under *shari'a*. Because three of the five "stans" border Afghanistan (and Tajikistan almost touches Pakistan as well), it has been easy for the IMU to seek refuge and sanctuary in the Federally Administered Tribal Areas (FATA) of Pakistan where it is believed that Osama bin Laden and Taliban fighters find refuge. There are known linkages between the Caucasus Emirate and the IMU, and multiple open source reports indicate that Chechen and Central Asian (IMU) fighters participate in the Afghan insurgency as well.

One of the most difficult things to discern is the *operational* (or midterm) objectives of the emirate. Long-range strategic goals are easy because they are broad and easily accepted by everyone—i.e., "get rid of the Russians." Short-term tactical objectives are also relatively straightforward—i.e., "conduct guerrilla attacks against Russian troops, gain support of specific areas of the population," etc. It is the operational-strategic objectives that are often the most difficult to plan and articulate because they bridge the tactical and strategic levels and define a course for a period of years. In a COIN environment, they are generally aimed at establishing and increasing governmental, military, economic, or informational *capabilities*.

The emirate's current operational (mid-term) objectives include continuing attacks on pro-Russian forces for the purposes of recruiting, training, and increasing legitimacy for the emirate, but not to decisively defeat or eject the Russians from the Caucasus. The emirate cannot conduct any major offensives against the Russians until the conflicts in Iraq and Afghanistan have been resolved simply because the insurgency in the Caucasus, although routinely mentioned in speeches by Al Qaeda and Salafist organizations, is still in the same position that it was a few hundred years ago—waiting for assistance from its Islamic brethren. As such, the Caucasus Emirate must continue to view the insurgencies in Iraq and Afghanistan as the "main effort" and wait until changes in those conflicts, regardless of the outcome, create opportunities. If, for example, either the insurgency in Iraq or Afghanistan were to be successful, then the Caucasus could expect to get an influx of recruits from all over the Muslim world eager to continue the struggle. If both of those conflicts end in defeat, then the emirate will still see an influx of experienced mujahadeen who have nowhere else to go to continue their fight.

Therefore, the primary operational objective of the Caucasus Emirate is to survive (not become decisively engaged); to stay relevant (by conducting well-planned attacks on high value targets that train the guerrillas, bring in new recruits, and garner sufficient media attention); and to avoid activities that will alienate the West (like specifically stating on their Web site that the Caucasus Emirate does not consider the United States to be an enemy and by not "officially" supporting the insurgents in Afghanistan or Iraq). This ensures that once the conflict in Afghanistan is over, the Caucasus Emirate can call for volunteers and the mujahadeen will make the trip from the Hindu Kush through Iran (or north through one of the "stans" and across the Caspian) into the Caucasus, probably through Azerbaijan.

Although not articulated by the emirate as such, statements from emirate leadership make it clear that the emirate is following the path described above. In a March 2009 interview, Anzor Astemirov, the former emir (leader) of the Kabarda, Balkaria, and Karachai vilayat (as well as one of the CE's primary ideologues, head of the emirate's Islamic Court, and the chief promoter of the emirate's creation until his death in March, 2010) gave a clear picture of the emirate's intermediate goals when he said, "We work according to a different program, which does not stipulate military activity at the current stage . . . although we provide more operations with more success than outside observers can see in news reports. A major portion of the population of so-called

Kabardino-Balkaria and Karachay-Cherkessia either latently or openly supports us."[15] This is a chilling understatement of latent capabilities if one takes into consideration that, when Astemirov made that statement, attacks in the North Caucasus had already increased by 58 percent in the first two months of 2009 compared to the year before.[16]

Notwithstanding the deliberate IO disinformation campaign, the Russians understand the real situation all too well, and despite the Russian government's consistent stance that there is no insurgency in the Caucasus, in March 2009, Russia's representative to NATO, Dmitry Rogozin, said that a U.S. defeat in Afghanistan would be a "great catastrophe for Russia" because fighters would spread across Central Asia (the "stans") and the Caucasus. He indicated that although an indefinite U.S. presence in Afghanistan would be best for Russia, he doubted that the United States would stay long enough to do the job.[17] As such, the Collective Security Treaty Organization (CSTO)[18] signed an agreement in 2009 to establish a joint rapid-reaction force, and called for each of the seven member states to provide a battalion. Rogozin stated that this force would step in to Afghanistan (or at least deploy to the shared border) in the event of an early United States withdrawal, for it is clearly understood that when Afghanistan is over, a significant portion of the fighters will head back to the Caucasus.

Now that the metamorphosis of the insurgency is clear and its concomitant parts have been exposed for analysis, it is time to see how the Russian COIN strategy adapted during the same period.

STRATEGY #6, VERSION II, CHECHENIZATION UNDER RAMZAN KADYROV

Before the assassination of Ahkmad Kadyrov in May 2004, his son had been in charge of the presidential security detail. After the elder Kadyrov's death, Ramzan became the heir apparent for the presidency; the only restriction being that he had to wait two years until he met the mandatory legal age of 30 to be a governor in Russia. The younger Kadyrov has publicly stated that the best way to deal with the insurgents in the mountains and forests is through their relatives, and after the assassination of his

15. Fatima Tlisova, "Exclusive Interview with Anzor Astemirov," *North Caucasus Weekly*, Vol. X, Issue 11, March 20, 2009 (Jamestown Foundation, Washington, DC).
16. North Caucasus Incident Database (NCID).
17. Dmitry Shlapentokh, "Russia has 'Chechnya' ploy for Afghanistan," *Asia Times*, March 11, 2009, http://www.atimes.com/atimes/Central_Asia/KC12Ag01.html; accessed on March 21, 2009.
18. CSTO is a Russian-led organization that could be referred to as "Warsaw Pact lite" and consists of Armenia, Belarus, Kazakhstan, Kyrgyzstan, Russia, Tajikistan, and Uzbekistan.

father and the Beslan attack, Ramzan, whose presidential security unit, the "Kadyrovtsy," already had a reputation for unrestrained behavior, was given free rein to prosecute the war as he saw fit.

It is important to remember that when the Kadyrovs gained power, it was still during the time of *bez predel*—or no boundaries—as far as the bulk of Russian troops were concerned. Whereas the Russian "carrot and stick" methodology of the past had been based on large-scale military offensives and wholesale destruction of villages as collective punishment, the Kadyrovtsy method of targeting the families of fighters was largely overlooked by the West because of its selectiveness—and because the Chechen terrorism campaign (and the corresponding Russian counterterrorism IO campaign) had dried up any support that the West had for the Chechen insurgency. Although holding an entire family responsible for the actions of a single member is not a novel phenomenon in Chechen culture, there is something new in the way that the younger Kadyrov has implemented it, and psychologists have already remarked on the ways that Chechen society has changed.

At the beginning of the 1999 war there were multiple Chechen splinter groups that sided with Moscow—the Kadyrovtsy, the Khakievs, the Yamadayevs—but it was Beslan Gantimirov's units that spearheaded the assault on Grozny and eventually gave victory to the Russians. Despite his effectiveness, Gantamirov and his troops nonetheless acted "within clearly-marked boundaries defined by the unofficial rules of Chechen behaviour. His men not only fought, but in some cases prevented the federals from harassing civilians. Moreover, it is still rumoured that during the blockade of Grozny they helped to transport wounded fighters from the city to hospitals outside it."[19] Gantamirov later lost his bid to become the president of Chechnya—in large part because of the restraint that he and his men demonstrated when dealing with their fellow Chechens.

The "blood feud" has always helped to mitigate Chechen-on-Chechen violence and a proscribed set of cultural traditions were immediately set into motion by family elders whenever a Chechen killed one of his own people, which helped to preserve the Chechen culture and preserve the population. However, that cultural life preserver was not consistent with Putin's expressed sentiments of "wiping them out in the shitters" and "a choice was therefore made in favour of those who demonstrated willingness to cleanse their souls and memories of any trace of the unofficial Chechen code of conduct. This was the path on which Akhmat-Khadzhi [Akhmad-haji] Kadyrov embarked."[20]

---

19. Valentin Tudan, "Every conflict always has a father," *Prague Watchdog*, February 14, 2009, available at http://www.watchdog.cz/?show=000000-000015-000006-000057&lang=1; accessed on February 16, 2009.
20. Ibid.

However, Kadyrov was the former grand mufti of Chechnya, so he tried to minimize violence and maintain good relations with the other Russian-backed Chechen groups as much as possible. When he became president, the Khakievs and Yamadayevs were each given a GRU special purpose battalion and Gantamirov worked for Kadyrov as his minister of press and information. The elder Kadyrov even went on record at a meeting of the Russian Security Council in 2002 and asked President Putin to hold accountable the Russian generals that were allowing "mop up" (*zachisti*) operations to take place saying: "When people disappear from their families and no one will say where they are located, and then their relatives find their bodies, this gives birth to a minimum of ten new rebels."

Unlike his father, Ramzan was not a religious leader. He also did not share his father's cooperative spirit and resented the other powerful stakeholders and their influence. After Ahkmad's assassination, Ramzan began to consolidate his power by removing rival power blocs—rivals who had helped establish a balance of power (and a greater sense of restraint against fellow Chechens) and prevented the elder Kadyrov from engaging in unrestrained violence. As the younger Kadyrov's power increased, so did his ability to act with impunity. Few spoke out against Ramzan and the increased violence—in part because his father's assassins were Chechens and had obviously received assistance from the local population. Akhmad Kadyrov's death made the conflict personal for Ramzan, and Beslan gave him the excuse to take off whatever gloves had been left on. In 2005, there were about 5,000 servicemen who reported directly to Kadyrov, then Chechnya's first deputy prime minister. Since then, these paramilitaries, known as "Kadyrovtsy," have been officially integrated into the interior ministry to man police units and the newly established south and north battalions of the interior troops.

Despite the fact that "human rights organizations and independent journalists have documented patterns of abduction, detention, disappearances, collective punishment, extrajudicial executions and the systematic use of torture by Russian and Chechen authorities, including Mr. Kadyrov,"[21] because Kadyrov appeared to make the large-scale violence dissipate, he was given even more autonomy. Moreover, because there was no press to report on Kadyrovtsy activities, because the international community turned away from Chechnya after Beslan, and because the new anti-terrorism laws gave him a veneer of legality, Kadyrov's actions were almost entirely ignored.

---

21. C. J. Chivers, "Slain Exile Detailed Cruelty of Chechnya's Ruler," *The New York Times*, January 31, 2009, available at http://www.nytimes.com/2009/02/01/world/europe/01torture.html?ref=world; accessed on February 1, 2009.

Nonetheless, if the policy was "all sticks and no carrots" there would be no support for Kadyrov in Chechnya at the moment—and that is not the case. After he was "re-elected" president in February 2007, Kadyrov began a major COIN program that, if not encompassing all the elements of a "hearts and minds" program, went at least as far as: "grab them by the balls and their hearts and minds will follow." Again, because this is a Russian/Chechen plan, it is hard to put in terms of U.S. doctrine and it makes more sense to use broader concepts.

Kadyrov began by mimicking the larger Russian strategy—the consolidation of power in a single executive authority, control of the narrative (information and the press), and a determined kinetic campaign. But in addition to the military and informational elements of national power, for the first time in the conflict, Kadyrov leveraged the other two as well—economic and cultural/diplomatic.

Restoration of Essential Services and Economic and Infrastructure Development[22]

When Kadyrov took over, Grozny was nothing more than a vast pile of rubble. Having already been declared the most destroyed city in Europe, the city had seen little improvement since it was leveled in early 2000. Following Putin's flyover of the city, he gave billions of dollars to Kadyrov and told him to fix it. Kadyrov, knowing that he owed his position to Putin, used the money wisely, and in an astonishingly short period rebuilt Grozny to such a degree that a delegation of journalists invited to visit the city in mid-2008 literally gushed like schoolgirls.

Despite the fact that there are cult-of-personality signs of Kadyrov and his father all over the city—and problems with corruption and poor quality construction persist, Kadyrov nonetheless rebuilt a surprising number of government buildings, apartments, schools, hospitals, parks, industrial buildings, and cultural centers in a little over a year. Moreover, Kadyrov built a brand-new mosque in Chechnya that is the largest in Europe—as well as one of the most ornate. Aided by the sad fact that the wars have decimated the population of Grozny— now listed as half as what it was prior to the 1994 war (about 225,000), Kadyrov was also able to put most people back in homes and restore running water, electricity, and sanitation.

Yes, Grozny is a "Kadyrov (Potemkin) village." Multiple reports indicate that utilities don't work all the time, and in some parts of the city they don't work at all. Apartment buildings stand empty because people

---

22. Although it's impossible to match up every element of Kadyrov's COIN campaign with a U.S. doctrinally approved line of effort (LOE), every effort is made to apply doctrinally correct terms for ease of analysis whenever applicable.

are afraid to move in due to poor construction or because pipes aren't hooked up. But considering that Grozny looked like a garbage dump in 2007, the fact that it has transformed so quickly is a statement to the Chechen people that someone is at least trying. The first step in establishing legitimacy is providing security, but after security, nothing increases government legitimacy like restoring water, power, sewage services, trash, medical services, and rebuilding homes, schools, and mosques. But Kadyrov didn't stop there; he also rebuilt the university, forced the kids to go back to school, and refurbished the football stadium so Chechens could have a real football team. Putin has promised to give another 5.1 billion dollars over the next five years to continue the reconstruction and expansion of businesses, industries, factories, colleges, institutes, hospitals, broadcasting facilities, roads, and transportation infrastructure.

However . . .

Because Grozny was rebuilt so quickly, with little or no interference from the guerrillas, some observers suggest that Kadyrov really did defeat the insurgents—otherwise they would be targeting the reconstruction efforts in an effort to show that the government is ineffective and illegitimate. Yet it has become clear that, despite the reconstruction boom, the Chechens haven't stopped supporting the local rebels. The insurgents half-laugh and half-snarl about this when asked, saying: "Why shouldn't the Russians rebuild the city, why shouldn't they rebuild our homes? They bombed our children and killed our wives and mothers. They were supposed to pay us to rebuild the city after the first war and they didn't. This time we'll let them spend their money and when it's nice and new again, we'll have a proper country to take control of."

As far as the insurgents are concerned, there really is no downside to allowing Kadyrov to rebuild the city. They believe that the majority of the people will turn on Kadyrov when given the opportunity because of his harsh methods and connection to Moscow, and in the meantime, their enemy will erect buildings (that they will one day be able to fight from), pay salaries to their supporters (who in turn use it to help the guerrillas), and rebuild lives so that future generations of fighters will be born and can be taught the lessons of their forefathers. The entire history of the North Caucasus conflict has been the same—periods of intense warfare and destruction followed by years of rebuilding, after which the people begin clamoring for independence again.

Job Creation and Wages

Cash incentives have always played a prominent role among warriors—even suicide bombers (the money goes to the family after the fact)—because there is honor in providing for one's family. Despite the fact that unemployment in Chechnya still runs about 50 percent, Kadyrov has nonetheless put tens of thousands to work in the construction industry alone—and taken them out of the insurgency. The 2008–2009 global economic crises hit Russia hard, but at the time of this writing, the Kremlin seems determined to honor its monetary promises to both Chechnya and Ingushetia (5 billion USD to each from 2008 to 2011). Although that money is focused on rebuilding infrastructure in order to create jobs and a long-term functioning economy, it appears as though the money will only provide Kadyrov with a short-term bump in publicity and a decrease in guerrilla attacks while the reconstruction continues.

It's unlikely that Kadyrov will be able to feed this chimera on his own, considering that revenues for 2008 amounted to only 4.6 billion rubles (about 140 million USD) accounting for only 13 percent of the annual budget. The rest came from Moscow.[23] By mid 2010, the Kremlin's portion had increased to 90 percent of the budgets for Chechnya and Ingushetia; Dagestan is not much better.[24] The Chechen oil industry only produces about two million barrels of oil per year, but even that revenue goes straight to the federal coffers. It's deemed too dangerous to give Chechnya control of its own natural resources because Kadyrov wouldn't be dependent upon the Kremlin.

So what will happen when the money dries up, the reconstruction stops, and Chechnya, Ingushetia, and Dagestan still haven't developed industries that will provide jobs? 2012 will be a watershed year for Kadyrov as the world economic crisis and construction of the 2014 Sochi Olympics venue means that he will not be getting another 5-billion-dollar multi-year package. Once Kadyrov is no longer able to artificially keep the economy afloat and pay salaries, the situation will deteriorate and even more men will join the insurgency—because the emirate will always be able to pay them. Average Russians, on the other hand, are upset because Chechnya, Ingushetia, and Dagestan receive government subsidies that far exceed those given to "real" Russian republics. With unemployment rising as quickly as consumer prices, preferential treatment for North Caucasians (already an ethnic group scorned by many Russians) causes resentment and even now it is not uncommon to hear strains of the 1994 mentality of "They're not Russian anyway—just let them go. Why pay so much money to keep them and have our own soldiers and police killed in the process?"

---

23. Simon Saradzhyan, "Putin's 'Pacification' of Chechnya," *ISN Security Watch* (Swiss Federal Institute of Technology, Zurich), April 1, 2008, available at http://www.isn.ethz.ch/news/sw/details.cfm?id=18808; accessed April 7, 2008.
24. Valery Dzutsev, "Khloponin's Innovative Approach to the North Caucasus Faces Uphill Struggle," *Eurasia Daily Monitor*, 7, 127, July 6, 2010 (Washington, DC: Jamestown Foundation).

There is also the short-term problem of ensuring the money actually gets to its intended use, since previous reconstruction and aid programs were shut down because so much money went straight into the pockets of administrators. This corruption, while endemic to all of Russia, is particularly bad in the North Caucasus, so even as Kadyrov has been working to increase his legitimacy, his functionaries have effectively been making the situation worse by systematically extracting kickbacks (usually 50 percent) from residents who received compensation payments for homes destroyed during the wars. Kadyrov apparently understands this, and has made efforts to stop corruption. In 2008 he started over 700 criminal fraud cases and acted to prevent further embezzlement from the heavily subsidized republic by hiring independent auditors for state-funded projects. Moscow has implemented its own regime of auditing as well, and the continued flow of money is dependent on responsible use of the funds. Ironically (or not), former Prime Minister and head of the FSB, Sergei Stepashin, is now the Chairman of the Accounts Chamber and responsible for ensuring that all the money going to Kadyrov is spent wisely. No one has offered an explanation of how Kadyrov paid for his menagerie of endangered species and his fleet of sports cars on his government salary.

Establishing Civil Control

Another significant portion of the new economic program has been to give jobs to ex-guerrillas. Establishing an amnesty and rehabilitation program for former insurgents is a best-practice approach and a continuation of the larger "divide and rule" campaign. Initially, the Kadyrovs, the Yamadayevs, and allied clans played a key role in fighting Maskhadov's forces once Russian forces and interior troops had secured all towns and strongholds by early 2001. But as part of his efforts to consolidate power, Ramzan Kadyrov has taken Chechenization to the lowest level and put a significant number of former fighters on his own payroll—giving him experienced counter-guerrilla fighters who know the families, the clans, the guerrilla bases, the trails, the tactics, the insurgent leadership, and how best to attack them. There is simply no better source of intelligence—nor better way to defeat an insurgency—and it was this practice in particular that caused such a decline in the insurgency following the mass defections after the death of Basayev.

In addition to a steady income, renewed status, the right to carry weapons, and the luxury of living at home (instead of sleeping in the snow and eating cold rations), the former fighters—many of whom still believe in an independent Chechnya—can justify their actions in this way: "The Kadyrov model of Chechen separatism has proven to be the most successful one and Russian jurisdiction is no more than a formality." These soldiers and militiamen make a fortune compared to the average Chechen; a captain makes $1,400 a month—which is a fine salary anywhere in Russia. As far as good COIN practices go, this is one of the best because it takes fighters away from the rebels while simultaneously increasing government forces.

Nonetheless, these ex-insurgents still have family and friends that know or work with the insurgents, so it is certain that a number of them pass information on to them and serve both sides—making them part of the mass base or even "fence sitters." This is why federal forces don't trust the locals and why the Russian regional commander stated that all the locals support the insurgents. This causes friction and coordination problems, especially when guerrillas attack remote posts at night. The local policemen generally do not respond to calls after dark because they aren't equipped to operate at night and are not willing to risk their lives now that they've left the insurgency. This ensures that insurgents will continue to "own the night" and why, despite the vast number of soldiers and security personnel in the region, the guerrillas are still able to take over villages and towns for short periods of time.

Support to Cultural and Religious Development[25]

In contemporary insurgency literature, culture is listed as being one of the "new" elements of national power. And although there are critics of this viewpoint, it is hard to disregard the concept when dealing with insurgencies like the North Caucasus. For centuries, religion and culture have been a central theme of the conflict and provided much of the ammunition for the ideological and informational campaigns on both sides. Kadyrov has waged an aggressive cultural campaign over the past few years that has surpassed even his father's efforts as grand mufti. In so doing, Kadyrov has snatched away much of the ideological underpinnings of the insurgent ideology and provided a fine example of one of Charles Callwell's ideas for successful counterinsurgency—seizing what the enemy prizes most—in this case, the moral high ground.

Kadyrov is trying to show that as the leader of the Chechens, no one is more Islamic than he is. And Kadyrov doesn't just say it, Kadyrov shows that Chechnya under Kadyrov doesn't oppose Islam (like the Salafists say), rather it *embraces* Islam—and moreover, a truer form of Islam that is consistent with Chechen culture as well as international Islamic norms. This is a significant *counter-ideology* to the current insurgent ideology because it convincingly argues that there is no need for

---

25. This is not listed as one of the seven doctrinal COIN Lines of Effort, but it should be. Although the activities discussed here are not the types of things military forces usually do (emphasizing the need for an interagency effort headed by civilian authorities), military forces deployed in Muslim areas could definitely provide support to these types of activities, especially in the areas of civic action projects designed to strengthen local religious and cultural norms.

another "outside" religion that claims to be a "better" and more "pure" form of Islam.

As part of this campaign, Kadyrov has built the biggest and most beautiful mosque in Europe. He has begun working with Arab countries and with the Organization of the Islamic Conference (OIC), he visits Muslim leaders and they visit him. In the past, the OIC had leveled accusations against Russia that it was fighting against Muslims and Islam in Chechnya, but Kadyrov has managed to turn things around and re-brand Chechnya and the North Caucasus as the "heart of Russian Islam." After opening the new mosque and an all-Islamic institute, Kadyrov even convinced the Palestinian president to visit Chechnya—legitimizing Kadyrov's Chechnya in the minds of millions of Muslims around the world.

In 2008, he brought an international Islamic conference to Gudermes, which was attended by hundreds of delegates from around the Islamic world, and in so doing legitimized the Chechen brand of Sufism. He established a "Center for Islamic Medicine" which mainly uses treatments based on *suras* (chapters) and *ayahs* (sections) of the *Qur'an* to heal people—as well as traditional "Chechen" methods that have been used by the locals for centuries. When Kadyrov opened the center he indicated the need for such an institution, and in so doing, linked himself, Islam, and Chechen tradition by stating Chechens need "precisely the kind of treatment using non-traditional methods that our ancestors fell back on."

Make no mistake, this is all part of the "dog and pony show in Kadyrov's Village." But as far as the ideological campaign, it just doesn't matter. The Salafists, the emirate, and Islamic scholars will argue that Kadyrov's efforts aren't "real," that the Chechens must adopt the *shari'a* and follow their strict brand of Islam. They will argue that Kadyrov shouldn't be visiting the shrine of Kunta-haji on feast days because idol-worshipping is forbidden—but nobody is listening to them. Instead, what people would be seeing—if they weren't so afraid all the time—is that Kadyrov's Chechnya is more Islamic than many of the "traditional" Islamic countries—and by association, Kadyrov himself. On March 8, 2009 (the birthday of the Prophet Mohammed), the Chechen government invoked one of the pillars of the Islamic faith (charity to the poor) by distributing 5,000 Russian rubles to 10,000 poor families, giving an additional 10,000 bags of flour and sugar to them and paying 50,000 rubles to every boy born on that day; Kadyrov stated he expects the families to name the boys after the Prophet.

But it's not all gimmicks; Kadyrov is serious about proving that there is no need for the Salafists. It's now mandatory for women to wear headscarves, hard liquor can only be purchased for two hours a day (forbidden completely during Ramadan), all the brothels have been shut down; Kadyrov even created an animation center to start producing cartoons to teach morals and proper Islamic behavior to children. He has gone on record to encourage polygamy and justified the honor killings of "loose women"—all in keeping with fundamentalist tradition—and in direct contravention of the Russian constitution which he has sworn to uphold.

Kadyrov made the government more "Islamic" by getting rid of the second house of the Chechen parliament because bicameral governments are inconsistent with Islamic tradition. Most remarkably, Kadyrov, an "elected" head of a Russian federal republic has publicly described women as the property of their husbands and says their main role is to bear children.[26] The unmistakable ideological message is that, even though he can't say it out loud, *shari'a is the law in Chechnya*—thus, *everything* that any "true" Chechen has ever wanted has been achieved. Even Shamil declared that Chechnya would be willing to live under Russia if they were allowed *shari'a*—and Kadyrov is showing the world—and especially the Chechens—that he has finally realized their dreams. Why would anyone—even the insurgents—want to fight against that, unless of course, their cause wasn't *really* about being Islamic.

This is truly significant. This is one of the few examples of a government fighting an ideological battle with jihadists and *winning*. Kadyrov is demonstrating that the CE has no legitimacy for Chechens because if they continue to fight against the Islamic society that Kadyrov has put in place, they are essentially proving that all the emirate really wants is power for themselves. The emirate's ideological counterpunch is that Kadyrov is merely a toady for the Russians, and the Chechens still desire independence. To which Kadyrov responds with even more cultural programs to erode that argument and show that under Kadyrov, Chechnya is more independent and "Chechen" than it has ever been.

Kadyrov can proudly claim that he has resurrected Chechen traditions that had been lost under Soviet times. Not only has he mandated teaching the Chechen language in schools, he has gone so far as to require core subjects be taught in the native language. His directive to teach math in the Chechen language makes Chechnya the first region in Russia to teach a major subject in public schools in a language other than Russian. The IO campaigns literally write themselves: "Kadyrov saves Chechen culture. Chechnya under Kadyrov has actually achieved independence."

It is a compelling narrative, especially in light of the fact that there are now jobs, a beautiful new mosque, the city is being rebuilt, and even more money is coming in. This "line of effort" (LOE) is producing

---

26. The newspaper references and quotes are too numerous to cite them all: start with "Pro-Moscow Chechen president upbeat on economy, worried at nationalist threat," *BBC Monitoring*. Source: Regnum news agency, Moscow, in Russian 1953 gmt 30 Jan 09; "Kadyrov Restricts Alcohol Sales," *Agence France-Presse* (AFP), February 17, 2009; Lynn Berry "Chechen leader imposes strict brand of Islam," Associated Press, *Miami Herald*, March 1, 2009; and *North Caucasus Weekly*, Vol. X, Issue 5, February 6, 2009.

results because Kadyrov is addressing all the elements of national power in one unified campaign. However, this strategy is not without risk because the government is essentially adopting the stated goals of the insurgents. Virtually every Russian newspaper article written about the end of the counterterrorism operation in April 2009 stated in one way or another that Chechnya is a part of Russia in name only, and that Kadyrov's economic, religious, cultural, and language programs merely encourage Chechen nationalism and sets up Russia for further conflict in the future.

Counter-Sanctuary and Additional IO Campaigns

To complement the aforementioned economic and cultural programs, Kadyrov has initiated a (forced) repatriation campaign and additional IO campaigns to promote legitimacy, marginalize insurgent influence, isolate parts of the population from insurgent forces, provide context for government operations, establish some legitimacy for his government, and create divisions between insurgency leadership and the guerrillas. What is most significant about these IO messages is that they are primarily focused on the local population. As discussed earlier, the previous "hearts and minds" campaign had been largely directed at the international and regional levels with the primary target being the Russian population. These new campaigns, while still resonating with the Russian and global audiences, show a more determined and focused approach to addressing what Western COIN theory would consider to be the center of gravity—the indigenous population. This is significant because it indicates that the Russians believe they have seized what they consider to be the key terrain in the conflict—the Russian population's support—and, therefore, they can now begin working on secondary objectives.[27]

The overriding theme of this campaign is: "There is no reason to oppose government because Chechnya has already achieved more independence now than it had ever hoped for in the past." The argument

---

27. To some extent, the identification of the sub-elements of the population is conceptually arbitrary. If one wants to look at the insurgency in the North Caucasus as a "Russian" insurgency, then one looks at the entire Russian population and directs appropriate I/O campaigns at the majority of the Russian population. Because the Russians have always considered the Caucasus to be a part of Russia, this is how they naturally look at the conflict and their strategy reflects that. Western theory focuses on insurgent ethnic groups and considers the mass base to be those civilians from a particular region or ethnic group that provides (or could provide) support to the insurgents and designs strategies to influence them.

is: "Chechnya has now been rebuilt, and it is better than ever. The separatists and the Islamists wanted Chechen independence, but they had no
idea what to do with it when they had it and instead of a successful
modern state, they created a mafia racket. Kadyrov knows how to run a
real Chechen state, and he isn't really subservient to Moscow. In fact,
Kadyrov routinely makes statements contrary to what the Kremlin is
saying and even mildly rebukes Russia now and again in the press,
which shows that he's independent." Kadyrov's religious and cultural
efforts further support this argument because it wouldn't be possible to
establish de-facto *shari'a* in Chechnya unless it really was already independent. This marginalizes the emirate's influence and isolates it from at
least a part of the population. This message plays well at home, but it is
also directed at the diaspora communities and the millions of refugees
that were displaced by the wars and have been too afraid to return.

And for the diaspora communities and refugees, the message
has been: "It's time to come home." This is a self-fulfilling campaign
(referred to as a "self-licking ice cream cone") because refugees are
being convinced to return—voluntarily or through coercive means.
Therefore *because* famous dissidents are returning home, things must
really be as Kadyrov and the media make them out to be. Because things
must be better, the rest of the refugees and dissidents should return
home as well; the more that return home, the stronger the argument.
This is an aggressive program that is not without benefit for some of the
returnees. Kadyrov is savvy enough to treat the more famous dissidents
with respect, offering them positions in the government and newly built
homes. These positions are well-paid (and funded with Kremlin money),
and provide the status and stability that is necessary to bring people
back to a region with 50 percent unemployment. Those who take the
offer (for whatever reason) provide tacit approval for the Kadyrov regime and convey legitimacy to the government. From a "diplomatic"
application of national power, this is also part of a larger strategy to
bring former fighters into the government, a "best practice" for COIN,
and part of establishing civil control by disarming, demobilizing, and
reintegrating ex-combatants.

An excellent example of someone who cultivates the legitimization
process is Bukhari Barayev, brother of the notorious Chechen field commander Arbi Barayev, and father of Movsar Barayev—the leader of the
terrorists who seized 900 hostages at the Dubrovka Theater in 2002. In
February 2009, Barayev resigned his position as the emirate's special representative in Europe and returned to Chechnya saying he had previously
been "blinded by fanatical ideas," but while living in Europe he had
learned about the changes taking place in Chechnya and "now sees no
reason to oppose Kadyrov's government." Barayev goes on to say, "The
idea of the holy war has nothing to do with today's realities and with

what is happening in Chechnya." He added that Kadyrov's Chechnya "does not oppose Islam."[28]

In general, governments who have successfully defeated an insurgency have done so by slowly "co-opting" the guerrillas; that is, bringing the insurgents into the government and the political process. Even if the former insurgents become the "opposition party," they now obtain legitimate political power and begin to get assimilated into the government. Their perks of privilege and power keep them from once again venturing back into the mountains and forests—the "power and money" motivation that provides much of the hidden motivations of insurgents.

There are two parts to this campaign: the first is a very public "wooing" of major figures to entice them back followed by publicity whenever significant numbers (or significant personages) make the return. The second is a coercive drive to bring the Chechens home, whether they want to or not—the idea that the only safe place for a Chechen to live is in Chechnya. The least coercive measure has been to simply close the camps where internally displaced persons (IDPs, or refugees) currently reside. IDPs living in other parts of Russia have been made to return to Chechnya and as recently as May 2009, the Moscow Helsinki Group's Chairman of the Committee for Protecting the Rights of Internally Displaced Persons reported that temporary residence facilities established for the Chechens in Ingushetia were being shut down—forcing the Chechens to return home. Electricity and other services were shut off, and they were warned that they would be forcibly evicted by police if they remained.[29]

Forcing Chechens who live outside of Russia to return home is more difficult because the majority of them have sought asylum in their new countries. Therefore, in addition to counter-ideological campaigns, there must also be a counter-sanctuary campaign to deny insurgents and their supporters a safe place to operate. As diasporas dwindle in other countries, it not only reinforces the "it's time to come home" narrative (above), it also makes it increasingly easier to shut down external support to the insurgency itself. Statements from both expatriate Chechens— as well as from those who have been sent to retrieve them—indicate that there is a program designed to bring the diasporas home—by force if necessary.

In an effort to facilitate the return of Chechen refugees, in 2009, Kadyrov began establishing Chechen "consulates" in countries with significant diasporas. The refugees state they do not wish to return to Chechnya, and

---

28. Interfax and *North Caucasus Weekly*, February 20, 2009, Vol. X, Issue 7 (Jamestown Foundation, Washington, DC).

29. Resettling displaced civilians and providing the populace with humane care and treatment is part of U.S. doctrine; however, the FM stipulates that this should be a positive measure to support the establishment of civil control.

some claim the consulates are actually designed to give the Kadyrovtsy "untouchable" diplomatic status while they are "hunting" the refugees (the consulates also support the "Chechnya is already independent" narrative because they make Chechnya the only sub-national "state" in the world to have its own diplomatic missions in other countries). Since 2004, notable Chechen expatriates have been killed in Muslim (Qatar, Turkey, Azerbaijan), as well as European countries (Austria, United Kingdom, and an attempt in Norway)—places where Chechen diasporas thought themselves relatively safe. The forced repatriation program is particularly effective because of the knowledge that the FSB (or Kadyrovtsy) will target those identified by the Kremlin as terrorists—even if they reside outside the borders of Russia. Bukhari Barayev (mentioned above), had been living in Vienna and despite his long association with the insurgents and terrorists, he nonetheless returned to Chechnya less than a month after another dissident was shot dead on the streets of Vienna using a signature FSB pistol. The murdered dissident, Umar Israilov, claimed he'd been followed in Vienna and asked the authorities for protection. They refused, saying there were insufficient grounds to warrant protection. Israilov was murdered a few weeks later, and Barayev returned home to Chechnya.

Barayev had been one of the most important members of the Caucasus Emirate outside of Chechnya and responsible for funneling money to the insurgency. As the father of Mosvar and the brother of Arbi (one of the most feared commanders after Shamil Basayev), Barayev was "resistance royalty"; he was comfortable and respected. His return to Chechnya was a blow to the insurgency and gave rise to another major IO theme: "There is no hope for the insurgency and no safety for the resistance." Having lost hope of winning the conflict through either guerilla warfare or terrorist attacks, hundreds of rebels have surrendered in Chechnya and Dagestan since 2002. Even in the absence of a formal amnesty, more than 300 rebels heeded a mid-July 2006 call by FSB director Nikolai Patrushev to come out of the woods and lay down their arms after Basayev was killed. When major resistance figures like Barayev give up, the average insurgent also begins to question why he is fighting; Kadyrov uses this doubt to his advantage. The idea that "Chechnya is rebuilt, Chechnya has achieved more independence than it ever dreamed of," coupled with the possibility of getting a job, is enough to make even the most hardened or indoctrinated insurgent wonder if there really is any reason to continue opposing Kadyrov's government.

If there are remaining doubts about whether to support Kadyrov's government, they are met by even more counter-ideological arguments. Kadyrov knows he can't turn the hard-core Islamists, but he can try and convince the non-Salafists that they would be better with him; after all, what did the Ichkerians actually do when they had power? According to Kadyrov, "nothing." As part of the "there is no reason to oppose the current regime," Kadyrov has embarked on a campaign to discredit the former Chechen Republic of Ichkeria and show that the Kadyrovs are the true heroes and liberators of Chechnya. Astonishingly, the primary spokesmen for this campaign have been the former rebel commanders and fighters themselves, who "voluntarily" appear on television to disparage their former leaders and their former cause. This IO message was clearly articulated by Kadyrov himself who stated at the beginning of one program: "Come home! Look at these fellows sitting in the room, they're alive and well, and so you don't need to feel threatened either. Listen to their stories—are these the men in whom you put your faith and followed?" Several hours of testimonials from long time field commanders and new recruits provided a compelling narrative—especially when the veterans shared stories about the Ichkerian heroes (Maskhadov, Basayev, and others) that discredited the idea of the "heroic Chechen resistance."

Viewers were left with the inescapable conclusion that even if the resistance had been able to stop the Russian army in 1999, it would have never been able to form a nation-state that could have operated independently from Russia. This message rings true for the average Chechen, because by 2003, even Maskhadov was willing to accept an arrangement with Russia that would have provided fewer freedoms than Chechnya now currently enjoys. Although this is a common theme coming from Kadyrov, the impact was overwhelming coming from the mouths of the former insurgents themselves.

Such an ideological attack forced the insurgents to go on the defensive, and Movladi Udugov, the head of the analysis and information service of the Caucasus Emirate released a statement the next day claiming, "Everything that is being told by these Russian puppets, including about Maskhadov—is a lie." Nonetheless, watching the former fighters give their own testimony on live television was far too arresting an image to have wiped away by an Internet statement from a man famous for his ideological framing of facts. Udugov goes on to attempt to rebut some of Kadyrov's other IO themes by saying, "We are existing in different dimensions which can never coincide, we are pursuing different goals which can never unite."[30] Veteran Chechnya observers will no doubt see the irony of Udugov attempting to counter an ideological attack, when in the past it was Udugov who was the master of such narratives.

Kadyrov is ambitious to say the least; he leaves no stone unturned and attempts to engage with and co-opt groups that even he can't reasonably expect to support him. In an astounding display of chutzpah, in 2008

---

30. Movladi Ugudov, "Everything told by the Russian puppets, including their words about Maskhadov—is a lie," posted on Kavkaz Center.com, available at http://www.kavkazcenter.com/eng/content/2009/02/20/10555.shtml; accessed on March 1, 2009.

Kadyrov even attempted to brand himself as a "human rights activist." As part of this media event, Kadyrov met with Memorial, the only human rights group that had not left Chechnya, and discussed human rights abuses with them. Despite the fact that Memorial has been Kadyrov's most vocal critic, he nonetheless met with them to discuss the situation in Chechnya. Kadyrov made a few promises, put the blame for the atrocities on the federal authorities, further criticized the federal government for not allowing a forensics lab to be established in Chechnya in order to identify human remains that are not accounted for, and scored a public relations coup that was written up in the papers. It was the old "admit nothing, deny everything, make counteraccusations" ploy, but it worked— and Kadyrov even got one of Memorial's leaders to state publicly that "Memorial is fully satisfied with the negotiations held with the Chechen authorities." Considering how vocally and consistently Memorial has criticized Kadyrov in the past, such a statement could only be interpreted as, "Kadyrov is changing for the better."

Further Controls on Information

Despite any forward momentum being made as part of the overall information engagement LOE, some IO measures are counterproductive to establishing civil control, supporting legitimate governance, and restoring institutions. Sanctions against the press and NGOs became even more restrictive in 2008, and although the counterterrorism operation ended in early 2009, none of the sanctions were lifted: "The government restricted the activities of some nongovernmental organizations (NGOs), in some cases moving to close the organizations through selective application of the laws and other mechanisms. Authorities exhibited hostility toward, and sometimes harassed, NGOs involved in human rights monitoring as well as those receiving foreign funding. A decree from the prime minister in June [2008] removed tax-exempt status from the majority of NGOs, including international NGOs, and imposed a potentially onerous annual registration process for those that met the proposed requirements."[31] Some organizations were taxed out of existence while others had their offices raided numerous times to discourage them from reporting on the situation in the North Caucasus. Still others became the victims of smear attacks on network television—with footage of Russian soldiers being beheaded by Chechens and statements that the human rights organizations justified such actions. When the "Foundation to Support Tolerance" held a memorial service for slain journalist Anna Politkovskaya in 2008,

---

31. U.S. Department of State, *2008 Human Rights Report: Russia*, available at http://www.state.gov/g/drl/rls/hrrpt/2008/eur/119101.htm; accessed March 1, 2009.

the FSB raided its offices, arrested some of its members, and froze its bank accounts, stating the foundation supported terrorism.

The Russian press has fared no better: "The government is still restricting media freedom through direct ownership of media outlets, pressuring the owners of major media outlets to abstain from critical coverage, and harassing and intimidating journalists into practicing self-censorship."[32] The U.S. State Department's official country report on human rights in Russia for any year from 2004 to 2009 lists pages of examples of how journalists are restricted from entering Russia—and the North Caucasus region in particular.

Moreover, throughout the Caucasus, government authorities are forbidden to give information to the media about insurgent attacks or casualty figures unless there is no way to keep it out of the public eye—like an injured soldier being taken to a civilian hospital. Journalists who continue to report the facts have been threatened, beaten, or have died under suspicious circumstances (like Ingushetia.ru news agency founder Magomed Yevloyev). So with few exceptions, there really is no reliable independent reporting coming out of the Caucasus.

REFRAMING THE CONFLICT—REWRITING HISTORY

Because Kadyrov and the Kremlin control the narratives, they have successfully reframed the conflict. There is no greater example of the effectiveness of IO campaigns over time than Prime Minister Putin's May 2008 statement to *Le Monde* that the Chechen insurgency had *never* been an attempt to achieve independence in the mid-1990s. With a straight face, Putin said that, from the very beginning, the conflict was started by the influence of a foreign type of Islam designed to "loosen Russia's place on the world stage." This statement is breathtaking—both for the scope of its disingenuousness as well as the realization of the fact that this view is now accepted by numerous people in Russia. This in turn makes it much easier for Putin to explain away the problems in the other North Caucasus regions as internal problems. Official Russian statements routinely refer to violence in Dagestan, Ingushetia, and Kabardino-Balkaria as "not related to any separatist movements—it is about an internal political struggle within the republics themselves."

What is truly significant about this campaign is that, for many years, the insurgents held and maintained the initiative regarding ideological

---

32. Ibid.

narratives and attacks; now, the opposite is true. The Russians and Kadyrov now own the "high ground" in the ideological and IO sphere. They control the dialogue by consistently launching their own campaigns and they have put the emirate on the defensive, forcing the insurgents to respond to their attacks instead of being able to initiate their own. Forget about all the tactical improvements that the Russian army implemented between 1996 and 1999—what really changed the conflict was the ability to win IO battles with the insurgents. The Salafist ideology *per se* does not resonate with the general Chechen population, and the emirate hasn't been able to construct an ideology that would convince the general population to support the insurgency either actively or passively.

ESTABLISHING CIVIL SECURITY AND SUPPORTING LOCAL SECURITY FORCES

Luckily for the emirate, they don't need to create a mobilizing ideology; the Kadyrovtsy and the Kremlin are doing it for them. The heavy-handed coercive tactics used in the region create enough resentment among the populace to drive young men into the insurgency and cause many civilians to quietly support the Salafists who, even if they are a bit extreme in their religious views, at least aren't burning down houses and "disappearing" their relatives and obliterating their remains. Mistrust of Russia and Kadyrov is still stronger than fear of the Salafists. Even as President Medvedev announced the end of the counterterrorism operation in May 2009, the human rights group Memorial stated that pressure from law enforcement organizations on the young men in the North Caucasus has only increased, and "this pressure is driving more and more young men to join the rebels." Until that situation changes, even the best IO campaigns will fail to end the insurgency.

And what are the pressures from law enforcement and military organizations? From 2005 until the end of the counterterrorism operation in 2009, there were two impulses at work in the North Caucasus—sometimes complementary, but more often at odds with one another. As part of the overall Chechenization strategy, Moscow has increasingly turned over control of government functions to Kadyrov—which is consistent with best-practice COIN doctrine that emphasizes the importance of establishing self-sufficient security forces. However, Moscow still maintains a large federal presence in the North Caucasus (about 300,000 in all) to ensure four things: that Chechnya will continue to answer to federal authorities; to emphasize the fact that the counterinsurgency (they refer to it as counterterrorism) effort is a national effort; to prevent any large groups of Chechens from reverting to their former roles and joining the insurgency; and to maintain Kremlin control of key terrain.

To effect this plan, police units from all 89 federal districts of Russia are sent twice a year to conduct six-month "combat tours" in the North Caucasus; some units as far as 10,000 miles away. The exact number and disposition of police deployments are unknown, but information available on open source networks makes it probable that at least several thousand Russian policemen rotate into the North Caucasus every six months. "Federal" police control all the major roads and checkpoints throughout the troubled region and "[Ethnic] Russian policemen are present in most strategically important checkpoints in Chechnya, such as the post near the village of Chiri-Yurt (Volgograd OMON) that is at the foot of the mountains, the Kavkaz-1 post (Kursk OMON) located at the administrative border between Chechnya and Ingushetia, and the post located near the village of Benoi in Vedeno District (Perm OMON). It seems that the Russian military still does not trust Chechen policemen to guard Chechen territory."[33] And despite Kadyrov's inexhaustible statements as to the reliability of Chechen internal security forces, every year a senior Russian general issues a statement about the need to maintain federal Russian forces because a large part of the local population is sympathetic to the insurgents.

Now that the CTO has "ended" and the Russians have announced a 20,000-man reduction in overall numbers in Chechnya, it is safe to assume that the majority of cuts will come from these rotating units which were expensive to deploy and maintain—especially as the CTO designation meant that they were all getting hefty bonuses for their participation.[34] The six-month rotations with extra pay is a double-edged sword: it provides a large number of motivated riot police to ensure Russian control of vital areas, but there is also the potential for a "cops gone wild" scenario for policemen whose motto is "We know no mercy and do not ask for any"—itself emblematic of the government's attitude toward the rule of law and basic security issues.

As for the military, it will remain, and despite Kadyrov's earlier attempts to remove federal troops from Chechnya, he now states that having Russian forces stationed just a few miles away from the capital is necessary to protect Russia's borders with Georgia and Azerbaijan. After

33. Andrei Smirnov, "The Geography of OMON Deployments in the North Caucasus," *North Caucasus Weekly*, Vol. 9, Issue 13, April 3, 2008 (Washington, DC: The Jamestown Foundation). The OMON are feared Ministry of Interior special purpose police squads.
34. At the time of this writing, three regions within Chechnya are under the CTO regime, allowing Kadyrov to have his cake and eat it too.

their 2008 victory in Georgia, the Russian troops are undoubtedly in much better shape than they were in the 1990s, but the majority of money invested in Russian military reforms over the past few years was used to pay salaries rather than finance new vehicles and weapon systems. As of this writing, the 42nd Motorized Rifle Division has the primary responsibility of maintaining a presence in the Caucasus. Although often referred to as being headquartered at the Khankala air base outside of Grozny, it is more likely that it is based out of Vladikavkaz (North Ossetia) with subordinate regiments based in Chechnya.

While one would expect that the 42nd would be one of the best equipped units in the Russian army—especially as it has the dual responsibility of keeping the North Caucasus quiet and protecting the border—only the newly established 33rd and 34th mountain brigades (stationed in Dagestan and Kabardino-Balkaria) have seen any significant injections of men, money, or equipment over the past few years. According to open sources, the 42nd has approximately 15,000 troops while the new mountain brigades will eventually supply another 4,500 soldiers to the region.[35]

The two mountain brigades have special "antiterrorism" training and are task-organized as independent maneuver brigades. Additional money is being spent to provide them with special bases, and a newly improved road connecting Botlikh (in Dagestan, on the border with Chechnya) with the rest of Russia is being constructed in a manner reminiscent of 18th-century road building and tree-clearing operations. The 42nd is also receiving new attack helicopters with night vision capabilities which will help it to guard the border as well as conduct operations against insurgents. However, the 42nd rarely operates with local forces, so their presence does very little towards the "best-practice approach" of supporting and empowering local security forces—or what the Russians refer to as "Chechenization."

In fact, Chechenization of the security forces has been largely counterproductive. The Zapad (West) and Vostok (East) Special Battalions were created by the GRU in 2003 and manned by non-Kadyrovtsy Chechens. The Zapad Battalion had been loyal to Moscow even in the first war, but the Vostok Battalion was composed of ex-militants loyal to the Yamadayevs to maintain a balance of power in the region. As mentioned previously, the Kadyrovs and the Yamadayevs were rewarded amply for their services to Russia. Kadyrov was given control of Chechnya while the Yamadayevs—the only family ever in the history of Russia to have three brothers receive the Hero of Russia award—were given a seat in the Duma and command of the Vostok Battalion. This strategy was designed to keep a system of checks and balances operating in Chechnya—to ensure that

---

35. C. W. Blandy, *North Caucasus: Advent of Mountain Brigades*, Advanced Research and Assessment Group, Caucasus Series, Defence Academy of the United Kingdom, 2007, 9.

none of the former factions would gain enough power that they could mount serious opposition to Russia.

This strategy worked well until Ramzan Kadyrov assumed the presidency and began a campaign to consolidate power. Kadyrov, although born in Tsentoroi, moved his private residence to Gudermes—a traditional area for members of his *teip* (the Benoi clan) in order to be able to constantly travel in and out of "Yamadayev territory" with his official entourage. Exchanges between the two sides were inevitable and continued to escalate. A significant firefight broke out between the two sides in 2008 when the president's official motorcade failed to stop at a Vostok battalion checkpoint. The incident was downplayed, but numerous reports indicate the number of dead exceeded 30. After the incident, Kadyrov began calling for the arrest of Sulim Yamadayev due to recently discovered evidence that implicated the Yamadayevs with numerous "disappearances" within Chechnya as well as hostage takings. The Yamadayevs responded with their own accusations, and veteran Chechnya observers waited for the inevitable showdown; the winner of that turf war would set the course for Chechnya's future.

The Kadyrov-Yamadayev conflict was symbolic of a larger battle within Russia—the rise of the FSB at the expense of the military establishment. Kadyrov was Putin's man—and Putin is the FSB. Yamadayev was the GRU's man—and the GRU (and the military as a whole) has lost its former elevated place within the system. In the past the military had been the final arbiter in the North Caucasus, the ultimate guarantor of Russian hegemony. So in June 2008, when a Russian GRU general stated that Sulim Yamadayev would remain the commander of Vostok and that "nobody plans to disband the Vostok and Zapad battalions," it was assumed that the Kremlin would continue its policy of "divide and rule" to ensure that Kadyrov did not become too powerful. Yet in the end, Kadyrov's shrewd manipulation of the political landscape coupled with his personal devotion to Putin made the difference.

Kadyrov—and the FSB—won. In September 2008, Ruslan Yamadayev, the eldest remaining Yamadayev (and former member of parliament) was assassinated in front of the British Embassy in Moscow enroute to a meeting with President Medvedev—allegedly to talk about Kadyrov's excesses in Chechnya. In November 2008, although conducting some of the heaviest fighting for Russia during the August War with Georgia, the Zapad and Vostok battalions were disbanded. In March 2009, Sulim Yamadayev, a Russian lieutenant colonel in the GRU and former commander of the Vostok Battalion, was gunned down in Dubai with a gold-plated Makarov pistol left at the scene. Two weeks later, Ramzan Kadyrov was photographed for an interview with Komsomolskaya Pravda holding a gold-plated Makarov pistol, which he said he always carried with him. As of this writing Interpol is still seeking extradition of Kadyrov's cousin Adam Delimkhanov (a member of the Russian parliament), for allegedly smuggling the gun into Dubai via diplomatic pouch.

The disbanding of Zapad and Vostok left Ramzan Kadyrov as the undisputed ruler of Chechnya. Nonetheless, Kadyrov still has a few Kremlin overseers to watch over him. In February 2010, President Medvedev appointed a new regional "governor" to administer the entire North Caucasus region. In addition to a new "boss," there is the army's 42nd Division, the FSB's Spetsnaz anti-terrorism center, and large numbers of FSB and ministry of internal affairs troops—including the 46th Separate Operational Brigade (approximately 16,000 men).

However, neither the Kadyrovtsy nor the federal forces are providing security for the Chechens, and their methods have provoked widespread resentment among the population. Calls for revenge have increased dramatically since two Spetsnaz officers publicly admitted to participating in the large-scale practice of "disappearing" Chechen civilians: torturing them, killing them, and using large explosive charges to "pulverize" their remains and prevent discovery of the event.[36]

This is a tragedy—and not only because of the shocking manner that Russian security forces are treating their own citizens. It is perhaps more tragic knowing that if the police and soldiers stopped abusing and killing the people that they have sworn to protect, then they might actually defeat the insurgency. Kadyrov and the Russians are doing the impossible—they are fighting an ideological battle with radical Islamists and *winning*. Yet everyday they are losing another ideological battle—the one they are creating themselves. When the population doesn't trust its own security organizations to protect them, the people intuitively understand that their government is not legitimate. A group of people who reject their political system and government and seek to withdraw from it and establish a new one are called secessionists.

So despite all the work being done by the Russians and Kadyrov, despite the newspaper articles touting the end of the resistance, the elimination of sanctuaries, the rebuilding effort, the influx of money, the return of refugees, the new Mosque, and the renewal of cultural traditions, the insurgency is strong, resilient, and gaining strength. And ironically, it is Kadyrov and the Russians who are empowering their most dangerous enemy—the secessionists. The foundations of both Putin and Kadyrov's ideological campaigns will crumble instantly if the Caucasus Emirate ceases to be the heart of the insurgency. Putin's "foreign terrorist construct" dissolves and Kadyrov's "Muslim heart of Russia campaign" becomes moot just as soon as secessionism becomes the dominant ideology of the insurgency again—especially since Russia justified its invasion of Georgia in 2008 on the grounds of supporting the right of independence for South Ossetia and Abkhazia.

---

36. Mark Franchetti, "Russian death squads 'pulverise' Chechens," *Sunday Times*, April 26, 2009, http://www.timesonline.co.uk/tol/news/world/europe/article6168959.ece.

Conclusions: The Future

Trying to determine the exact state of the North Caucasus insurgency is difficult, in no small part because the determinants of success—the metrics[1]—are, at their best, always partly relative, and, at their worst, contradictory; it's like comparing apples to oranges. One metric frequently used in U.S. COIN operations is: "number of schools built." School construction, which is definitely a point on the "support to economic and infrastructure development" line of effort, can have a definite impact on the long-term success of a COIN campaign. However, that metric is not as important in assessing overall success as the number of recruits that join an insurgency on a monthly basis. A U.S. colonel once told a North Vietnamese officer that the North Vietnamese had never defeated the U.S. Army on the battlefield. The Vietnamese officer admitted that the statement was true—and also completely irrelevant to the outcome. Determining success through metrics not tied to ultimate victory (winning the battle but losing the war) was extremely problematic during the Vietnam War, and the problem is no less difficult today for the conflict in Chechnya.

To begin with, there are multiple theoretical constructs for determining success, and if each was applied to the North Caucasus insurgency, each would yield different conclusions. Moreover, what can be used as a successful metric in one conflict is not necessarily applicable for use in another, and as attack data already presented in this book shows, numbers are easy to manipulate and there is a natural human tendency to stress data that is readily at hand or that supports the authors own bias.

For instance, one can easily accept the Kremlin proposition which says that Russia has waged a successful COIN campaign based on Russia's original declared end state. Chechnya has not seceded, Russia has a secure border, terrorist attacks within Russia are considered manageable, and violence in the North Caucasus is generally localized and rarely

---

1. Referred to as "measures of performance or effectiveness" in U.S. COIN doctrine.

affects those outside of the region—making it acceptable to the average Russian. And because Russia has the ability to control the information coming out of the Caucasus and has taken control of the narratives, the general Russian population does not consider the cost of current operations to be too high and other countries do not attempt to "interfere in Russia's internal affairs and its fight against international terrorism."

THE QUESTION OF LEGITIMACY

Given that the international community no longer supports the Chechens and the Russians support their government, it doesn't matter whether the Kremlin and the Kadyrov regimes' actions are illegitimate and undermine long-term COIN efforts. If there is no perceived illegitimacy outside of the Caucasus, then the insurgency will not get significant external support from within Russia or the international community (strategies 2, 3, and 5 discussed earlier), which ensures that the North Caucasus insurgency will not progress beyond its current state.

The Russians also believe that as long as Russia is important to the West for natural gas and geopolitical cooperation on sensitive issues like the Iranian or North Korean nuclear armament programs, the West will continue to treat the conflict as a Russian internal affair. Increased Russian engagement with the Arab nations and Turkey will ensure that Muslim support for the Caucasus Emirate will be marginal.

So if Ramzan Kadyrov is able to maintain the current state of security (seen as flawed, but acceptable), then chances are the Kremlin will allow him to continue running the republic as he sees fit. Moscow will handle the big issues of denying external support, controlling the press, and providing huge sums of cash while Kadyrov will have the task of trying to crush any remaining pockets of resistance. Despite the brutality, as more and more Chechens adopt the "he may be a bastard, but at least he's our bastard" mentality, the Kremlin will attempt to export all or part of Kadyrov's methodology to Ingushetia and Dagestan.

So why isn't this approach working? The number of attacks in the North Caucasus has increased, formerly quiet regions like Kabardino-Balkaria are now involved, and even the Russians are admitting the number of active fighters seems to be increasing.[2] Part of the conundrum about determining the success of one side or another lies in the inherent paradox of insurgent warfare: both sides are fighting each other, but both sides are fighting a *different* war—at least during the

---

2. Statement of Alexander Bastrykin, Head of the Investigative Committee of the Russian Prosecutor General's Office, official press conference, May 20, 2009. Bastrykin put the number of active fighters in the Caucasus at 1,500. Available at http://lenta.ru/news/2009/05/20/boevicks.

latent and incipient and guerrilla warfare stages, where the majority of the conflict takes place. Different wars mean different metrics; for the insurgency, success equals survival and the ability to conduct attacks.

For the Russians, however, it has been important to assess progress in a way that reinforces the national will to sustain the current levels of operations—regardless of what the NGOs and press have to say about human rights abuses or the legitimacy of Kadyrov's government. We may not agree with how the Russians conduct their operations, but the Russians are unconcerned about what we think. The Russians have used the "means" they have available in "ways" the public has deemed acceptable to accomplish "ends" the government has directed. The West will not change the way the Russians conduct COIN or CT operations; only the political process can change that, demonstrating once again why "politics" is the most important aspect of any "military" campaign.

This leaves the West in a difficult dilemma: if one accepts the rhetoric that Russia, many journalists, and even some U.S. intelligence agencies espoused in 2009—that the Chechen insurgency was over—it necessarily requires one to accept that Russia's coercive methods are effective, and thus the "carrot and stick" approach to COIN is valid. If, however, one accepts Western doctrine which states that governments are responsible to their people and, to defeat an insurgency, the focus must *always* be on government legitimacy and the security of the population, *then we must accept that the Russian strategy is insufficient and the North Caucasus insurgency cannot be over and will not end* until the Russians change their strategy. It was a failure to understand this dilemma (and insurgency warfare in general) that led some analysts to declare the Chechen conflict "over" in 2007 when insurgent attacks (the wrong metrics) were down.

DETERMINANTS OF CONTROL AND MEASURES OF UN-SUCCESS

Successful COIN forces must align their metrics with those of the guerrillas to learn what the population considers "government legitimacy" and use that as the "metric" for success. To put it in the vernacular, "It is not enough to know math, COIN forces must learn G-math (guerrilla math)." In "normal" math, the figure "11" means "eleven"; however, in programming language, the figure "11" means "two." To defeat an insurgency, COIN forces must not be socio-centric; they must get into the heads of the insurgents and learn to use their metrics.

David Galula goes even further and says that in order to be successful, the side that eventually wins must *become* like the other side: insurgencies have to get large at some point (war of movement) and governments must get small—that is, to start working in smaller units and at the lowest levels of engagement (i.e., villages and hamlets). This is what the "Chechenization" of the conflict was designed to do, and Kadyrov has taken to this concept with alacrity—enabling him to rob the insurgents of much of their former legitimacy, co-opting insurgent goals for his own use, and creating narratives that have seized the initiative from the insurgents and put them on the defensive.

Nonetheless, in the end, the ability to exert control in the North Caucasus is not determined by who has the most firepower, but by who has the biggest base of sympathizers. Kadyrov's "hearts and minds" campaign may be addressing many of the "approved" lines of effort (winning battles), but he's not reducing the mass base of the insurgents (losing the war). The support of the people may not be vital to the government's ability to maintain order through fear and coercion, but it is absolutely necessary for the insurgents—who depend on them for food, shelter, recruits, and intelligence. If we look at the indicators for those last two prerequisites (below), we can plainly see that there are many that suggest large-scale support—even if silent—for the insurgents.

I submit that the following metrics are more relevant to ultimate victory in the North Caucasus than those that have been applied thus far, and although they are not nearly as conclusive as late-stage indicators of successful insurgencies, they nonetheless tell us that the North Caucasus insurgency is far from over.

- The populace fears the government more than they fear the insurgents (safe, secure, and stable environment has not been established)
- The populace does not trust law enforcement (local or federal) and does not support them
- The local population is highly skeptical of government propaganda (indicating illegitimacy)
- Local and federal government repression is seen as indiscriminate and illegitimate
- The local population does not support the government's methods for eliminating the insurgents (less true in Dagestan where large groups do support elimination of the Wahhabis)
- The populace (in Chechnya) believes that the region is run by "rule of Kadyrov" and not "rule of law"; other regions feel the same
- The populace (in Chechnya and Ingushetia) has no say in local governance, and the government in power requires external support
- Even with the intense construction boom, which cannot be sustained indefinitely, unemployment for the region is still over 50 percent
- Insurgent forces are still able to take over and control villages or larger areas for short periods of time

- There is a high degree of corruption at all levels of government
- Despite highly coercive measures, the number of recruits joining the insurgency is not decreasing
- The new recruits are almost exclusively comprised of local residents—some are women
- Government services are perceived locally as inadequate
- Government quick reaction forces (police, MIA, or military) do not respond quickly and effectively to guerrilla attacks—especially at night
- Russian soldiers and federal police are viewed by the locals as threatening outsiders and not allies
- The insurgents are largely perceived as being more aggressive, professional, and effective than all but the Spetsnaz commandos

A "SLUSHY" CONFLICT: NOT FROZEN, NOT BURNING, BUT DEFINITELY NOT OVER

The North Caucasus is heating up; as this book goes to print, insurgent and terrorist attacks have increased by at least 20 percent in 2010, and the violence has continued to spread westward. The Kremlin is hoping that time, money, apartments, and Kadyrov or Khloponin (or somebody) can find a way to remove some logs from the fire and eventually end the conflict; hoping that the mountaineers will forget the old wars; and hoping the instability in the rest of the North Caucasus can be contained. They are hoping that globalization and Chechenization will eventually convince the Sufis that it is better to be an autonomous region inside of Russia than to constantly get crushed by Russian military might—especially in light of the knowledge that Russia will never give up the Caucasus due to its geo-strategic position. But "hope" is not a method.

The Chechens are waiting. The secessionists are waiting for the next opportunity to assert themselves again. They must have time to build up their strength and grow to maturity while giving outward signs of servitude. And "indeed, that is exactly what Kadyrov junior was not abashed to say out loud a few years ago, when explaining why he was working for the Russians."[3] As for the Caucasus Emirate, fighters are beginning to flow their way again from Arab countries as their cause has been taken up on the Internet by Salafi-jihadists who support the emirate. They are

---

3. Andrei Babitsky, "Why has Timur Mutsurayev returned (or not returned)?" *Prague Watchdog*, May 22, 2008.

waiting for the fighting in Afghanistan to come to a lull so that more money and fighters will start to flow their way again.

In addition to the above-mentioned metrics, I believe one of the most significant indicators in the conflict is the lack of a functioning security-intelligence cycle in most areas of the North Caucasus. As discussed earlier, making the population feel safe is not exclusively for good governance and higher ideals; at the tactical level, safeguarding the people results in trust, and trust results in information about the insurgents, which results in actionable intelligence, which provides an even greater level of security, which motivates the population to give even more information. This is why the European method of counterterrorism and counterinsurgency favors domestic police work—because when it's done right, when a government is legitimate and society is sufficiently stable—then local police walking the beat can be a highly effective tool against terrorism and insurgency.

Unfortunately, this view has not been embraced by the Russians—in fact the opposite is true. The most recent (2007, 2008, 2009) U.S. Department of State's Country Report on Human Rights Practices in Russia bluntly states: "Security forces reportedly engaged in killings, torture, abuse, violence, and other brutal or humiliating treatment, often with impunity." Amnesty International's 2009 report is even more explicit: line one of the Russian reports reads, "The North Caucasus remained volatile and reports of human rights violations, including killings, enforced disappearances and torture, were frequent." These "zachisti" (clean-up operations and "disappearances") erode security, and without security there is no real intelligence, and as any battalion-level staff officer will tell you: intelligence drives operations. Moreover, such violations drive fence-sitters into the arms of the insurgents "not because they sympathize with radical or extremist ideology, but because they feel powerless to do anything else in response to violations committed against them and their loved ones by the security forces."[4] The sad truth is that young men are joining the insurgency because it is safer in the mountains and forests than it is at home, where at any moment they might be seized by the security services. Some of those who are taken are merely tortured and allowed to return home; others are killed and their names are added to the list of terrorists who've been killed during an anti-terrorism operation. If they join the insurgents, at least they have some control about how they will live; if they die, they will die like their heroes and their ancestors—with a gun in their hands fighting back. In their villages and cities, they constantly live in fear.

---

4. Simon Saradzhyan, "Putin's 'pacification' of Chechnya," *ISN Security Watch* (Zurich: International Relations and Security Network, Swiss Federal Institute of Technology), available at http://www.isn.ethz.ch/news/sw/details.cfm?id=18808; accessed on April 7, 2008.

And so, regardless of the amount of money that the Kremlin spends in reconstructing or improving infrastructure, until the local population starts to fear the insurgents more than they fear the local authorities, there will be no peace in the Caucasus. This "security-intelligence cycle" is borne out by research, and should no longer be brushed aside by those who tend to regard such niceties as "not bombing their own citizens" as something of an inconvenience and not contributing directly to tactical and operational objectives. In a study of fifty 20th-century insurgencies around the world, the most successful COIN practice has been to emphasize intelligence gathering and the second-most successful has been to "focus on population, their needs, and security." Conversely, the top unsuccessful practice has been the "primacy of military direction of counterinsurgency" and the second least effective has been the "priority to kill-capture enemy, not on engaging population."[5]

The Russians have their own theories and doctrine on how to fight insurgency, and some of those techniques have brought them medium and short-term success; Kadyrov's counter-ideological campaign against the Salafists is an excellent example. Likewise, the Russians would argue that their special services (including the FSB, MVD, and others operating in the region) have emphasized intelligence gathering. Yet, one can simply look at the current situation to determine whether the overall intelligence effort in the North Caucasus has been successful. Although there have been occasional intelligence windfalls that generated successes, the inability to establish the "security-intelligence cycle" ensures that no long-term solution is in sight and the insurgency will continue to survive for the foreseeable future.

Much of the problem comes from two endemic problems within Russia— problems that the Russians themselves admit to: lack of professionalism among the lower ranks in the military and corruption throughout all layers of government, but especially within the law enforcement bodies. It is sadly ironic that in a June 2009 poll, the average Russian considered the police to be the most corrupt of all government organizations. Unprofessionalism and corruption can only add to the perception of illegitimate government, and without legitimacy, there cannot be long-term COIN success.

Examples of military unprofessionalism abound, but two recent examples include drunken Russian soldiers shelling the village of Gheki in retaliation for an attack on their fellow troops—25 kilometers away from the village—and a special operation (caught on tape) that killed a young boy with stray gunfire—despite the fact that the soldiers were not in contact with enemy soldiers.[6] Videos of such operations (widely

---

5. Kalev I. Sepp, "Best Practices in Counterinsurgency," *Military Review* (May-June 2005), 8–10.
6. U.S. Department of State Country Reports on Human Rights Practices, 2007, Russia, available at http://www.state.gov/g/drl/rls/hrrpt/2007/100581.htm.

available on YouTube) routinely show soldiers firing their weapons into rooms and cellars before actually determining if there are civilians inside. And according to a recent report by the Memorial human rights group, the number of kidnappings in Chechnya and people killed in violence in Ingushetia increased between January and April 2009, compared to the same period in 2008. Although Russia has planned major military reforms, most analysts don't believe that there is any hope that Russia will be able to create a modern and effective army in the next ten years. The most promising of the reforms is an initiative to require all sergeants to attend a two-year development course in the hopes of jump-starting a professional NCO corps. Unfortunately, the first graduates of that course will not be ready to join a line unit until 2012.

So without any substantive military reforms, there is little hope of creating large-scale military forces that can conduct counterinsurgency operations that would create a net gain for government legitimacy. The Russian military, despite its advances, still does not have the requisite command and control platforms essential for the types of decentralized operations required by COIN and counterguerrilla operations—thus making convoys and patrols vulnerable. And at the individual soldier's level, there is no real motivation to fight. The Russian troops do not want to close with the rebels and the Kadyrovtsy are unable to do the job without them, meaning that the insurgents will continue to thrive and have success and provide motivation for young men to fill their ranks and continue the conflict. Local policemen on Kadyrov's payroll do not venture out at night and do not provide assistance to federal troops that are caught in ambushes. They are on the payroll, but they are not committed, they are not professional; some are even helping the insurgents.

Moreover, as part of the announced military reforms, the Russians have already indicated that the total number of soldiers will *decrease* by a few hundred thousand, and reduce conscription periods to one year— making the chances that large numbers of well-trained troops will be available for COIN even less likely. In addition, new equipment or new types of equipment are not forthcoming, as the Russian military-industrial complex is facing a deep crisis and is in danger of losing key export contracts due to poor quality control and missed deadlines. Without the export business, the chances of Russian troops getting substantial amounts of new equipment are slim.

As for corruption and illegitimacy, even President Medvedev has spoken at length about the pervasive nature of corruption within Russia and made it the top priority of his administration. Nonetheless, despite any efforts that the Kremlin might make, Kadyrov's government seems increasingly removed from the people. A recent case in point is renaming streets in Grozny after Russian paratroopers who participated in the second war— even though the average Chechen referred to them as "those who handed out the most brutal treatment to the population." It has been compared to the mayor of Tel Aviv renaming a street, "Nazi Boulevard"; a local resident summed it up by stating: "Naming one of the streets of our capital city in their honor is, I believe, a genuine blasphemy and mockery of our people." Yet Kadyrov continues to unabashedly move important monuments to Chechen history and make other changes that under-cut the gains of the cultural and religious programs that succeeded in co-opting insurgent goals. While Kadyrov may not see any inconsis-tency in this policy (especially as he considers Putin and the airborne troops as heroes who liberated Chechnya), it cannot help but make the average Chechen (the mass base) wonder if all the other "re-forms" are just for show and will, in time, disappear like so many others before it.

Finally, as mentioned at the beginning of this book, properly defin-ing the conflict, although seemingly a pointless exercise in semantics, is absolutely critical to finally ending the conflict once and for all, and that is not being done by the Russians—at least in public. Counterter-rorism operations are fundamentally different from counterinsurgency operations; by not addressing the conflict as it *really* is—a regional in-surgency—the Russians aren't able to design a strategy that might con-clusively end a conflict that has endured for close to 300 years. Putting Kadyrov in charge and giving him free rein will keep things quiet for a while, but it will not ultimately resolve the conflict unless Kadyrov somehow manages to create a lasting "independent" state inside of Russia that will be acceptable to the Chechen people; but that doesn't help the Ingush or the Dagestanis or the Kabards.

The Caucasus Emirate now operates across the entire region and it is able to exploit the boundaries between the republics, making it clear that the insurgency is no longer the Chechen insurgency, but once again it has become the North Caucasus insurgency. Kabardino-Balkaria has seen a steady and significant rise in violence since March of 2010; insurgents even successfully attacked and disabled a hydroelectric plant in July 2010, less than 175 miles away from the site of the 2014 Sochi Olympics. It is clear that there is no consolidated, overall counterinsurgency plan designed to combat a *regional* insurgency, and despite occasional attempts to conduct joint and combined operations across borders, each republic conducts its own COIN or CT campaigns. It remains to be seen whether the new North Caucasus regional governor, former businessman Alek-sandr Khloponin, can get the individual republics to cooperate, but it is doubtful that Kadyrov will deviate from what he considers to be a suc-cessful policy.

In July 2010, Khloponin announced a new regional initiative to create industry, lower unemployment, and invigorate the entire region. He wants to build highways and train lines that will traverse the entire

Transcaucasus region, build new ports, and create low or zero tax zones to attract outside investment. Shortly thereafter, Prime Minister Putin followed up saying he was going to create 400,000 jobs in the region over the next ten years. However, given that the money to invest in these measures will come from the Kremlin (which is already strapped from the financial crisis and construction costs for the Olympics), it is doubtful that Khloponin's plan will be approved. Moreover, given that the Kremlin has already spent 27 billion dollars[7] from 2000 to 2010 in the region without much success, it is doubtful that these new measures, even if approved, will bear fruit. This is because, although the economic factor is a strong one, it will still not remove the central obstacle to long-term COIN success—government legitimacy expressed as an ironclad rule of law and security elements that don't frighten the locals more than the insurgents do.

Meanwhile, the FSB, MOD, and MVD all run their own independent operations—which do span borders—but are rarely coordinated between agencies or republics or even local branches of their own agency. In its simplest terms, this means there are at least 15 agencies operating independently within Chechnya, Dagestan, and Ingushetia alone. The government of Russia, despite its rhetoric about having to worry about Islamic terrorism in the region is hamstrung by its earlier statements that the insurgency in Chechnya is over and that the counterterrorism operation is complete. Because of that, they can't really undertake any large operations in the area, otherwise it will look like Putin *hasn't* actually done what he said—namely, tame the Chechens. As a result, this continued piecemeal action, performed by troops that have not been sensitized to the long-term ramifications of brutality on the conflict, will result in more strong-armed tactics and ultimately lose more legitimacy in the eyes of the local populace.

What is needed is a regional plan that specifically names and *targets* the Caucasus Emirate, led by uncorrupted politicians and generals, operating from a single headquarters, utilizing all economic, diplomatic, cultural, legal, security, and informational means of national power with the full support of the Kremlin, the Russian and North Caucasus populations, and all other power and security organizations. Until then, *if the Russians are lucky*, the insurgents will merely continue to move from one area to another while attacking government targets at will. Kadyrov and the Russians have made progress over the past 15 years, but the insurgency has not been defeated, and in the paradox-ridden world of counterinsurgency warfare, the insurgent wins if he does not lose and the counterinsurgent loses if he does not win.

---

7. Speech by Prime Minister Putin, July 6, 2010, available at http://www.premier.gov.ru.

Selected Bibliography

Abubakorov, Taimaz. *Rezhim Dzhokhara Dudayeva: Pravda I vymyse.* Moscow: INSAN, 1998.

Ahmadov, Sharpudin. *Imam Mansur: Narodno-osvobitel'noe dvishenie v Chechne I na Severnom Kavkaze v kontse XVIII v.* Grozny: Kniga, 1991.

Akaev, Vakhit. *Religious-Political Conflict in the Chechen Republic of Ichkeria.* Stockholm: CA & CC Press, 2005.

Albats, Yevgenia, and Catherine A. Fitzpatrick. *The State Within a State: The KGB and Its Hold on Russia—Past, Present, and Future.* New York: Farrar, Straus and Giroux, 1994.

Aldis, Anne, ed. *The Second Chechen War.* Shrivenham, UK: The Conflict Studies Research Centre, Strategic and Combat Studies Institute, 2000.

Algar, Hamid. *Wahhabism: A Critical Essay.* Oneonta, NY: Islamic Publications International, 2002.

Algar, Hamid. "The Naqshbandi Order: A Preliminary Survey of its History and Significance." *Studia Islamica* 44 (1970): 124.

Ali, Fadhil. "Sufi Insurgent Groups in Iraq." *Terrorism Monitor* VI (January 2008): 2, 7, 24.

"Al-Qaeda Financed Seizure of Russian Hostages," Sofia News Agency, September 3, 2004. http://www.novinite.com.

Amitai-Preiss, Reuven. *The Mamluk-Ilkhanid War.* Cambridge, UK: Cambridge University Press, 1998.

Amnesty International Report 2008, State of the World's Human Rights, Russian Federation. http://thereport.amnesty.org.

Anderson, Benedict. *Imagined Communities, Reflections on the Origin and Spread of Nationalism.* New York: Verso, 1991.

Anderson, Lisa. *Political Islam, Revolution, Radicalism or Reform,* Boulder, CO: Lynne Reinner, 1997.

Anderson, Scott. "None Dare Call It Conspiracy." *Gentleman's Quarterly* (September 2009): 246.

Applied History Research Group, University of Calgary. *The Chagatai Khanate, The Islamic World to 1600.* http://www.ucalgary.ca.

Astvatsaturyan, L. I. *Oruzhie narodov Kavkaza.* Nalchik: El-Fa, 1994.

Atwood, Christopher P. *The Encyclopedia of Mongolia and the Mongolian Empire.* New York: Facts on File, Inc., 2004.

Baddeley, John F. *The Russian Conquest of the Caucasus.* London: Longmans, Green, 1908.

Bakier, Abdul Hameed. "Ex-Baathists Turn to Naqshbandi Sufis to Legitimize Insurgency." *Terrorism Focus* 5 (January 8, 2008): 1.

Baluyevskiy, Yu. "Kavkazkaya liniya: istoriya, politika, uroki." *Krasnaya Zvezda,* May 16, 2000.

Barber, Tony. "Fog of Battle Clouds Pervomayskoye's Ugly Truth." *The Independent,* January 20, 1996.

Basayev, Shamil, interview, *Nightline,* ABC News, July 29, 2005. Originally broadcast on British Broadcasting Company (BBC).

Bastrykin, Alexander. *Official Statement of the Committee of the Russian Prosecutor General's Office,* May 20, 2009. http://lenta.ru/news.

Baumann, Robert F. *Russian-Soviet Unconventional Wars in the Caucasus, Central Asia, and Afghanistan.* Fort Leavenworth, KS: Combat Studies Institute, U.S. Army Command and General Staff College, 1993.

Bell, Gertrude, CBE. Letter to her father, Gertrude Bell Archive, Newcastle University Library. http://www.gerty.ncl.ac.uk.

Bellavia, David. *House to House, A Soldier's Memoir.* New York: Free Press, 2007.

Bennigsen, Alexandre, and Marie Broxup. *The Islamic Threat to the Soviet State.* New York: St. Martin's Press, 2000.

Bennigsen, Alexandre, and S. Enders Wimbush. *Mystics and Commissars.* Berkeley: University of California Press, 1985.

Bennigsen-Broxup, Marie, ed. *The North Caucasus Barrier: The Russian Advance Towards the Muslim World.* London: Hurst, 1992.

Berseneva, Anastasiya, Irna Masykina, and Alexandr Rybin. "Sostayanie krainei tyazhesti: Informatsiya ovzryve u 'Rizhskoi' poka skudna I protivorechna." *Novye izvestiya* (September 2, 2004): 3.

Bin Laden, Osama, videotaped statement, Al-Jazeera Television, November 2, 2001. http://news.bbc.co.uk.

Blandy, C. W. *North Caucasus: Advent of Mountain Brigades.* Advanced Research and Assessment Group, Caucasus Series, Defence Academy of the United Kingdom, 2007.

Bostom, Andrew G. "Sufi Jihad." *American Thinker,* May 15, 2005. http://www.americanthinker.com.

Boucher, Richard, press conference. *U.S. Department of State, Daily Press Briefing Index,* September 3, 2004. http://www.globalsecurity.org.

Boyle, J. A., ed. *The Cambridge History of Iran: Volume 5, the Saljuq and Mongol Periods.* Cambridge University Press, reissue ed., January 1, 1968.

Brachman, Jarret. "Abu Yahya's Six Easy Steps For Defeating Al Qaeda." *Perspectives On Terrorism* I:5 (2007).

Bransten, Jeremy. "Russia: Putin Rejects Open Inquiry into Beslan Tragedy as Critical Voices Mount." Radio Free Europe/Radio Liberty, September 7, 2004. http://www.rferl.org.

Byman, Daniel. *The Five Front War: The Better Way to Fight Global Jihad.* Hoboken, NJ: John Wiley and Sons, 2008.

Byman, Daniel, et al. *Trends in Outside Support for Insurgent Movements.* Santa Monica, CA: Rand, National Security Research Division, 2001.

Callwell, Charles E. *Small Wars: Their Principles and Practice.* Lincoln: University of Nebraska Press, 1996.

Chaliand, Gerard. *Guerrilla Strategies: An Historical Anthology from the Long March to Afghanistan.* Berkeley: University of California Press, 1982.

Chambers, James. *The Devil's Horsemen: The Mongol Invasion of Europe.* New York: Atheneum, 1988.

Chivers, C. J. *Slain Exile Detailed Cruelty of Chechnya's Ruler.* The New York Times, January 31, 2009. http://www.nytimes.com/.

Colton, Timothy J., and Michael McFaul. *Popular Choice and Managed Democracy, The Russian Elections of 1999 and 2000.* Washington, DC: Brookings Institution Press, 2003.

Coughlin, Stephen C. *To Our Great Detriment, Ignoring What Extremists Say About Jihad.* Washington, DC: National Defense Intelligence College, 2007.

Cracraft, James, ed. *Major Problems in the History of Imperial Russia.* Lexington, MA: D. C. Heath and Company, 1994.

Craddock, John, remarks given at the Heritage Foundation, Washington, DC, May 8, 2008.

"Crisis in Chechnya: Causes, Prospects, Solutions." Princeton University Conference Summary, March 3–4, 2000.

Dalgaard-Nielsen, Anja. *Studying Violent Radicalization in Europe I, The Potential Contribution of Social Movement Theory.* Copenhagen: Danish Institute for International Studies, 2006.

Defense Intelligence Agency. *Declassified Intelligence Report NC 3095345,* October 16, 1998.

Demograficheskii ezhegodnik Rossii, ofitsial'noe izdanie. Moscow: Goskomstat Rossii, 1990–2003.

Derlugian, Georgi M. *A World History of Noxchi.* (work in progress), http://www.yale.edu/agrarianstudies/papers/11noxchi.pdf.

Derlugian, Georgi M. "Che Guevaras in Turbans." *New Left Review* (October–November 1999): 237.

Department of the Army. *Human Factors in Underground Movements, Pamphlet 550-104–Appendix B.* U.S. Government Printing Office, 1986.

Department of the Army. *Tactics in Counterinsurgency (US Army Field Manual, 3-24.2).* U.S. Government Printing Office, 2009.

Department of the Army. *Counterinsurgency (US Army Field Manual, 3-24).* U.S. Government Printing Office, 2006.

Department of the Army. *Foreign Internal Defense: Tactics, Techniques, and Procedures for Special Forces (US Army Field Manual, 31-20-3).* U.S. Government Printing Office, 1994.

Department of the Army. *Counterguerrilla Operations (US Army Field Manual, 90-8).* U.S. Government Printing Office, 1986.

Department of the Army. *Military Operations in Low Intensity Conflict (US Army Field Manual 100-20)*. U.S. Government Printing Office, 1990.

Department of Defense. *Department of Defense (DOD) Dictionary of Military and Associated Terms, Joint Publication 1-02*. U.S. Government Printing Office, 2010.

Department of Defense. *Joint Tactics, Techniques, and Procedures for Foreign Internal Defense (FID), Joint Publication 3-07.1*. U.S. Government Printing Office, 1996.

Dershowitz, Alan M. *Why Terrorism Works*. New Haven, CT: Yale Publishing, 2002.

Dilegge, David P., and Matthew Van Konynenburg. "View from the Wolves' Den, the Chechens and Urban Operations." *Small Wars and Insurgencies* 13, no. 2, (2002): 171.

Dodd, Vikram. "Time to talk to al-Qaida, senior police chief urges." *The Guardian,* May 30, 2008. http://www.guardian.co.uk.

Dubrovin, N. F. *Istoriia voiny I vladychestva russkikh na Kavkaze*. St Petersburg: Tipgrafiia Departmenta Udelov, 1886.

Dunlop, John B. *Russia Confronts Chechnya, Roots of a Separatist Conflict*. Cambridge, UK: Cambridge University Press, 1998.

Dunn, Stephen P., and Ethel Dunn, eds. *Introduction to Soviet Ethnography*. Berkeley, CA: Highgate Road Social Science Research Station, 1974.

Edwards, Sean J. A. *Mars Unmasked: The Changing Face of Urban Operations*. Santa Monica, CA: Rand, 2000.

Evangelista, Matthew. *The Chechen Wars: Will Russia Go the Way of the Soviet Union?* Washington, DC: Brookings Institution Press, 2002.

Faurby, Ib, and Marta-Lisa Magnusson. "The Battles of Grozny." *Baltic Defense Review,* February 1999.

Ferguson, Niall. *The War of the World: Twentieth-Century Conflict and the Descent of the West*. New York: Penguin Press, 2006.

Fine, Jonathan. "Contrasting Secular and Religious Terrorism." *Middle East Quarterly,* Winter Edition, 2008.

Finkel, Caroline. *Osman's Dream: The History of the Ottoman Empire 1300–1923*. New York: Basic Books, 2006.

Franchetti, Mark. "Russian death squads pulverize Chechens." *The Sunday Times,* April 26, 2009. http://www.timesonline.co.uk.

Frazer, Ian. "Invaders, Destroying Baghdad." *The New Yorker,* April 25, 2005. http://www.newyorker.com.

Gall, Carlotta, and Thomas de Waal. *Chechnya: Calamity in the Caucasus*. New York: New York University Press, 1999.

Galula, David. *Counterinsurgency War, Theory and Practice*. London: Praeger, 2006.

Gammer, Moshe. *The Lone Wolf and the Bear, Three Centuries of Chechen Defiance of Russian Rule*. Pittsburgh: University of Pittsburgh Press, 2006.

Gammer, Moshe. *Muslim Resistance to the Tsar: Shamil and the Conquest of Chechnia and Daghestan*. London: Frank Cass, 1994.

Gannon, Kathy. "Al-Qaida draw more foreign recruits to Afghan war." Associated Press, July 17, 2008. http://ap/google/com/article/ALeqM5gqv2wf9405P DAxxMjAGhRRNcuE1QD91VQ2P80.

Goldfarb, Alex, and Marina Litvinenko. *Death of a Dissident: The Poisoning of Alexander Litvinenko and the Return of the KGB.* New York: Free Press, 2007.

Gordin, Yakov. "Kavkaz: zemlya I krov." *Zvezda* 121, 2000.

Gordon, Michael R. "Summit in Turkey: The Overview; Yeltsin and West Clash at Summit Over Chechen War." *The New York Times,* November 19, 1999. Available at http://www.nytimes.com.

Gordon, Philip. *Winning the Right War: The Path to Security for America and the World.* New York: Henry Holt and Company, 2007.

Graham, Thomas E. "The Friend of My Enemy." *The National Interest,* May/June 2008. http://www.nationalinterest.org.

Grau, Lester, and Timothy Thomas. *Russian Lessons Learned from the Battles for Grozny.* Fort Leavenworth, KS: Foreign Military Studies Office. (Article originally appeared in the *Marine Corps Gazette,* April 2000.).

Griffith, Samuel B., trans. *Mao Tse-Tung on Guerilla Warfare.* New York: Praeger, 1961.

Guevara, Che. *Guerrilla Warfare.* Lincoln: University of Nebraska Press, 1998.

Gurr, Ted R. *Why Men Rebel.* Princeton, NJ: Princeton University Press, 1971.

Hafez, Mohammed M. *Why Muslims Rebel, Repression and Resistance in the Islamic World.* Boulder, CO: Lynne Reinner Publishers, 2003.

Haraszti, Miklos. "Report on Russian Media Coverage of the Beslan Tragedy: Access to Information and Journalists' Working Conditions." Organization for Security and Cooperation in Europe (OSCE), official report, September 16, 2004.

Hayes, Robert Wingfield. "Scars remain amid Chechen revival." BBC News, March 3, 2007. http://news.bbc.co.uk.

Herrera, Yoshiko M. *Imagined Economies, the Sources of Russian Regionalism.* Cambridge, UK: Cambridge University Press, 2005.

Herspring, Dale R. *Putin's Russia, Past Imperfect, Future Uncertain.* Lanham, MD: Rowman and Littlefield Publishers, 2005.

Hildinger, Eric. *Warriors of the Steppe: A Military History of Central Asia, 500 B.C. to A.D. 1700.* Cambridge, MA: Da Capo Press, 2001.

Hoffman, Bruce. *Insurgency and Counterinsurgency in Iraq.* Washington, DC: Rand, 2004.

Hoffman, Bruce, and Jennifer Morrison Taw. *The Urbanization of Insurgency.* Santa Monica, CA: Rand, 1994.

Hovannisian, Richard G. *Armenia on the Road to Independence, 1918.* Berkeley: University of California Press, 1967.

Hovannisian, Richard G. *The Republic of Armenia, Volume I, The First Year, 1918–1919.* Berkeley: University of California Press, 1971.

Howard, Marc Morje. *The Weakness of Civil Society in Post-Communist Europe.* Cambridge, UK: Cambridge University Press, 2003.

Human Rights News and Archives 1999–2009, http://www.memo.ru.

Hunt, Thomas F. *The Cereals in America.* London: Orange Hall, 1904.

"International Terrorist Gang Headed by Militant Thought Dead." Mos News carried by NTV, September 3, 2008. http://www.interfax-religion.com/?act=news&div=5134.

Iraq Coalition Casualty Count Web Site. http://icasualties.org.

Isriev, Enver, and Robert Ware. "Conflict and Catharsis: A Report on Developments in Dagestan Following the Incursions of August and September 1999." *Nationality Paper* 28, no. 3 (September 2000): 87.

Jack, Andrew. *Kremlin Candidate Wins Chechnya Election. The Financial Times*, August 29, 2004.

Jaimoukha, Amjad M. *The Chechens: A Handbook.* New York: Routledge Curzon, 2005.

"Kadyrov laments Chechen youth doesn't observe the holy month of Ramadan." Interfax Information Services Group, September 3, 2008. http://www.interfax-religion.com.

Kagan, Robert. *Of Paradise and Power: America and Europe in the New World Order.* New York: Random House, 2004.

Kesaeva, Ella. "Terrposto-agenti, Neizvestnie podrobnosti beslanskoi tragedii." *Novaya Gazeta*, November 20, 2008. http://www.novyagazeta.ru.

Killcullen, David. "Countering Global Insurgency: A Strategy for the War on Terrorism." *Journal of Strategic Studies* 28, no. 4 (August 2005): 597–617.

Killcullen, David. "Road-Building in Afghanistan." *Small Wars Journal*, April 24, 2008. http://www.smallwarsjournal.com.

Kissinger, Henry. *Diplomacy.* New York: Simon and Schuster, 1994.

Kitson, Frank. *Low Intensity Operations: Subversion, Insurgency and Peacekeeping.* London: Faber and Faber, 1971.

Kramer, Mark. "Guerrilla Warfare, Counterinsurgency, and Terrorism in the North Caucasus: The Military Dimension of the Russian-Chechen Conflict." *Europe-Asia Studies* 57, no. 2 (March 2005): 209.

Lapidus, Ira M. *A History of Islamic Societies.* Cambridge, UK: Cambridge University Press, 1989.

Lawrence, T. E. *Seven Pillars of Wisdom: A Triumph.* New York: Anchor, 1991.

Lehmann, Susan G. "Islam and Ethnicity in the Republics of Russia." *Post Soviet Affairs* 13, no. 1 (1997).

Lesser, Ian O., et al. *Countering the New Terrorism.* Santa Monica, CA: Rand, 1999.

Lewis, Bernard. *The Crisis of Islam: Holy War and Unholy Terror.* New York: Modern Library, 2003.

Lewis, Bernard. *The Middle East and the West.* New York: Harper and Row, 1966.

Lieven, Anatol. *Chechnya, Tombstone of Russian Power.* New Haven, CT: Yale University Press, 1999.

Lukin, Vladimir P. "Remaking Russia: Our Security Predicament." *Foreign Policy* 88 (Fall 1992).

MacKenzie, David, and Michael Curran. *A History of Russia and the Soviet Union.* Belmont, CA: Wadsworth Publishing Company, 1987.

Madsen, Wayne. "Did NSA Help Russia Target Dudayev?" *Covert Action Quarterly* no. 61 (1997): 47.

Manchuk, Andrei. "Shamil' na pecherskikh holmakh." *Gazeta po-kievski.* http://pk.kiev.ua.

Mansfield, Laura. "Chechen terrorists follow al-Qaida manual." *World Net Daily*, September 4, 2004. http://www.worldnetdaily.com.

McConnell, J. Michael. *Annual Threat Assessment of the Director of National Intelligence.* February 5, 2008.

McFaul, Michael. *Russia's Unfinished Revolution, Political Change from Gorbachev to Putin.* Ithaca, NY: Cornell University Press, 2001.

Meskhize, Julietta, and Mikhail Roshchin. "Islam v Chechne." *Biblioteka Yakovo Krotova*, 2004, http://www.krotov.info.

Metz, Steven, and Raymond Millen. *Insurgency and Counterinsurgency in the 21st Century: Reconceptualizing Threat and Response.* Carlisle Barracks, PA: U.S. Army War College, 2004.

The Mogul Conquests. Alexandria, VA: Time-Life Books, 1989.

Mohammed, Khalid Sheikh, et al. "The Islamic Response to the Government's Nine Accusations." Official statement of the 9/11 Shura Council. March 1, 2009. http://www.defense.gov.

Morgan, David. *The Mongols.* Cambridge, MA: Blackwell, 1990.

Morganthau, Henry. *Ambassador Morgenthau's Story.* Detroit, MI: Wayne State University, 2003.

Morganthau, Henry. Official U.S. State Department Cable, Constantinople, July 20, 1915. http://enlwikipedia.org/wiki/File:AmbassadorMorgenthau telegram.jpg.

Murphy, Paul. *The Wolves of Islam: Russia and the Faces of Chechen Terror.* Washington, DC: Brasseys, 2004.

Nasiri, Omar. *Inside the Jihad: My Life with Al-Qaeda, A Spy's Story.* New York: Basic Books, 2008.

National Society of Defense: The Seat of the Caliphate. *A Universal Proclamation to All the People of Islam.* Muta'at al Hairayat: The Ottoman Empire, 1915; trans. American Agency and Consulate, Cairo, in U.S. State Department, document 867.4016/57, March 10, 1915.

Nicolle, David. *The Mongol Warlords.* Leicester, UK: Brockhampton Press, 1988.

Nowak, David. "Police Go On Alert After Three Killings." *Moscow Times* (February 19, 2008): 3.

Ocherhadji, Magomed. "The Mop up of Europe." Interview. *Prague Watchdog*, March 6, 2009. http://www.watchdog.cz.

O'Conner, Eileen, and Steven Harrigan. "Scores dead at end of hostage siege." Cable News Network (CNN), January 18 1996. http://www.cnn.com.

Oliker, Olya. *Russia's Chechen Wars 1994–2000.* Santa Monica, CA: Rand, 2001.

O'Neil, Bard. *Insurgency and Terrorism, Inside Modern Revolutionary Warfare.* Dulles, VA: Potomac Books, 1990.

"Over 70 killed in racial violence in Russia this year." *RIA Novosti*, September 23, 2008. http://en.rian.ru.

Pain, Emil, and Arkadii Popov. "Rossiiskaya politica v Chechnye." *Izvestiya* (February 7, 1995).

Perrie, Maureen, ed. *The Cambridge History of Russia, Volume 1: From Early Rus' to 1689.* New York: Cambridge University Press, 2006.

Peterson, Scott. "Heavy civilian toll in Chechnya's 'unlimited violence.'" *The Christian Science Monitor* (December 11, 2000).

Pilipchuk, Andrei. "Stereotip 'chernoi dyry." *Krasnaya zvezda* no. 12 (December 2003): 37.

Pipes, Richard. *The Formation of the Soviet Union: Communism and Nationalism, 1917–1923.* Cambridge, MA: Harvard University Press, 1957.

Pointing, Clive. *The Crimean War: The Truth Behind the Myth.* London: Chatto & Windus, 2004.

Politkovskaya, Anna. *A Small Corner of Hell, Dispatches from Chechnya.* Chicago: University of Chicago Press, 2003.

Polk, William R. *Understanding Iraq.* New York: Harper Collins, 2005.

Pravosudov, Sergei. "Bloka OVR voobsche moglo I ne bit." *Nezavisimaya Gazeta* (January 2000).

"Pravovaya otsenka deistviy organov vlasti v Chechenskoy respublike." Official statement, Ministry of Justice, Russian Federation, October 12, 1999.

Pushkin, Aleksander S., "Kavkaskiy plennik." http://publiclibrary.narod.ru.

"Putin links Chechen fighters to international terror." The Associated Press, August 31, 2004.

Putin, Vladimir, televised speech at the Kremlin, September 4, 2004, translated by *The New York Times.* http://www.nytimes.com/2004/09/05/international/europe/05rtext.html.

Rabasa, Angel. "Ungoverned Territories." Testimony before the Subcommittee on National Security and Foreign Affairs, Washington, DC, February 14, 2008.

Radio Free Europe–Radio Liberty. "Daily Report," November 21, 1994.

Radio Mayak. "Na etom etape' mi dolshni bit' bditel'nie." September 8, 2004, transcript available at http://old.radiomayak.ru.

Rashid, Ahmed. "Jihadi Suicide Bombers: The New Wave." *The New York Review of Books* 55, no. 10 (June 12, 2008). http://www.nybooks.com.

Reagan, Geoffrey. *The Guinness Book of Decisive Battles.* New York: Canopy Books, 1992.

Rechkalov, Vadim. "Deneg Basaeva. Pochemu spetzsluzhbi ne mogut poimat' Shamilya Basaeva. Prichina nomer tri," *Izvestia* (December 9, 2004).

Rechkalov, Vadim. ". . . And Other Bastards." *Moskovsky Kossomolets* 28 (February 8, 2008).

Regioni Rossiiskoy Federatsii, sotsial'no-ekonomicheskie pokazateli, Moscow: Goskomstat Rossii, 1990–2003.

Registrar of the European Court of Human Rights, "Chamber Judgments in Six Applications Against Russia," news release, 2005. http://www.echr.coe.int.

Reporters without Borders Web Site. "Russia–2008 Annual Report," http://www.rsf.org.

Riasanovsky, Nicholas V. *A History of Russia.* New York: Oxford University Press, 2000.

Rogozhin, Nikolai, press conference, January 11, 2008, *RIA Novosti,* and *Johnson's Russia List* 2008-#11.

Roi, Yaacov. *Islam in the Soviet Union: From World War II to Gorbachev.* London: Hurst, 2000.

Royle, Trevor. *Crimea, the Great Crimean War, 1854–1856.* New York: St. Martin's Press, 2000.

Russia: The Ingush-Ossetian Conflict in the Prigorodnyi Region. Helsinki: Human Rights Watch, 1996.

Sageman, Marc. *Understanding Terror Network*. Philadelphia: University of Pennsylvania Press, 2004.

Saradzhyan, Simon. "Attack Creates Dilemma for Putin." *The Moscow Times*, September 22, 2004.

Saradzhyan, Simon. "Putin's 'pacification' of Chechnya." *ISN Security Watch* (April 1, 2008). http://www.isn.ethz.ch.

Saunders, J. J. *The History of the Mongol Conquests*. London: Routledge & Kegan Paul Ltd., 1971.

Schaefer, Robert W. "The Imagined Chechen Economy 1990–1994." Author paper presented at the Fourteenth Annual Russian, East European and Central Asian Studies (REECAS) Conference, 2008.

Scheuer, Michael. "Al-Qaeda's Insurgency Doctrine: Aiming for a 'Long War.'" *Terrorism Focus* III, no. 8 (February 28, 2006).

Scheuer, Michael. "Victory in Death: The Political Use of Islamist Martyrs." *Terrorism Focus* V, no. 19 (May 13, 2008).

Sepp, Kalev I. "Best Practices in Counterinsurgency." *Military Review* 85:3 (May-June 2005): 8–12.

Shah, Pir Zubair, and Perlez, Jane. "Pakistani Prime Minister Acknowledged for the first time that fighters from Chechnya, Uzbekistan and Tajikistan were there." *The New York Times*, July 19, 2008. http:www.nytimes.com.

Shlapentokh, Dmitry. "Russia has 'Chechnya' ploy for Afghanistan." *Asia Times*, March 11, 2009. http://www.atimes.com.

Shoemaker, M. Wesley. *Russia and the Commonwealth of Independent States*. Harpers Ferry, WV: Stryker-Post Publications, 2000.

Sicker, Martin. *The Islamic World in Ascendancy, From the Arab Conquests to the Siege of Vienna*. Westport, CT: Praeger, 2000.

Sidahmed, Abdel Salam, and Anoushiravan Ehteshami, eds. *Islamic Fundamentalism*. Boulder, CO: Westview Press, 1996.

Smirnov, Andrei. "The Geography of OMON Deployments in the North Caucasus." *North Caucasus Weekly* 9:13 (April 3, 2008).

Smith, Sebastian. *Allah's Mountains, The Battle for Chechnya*. New York: St. Martin's Press, 2006.

Smith, William. *Dictionary of Greek and Roman Geography*. London: Walton and Maberly, 1854.

Snow, David A., and Robert D. Benford. "Master Frames and Cycles of Protest." *Frontiers in Social Movement Theory*. New Haven, CT: Yale University Press, 1992.

Soucek, Svat. *A History of Inner Asia*. Cambridge, UK: Cambridge University Press, 2000.

Souleimanov, Emil. "Chechnya, Wahhabism and the Invasion of Dagestan." *Middle East Review of International Affairs* 9:4 (December 2005): 50.

Stanley, Alessandra. "Russia Backs Group Fighting Secession in South," *The New York Times*, September 27, 1994. http://www.nytimes.com.

Stanley, Alessandra, "Yeltsin Criticized for Handling of Chechen Hostage Crisis," *The New York Times*, January 20, 1996. http://www.nytimes.com.

Sweeney, John. "Revealed: Russia's worst war crime in Chechnya." *The Guardian*, March 5, 2000. http://www.guardian.co.uk.

Sweetman, John. *Crimean War, Essential Histories 2.* Oxford, UK: Osprey Publishing, 2001.

The Columbia Encyclopedia, s.v. "Daryal," http://www.bartleby.com/65daDaryal.html (accessed on February 6, 2008).

Tishkov, Valery. *Obshchestvo v vooruzennom konflikte: Etnografiya chechnsko voyny.* Berkeley: University of California Press, 2004.

Tlisova, Fatima. "Exclusive Interview with Anzor Astemirov." *North Caucasus Weekly* X:11 (March 20, 2009).

Tolstoy, Lev. *Hadji Murat* (trans. by Louise and Aylmer Maude). Adelaide: University of Adelaide Library, 2010. http://ebooks.adelaide.edu.au.

Tolz, Vera. *Inventing the Nation, Russia.* New York: Oxford University Press, 2001.

Tse-Tung, Mao. *Strategic Problems of China's Revolutionary War*, December 1936. http://www.marxists.org/reference/archive/mao/selected-works/volume-1/mswv1_12.htm.

Tudan, Valentin. "Every conflict always has a father." *Prague Watchdog*, February 14, 2009. http://www.watchdog.cz.

Ugudov, Movladi. "Everything told by the Russian puppets, including their words about Maskhadov—is a lie." http://www.kavkazcenter.com/eng/content/2009/02/20/10555.shtml.

United States Code Electronic Edition, s.v. "United States Code 2331," http://www.access.gpo.gov/uscode/index.html.

U.S. Department of State. *Country Reports on Human Rights Practices, 2007–2009, Russia.* http://www.state.gov/g/drl/rls/hrrpt/2007/100581.htm.

United States Marine Corps. *Small Wars Manual.* Washington, DC: U.S. Government Printing Office, 1987.

United States-Russia Working Group on Counterterrorism Joint Press Statement and Fact Sheet, June 20, 2008, http://Moscow.usembassy.gov/factsheet_ctwg.html.

Usmanov, Lema. *Nepokorennaia Chechnia.* Moscow: Isdatel'skii dom Parus, 1997.

Vatchagaev, Mairbek. *Chechnya in the 19th Century Caucasian Wars.* Moscow: 1995.

Vatchagaev, Mairbek, "Dokka Umarov Suffers Setback in Turkey." *North Caucasus Analysis* 10, no. 9 (March 6, 2009).

Vatchagaev, Mairbek. "The Role of Sufism in the Chechen Resistance." *Chechnya Weekly* 6, no. 16 (April 28, 2005).

Vatchagaev, Mairbek. "Uzun Haji's and Dokka Umarov's Emirates: A Retrospective." *Chechnya Weekly* 9, no. 10 (March 13, 2008).

Wa Islamah News Network. "Biography of the Sword of Islam Khattab." *Contemporary Heroes of Islam Series.* http://www.youtube.com/watch?v+wCqR-A1Z0Yk&feature=related (accessed July 20, 2008).

Warren, Marcus. "Rebels March Over Mines to Save Their Comrades." *The Telegraph*, February 6, 2000. http://www.telegraph.co.uk.

Weiszhar, Attila, and Balazs, Weiszhar. *Lexicon of Wars.* Budapest: Athenaeum Publishing, 2004.

Wetzel, David. *The Crimean War: A Diplomatic History.* New York: Columbia University Press, 1985.

"Who Gains From the Moscow Apartment Bombings?" *Global Intelligence Update*, September 14, 1999, Strategic Forecasting (STRATFOR).

Williams, Brian Glyn. "Allah's Foot Soldiers, An Assessment of the Role of Foreign Fighters and Al-Qaida in the Chechen Insurgency." http://www.briangylnwilliams.com.

Williams, Brian Glyn. "The Chechen Arabs: An Introduction to the Real Al-Qaeda Terrorists From Chechnya." *Terrorism Monitor* 2, no. 1, (January 15, 2004).

Williams, Brian Glyn. "Shattering the Al Qaeda-Chechen Myth: Part I." *Chechnya Weekly* 4, no. 35 (October 2, 2003).

Winston, Brian. "Triumph of the Will." *History Today Magazine* 47, no. 1 (1997).

Witorowicz, Quintan, ed. *Islamic Activism, A Social Movement Theory Approach.* Bloomington: Indiana University Press, 2004.

"Worst Places to be Terrorist 2008." *Foreign Policy Magazine* Online. http://www.foreignpolicy.com.

Yanderbiyev, Zelimkhan. *V preddverii nezavisimosti.* Grozny: Author publication, 1994.

Yemelianova, Galina M. *Russia and Islam, A Historical Survey.* London: Palgrave, 2002.

Yemelianova, Galina M. "Sufism and Politics in the North Caucasus." *The Nationality Papers* 29, no. 4 (2001): 663.

Zubov, Mikhail. "Interview with Gleb Pavlovsky." *Moskovskiy Komsomolets*, November 18, 2008 (available in English at Johnson's Russia List, 2008–#212, November 19, 2008).

Index

Abbasid dynasty, 70
Abkhazia, 4, 92, 116, 118–120, 191, 271
Abu Nidal Group, 38–39
Afghanistan, 40, 67, 78, 277; Al Qaeda in, 151, 153; casualty figures, 3, 238; Chechen "ghosts" fighting in, 248; effect of war on Caucasus Emirate activities, 248–250; government support to Chechnya, 77, 112, 127, 235, 246; Soviet involvement in, 214; U.S. involvement in, 2–3, 5, 7, 196, 206–207, 235, 250
aid workers. *See* non-governmental organizations
Alexander I, Emperor, 58
Alexander II, Emperor, 67
Alexy II, Patriarch, 169
Ali Bek-haji's revolt, 81–83
Al Qaeda, 14, 24, 35, 37, 42–48, 153; Chechen links to, 166–167, 208, 219, 222, 248–249; goals, 33, 41; ideology, 44–45, 150; as insurgency, 39, 42; in North Caucasus, 4, 144, 163–168; strategy, 42, 44–45

Al Qaeda in Iraq (AQI), 35, 37; Islamism, 41, 47
ambush, 25–27, 57, 58, 63, 79, 128–130, 141, 191, 193, 279
Angola, 24
Anna, Empress, 54
Antony, Mark, 50
Aquinas, Thomas, 147
Armenia, 50, 95, 110–111, 119, 210, 250; and Ottomans, 81, 82, 85; resettlement, 86; World War I, 85–91
Armenian Orthodox Patriarch in Constantinople, 82
Army of Islam, 91
Astemirov, Anzor, 249, 250, 292
Atayev, Musa, 220, 245
Austria, 54, 89, 92, 221, 263
Autonomous Soviet Socialist Republic (ASSR), 105–106, 111, 113
auxiliary, 244; in insurgency, 21, 25, 29
Avturkhanov, Umar, 122
Azerbaijan, 50, 59, 84, 166, 249, 263, 268; external support, 210, 246; Soviet Union, 91, 95, 110, 119
Azzam, Abdullah, 150–151, 165, 175

About the Author

LIEUTENANT COLONEL ROBERT W. SCHAEFER is a highly decorated U.S. Army Special Forces (Green Beret) and Eurasian Foreign Area Officer. For more than 20 years he has served in a variety of special units and he has participated in virtually every U.S. overseas operation since 1990. He has extensive experience with counterinsurgency and counter-terrorist operations around the world and has lived and worked in many countries of the former Soviet Union. LTC Schaefer was the recipient of the Special Operations Command (US SOCOM) Award of Excellence in 2001. He obtained his Masters Degree in Russian, Eastern European, and Central Asian Studies from Harvard University in 2005, served as a consultant for the PBS news program "Worldfocus," and hosted National Public Radio's Memorial Day Special in 2007 and 2008.